Some Talk of Alexander

Some Talk of Alexander

FREDERIC RAPHAEL

with 106 illustrations

Thames & Hudson

For my granddaughter Natasha

My thanks are due, as always, to Beetle for her patient reading, rereading and
annotations of many versions of the text. I am also grateful to Mark Glanville for
his encouraging and helpful remarks. Alison Austen has been an invaluable
copy-editor. Stanley Baron suggested that I write this book at a time when his
sponsorship was particularly needed. Paul Cartledge has been boundlessly
patient and stringently tactful in saving me from myself. Peter Green has always
encouraged my unacademic forays into the ancient world.

Frontispiece Travelling heroes.

First published in the United Kingdom in 2006 by
Thames & Hudson Ltd, 181A High Holborn, London WC1V 7QX

www.thamesandhudson.com

© 2006 Frederic Raphael

British Library Cataloguing-in-Publication Data
A catalogue record for this book is available from the British Library

ISBN-13: 978-0-500-51288-3
ISBN-10: 0-500-51288-4

Designed by Liz Rudderham

Printed and bound in Slovenia by MKT Print d.d

Some talk of Alexander and some of Hercules,
Of Hector and Lysander, and such great names as these...
—*The British Grenadiers*

Introduction

*W*hen I first went to preparatory school in England, nothing was more taken for granted than the importance, and even the usefulness, of a classical education. What else should we be prepared for? Generations of those who crept unwillingly to school were promised that familiarity with the golden ages of Greece and Rome – the fifth and fourth and the second and first centuries B.C. (plus the early decades of the first A.D.) respectively – was a certificate of entry to the Church and the Civil (and Colonial) Service. Even duds in the Army Class could profit from them: Alexander the Great's victories were refought, and his tactics advertised, on the blackboards and sand tables of Sandhurst Military Academy. Ancient rhetoric infected politics and the law; Greek was the basis of medical jargon, Latin of legal. Civilization was based on the study of two languages which, half a century later, have been officially stigmatized as useless.

The glory of Greece and the grandeur of Rome long supplied warrants for empire, tabulated precedents for architectural orders, prescribed forms for art and furnished matrices for political rhetoric. Parliamentarians graced their reputations by capping each other's quotations from Horace: their boroughs might be rotten, but their citations had better be word-perfect.

As late as the 1960s, Harold Macmillan could expect to be widely understood when he claimed, wistfully, that Britain could play Greece to America's Rome. Did not everyone know that defeated Greece conquered its conqueror? Macmillan took Great Britain to be an educated country, and by education he meant the classics. But the Age of Satire was upon him, and us: the style of Aristophanes, who had no time for tragic solemnities and culled laughs from farts and fucks, was more to modern taste than Sophocles' piety or Euripidean ironies.

More style than content, Macmillan was the last patrician. Subsequent politicians, left and right, advertised their breach with the classical world and, coincidentally, with what Shelley called "antique courtesies", which, even as a romantic revolutionary, he insisted on honouring. Latin – once the lingua franca of Christendom and of scholarship – is no longer required for Oxford entrance. When I took my scholarship to Cambridge in 1949, some six hundred candidates offered Greek in applying to my college alone. That language now has fewer than three hundred students in the whole university.

The traditional *paideia*, which had origins at least as far back as Periklean Athens, has come to a largely unmourned end. The decline in religious credulity means that the study of sacred texts, which were encrypted in Greek and Latin, as well as in Hebrew, is no longer a common guide to salvation: success is modern man's god; a good pension his idea of an afterlife.

In the 1960s, classicists threw in the sponge, rather as Ludovico Manin, the last doge of Venice, tossed his ducal hat into the Mediterranean. Even in France, where the classics underwrote a Latinate culture, Edgar Faure, the conservative intellectual minister of education, was panicked by the events of 1968 into jettisoning what had been denounced by the Left as a system for promoting mandarinism.

Since then, the triumph of science and of classlessness (its social correlative) has rendered the old humanities irrelevant and – worst of all in modern eyes – unprofitable. Against the odds, however, interest in Greece and Rome (though not in their intricate linguistic syntax) is greater, in some ways, than when their dreaded dust was sifted over every schoolboy's curriculum. Small Latin and less Greek were beaten into too many sullen pupils for their vanished supremacy to be widely lamented. It is, however, crass to insist that the priority of Latin and Greek was a toffs' ramp, calculated to exclude the unprivileged. For centuries, scholarly talent advanced the prospect of boys who might otherwise have been condemned to provincial obscurity, exclusion or even death: Ben Jonson's learning secured him "benefit of clergy" and reprieved him, literally, from the gallows. In his 1609 play *Epicene*, someone observes of an impostor pretending to be a parson, "When he spoke Latin, every word was a mistake". The same was never true of the author.

A century later, Samuel Johnson's erudition gained him the title of the Great Cham of Literature. The quondam Lichfield Grammar School boy became one of the sights (and sounds) of London, though he was hardly handsome, or hygienic. The classics supplied common ground on which new men might display a wit which recommended them to their betters. That capacity to open doors continued until recent times. My friend, the late J.P. Sullivan, was the son of a Liverpool Irish docker. Even in 1950, when we both went up to St John's College, Cambridge, he might never have transcended his father's limited social horizon had not the Jesuits beaten so much intelligence into him, A.M.D.G. (*ad majorem dei gloriam*), that he became the leading Latinist of his generation. He was first Dean of Lincoln College, Oxford and, finally, Professor of Classics at the University of California at Santa Barbara. Latin was his passport and his passion, though rarely his only one.

In scholarship, there was – in principle, at least – neither Jew nor Gentile: when Eduard Fraenkel was thrown out of his chair by the Nazis (with no protesting word from his ex-colleague Martin Heidegger, who proscribed him as "the jew Fraenkel"), he was received with respect at Oxford. If bigoted or envious men whispered against him, and questioned his morals, none openly disputed his qualities (even though, as his bizarre translation of Aeschylus's *Oresteia* reveals, they never extended to a mastery of speakable English). While Fraenkel and many others were given sanctuary in English universities, the British Medical Association was barring refugee doctors from practising, or teaching, on the grounds that local medicine had nothing to learn from foreigners.

Now science supplies the lingua franca. In its terminologies, heavy with derivatives from Greek and Latin, there is little place for metaphor, irony and allusion. Multiculturalism is impatient with the tyranny of the well-spoken; nuance and subtlety are divisive. In principle, we are all moderns now. Yet the ancient world is visited, admired and exhumed. Television packages tours to it; computer-generated imagery reconstitutes it; Hollywood stars fight in the virtual reality of its arenas. Translations, whether direct or fanciful, abound. Ancient ideas remain tenaciously relevant to modern life. Fanatics and fundamentalists echo antique polytheism and philosophies; Eros and Aphrodite rule; the Great God Pan has come to life again and lives not only in Arcadia but *un peu partout*.

Scholars such as Charles Freeman, in his *The Closing of the Western Mind*, discover more charity in Julian the Apostate – the tolerant, short-lived, ex-Christian emperor, who sought to revive the Olympian gods – than in Constantine the Great, who had homogenized the Roman Empire's religion under a single Trinity. Although the pagan world could be vigilantly, and sometimes vindictively, pious (Pheidias, like Socrates a generation or so later, fell foul of Athenian religious conservatism), doctrinal deviance was unknown before Constantine proclaimed that he had "received from divine providence the supreme favour of being relieved of all error". If the emperor had little idea of what Christianity demanded of him, he was clear that it gave him the certificate of infallibility. Tyrants have claimed it ever since. The one-party state begins, in practice, with Christianity rather than in Plato's advocacy of the "closed society".

The fancy of historians is free to toy with the possibility that, if the Apostate had lived as long as Augustus, we might still be sacrificing cocks to Aesculapius. The retreat of Christian conviction into costumed nostalgia and purple

1 Well-marbled Paros walled its *kastro* with builders' leftovers.

2 Johann Winckelmann, at his day job.

moralizing has made way for the study of pagan texts which, in my school-days, were too improper, or too spicy, for proper attention. The Golden Ages, Greek and Roman, remain the source of most of our revered texts, but the determination to manipulate the best ancient literature, as well as the Old Testament, into a prefiguring of Christianity has lost its plausibility.

The more we know about the ancient Greeks, their social habits and sexual ambivalences, the less they seem like voices crying in the wilderness, "Prepare ye the way of the Lord". Yet who can deny that much of Christian morality is transposed, cannibalized and quarried, as early churches were, from the society and institutions to which it put paid? The umpteenth three-dimensional instance is the temple of Artemis on the shore of the Greek island of Ikareia, whose stones were transported inland and uphill, to the citadel of Christos Rachon, to furnish the walls of the village church. Nietzsche's *aperçu* that without the temples of now disempowered gods we should have no architecture can be carried further: without the compost of pagan beliefs and the family relationships which gave grammar its mythical structure, the modern world would never have the language or concepts which arm its dismissal of antiquity.

For the Romantics, the charm of the Greek world derived from its seeming to offer an immutable vision of Arcadia. "Ah, happy, happy boughs! that cannot shed / Your leaves, nor ever bid the spring adieu", was what John Keats read into his (unattributed) Grecian urn. He concluded that its imagery and literature were set for ever. In recent times, however, the beauty and truth of antiquity have been radically reconsidered, in a variety of modern lights. Its aesthetics, sociology, topography (Apollonia was once in Galatia, but is now said to be in Pisidia) and chronology are constantly being challenged. The literary corpus has been fattened by important manuscript discoveries in the Egyptian desert; modern technology may soon decipher the scorched scrolls in the library at Herculaneum which belonged to Lucius Calpurnius Piso, the father-in-law of Julius Caesar.

Neither ancient history nor scholars' estimates of its literature and art can ever be immune to revision. Johann Winckelmann (1717–68) was one of the great scholars of his day. Few did more to sponsor enthusiasm for the "noble simplicity" of Greek sculpture. In his own mind, at least, he fixed its aesthetic standards. But who now would gush, as he did, over the Vatican's Laocoön – a post-classical first-century B.C. collaboration between three Rhodian sculptors – or agree that the Apollo Belvedere (a Roman copy of Leochares' original) is a divine instance of classical male beauty? Winckelmann made fundamental contributions to both archaeology and art history, but if he set the tone for German appreciation, and appropriation, of ancient Greece, his aesthetics were less durable than his scholarship.

The Laocoön depicts the legendary Trojan priest and his sons wrestling in vain with the demonic sea-monster sent, by the furious Apollo, to destroy them. Leochares' Apollo, on the other hand, stands calmly above the fray, all passion spent, like a professor surveying his class. Was the orderly grace which Winckelmann wished on the Greek sensibility a projection of his own craving for self-control? Scholars have private demons too: as his contrasting icons

3 Catherine the Great's counsellor, Prince Cyril Razumovsky, grand-touring the Vatican: Laocoön, Apollo Belvedere and a couched Ariadne in his curriculum.

suggest, Winckelmann led a double life. His night job may have been as a secret agent. Was he murdered, in Trieste, while operating under academic cover as a Prussian courier? Travelling incognito, he most likely took time out for some rough trade. His choice, a local cook, robbed and stabbed him. Two centuries later, Marcel Detienne wrote a study of Apollo entitled *Apollon, le couteau à la main* (Apollo, knife in hand). The god whose self-control appealed to Winckelmann was, Detienne reminds us, himself a killer.

Do we know better, or see more clearly, than Winckelmann because we have shucked the coils of scholarly cant? Nietzsche was its first great unraveller. In his *The Birth of Tragedy*, he challenged Winckelmann's (and Keats's) plaster-cast vision of Greek character and gods. Jane Harrison's *Prolegomena to the Study of Greek Religion* (in its turn excited by Sir James Frazer's *The Golden Bough*) was its Anglo-Saxon by-blow. Dated or derided as she – and her ubiquitous *eniautos daimon* – may now be, Harrison changed for ever our accepted view of the Olympian gods: she saw undying divinity in the snakes at home in the underworld and sensed the instability behind the marbled pretensions of the official theocracy.

It is typical of my experience of classical studies that I never read Harrison's *Prolegomena* until I had graduated from Cambridge, and that I discovered the text in an American paperback edition. European academics may deplore the decline of philology, and the almost universal American habit of relying on translations, but American scholars have brought energetic irreverence to the old game. Without an orthodoxy to judge their merits, or blight their careers, academics are ready for – not to say obliged to – ingenious provocations. Heterodoxy is almost everybody's doxy now. The brashness which destroyed Nietzsche's hopes of professorial advancement would today embellish them. Structuralist *avant la lettre*, Nietzsche proposed the polar antithesis of Apollo and Dionysus. By doing so, he released new dynamics in what had been a static view of antiquity. As a result, anthropology and sociology have displaced the centrality of the philological pedantry of which Nietzsche, at twenty-three, was a precocious professor.

Claude Lévi-Strauss's structuralism supplied a new grid of relations and readings from which the great modern French scholars, Jean-Pierre Vernant, Marcel Detienne and Pierre Vidal-Naquet, Nicole Loraux, François Hartog and Françoise Frontisi-Ducroux, have revolutionized our understanding of ancient society (their founding father was Louis Gernet). Among English post-war scholars, none has been more enduringly daring, or more foot-sloggingly investigative, than my friend Peter Green, whose genius is as copious as it is unflagging. Not the smallest pleasure of the classics lies in the willingness of professionals, such as Peter Green and Paul Cartledge, to mark the cards of importunate amateurs.

Soon after my arrival in Cambridge, Peter and John Sullivan made it clear to me that I was never destined, or qualified, to be a classical scholar. With small wish to be an also-ran, I abandoned classics for philosophy. Chance (which Hellenistic Greeks worshipped as *Tyche*, the Romans as Fortuna) was generous. I had chosen St John's College only because Ivor Gibson, my sixth-form master at Charterhouse, had spread his runners across the Cambridge spectrum so that they should not compete with each other. I could not, in the event, have been more happily placed. Although my tripos results were not of the best, my scholarship was extended to a fourth year. Then, thanks to my director of philosophical studies, the late Renford Bambrough, I was recommended for a studentship reserved for would-be creative writers (an exiguous band in those days of respectable ambitions). The award was designed to give its recipient a year of mind-broadening foreign travel.

In 1954, thanks to the Reverend Harper Wood's legacy, I travelled to Provence, to Spain, to Morocco and then to Italy. My landfall there was at Naples, the Greek Neapolis, which stood near the high-tide mark of Magna Graecia, that great palimpsest where Greece and Rome were impacted on each other. Eye-opening days in Pompeii and Paestum, and in the Naples museum, alerted me to why I should have been more diligent in the years when I thought it was enough to be clever. Ancient dust swarmed into life. It was too late to be a proper scholar, but I was belatedly hooked on what I had renounced.

This book is the eclectic consequence of travels, real and imaginary, literal and literary, over half a century. During that time, I have read and reread ancient writers and become addicted to books about them. In my unsystematic persistence, I have tried to apologize to myself, and to my teachers, for student failings. I still know that if I was clever enough to get scholarships, I was never a scholar. A *flâneur* without formal scheme or speciality, I hop from one aspect of the Greek world to another, guided only by prejudice and curiosity. *Some Talk of Alexander* does not pretend to be more than a rambling catalogue, only somewhat *raisonné*, of my version of André Malraux's "*musée imaginaire*".

My collection is avowedly incomplete and its documentation patchy. But then not every museum can, or should, be comprehensive. The great collections of London and New York, or Munich and Paris, rightly attract the largest crowds, but I have a penchant for little frequented and underfunded museums, like those in Odessa and Constanta (the ancient Tomis), where the collections have been dumped in dusty cases and where the guardians greet the rare visitors with informative gratitude. There you can still have the sweet illusion of being almost the first to see the provincial oddities which have been spared summary transportation to great private or national collections.

In Odessa, I could lie on the floor to look more closely at a pig-faced libation cup designed, surely, for the porcine rites of some local *Thesmophoria*, the female festival so relished by Jane Harrison in her *Prolegomena*. In Tomis, we were shown the local totem, a triple monster with the head of a lamb, the trunk of a lion and the tail of a snake. The Romanian guide told us that it represented "Air, Earth and Fire, which the ancients regarded as the key elements". A temptation to repeat the pedant's sneer, "*Vous avez un texte, monsieur?*", had to be repressed. I did speculate, however, that perhaps the curious hybrid (the work of a local mason during the second century A.D.) represented the dragon which guarded the Golden Fleece. The improbable affixing of an ovine head to what seems an intimidating statue suggested that some local cult was being served, possibly by an image of the "dragon" which guarded the Golden Fleece and which itself might have had a sheepish aspect. Colchis – where Jason went to kill the dragon (aided by Medea's local knowledge) – was many miles to the east, but Tomis had a link with the legend of the *Argo*: Medea's father supposedly put in to Tomis to reassemble his son, Apsyrtus, who had been cut in pieces by his half-sister, and strewn on the waters, in order to inhibit her father's pursuit of Jason's ship.

Readers of scholarly work are accustomed to regular chronology and to the assembly of topics under discrete headings: history, religion, philology, tragedy, comedy, politics tend to be found in distinct chapters or volumes. Historians deal with, for instance, the Persian or Peloponnesian wars; political scientists with the laws and constitutions of city-states; literary pundits tell us exactly where this or that character in tragedy made his entrance or his exit (although no ancient author specifies such things); and anthropologists analyse myth in the light of this or that theory. What interests me most is how all these things, and many more, reacted on each other *all at the same time*.

Even comedy and tragedy could depend from the same mythical pegs. Perverse frivolity and reckless vanity, piety and outrage, superstition and *realpolitik* jostle in a world where myth is both revered and derided, where reason is important because unreason is so widespread: who can say what the *real* reason was for the Spartans' failure to march promptly to Marathon in 490 B.C.? Did they hope – as some local Bismarck might have – that the Athenians would succeed in hampering the Persian invaders, but with losses serious enough to abate their own ambitions, or were they *seriously* afraid to curtail the rites of the Karneia, which might excite the anger of the gods?

The Greek world was one in which – as Heracleitus said – everything was in a state of flux. Motive itself is a dubious notion in many cases: it interiorizes and individualizes social habits in a false reading of antique psychology. Interiorization was a distinctly *feminine* characteristic; the male-dominated official world regarded it with suspicion and alarm. Men did, straightforwardly, what men did; women did, deviously, what their stomachs/wombs and antisocial habits prompted. Where, as Heracleitus again said, "war is the king and father of all things", women are dangerously Other, as the modern cant puts it; and yet duplicity haunts the Greek mind and vocabulary, and the female with it: Hellas itself was a feminine noun.

It would be tedious, and affected, to annotate every passage in which I should acknowledge the scholars on whom I have depended or from whom I have differed. In many cases, I have so assimilated what I happen to have read that I am too often unable to identify my sources. To acknowledge at least some of my debts, I append a bibliography, culled largely from my own library.

—F.R.

Every man with a bellyful of the classics is an enemy to the human race.

—*Henry Miller*

4 Alexander the Great, the glory boy.

My first landfall in mainland Greece, over forty years ago, was in the north-west, at Igoumenitsa. The ferry from Brindisi – where Rome's generals, proconsuls, exiles and renegades embarked for the East – put us down in cold Epirus, once the mountain kingdom of Pyrrhus. Distantly related to Alexander the Great, and hardly less aggressive, Pyrrhus lived by the sword and, in 272 B.C., died by it. War was in his blood: Neoptolemus, the son of Achilles, was one of his royal predecessors. Myth often leaked into, and embellished, ancient genealogies: real kings boasted of, or fabricated, heroic and divine ancestors. Alexander the Great went, without fancy escort, to the oasis of Siwah, in the Egyptian desert, to discover if he would be recognized by the oracle of Zeus Ammon as "the son of Zeus". His witch-mother, Olympias, was said to have enjoyed a snake in her bed on the night of his conception; why should his father not be Olympian?

Shakespeare's "rugged Pyrrhus" was one of the first Greek generals to confront the expanding power of Rome, early in the third century. Having accepted command of the Greek cities in southern Italy, he campaigned with success against Roman encroachment in Calabria, where Greek colonists had themselves been encroaching for at least three centuries. He blenched, however, at the cost of beating the legions at Asculum in 279 (dates are B.C. unless otherwise stated, or obviously not): "One more such victory", he said, "and we're done for."* The Hellenes were done for anyway: they lost ground to

---

*So-called Pyrrhic victories were called "Cadmeian" by the Greeks. Cadmus, founder of Thebes, sowed the dragon's teeth, from which sprang warriors whose first action was to kill each other.

the uncompromising spread of Rome until all Hellas became a province of the westerners to whom Greeks never quite ceased to condescend, if from below. Their Golden Age, always enshrined in the past, receded into myth. Dreams of return were more powerful, among Greeks, than hopes of progress: at least until the fiasco of A.D. 1922, "the Great Idea" – of reconquering Byzantium – dominated their modern patriotic ambitions.* Hesiod's Golden Age long preceded his own, in which greed and toil were the sorry human lot. Plato made a retrospective myth of an Edenic lost Atlantis. Literalists site it on the island of Thera (today's Santorini), before the volcanic eruption of the second millennium B.C. scorched its beaches black and rolled killing clouds and swamping waves over Minoan civilization.

Greek muscle might be despised by the Romans; Greek muses were envied. During the centuries of Roman hegemony, Hellenes gave their masters lessons in everything but war, and cohesion. The impacted civilizations of Greece and Rome generated that of Europe, on a basis of political organization, schism, curiosity, wit, credulity, doubt, rhetoric, reason, prejudice, scholarship, tyranny, conceit, self-criticism, democracy, law, violence, art, carnage, justice, superstition and ruthlessness.

Having studied ancient Greek for more than a decade of grim English education, I was over thirty before setting foot in the country where all those arcane figures of speech – *tmesis, chiasmos, krasis, asyndeton* – and textual conundrums, irregular verbs and convoluted legends proliferated. Our schoolmasters' scholarship was primly philological: grammatical irregularities, the rules of Greek accentuation – unknown to ancient Greeks – and elegant models for prose and verse were extracted from a culture in which incest, polymorphous sex, human sacrifice and treacherous self-advancement were at least as common as steadiness under fire, the team spirit and clean living.

To those educated in Dr Arnold's long shadow, Socrates was at once example and exception. The quest for truth and conscientious interest in "the examined life" might be admirable, but Socratic moderation had, embarrassingly, to be explained in the light of the unmentionable propensities of many other Greeks: clearly, none of his contemporaries would have matched Socrates' "Christian" reluctance to have sex with dishy Alcibiades. Our squeamish teachers might have preferred that Plato's *Symposium* – in which the matter was amusingly aired – be ejected from the syllabus, along with many uncanonical celebrations of the erotic. Classical texts, like the Old Testament, were at once seminal and serviceable in Christian eyes: both were often skewed, or mistranslated, to

---

* Byron's philhellenism was as nostalgic as his proto-Zionism: those who had fallen from grace appealed to his own decadence.

make them seem to predict what their authors never had in mind. Ideas too need divine genealogies. Jesus was said to be Isaiah's "suffering servant" in order that his coming be rooted in the prophets, whose writings were preserved – like the wandering Jews themselves – to bear witness to the moral, and theological, superiority of Christianity. The Church, primed by scholars such as St Jerome, destroyed unserviceable pagan texts (as later pietists, St Louis *en tête*, did the Talmud) and retained what best certified its own authority. Accident or arson also destroyed ancient texts: 400,000 manuscripts were torched by the Arabs, possibly for fun, in the first great fire of the two famous libraries of Alexandria; 200,000 in the second, though fanatical Christians had already done much damage to the fabric and collected manuscripts in A.D. 491.

Umberto Eco's *The Name of the Rose* makes a medieval murder story out of a fanatical monk's destruction of the last manuscript of Aristotle's *On Comedy* because he thought humour a danger to faith: God was not to be mocked. As a Calvinist preacher said to the young Byron, when he giggled during a sermon, "No hope for them as laughs".

Romantics also travestied pagan society and literature so that they lent credibility to an idealized, unvisited, Greece. Schiller's poem *The Gods of Greece* lamented their eviction from earth. His opening salvo apostrophized "...Exquisite beings of the land of myth / Ah when your worship, full of joys, was still at its brilliant peak / How the world was different then!" In the introduction to his *Hellas*, Shelley announced that "The human form and human mind attained...perfection in Greece". His *Prometheus Unbound* was Percy Bysshe, in antique drag, empowered to free mankind from the tyrannical (Christian) God.

Christians, by contrast, have seen Socrates, for particular instance, as a prototypical Jesus. To Nietzsche, however, he would seem morbidly introspective (and too like Nietzsche); while Heidegger read the pre-Socratics – with their alleged reverence for Being – as prototypically Heideggerian. Heidegger has been accused of mistranslating a passage in Sophocles' *Antigone* in order to give a noble pedigree to his own ideas about Nothing.

If Heidegger construed the first philosophers in his own latter-day light, he scarcely ever visited Greece itself; nor did the great scholar Johann Winckelmann, who, while resident in Rome in the eighteenth century, promoted the "noble simplicity" and "quiet grandeur" of classical sculpture. His evangelical aesthetics incited more Grand Tourists to become predatory collectors than refined souls. Lord Elgin was only the most enterprising, as he is still the most abused, of them.

Winckelmann's enthusiasm led his contemporary, the Danish sculptor Bertel Thorvaldsen (also resident in Rome, where a piazza is now named after him), to "improve" – that is, "skin" – the marbles filched from the pediment of

5 Thorvaldsen and expat friends in the Osteria Gensola.

the little Doric temple of Aphaea, the Lady Who Vanished, on the island of Aegina, before sending them to Munich, where they remain. Did their arrival prime "mad" King Ludwig's wish to build Greek temples? The bereft temple still sits in its pine grove on an aromatic hilltop where I once mused for an hour, or less, with a bag of excellent pistachios, an Aeginetan speciality.

Winckelmann articulated the supposed affinity between Hellas and Germany which – thanks to Arminius's defeat of Varus's legions in A.D. 9 – was little infected by Latin culture. Yet his respect for antique proportion was based on Roman marble copies of Greek bronzes, mostly from what purists consider a period of decline: the tendency of sculptors such as Praxiteles to infect their work with feeling is often regarded as sentimental. The Anatolian/Egyptian inscrutability of sixth-century *kouroi* conveyed a more comely, impersonal reticence. Even now, it is hard to share Winckelmann's (and the elder Pliny's) enthusiasm for the first-century Laocoön – made in Rhodos by a troika of sculptors – or for the *Apollo Belvedere*, buttressed by his marble tree trunk.

After a decade and more of falling asleep over texts and notes, postgraduate travels took me to the sites, and sounds and smells, of ancient Greece and

Rome. I was drawn first to Magna Graecia, where Greeks, Romans and others clashed and fused. If Paestum (ancient Poseidonia, modern Pesto) and Sicily were not in geographic Greece, they were unarguably Greek: the so-called Temple of Neptune (actually of Hera) at Paestum, the russet temple of Zeus at Agrigento, the ruins of daisy-yellowed Selinunte and what was billed as the unfinished Doric temple in Segesta* owed no other aesthetic allegiance. Somewhat late in the day, I woke to, and in, an ancient world purged of Anglo-Saxon dust.

Ancient Hellenes were never defined by the boundaries of modern Greece: the Mediterranean, and far beyond, was probed by their ambitions, and stitched with their appropriations. Homer spoke of the "pathless sea", but Greek boats scored its surface from the earliest times. Hellas was a movable feast: its mythical gods and heroes were travellers. Jason, Odysseus and Theseus, Herakles, Dionysus and Hermes (who rarely hung up his frequent-flyer's hat or put down his staff) were seldom at rest.

In historic times, the Corinthians are credited with the first triremes. Less sophisticated, undecked ships from Athens (sailing east for New Ionia on the coast of Asia Minor) and even from Sparta (on the way to Taras, the modern Taranto), carried colonists to a wide spread of destinations, from the eighth century onwards. Some form of sea travel may have begun much earlier: there is evidence of Minoan/Mycenaean trade, in prehistoric times, with what was later Magna Graecia and also in eastern Iberia.

The Corinthians, who had easy access to western waters, were quick to colonize Corcyra (Corfu), which later became their sour enemy: the first recorded naval battle, in the seventh century, was between the island and its city of origin. Most expatriates retained sentimental ties, though only Athenian "cleruchs" kept voting rights, in their mother-cities. There was charm and danger in such umbilical allegiance: great cities could become embroiled in their satellites' quarrels. In the fifth century, Corcyra's recurrent stand-off with Corinth supplied the *casus belli* for the first rounds of the Peloponnesian War. The Corinthians regarded Athenian support for Corcyra's democrats as interference in their own internal affairs.

The successful Ionian cities in Asia Minor in their turn spawned further colonies. The Milesians were probably the first Greeks (after Jason and his Argonauts) to venture into the Black Sea, where they founded Sinope in the eighth century. The city was named for Asopus's daughter to whom the amorous Zeus promised any gift she wanted. The clever girl chose virginity,

---

* The non-Greek, Elymian population graced themselves with a Greek peristyle, probably to define the area of an open-air altar.

the last thing the god had in mind. Apparently, he granted it with a good grace and she lived in unruptured seclusion ever after. Sinope is the right place to find it: even today, it is almost impervious from the landward side, though easily reached by sea. Only vestigial rudiments of antiquity give the modern Turkish town its small charm: the once notorious gaol (closed after a riot in the 1970s) has had to be promoted to a tourist attraction. Contemporary Sinope is curious only for the number of shops which sell model yachts of various sizes, quite as if they were a form of local currency. Greek title to the port was based on the myth that the *Argo* called in there when Jason needed replacement oarsmen for the long pull to Colchis.

* * *

Now a backwater, Sinope knew great days: it was the birthplace both of Diogenes (400–325), the showboating cynic whose long, asocial life was spent demonstrating that life was not worth living, and also – when the town was the capital of the kingdom of Pontus – of the scheming Mithridates, Rome's oriental bogeyman during the first century B.C.

Mithridates masterminded a synchronized terrorist attack on all Romans living in Asia Minor: eighty thousand are said to have been murdered in an orgy of slaughter like that of the Sicilian Vespers (in A.D. 1282, the islanders rose and, at a stroke, more or less annihilated their alien, Frankish rulers). By no means all Asians rallied to Mithridates: the fine city of Aphrodisias, fifty miles inland from Ephesus, stayed loyal to a beleaguered Roman general, whose alien administration was evidently preferable to that of an indigenous despot.

Known earlier as Ninoe, the honey-coloured city – appropriately placed in a fertile plain – was probably first dedicated to Akkadian Ishtar, the Asiatic Aphrodite. Inhabited by Karians and Anatolian Greeks and dominated by Rome, Aphrodisias was a palimpsest of cultures with a temple of Love at its heart. The genetically mixed population was reconciled not least by sport and, one guesses, gambling: the still impressive hippodrome could seat thirty thousand fans. However, small relics are often more moving than grandiose ruins: there is a marble well-head at Aphrodisias which is scored by the countless ropes that were let down through it. One senses the urgent daily life of countless anonymous Rebeccas.

Thirty miles away is the hilltop city of Pammukale (ancient Hierapolis). Its hot springs ooze into a descending series of limestone basins, ribbed like white tweed. You can swim in an outdoor tepidarium and look down through the clear water at the fallen pillars of the Roman baths. Nearby is the steamy vault in which priestesses delivered oracular messages and initiates underwent rituals of Orphic rebirth.

The Romans reacted to Mithridates' rebellion with typical, phlegmatic ruthlessness. Their policy of "as long as it takes" at length paid off when Mithridates was driven to suicide. Mithridates had trusted his friends little more than his enemies: from an early age, he took prophylactic doses of arsenic to avoid the lethal surprise of being given a larger, unprescribed one. As a result, he was unable to poison himself even when he was cornered and wished to do so. He less committed suicide than had it committed on him: a slave had to be ordered to stab him.

Mithridates was a serious menace to Rome when he was alive, and furnished a nice excuse for righteous extortion, but he lost his bogeyman status after his death. Hannibal remained the essential symbol of barbarian menace. After his defeat at Zama, in 202, he took refuge in Bithynia, later part of Mithridates' kingdom. Hannibal did manage to poison himself, when he learnt that his host was about to hand him over to the Romans. In Virgil's *Aeneid*, book IV, Dido predicts Hannibal's mission to destroy Rome: "*exoriare aliquis ex nostris ossibus ultor*" (from our bones may someone arise as an avenger). Mithridates was, however, the subject of an opera by the fourteen-year-old Mozart, *Mitridate Re di Ponto*, which is soon to receive a new production.

On Mithridates' death, Asia was sliced into provinces and became the treasure house from which Sulla, and his no less predatory successors, enriched and – by using its wealth to fund their careers – corrupted Rome. Lucius Licinius Lucullus was one of the first generals to plunder the East in a big, tasteful way, but – frustrated in politics – he then applied himself to gastronomy. Among his rich pickings was the original cherry tree to be imported into Europe. The elder Pliny says that, in retirement, Lucullus committed suicide after his cherry crop failed.

After the Great War, T.E. Lawrence (a trained classicist) urged the greedy Allies to leave the oil under the Arab sands and not to revise the geography of the Middle East into factitious kingdoms and emirates which would cause endless trouble. Greed prevailed; turmoil followed. Elie Kedourie argued forcefully that the wilful dissection of the Ottoman Empire was far the most catastrophic of the economic (and political) consequences of the post-Great War Treaty of Versailles. But then Alexander the Great and his *diadochoi* (successor generals) set the style when they wantonly gave the Persian Empire the chop.

* * *

*B*efore the flood of tourism, the hills of Epirus were bare and bony in the bright, chilly sunshine of early March. To drive to once-famed Dodona we had to wheel through steep bends on a narrow, uneven road. The oracle is in a high valley, almost five thousand feet up. Heavy flocks tugged at tilted, rocky pasture. Shepherds in shaggy fleeces – some dyed saffron, others blanched – huddled in intent vigilance, knees to chin for warmth. Long white crooks posted question marks in the sharp air.

The sanctuary was unfenced and unguarded. There were lichened remains of a theatre and the pediment of a temple to Zeus. Established by Deucalion and his wife, Pyrrha, the original oracle was sacred to Zeus and to Dione, his local consort. Her name is a feminized version of Zeus, little cited elsewhere. She was first worshipped by a trio of priestesses, the Peleiades, whose group name was literally mud (*pelos*).

We wandered through overgrown traces of two small early temples in Dione's honour, as well as one to Aphrodite. As the fate of Hippolytus proved – when Aphrodite contrived his death for venerating only Artemis, goddess of hunting – Love was never a force to ignore: unlike female virginity, male chastity was a vanity without virtue. With tactful etymological convergence, "venery" came to mean the pursuit both of wild game and/or of sexual pleasure.

Many other oracles would serve, and trade on, the inquisitive piety of pilgrims, but only Deucalion's is mentioned in Homer. When Achilles prays Zeus to allow Patroklos to take his place in driving the Trojans from the ships, he addresses "Lord Zeus...ruling over hard-wintered Dodona, and around dwell the Selli, your interpreters with unwashed feet, sleeping on the ground."

Of all ancient sites, which is as numinous as lofty, leafy Dodona? Michael Ayrton nominated Cumae. Near modern Pozzuoli, it lay at the northern limit of Magna Graecia, home of the Sibyl, whom Virgil's Aeneas consulted. Her cave gave Ayrton suggestive shivers. The Latin *numen* refers to the divine nod: exactly what pilgrims came for. The Cumaean Sibyl inscribed her sayings on palm-leaves later enshrined in the so-called Sibylline books, which the Romans consulted at times of grave crisis. Roman practicality, like Greek reason (rarely a last resort), often yielded to superstition, by which the cynical could manipulate the credulous, but to which they themselves were rarely immune.

In the second century A.D., Pausanias – the most exhaustive, and unassuming, of travel-writers[*] – tells of an earth-goddess having cult at Dodona, where Zeus's icon, the sacred oak, had its roots in the earth. If the tree drew strength

---

[*] An invaluable, pedestrian source, Pausanias's odyssey (he had wanted to be a Homeric scholar) took inventory only of pre-Roman Hellas; he ignored all subsequent monuments.

from soiled feet, as it were, might not the muddy priestesses do the same? The rustling foliage of the oak spoke to the hierophants, who gave pilgrims lead "leaves" as mementos. Worship centred on the oak because it was associated with the god of thunder. Zeus's appropriation of the site prefigures the stand-off between him and Demeter. It had a Christian sequel in the Middle Ages, when Nature was honoured as a distinct, if subordinate divinity. Mariolatry is a modern derivative of this cult.

There was a site in Boeotia, many miles south-east of Dodona, where suckling pigs were sacrificed and their bodies thrown into a shrine in a wood sacred to Demeter, Earth-Mother, and to her daughter, Persephone, bringer of spring. The following year, worshippers claimed, the pigs were resurrected at Dodona.* A similar belief was honoured at Athens in the autumn *Thesmophoria*, another of Demeter's festivals: the remains of piglets previously thrown into a pit were retrieved (by women called "pullers-up") and, mixed with seed, scattered as sacred fertilizer.

The mythical back-story was that a herd of pigs had fallen into the crack in the earth through which Minos, King of the Underworld, abducted Persephone. Sicilians will tell you that the maiden's subtraction took place near Lake Pergusa on the plain below Enna, a hill town that rides on a towering crag of rock from which the citizens may have had a grandstand view of Minos's eruption from his basement palace. Do not, however, expect to be able to park your car in Enna's tight and black-flagged, volcanic streets. A Fragonard drawing shows Demeter, who has lit a torch from the crater of nearby Mount Etna, being borne by a chariot pulled by dragons as she searches for her daughter.

It may seem improbable that sacrificial pigs travelled underground all the way from Sicily to Dodona, but if faith moves mountains, why might it not also transport pigs? To scare off snakes,

6 A great mother and litter.

---

* In Virgil's *Aeneid*, an oracle tells Aeneas to look out for a white sow, with a litter of thirty piglets, and there establish his permanent base in Italy. Pigs promise fertility.

the all-female *Thesmophoroi* made rattling noises while the pigs' remains were retrieved. Were pigs sacred to serpentine gods who could no longer be worshipped openly? The witch in Petronius's *Satyrica* uses "antique fragments of pig's head" to alleviate Encolpius's impotence. *Choiros*, the "pig", was also slang for the hairless female pudenda (cf. the modern "pussy",* for the furred version). The term may have originated in Corinth, where the famous erotic bazaar began – so the first-century geographer Strabo says – with sacred prostitution: even aristocrats sent their daughters to sell their virginities to strangers. Such girls were known as "Daughters of *Peitho*" (persuasion), but seem to have needed little persuading. As for the true professionals, in the fourth century, Leaina – the Lioness – was famed, James Davidson tells us in *Courtesans and Fishcakes,* for riding her clients like a jockey. She was applauded by Demetrios the Besieger, who evidently laid her without a siege.

In our Latin grammars, the word quivis (whoever you like) was illustrated – in the dative – by the hexameter, "*Non cuivis homini contingit adire Corinthum*": not any old body has the luck to go to Corinth. It was a Roman tag tied to a city which Lucius Mummius supposedly levelled, and certainly sacked, in 146. At the end of the eighteenth century, John Lemprière, in his *Classical Dictionary*, links the proverb, prudishly, only with "an arduous undertaking". Lemprière, who came from Jersey in the Channel Islands to go to Winchester and Oxford, may have remained French enough to relish the hot-blooded implications of ardour. The visitors' luck lay, in fact, in their access to Corinth's delectable whores.

Inaccessibility added to Dodona's aura, but Delphi was so central – and its Apolline oracle so ingeniously and memorably garrulous – that, as time went by, the Pythian priestess proved a greater attraction than the remote, unsavoury Selli. Nevertheless the theatre at Dodona could seat – and presumably attract – 18,000 spectators as late as the third century, when it was built by King Pyrrhus. Although it had lost its worldwide lure, the site remained the social centre for Epirots.

Delphi's priestess was, for centuries, the frequently solicited primate of divinely received opinions. Whether dictated by Apollo or inflected by political and financial motives, the force of her pronouncements surpassed that of The Thunderer in the days when *The Times* of London was taken to be the voice of Britannia herself. Delphi's venality less detracted from its authority than encouraged the rich and famous to place confidence in edicts which they had

---

* Recent research shows that "eating the hairy dog" is American all-girls-together slang for fellation.

28

sweetened by their donations. Alien Hellenophiles such as Lydia's King Croesus pampered the oracle, and Apollo, rather as plutocrats acquire newspapers whose leading articles then endorse (as if independently) their corporate or political purposes. Non-Greek benefactors were never unwelcome at Delphi: its venality was of a piece with its lack of bias.

Dodona's antiquity – Aristotle says that "Hellas" referred originally to just this area – never became entirely obsolete. A bizarre Byzantine poem refers to "cauldrons that cannot be silent, but incite the brass to sound articulately, the first responding to the second, and the third transferring the sound to the fourth, but if the motive force (the wind) does not blow, the cauldron is voiceless...." This convoluted passage probably refers to a late practice at Dodona, perhaps a gimmick devised to attract pilgrims, in which Zeus, mediated by the wind, clashed brass cauldrons together to convey his will. Modern desktop toys, in which one ball swings and strikes another, and the second the third, the third the fourth, have the same knock-on effect.

Dodona's talking oak trees were vestiges of the time when timber was divine. *Xoana*, the earliest images of the gods, were planks of wood: the Greek for totem poles. Pagans bowed down to wood before they did to stone. The Wooden Horse, with its elaborate trappings, was devised by cunning Odysseus to appeal to the Trojans as a divine offering, if not a divinity: Poseidon raised horses no less than storms. If the plank-flanked monster that now stands near the café on the site of ancient Troy at all resembles the Greeks' gift, the original owed more to commodious fancy than to equine verisimilitude.

* * *

*E*ven when felled, wood never became mere dead material: kidnapped by pirates, the tree-god Dionysus – angered by their disrespect – established his identity by bringing the ship's timbers back to burgeoning life. The mast sprouted branches; the branches, leaves and fruit; vines flagged the rigging. The terrified pirates walked the greening planks and jumped into the sea. Dionysus was the generator of moisture, and hence of wine, as well as patron of the drama. By causing the seasoned ship to become sappy again, he combined his functions in springing a *coup de théâtre*.

Until the seventh century, temples were made of wood: even when marble or limestone came to be used, probably in imitation of Egyptian styles, grooved triglyphs and unadorned metopes mimicked the planks whose ends protruded where stone elements were later mounted. Concrete sections of Basil Spence's complex on the South Bank in London, built for the 1951 Festival of Britain, are grained with the brutalist imprint of planks which braced them as they dried, unconsciously echoing "true joints of cypress, welded together with Chalybean axe and bull's hide glue".

Some scholars read classical columns as idealized tree trunks, with fluted bark, and the temple itself as a petrified forest clearing: *nemos* (Latin *nemus*) designated a sacred grove of the kind where Frazer's Golden Bough might be found. Pausanias reports that the antique *Altis* (sacred enclosure) at Olympia was planted with plane trees, wild olives, poplars, oaks and pines. The Greek failure to make wide use of the arch suggests some inhibition against deviating from pious precedent: since planks could not easily be warped into arcs, it might be that some touchy god would take offence at engineering stone forms that deviated too flagrantly from antique precedent.

The sacred wild olive tree, from which Olympic victors' wreaths were culled, had been brought by Herakles from the lands of the Hyperboreans. Since the latter lived "beyond the North Wind", where they worshipped Apollo (a deity no more welcome at Olympia than Dionysus), Macedonia's "north Greeks" may, after all, have been entitled to claim the right to compete in the Olympic Games,* although they did not enjoy it until Philip of Macedon's endowment of a new, immodest monument, the Philippeion. An architectural amalgam (Corinthian within, Ionic outside), the circular *tholos* was begun after his victory at Chaeronea, in 338, over the very Greeks whose club he now sought to join.

After Philip's murder in 336 in distant Vergina – possibly contrived (and certainly exploited) by his son Alexander and his savage mother, Olympias,** who had been set aside in favour of a younger, now pregnant woman – the Philippeion was graced with the late king's image and with that of the newly enthroned Alexander. The sculptural genius of Leochares could not abate the indignation of Hellenes who were expected to welcome a marble parade of Macedonian upstarts. Alexander's fresh-faced ruthlessness was less shameful, to Macedonians, than evidence of leadership qualities: he was "elected" king by warriors who clashed spears on shields in ritual acclamation. Prime ministers, they say, have to be good (metaphorical) butchers: as king of Macedonia, Alexander would prove one of the greatest slaughterers in history.

Wood came to have innumerable secular uses. It was vital for fuel, for building and for the machinery of war, especially ships and siege equipment. Over the centuries, the Mediterranean world was stripped of its forests. Later, in a blame-shifting exercise, goats were accused of having destroyed the

---

* Herodotus tells of an earlier, less than great Macedonian Alexander, who had to prove his "Argive descent" before being admitted to the foot-race, in which he dead-heated for first place.
** She was Philip's fourth wife, the youngest queen his seventh.

saplings and hence of responsibility for environmental impoverishment (and climate change). In truth, the greediest animals were human beings: today's arid Ephesus was once in a bosky landscape; Asia Minor enjoyed fertile valleys and a refreshing annual rainfall.

After the forests were felled, the soil was eroded and washed down the mountains and through the valleys. The harbour of Ephesus became silted up: as at Miletus, the old city is now some miles from the sea (you walk away from the great library and theatre down an avenue whose sidewalks are ancient jetties). By the first century B.C., pine for shipbuilding had to be imported from the Caucasus: Catullus's *phaselus*, little boat, started life, he says in poem 4, "on a high Cytorean ridge".

7 Goat at the site of his alleged eco-crimes.

Mount Cytorus, in Paphlagonia, was remote enough still to be thick with boxwood. The agile *phaselus* was probably first built by the piratical inhabitants of Phaselis, a small, nicely sited Greek city some few miles south of Antalya in today's south-western Turkey.

* * *

Zeus's sacred grove at Dodona is twelve miles from Ioannina, where we ate our first Greek meal – *arnaki tou fournou* (braised lamb) – in a basement taverna. The bill was the equivalent of a few shillings. Early 1960s Greece – before charter flights and after a civil war at least as savage as the fifth-century *stasis* (internal violence) on Corcyra – seemed marooned in pastoral peace as timeless as it was, in fact, temporary. Superficially, little had changed since Henry Miller, in *The Colossus of Maroussi*, made much of the tall glasses of spring water which, as in the 1930s, accompanied every tiny cup of coffee (*glyko*, *metrio* or *sketo*: sweet, medium or neat). In the early sixties, old Greeks continued to wear "Turkish" trousers and assessed water and distinguished its source as Masters of Wine do vintages. Their connoisseurship was matched, if not initiated, by the Great Kings of Persia, whose luggage, when they went on campaign, included water from the River Choaspes, sealed in silver jars.

On the 1809–11 tour which he versified in *Childe Harold*, Byron was entertained *en prince* in Ioannina, by Ali Pasha, a Turkish satrap with small respect

8 Ali Pasha's Ioannina.

for his distant overlord in Istanbul. Appropriating Epirus as his private fief, the syphilitic scoundrel had all but seceded from the Sublime Porte. Later, he would pay for his impudence with his life. Meanwhile, he revelled in it. The reflected minaret of Ali's mosque still needles the lake outside Ioannina. The town, with its tall, rectilinear bay windows at first-floor level, recalls Toledo and its equally trim traces of Islam.

On entering Ioannina, Byron was shocked to see a human arm and hand hanging from a gibbet: all that remained of a Greek patriot called Evtinnio, who had been tortured for three months, before being hanged, drawn and quartered. Did Byron remain conscious of him when the passionate Pasha admired his "fine, white hands" and small ears? "I am very partial to Englishmen", Ali told him. "I particularly love English sailors".

Exemption from their brutality lends autocrats grace in the eyes of star-struck visitors: British Socialists fawned on Stalin, and some on Saddam Hussein. There is a perennial frisson in shaking hands with blood on them. However disgusted he may have been by Turkish cruelty in Greece, when visiting Istanbul Byron was at pains to make a good impression on the Grand Turk.

The revolutionary poet bridled only after the Grand Chamberlain denied due precedence to his English peerage. Nevertheless, his lordship was glad to pose in Turkish dress (tyrants often have good costumiers). More than a few ancient Greeks made their peace, and sometimes their fortunes, with barbarian grandees. In the 470s, ostracized by his ungrateful countrymen, Themistokles changed into barbarian trousers and became a high official of the very Persians whom his triumph at Salamis had repelled from Hellas. He died as the governor of Magnesia, a Greek city where – though he had taken a crash course in Persian – he cannot have lacked conversation in his native tongue. Many Anatolians were descended from Hellenes displaced by misfortune (or ambition) or evicted by political enemies. At least as many Greeks fought for Xerxes as against him. However, the Great King's conscripts often proved accessible to seduction, either by propaganda – a speciality of Themistokles in his patriotic days – or when a battle turned against the king and relicensed primal loyalties.

In 480, Themistokles incited Xerxes' Ionian contingents to desert by painting patriotic slogans, in huge letters, on rocks and cliffs which were bound to be seen as Persia's conscripts pulled into the harbours from which the Greeks had retreated on the way to regroup around Salamis. At best, Themistokles hoped, Xerxes' "ethnic Greek" sailors would desert; at worst, the Great King, doubting their fealty, might hesitate to deploy them in key positions. Apart from Xerxes' elite corps of ten thousand "immortals", the Persian forces had to be whipped into battle, in contrast – as his honest fellow-traveller, the Spartan, ex-King Demaratus, told him – with the willing valour of free Hellenes.

Like Byron, on that first trip to Greece, we headed south from Ioannina towards Athens, down the jagged western coast where the poet indulged his *nostalgie de la boue* by picnicking with a set of Albanian *klephts*, thieves both by name (*klepto* meant "I steal") and, they boasted, by calling: "Robbers all at Parga" was their loud theme song. They might have been descendants of the pirates with whom Julius Caesar hung out, in much the same area, when they had made him prisoner, and whom he came back to hang in earnest, once he had been ransomed. *Klephts* were viewed more indulgently by Ali Pasha than were Greek patriots. Tyrants often patronize folklore: it is a form without a future. Stalin made Khrushchev squat and dance the peasant's *plyasat' vpisyadku*.

A few weeks after hobnobbing with Ali in Epirus, Byron swung to the philhellenic camp. He had been dining, in civilized style, with Andreas Londos, a young Greek employed in the Turkish administration. Since the Phanariotes – functionaries drawn mainly from the Greek quarter in Istanbul, which was topped by a *phanari* (lighthouse) – were highly privileged, Byron was astonished when Londos leaped onto the table and sang a banned patriotic song, "*Thefte, pethes ton Ellenon!*" (Arise, you sons of Greece!).

Did Byron's classical knowledge spring to making the connection with an elegiac poem written by Callinus of Ephesus, in the seventh century? In "*Mechris teo katakeisthe?*" (How long are you going to lie around?), Callinus reproached fellow-Ionians for failing to rise against the Lydians, whose territory coincided with that controlled, in Byron's day, by the Ottomans. A century and a half after Callinus, the Ionians of Asia Minor – excited by promises from their mother-city, Athens – did indeed rebel, with ruinous consequences.

After the insurgents had been crushed, and their cities pillaged, Darius instructed a slave to say to him, three times, whenever he sat down to dinner, "Remember the Athenians". Their sin was compounded by active involvement in the burning of Sardis, after which Darius could be excused for firing an arrow in the air and saying, "God grant that I punish the Athenians".

Darius and his son Xerxes' punitive expeditions against Greece, in 490 and 480, were primed either by justified indignation or by barbarian insolence, depending on whose justice, and which gods, you favoured. The Athenians reacted with outrage when the Persians did indeed burn the temples on the Acropolis, and in their turn vowed revenge. "War", said Heracleitus of Ephesus at the beginning of the fifth century, "is the king and father of all things", not least the bloody stand-off which has led East and West to define themselves in the light of their differences: the "oriental" Persians wore trousers, which the skirted Greeks regarded as effeminate. Furiously symbiotic, their antagonisms generated religions, arts and hatreds unthinkable without cultural cross-breeding.

Heracleitus's gnomic philosophy, which at once says and does not say what its author means, is at the root of the enigmatic thinking that has given western philosophy its cryptic course. His native city, Ephesus, stood on the fault-line between Persian and Greek civilization. Heracleitus's ambiguous view of humanity is the product of their discordant synthesis. When he writes of "the force / god that does and does not wish to be called Zeus", he straddles both sides of the dialectic. He seemed to question the gods, but left his work for safekeeping in the temple of Artemis. Truth was more noble in Persia than in Hellas: the Persian upper class was brought up to tell it (and to ride a horse and use the bow). The first philosophers – who often doubled as diplomats – were at home in the logically excluded middle: yes *and* no is still a philosophical answer.

* * *

One of the effects of Byron's youthful visit to Athens was to encourage him in a love affair with Nicoló Giraud, the brother-in-law of Lord Elgin's agent, Lusieri, who was negotiating with the Turks for the removal (to safe keeping) of the Parthenon marbles. Unable to resist an opportunity for satire, Byron later lampooned Elgin as a looting philistine. In truth, however, the Turks attached no importance to antique marbles, which were often

9 Byron lording it in oriental drag.

broken up in the manufacture of quicklime. If Elgin had not appropriated and shipped out the Parthenon frieze and metopes, they would almost certainly have been recycled, thus aborting for ever the occasion first for Byron and then for modern Greeks to strike reproachful attitudes.

Byron's bisexuality is beyond doubt, but is it right to accuse him of paedophilia, if this is supposed to mean love of small boys? Nicoló was "fifteen or sixteen" and was, it seems, as passionately attached to Byron as his lordship to him: in his will, Byron left Nicoló the vast sum of seven thousand pounds. The flagrancy of his passion probably owed something to the location in which it was expressed. Byron was nothing if not susceptible to the *genius loci* of almost everywhere he went. Athens moved him to sentimental lamentation: "Look on this spot – a nation's sepulchre! / Abode of Gods whose shrines no longer burn..."

Byron was a chameleon,* hot for local colour. His romance with Nicoló Giraud honoured Greek tradition no less than personal appetite. Classical studies at Harrow encouraged "imitation" of ancient models: Byron's juvenilia included versions of Euripides, Anacreon and Catullus (as Catullus's did of Callimachus). Education and emulation were much the same thing. He must have seen himself and Nicoló in an ancient light, lovers in the Greek tradition, although Giraud was, in truth, rather old for ancient taste: "I delight in a boy of twelve,"** wrote Strato of Sardis, in the second century A.D., "but thirteen is more desirable, much. A fourteen-year-old is an even sweeter flower of love, fifteen still more delicious, the sixteenth is heavenly, but seventeen...that's maybe cool for Zeus, but not for me.... Your beard will come, last of evils, and the worst, and then you'll discover what it is to have no friends."

John Donne, in his *Sappho to Philaenis*, catches the Greek attitude with, "His chin, a thorny hairy unevenness / Doth threaten, and some daily change possess". Body and facial hair presaged unlovable maturity. To be *melanpygos*

---

* Plutarch said the same of the versatile Alcibiades.
** Shaping dough into tight buttocks, the homosexual chef in Denys Achard's film *Le Déclin de l'Empire Américain* makes an identical observation.

("black-arsed") symbolized erotic obsolescence, in the eye of an adult *erastes* (mature lover): in the first century B.C., Meleager warns a boy, "Don't be too grand with me. A Nemesis is creeping on you from behind." In one poem, Meleager is exasperated into preferring sex with women to hairy boys.

In the seventh century, that poetic sergeant-major Archilochos also used *melanpygos* to advertise shameless virility. Robert Graves's "giants of old", with their "long yards and stinking armpits", stood for the same blatantly hirsute style. Today's Hollywood male film stars revive Strato's cult of immaturity by waxing their hairy chests to smoothness.

Hair has a rhetoric of its own: the Spartans were famous for combing their long locks in the hours before going to their glorious deaths in the pass of Thermopylae, in 480, but an earlier generation of Spartiate warriors is said to have favoured short hair when they were fighting Argos for mastery of the Peloponnese. Until the so-called Battle of the Champions in – it is thought – 545, the Argives wore their hair long. After it, the latter shaved their heads, in shame; the previously crew-cut Spartans grew theirs, in pride. Spartan boys are said to have had their heads shaved as recruits to their *agelai*, the boarding houses in which they were hardened for entry to the *boua*, the heifer herd, the next stage on the way to full citizenship.

The language of gesture often involves hair: Samson's virile strength was a function of abundant locks; at Erythrae, in Karia, the local cult statue of Herakles – the Greek Samson – was hauled ashore annually with a "rope of tresses". Jewish brides wear wigs in public, sometimes having first shorn their hair. A Spartan girl's hair was cut on her wedding night (and she was dressed in male clothing), just before her husband came to her. In the Christian world, girls who were taking the veil were similarly shorn, as brides for Jesus. Herodotus says that girls on Delos cut a lock of their hair and, before they marry, lay it on the tomb of two Hyperborean girls in the temple of Artemis.

Robert de Niro, in *Taxi Driver*, shaved part of his head before going into battle, with only a springing stripe of hair on top of his head, like a Native American warrior. The crested helmets of Homeric heroes (Hector's plumes alarmed his small son, Astyanax) were glorified topknots. In Aeschylus's *Libation Bearers*, Orestes leaves a lock of hair on his father's tomb, where it is discovered, and recognized, by his sister Elektra (Robert Lowell's translation has him leave "feathers", which is fatuous). Some two hundred years after the *Oresteia*, Callimachus wrote a poem – the fourth of his *Aitia* – about a lock of hair cut and dedicated, in the temple of Aphrodite, as a thank-offering for her husband's safe return from the wars, by Queen Berenice (wife – and sister – of Ptolemy Euergetes). Her name is a Macedonian version of Pherenike, the victory-bringer. When the lock disappeared a day later, the astronomer Conon, "eager to

10 Crested hero from Aegina, sixth century B.C.

11 Crested London rocker, twentieth century A.D.

12 De Niro's taxi driver on the warpath.

curry favour", pointed to the heavens and divined that the regal hair had been elevated into a "shapeless group of seven stars". Callimachus lends his poetic voice to the exiled tress, which still regrets its severance from the royal head. Alexander Pope's *The Rape of the Lock* is a variant *hommage* on a similar theme.

Like dyed hair, depilation was a way to delay signs of age. In the second century A.D., the Roman emperor Hadrian's young Greek lover, Antinous, soaked his cheeks in milk when, at the advanced age of twenty, he was striving to remain the emperor's baby-faced darling. Hadrian's admiration for Hellas – among many benefactions, he completed the sixth-century temple of Zeus at Athens – and his sexual habits led the Romans (who might practise Greek vices, but did not preach or sentimentalize them) to call him *graeculus*, Greekling: it implied furtive scorn for a dutiful *princeps* of whom few Romans spoke well. A much more despicable emperor earned the affectionate diminutive Caligula, "Little Boot", while strutting, as a boy, in miniature military uniform when on campaign with his father, the great Germanicus.

After Antinous drowned in the Nile – which some read as a deliberate Osirian gift of his youthful soul to his emperor/lover – Hadrian shaved off his own beard, as if the boy's sacrifice had indeed rejuvenated him. He alone was fooled, but not for long: he fell into a depression and finally retreated to Tivoli, some sixteen miles north-east of Rome, which was never his favourite city. The eclectic architecture of his so-called villa – in fact, a huge estate – supplied a theme park in which he could rehearse happy oriental days: a marble crocodile still decorates the ornamental pool. Hadrian's now tenantless private Pompeii,

37

with the Villa d'Este a few hundred yards away, was a favourite weekend haunt when we and our children lived in Rome in the early 1960s.

On mature men, a well-groomed beard could be a sign of strength: a vase painting of the seventh century, in the British Museum, shows the centaur Nessus asking for quarter by the traditionally submissive gesture of touching Herakles' beard, after the centaur had made a fateful pass at the hero's wife, Deianeira, while ferrying her across a river. A not dissimilarly pleading gesture, but towards the genitals, was used to proposition boys. The timidity of a defeated foe became that of a prospecting *eromenos* (juvenile beloved). As Shi'ite Muslims continue to illustrate, when they proffer both hands to Allah, palms upwards, the gesture is disarmingly imprecatory. In his *Satyrica*, Petronius has a woman "holding out supine hands towards your knees" as she begs Encolpius not to reveal her secrets. As for beards, Saddam Hussein's repeated caressing of the one he grew in hiding was said to indicate that he had been betrayed.

* * *

*H*erakles was not appeased by Nessus, though it might have been wise to be so: he later died in agony after putting on a shirt steeped in the centaur's blood, which Deianeira had preserved after Nessus's dying promise that it would supply a prescription for retrieving her husband's love.* Instead, it burnt him so inextinguishably that the hero prayed to be allowed to die. Granting his wish, Zeus assumed him into heaven as a supplementary immortal. Only then was Herakles reconciled, in Olympian solidarity, with his stepmother, Hera, who had pursued him during his mortal life with implacable malice.

If the ancient Hellenes made a noble fuss when invaded by the Persians, how often did they hesitate to intrude on barbarian soil? Not only the far reaches of the Black Sea to the east, but also distant Spain, to the west, became somewhat Hellenized. Tartessos (the biblical Tarshish) is usually identified with Cádiz. It was colonized first by Phoenicians, early in the twelfth century, but Greek metal-traders from Samos soon penetrated the Pillars of Herakles to reach its profitable shores. Posidonius reported that precious metals were so common that the first Phocaeans were welcome to exchange their iron anchors for silver ones.

Outside Sevilla, you can see a pillar topped by Herakles, still the patron, if not the saint, of the city. The Greek super-odd-job-man visited what would become Andalucía on the tenth of his labours of atonement – in servitude to

---

* Herakles was not always irascible with centaurs: a fifth-century vase in the Villa Giulia in Rome shows the hero, club at ease, over his shoulder, shaking hands with a venerable and unexcited member of the breed. Varieties of mood were common to both.

King Eurystheus – for a fit of madness (wished on him by Hera) during which he slaughtered his own children. In curious reciprocation, in the thirteenth century, the Catalans, under Roger de Flor, briefly conquered some of Greece, after which the kings of Aragón incorporated "Duke of Athens" in their titles.

Hesiod has Herakles sailing to Erythea, a mythical "island beyond the sunset", nevertheless identified with Cádiz, on a mission to steal the cattle of Geryon, a three-bodied giant who presented a savage challenge to rustlers: "...Fancy a fight with Mr Three-in-One? / I'd frankly sooner see than be in one."

Being outnumbered was the constant problem of Greek generals: the weight of enemy numbers defeated Leonidas, the Spartan hero at Thermopylae, but – a century and a half later – Alexander the Great turned speed and discipline into a dynamic force that drilled into and shattered the massed, and static, Persians. For all his strength, even Herakles had to display cunning to achieve what seemed impossible. How could Geryon's three bodies be lanced by the single javelin available to the hero? Herakles prevailed by a flanking attack which spitted all three of the giant's trunks with one threading thrust: "With but one dart Geryon's fate is sealed. / Six eyes enjoy their last glimpse of the sun; / Three heads can sometimes be out-thought by

13 Herakles labouring with triple Geryon.

one." Pictorial representation of myth could be more literal than poetic fancy: a fifth-century vase in the British Museum shows a Geryon with three distinct bodies and pairs of legs: a trio of brothers rather than the triune triplets which one imagines. There was a pseudo-historical King Geron of Tarshish, who reigned over an area famous for its fighting bulls.

Herakles remained the essential Greek hero, at once fearless warrior and holy, sometimes demented, buffoon. Credited with prodigious appetites in all departments, he deflowered fifty virgins in a single night. He was also notorious for spicing his virility with gay passades and cross-dressing. In addition, he was an important founding father, not least of the Olympic Games, by whose quadrennial pan-Hellenic festivities the Greek calendar came to be calibrated. The Olympics are generally held to have started in 776, though that is only the postulated date from which the names of victors began to be recorded; it would be literal-minded to infer that Herakles must have been alive at that time. Folklore is as innocent of reliable chronology as it is of historical probability. Yet even Thucydides (who disdains oracles and omens) speaks of mythical characters, such as Helen, without distinguishing them from historical ones. As Moses Finley pointed out, there is a five-hundred-year lacuna, without a landmark date, between the Dorian invasion of the Peloponnese, in the twelfth century, and the widespread use of written records at the onset of the seventh, when the Corinthian Ameinocles is known to have built four ships for the Samians.

Greek heroes were advised not to boast too grandly: none escaped if he or she claimed to emulate the gods, or not to need their favour. In Sophocles' play, Aias falls foul of Athene by claiming that his victories owe nothing to divine sponsorship. That emulous mortal seamstress Arachne needled the same skilled, spiteful goddess by weaving a wittier tapestry, and was turned into a spider. After producing a large family, Niobe affected to have outscored Leto, the mother of Apollo and Artemis. Recruited to avenge the insult, Apollo shot Niobe's ten sons, Artemis her ten daughters, leaving the bereaved mother "all tears". To distribute death with impunity was the mark of an immortal.

To remain on the right side of the gods, prudent heroes let myth, and the poets, blow their trumpets for them. In due time, art would apologize to those whom spiteful gods had punished. Praxiteles' statue of Niobe bore the anonymous inscription, "From a living woman, the gods turned me to stone; / But from stone, Praxiteles made me alive again."

Art both celebrates the gods and, by humanizing, diminishes them. Jewish law prohibits not only the representation of the divine but *all* "naturalistic" depiction, lest it involve an inadvertent slur on G-d or encourage the worship of an image – such as the Golden Calf or a celebrity pin-up – in His place.

Islam mimics this caution. In Christian Byzantium, iconolaters and icono-clasts fought for and against holy images with the same ferocity as the same city's sports fans for the Greens or the Blues. Renaissance popes commis-sioned handsome advertisements for the True Faith, but their painters' visual parables, based on ancient myth, prompted the luscious depiction of the nude. What was, above all, reborn with the Renaissance was the pagan world, its polymorphous duplicity and allegorical iconography.

* * *

*A*t the beginning of the fifth century B.C. – the hinge on which Hellenic minds turned to questioning folkloric credulities – the historian and diplomat Hecataeus of Miletus doubted whether Herakles could "really" have gone rustling as far afield as Spain. As a more likely location, he proposed the countryside near Ambracia, on the Greek mainland. Piously sceptical, he dared to question Herakles' range, but not his achievements. It would, he promised, still be "no small labour" to make off with a three-headed giant's herd. Rustling cattle was a common feat of daring, as the newborn Hermes proved. He got away with it because Zeus was amused at the god-child's ingenious nerve when Hermes caused Apollo's oxen to back into the cave where he hid them, thus giving their owner the impression that the hoof-prints led away from their hiding place. Critical theorists might read this as an omen: hermeneutics also take you away from the truth. Mortal rustlers were less indulged than Hermes. When Odysseus's crew barbecued the Sun's sacred cows, Circe turned them into the pigs they had made of themselves.

Hecataeus was unlucky not to be dignified by posterity with the title "the Father of History", with which Herodotus, his disciple, was crowned. Most of his pioneering work was lost. His genealogies offered a prosaic challenge to the rapturous mythography of Hesiod; but if scornful about Greek "lies", the Milesian master still claimed divine descent for himself.

Sevillian legend continues to insist that Herakles came west. Galician Spaniards say the same of St James. Although it is improbable that the brother of Jesus ever got as far as Santiago de Compostela, pilgrims continue to trudge to his alleged tomb and crave the favours he granted the *conquistadores*, who slaughtered Aztecs and Incas on the pious cue, "Santiago!" "*In hoc signo vinces*" was the crucial rubric that confirmed the emperor Constantine's politic decision to adopt Christianity. After converting the empire to monotheism, he saw no inconsistency in having a huge temple built in his own and his family's honour. He was actually baptized only towards the end of his life, when in sight of paradise (the Cathars had the same habit in the thirteenth century).

Constantine's mother, Helena, was more zealously faithful. On a visit to Palestine, she claimed to have found the True Cross and brought back to Europe the Seamless Robe which Jesus wore at his crucifixion. Supposedly still preserved in the Catholic cathedral at Trier, it was paraded at a ceremony in 1933, soon after Adolf Hitler became chancellor. The bishop declared that he and his congregation had "entered the new Reich and...are prepared to serve it with all the might of our body and soul". Whether B.C. or A.D., worldly success confirms divine favour. "The Mandate of Heaven" warranted Chinese emperors whose failures were taken to be evidence of its retraction; Allah has his Will, which grants and withdraws favours with equal inscrutability.

Like "Christendom", Hellas was a term that embraced a culture rather than defined a territory. Hellenism announced citizenship in a civilization with no single ruler or capital, no predominant political system, still less with a clerical class. Heresy was no scandal among pre-Christian Greeks; the term derives from *hairesis* (choice), a normal practice in polytheism. In the *Iliad*, book II, Homer assumes that everyone sacrifices to his preferred god. As for myth, there were variations, apocrypha and parodies. None was "gospel": mythical lilies were constantly gilded. Lack of dogma did not, however, prevent Hellas defining itself in terms of shared pieties. The temples of Greek enemies demanded respect. Treaties were sealed with pious libations and the undertaking to observe oaths unless – the small print stipulated – "Gods or heroes" (always out for blood) should intervene. Although the mathematician Hippodamus, born in Miletus in Asia Minor, around 500, furnished the grid-system plan on which Hellenic cities – from Pella to Sinope – were disposed, there was no users' guide to their proper administration, nor any recommendation to a specific political system, although the blueprint's open spaces implied a public arena for markets and debates. Greek culture was vested in common deities and a (more or less) common language. The variety and mutability of their gods, and the elasticity of their imagery, gave Hellenes the material for inventive, sometimes skittish, diversity.

Reason and art less banished myth than renovated and revised it. The durability of a myth was dependent on its mutability: the more it could be stretched into variant or entertaining versions, the more likely its use in either drama or art. Plato's so-called myths were often extravagantly far-fetched: he makes a didactic fancy of the story, told matter-of-factly by Herodotus, of Gyges, the insolent usurper of the throne of Lydia, whom Plato graces with a helmet of invisibility. My novella *The Hidden I* is a recension of the same myth.

Other stories lost their more outlandish elements: Perseus's rescue of Andromeda at first centred on his slaying of her dragon-gaoler, but romantic painters chose to dwell on the heroine's naked gratitude when rescued from her crag. Giorgio de Chirico turned Ariadne into a series of literally statuesque,

14 Perseus loops the loop to rescue Andromeda.

draped figures. There is a particularly fine Greco-Roman more-than-life-size statue of a seductively pneumatic Ariadne, reclining on what looks like a marble lilo. Originally found in Perge, it is now in the excellent new museum at Antalya, in south-western Anatolia. Oedipus's myth rarely primed pictorial imagination (Ingres is the exquisite exception), though it furnished a maquette for many plays and for Freud's knowing misrepresentation of the king's "desire" for his mother (Jocasta probably went with the throne, or vice versa).

Whatever the compost – social and linguistic – in which the Greeks plunged their roots, and which coloured their vanities, the flowering of their culture was a hybrid entirely their own. The expansive qualities of myth were repeated in speech: Aristophanes was famous for tongue-twisting neologisms such as the longest word in Greek, *orthro-phoito-sycophanto-diko-talaiporos*, rendered by Liddell and Scott as "early-prowling-base-informing-sad-litigious-plaguy", a portmanteau adjective attached to parasites who made a living as

15 Roman marble Ariadne/Arianna, draped.

16 De Chirico's twentieth-century Ariadne, a *maja semi-desnuda*.

professional prosecutors in the Athenian courts. The question of whether the Greeks "believed" in their myths is as much beside the point as asking if they believed in their language.

In *The Republic*, Plato scowls at poets for fabricating tales which prompted, in particular, the fear of death. But then his myth of Er, later in the same dialogue, depicts the souls of the dead alarmingly adrift in a kind of limbo. Plato substitutes his own sanitized myths for the toxic legends of the unenlightened. Communism too would disparage old credulities the better to replace them with blind faith in dialectical materialism. Epicurus's pupil and disciple Colotes (*c.* 310–260) was a more honest materialist who advocated unprogrammatic empiricism rather than Platonic (or any other) prescriptive faith. No good deed goes uncensured, however: in Cicero's *De natura deorum* – written in the first century B.C. – Cotta the Academic (that is, meta-Platonist) accuses Epicureans of denying "divine benevolence" and hence promoting egocentric utilitarianism. And so it goes.

* * *

What are the islands to me?
What is Greece? What is Rhodos, Samos, Chios,
What is Paros facing West,
What is Crete?   —*H.D.*

*T*he first house we ever owned – a converted donkey shed – was on the Cycladic island of Ios. We arrived there by honouring an oracular hint: uncertain of which Greek isle to choose, we consulted a travel agent in Athens who was a friend of a friend. While we sat musing in her office, drinking coffee (she gave the children spoonfuls of vanilla in a glass of cold water), Thalia – named after the muse of comedy and bucolic poetry – happened to be telephoned by a ship-owner who had once been minister of marine, for a week or two. "This is a sign for you," she said.

Artemis Denaxas was the owner of big estates on unfavoured and depopulated Ios. A blazered Anglophile, with dogs called Dick and Rover, he was eager to have English expatriates settle on his native island. In the early 1960s, the Cyclades were as difficult of access as they were free of tourists. Mykonos was a flashy exception that proved the obscurity of the rest. Its homosexual clientele had enriched a flat island proverbial, in antiquity, for extreme poverty. The seventh-century poet Archilochos speaks scornfully of it, but – heaven knows – not only of it: he was a master of vituperation.

A century and a half after him, the Athenian pundit Solon equated lack of initiative with settling for a quiet life on uneventful Pholegandros or idyllic Sikinos, which is visible across the narrow sea from our house on Milopota bay: the sharper its humped profile, the more ominous the weather. Was there latecomer's spite in Solon's scorn for obscure and peaceful islands? The Cyclades had been rich, and brilliant with art, when Athens was a talentless village. According to Homer's roll-call, Athens was too insignificant for mention among those thousand ships sailing to Troy. However, once they were dominant, Athenian propagandists interpolated lines in the *Iliad*, asserting that their city had made an important contribution: an early instance of the Stalinist rescripts that edit the past to buttress the present. Classical scholars with ingenious theories about ancient life were often challenged with, "*Vous avez un texte, monsieur?*" The Athenians had the wit, and nerve, to supply one.

The story of Theseus is the most blatant instance of the Athenian capacity for pluming their history with mythological gloss. The emblematic hero was decked with stupendous achievements and manly qualities which Athenians could then deduce to be innately typical of themselves. The culmination of Theseus's cult came when, in 475, the great admiral Cimon obeyed an oracle requiring him to repatriate the bones of a gigantic man whom he discovered to have been buried on Skyros. Cimon culled kudos by commanding the vessel in which the heroic relics were ferried home to Attica. They were laid to ostentatious rest in a specially constructed Theseum, as the great Napoleon's were in Les Invalides. The Athenians' best-known unknown soldiers had an extramural place in the communal mound on the site of Marathon where they had fallen; those missing in battle were traditionally remembered by the carrying of an empty bier in the procession for the public burial of war dead, but Athens' best-known hero, Theseus, was centralized as a focus for emulation.

The importance of bones, as giving title to a hero or to a property, is borne out by a Delphic pronouncement, again cited by Herodotus, which lends convenient piety to the inquirers' territorial ambitions:

> There is in Arcadia Tegea, on a level plain
> Where two winds blow with driving force,
> Blow and counter-blow, and woe alike on woe.
> There the life-giving soil holds Agamemnon's son.
> Bring him back home, and Tegea is your prize.

The beneficiary of this go-get-him promise, Orestes, is a victim-figure who has been compared with Hamlet: he too feels revulsion from his mother, Klytemnestra, and hatred for her lover (and has a taciturn Horatio in Pylades). Orestes' conscience does not quite make him a coward, but – once he has screwed himself up to kill Klytemnestra – he is tortured by inner demons. Since Aeschylus's trilogy is named in his honour and culminates in his vindication, Orestes should, like Theseus, rate as an exemplary hero, but priggishness makes him more woebegone than charismatic. Klytemnestra's vengeful hatred for Agamemnon – she cannot forgive his politic sacrifice of their daughter, Iphigeneia – seems better justified than her son's matricidal hardness.

It is difficult for modern moralists to accept the relative unimportance of family *affection* as a motive among the ancients, especially males. Perikles' wartime admonition to Athenian mothers and widows not to indulge in protracted grief over dead warrior sons and husbands insists on the primacy of political over personal bonding.

The *Oresteia* is an early example of a work of genius which defeats its author's presumed intentions. With the exception of Elektra (like Athene, "strong for the father"), the females are either venomous, like the Furies and Klytemnestra, or pathetic, like the doomed Cassandra and the sentimental (and intentionally comic?) nurse. What is important should be men's business. Yet female characters dominate the stage. Even Klytemnestra's revenant shade, in *The Eumenides*, has an accusatory dignity to match that of Hamlet's father.

The Furies are finally persuaded to abate their rage against Orestes, but Athene needs Portian skill to procure their climbdown. She has to offer them a comfortable dower house, appropriate annual tribute, and – in the English style – a lordly title (Eumenides, the Kindly Ones), before they consent, reluctantly, to become domesticated deities rather than remain the hounds of hell. We are told that the play ended with a procession like that of the Panathenaea. The pensioned Furies were accompanied to their new homes with patriotic enthusiasm. The audience was encouraged to applaud both the author and its own magnanimity.

Once vindicated, Orestes leaves to resume the throne of Argos, but makes no memorable mark. Like Aeneas, he does the god-ordained thing without exciting sympathy or admiration. What actor ever craved the part of Orestes? Even Elektra, who scarcely speaks once her mother has been killed, has a more fiery role, although her abrupt marriage to taciturn Pylades, king of Phocis, smacks more of political deal-making than of eager passion. As for female independence, Elektra – like the suicide bomber – is her own woman only as long as she serves a male policy.

* * *

W hy do we like Odysseus so much more than Orestes? He was by Homeric definition a crafty, often dodgy operator. Seldom portrayed as a superman, he rarely shirks a fight, but never seeks a fair one: he prefers an ambush or a ruse. He gets what he wants even if he has to break his word, as he does with Dolon, the Trojan scout whose life he and Diomedes promise to spare, if he will give them information. Once he has, they cut his throat. The episode puns cruelly on Dolon's name, which Robert Graves translates as "ensnarer" (*dolos* is a trick or ruse).

Metis, cunning intelligence, makes Odysseus an able, because unprincipled, diplomat: in *Philoctetes*, Sophocles portrays him as a promise-him-anything deceiver. His cynical attempt to induce the gangrened archer to return to the siege of Troy, which cannot be defeated without the deadly accuracy of his famous bow, disgusts his fellow-envoy, the naive Neoptolemus. Yet the sly hero retains our affection, regardless of the fact that he himself once tried to evade the draft by pretending to be mad. When Agamemnon, Menelaus and Palamedes came west to Ithaka to recruit him, they found Odysseus literally playing the fool. Warned by an oracle that he would be away for twenty years if he took ship to Troy, he had put on a silly hat, shaped like

17 Dolon, the ensnarer, snared by Odysseus and Diomedes.

half an egg (in 1960s Macedonia, I saw Muslim peasants in similar oval white skullcaps working their land), yoked together an ass and an ox, and ploughed his fields – some say the beach – while sowing salt over his shoulder, like a demented version of Deucalion throwing the rocks.

Palamedes – another byword for cunning – responded to Odysseus's performance like some ancient Mycroft Holmes outwitting young brother Sherlock: he took baby Telemachus from his mother Penelope's arms and put him on the ground right in line with Odysseus's advancing ploughshare. Unable to sustain his lunatic charade, the paternal ploughman had to halt his oddly-coupled team. Certified as sane, Odysseus could no longer resist the call to arms.

Odysseus never forgave Palamedes, not least since the oracle had added a rider that he himself would return empty-handed and alone from Troy. The hero was additionally incensed by the shipments of booty which the gloating

Palamedes sent back regularly from Troy. Contriving the least lovely of his wiles, Odysseus forged a letter from King Priam of Troy, in which he offered Palamedes a fortune if he would betray the Greeks. Odysseus buried a stash of gold near Palamedes' tent, together with the covering letter. He then arranged for the Achaeans to detect both. Palamedes was arrested and locked up, pending trial.

Since his father Nauplius was king of Evia (Euboea), across the Aegean from Troy, Palamedes tried to contact him by writing messages on oar-blades, which were launched on the waters, in the hope that they would drift to Evia with the help of his grandfather, Poseidon. This variation on putting a message in a bottle proved unsuccessful. Odysseus and his crony Diomedes prosecuted the framed Palamedes,[*] who was convicted and stoned to death. Killing at a distance avoided blood-pollution.[**]

Palamedes is unlucky to rate among the also-rans of myth. He is credited with having invented some letters of the Greek alphabet, as well as the games of dice, draughts and knuckle-bones. His name – like that of Palaemon, the wrestler, an early name for Herakles – implies handiness (from *palame*), though Graves derives its prefix from *palai* and reads Palamedes as incarnating "ancient wisdom". Is that why Marcel Proust baptized the Baron de Charlus "Palamède"? Or did that archly Homeric poseur and classicist Bloch suggest it?

One wonders if Odysseus managed to give evidence against Palamedes without swearing an oath, which might have incurred more miasma than contriving his rival's death (no great scandal in the ancient world). He and that archetypal slyboots Daedalus were equally artful in turning *metis* to self-advancing purpose.

War made Greeks hard. In *Philoctetes* young Neoptolemus is disgusted by Odysseus's duplicity. Not long afterwards, however, he grew callous enough to become the murderer of Hector's infant son: Astyanax was thrown from the same battlements on which – in that touching scene in the *Iliad* – he had been alarmed by the flaring plume on his father's helmet. Neoptolemus was also the instigator of the sacrifice of Priam's daughter, Polyxena, to his father Achilles' angry ghost. Odysseus's queasy accomplice in the duping of Philoctetes became a pitiless, impious killer. The demands of his dead father for the blood of an innocent living victim, and the son's obligation to honour it,

---

[*] For whom the sophist Gorgias composed a posthumous apologia.
[**] In *The Evolution of the Gospel*, Enoch Powell persuaded himself, if no one else, that Jesus was not crucified by the Romans, but stoned by the Jews, who abhorred direct contact with blood and, in any case, lacked licence to crucify people. Powell's scholarly evidence was that there was none: the Jews – manipulators of the media from way back – had kept it out of the Gospels.

suggest that human sacrifice was never alien to archaic tradition, though only occasional instances can be glimpsed through the torn veil of myth.

Do we persist in relishing Odysseus's company because we sense his distaste for high politics and ostentatious spoils? Neither glorying in conquest nor craving bloody fame, he sets out to win the war only in order to go home to his wife and son. If Odysseus had kingly qualities and endorsed autocracy (he says, in the *Iliad*, "Let one man be master and one the king"), he was scarcely a gentleman in the snobbish sense of someone without time or taste for physical labour. What Plato and Aristotle disdained as "banausic" was no shame to earlier generations (modern Greeks call all work *douleia*, the ancient word for slavery).

The *metis* with which Odysseus was blessed by Athene – whose unacknowledged mother was the divine impersonation of it – was not mere intellectual

agility: it could involve weaving material no less than stratagems. When Odysseus blinded the Cyclops Polyphemus in order to find a way out of the cave in which he (and his crew) had been penned, Homer describes how he heated a beam and screwed it into Polyphemus's single eye, twirling it around "...as a man would pierce the timbers of a ship, / With an auger, and others keep it spinning with a strap beneath, / Holding it at each end, and the auger drills on and in".

18 One in the eye for Polyphemus.

This episode is probably among the most frequently illustrated in all mythology: you can see fragments of it on what is left of the vaulted ceiling of Nero's *Domus Aurea* in Rome. The all-together-boys aspect of the scene, which is often depicted with a trotting troop of crewmen ramming the sharpened trunk into Polyphemus's eye, is a contrast with the solitary achievements of Herakles. Odysseus and Polyphemus figure on the superb mosaics in Piazza Armerina, near Enna in Sicily (in the villa probably built at the beginning of the fourth century A.D. by the emperor Maximianus, as a hunting lodge).

When Odysseus decides to leave the island where he has been hanging out with the beautiful and immortal Calypso, he uses his craftiness to construct a vessel to carry him home to his mortal wife, Penelope, despite Calypso's offer to vest him with immortality. Calypso ("she who hides") is a seductress who stood – Neoplatonists said – for both Death and Nature, which hides its secrets. Having unveiled Calypso, Odysseus ceased to fancy her. Both regal and banausic, he himself had built the conjugal bed to which he craves, slowly, to return. His mainland neighbour, sober old Nestor, was similarly versatile: sagacious in counsel, the king of Pylos could also sink a bigger bumper of wine than lesser men could even lift. From the high plateau of his palace, you can see the island of Sphacteria, where the Athenian politician-turned-general, Cleon, literally, and unsportingly, smoked out an elite detachment of Spartans in 425 and, by doing so, procured the prompt offer of an armistice from Sparta. It turned out to be the best chance the Athenians had of quitting while they were ahead. They lacked a Nestor to advise them.

* * *

*I*n Sophocles' *Aias*, Odysseus appears in a more pleasing light than in the same playwright's *Philoctetes*: he argues for the humane treatment of Aias's family after the dead hero has been anathematized by Agamemnon and Menelaus. When the commanding generals want to deny the rites even of a decent funeral to the disgraced suicide, Odysseus – Agamemnon's most trusted friend – deplores their vindictiveness:

> You're blind with hate. Deny him burial
> and trample justice! I loathed him,
> More than any other Greek in camp.
> I detested all he was – and still I say
> he was the bravest man I ever saw,
> except for Achilles, the best and bravest
> Who ever came to Troy. Admit it!

Although he and Aias were always at odds, Odysseus is disgusted by Agamemnon's pettiness. He is stirred by common decency rather than by remorse: he may have triumphed over Aias, by being awarded the arms of the dead Achilles, but now that the son of Telamon has gone mad and slaughtered a flock of sheep, while imagining that they were the ungrateful commander-in-chief and his staff, rivalry yields to pity: a great warrior should never have been driven to ignominious self-destruction. As the *Aias* opens, we see Odysseus delighted by Athene's gloating attitude towards Aias's folly. Later, however, he shows more magnanimity than his divine patron. Man may be frail, corruptible and short-lived, but Odysseus proves capable of forgiveness, and compromise. How many deities have followed his example?

Aias's slaughter of the cows and sheep which, in his hallucination, he takes to be Agamemnon and Menelaus, is a tragic case of uncontrolled rage which

19 And the arms go to...Odysseus, awarded Achilles' kit.

issues in treason. Odysseus's attitude to his commanding officers is not markedly more respectful, but it is within the limits of civility. As with his wife Penelope, he is faithful only in his fashion, and for his own reasons: since Penelope's suitors hope to win the throne of Ithaka through marrying its queen, there is a charmless possibility that Odysseus acquired it by the same means. His fidelity tends to be one of the causes for which he raises no more than two cheers.

Despite being Athene's protégé, Odysseus honours the Apolline golden rule: knowing himself, he has an unblinkered sense of his own character and limitations. When he struggles ashore, naked and salt-caked, among the Phaeacians, he is ashamed to show himself to their princess, Nausicaa, and affront her innocence. He remains incognito at dinner in the palace, until his all-too-human tears at the rhapsode Demodocus's song about the men who fought at Troy blow the hero's cover. He is more of a man for being unmanned; when did Agamemnon weep?

Odysseus's courage is not in question, but his resource – like his dexterity – suggests a certain femininity. By supplementing muscle with guile (*metis* is essentially female), he is able to be more of a man. The vanity of those who despise women leads them into folly and *hubris*, the violent pride that brings them down. Something about Odysseus/Ulysses has made him endlessly adaptable as a subject: Nikos Kazantzakis wrote a 33,333-line sequel to the *Odyssey*. In it he trades on the myth that, after his return to Ithaka and reunion with his paragon of a wife (Penelope has the chastity which Helen lacked, and the constancy that the latter's sister, Klytemnestra, betrayed), Odysseus found conjugal life in his petty kingdom too sedate and set off once again on his travels.

Agamemnon can never be credited with an inner life: he is a strutting commander, never seen where the battle is hottest, and nothing more. And when is Menelaus anything but a loud-mouthed, cuckolded adjutant, whom everyone knows to have been slow with his wife? Odysseus can dispense with uniform, and office, and remain recognizably himself: James Joyce makes Ulysses/Bloom into an Irish mutation of the wandering (half-)Jew, a character somewhat indebted to Italo Svevo/Ettore Schmitz, the great Triestine novelist whom Joyce met (and later fostered) when taking Italian lessons from him. Joyce's sense of exile was as acute as Odysseus's, but he never went back to Dublin.

In his *Ithaka*, Cavafy too offered a wry gloss on the *Odyssey*:

> When you set off to go to Ithaka,
> Pray for it to be a long way away,
> And full of adventures, full of discoveries.
>
> The Laestrygonians,* and Cyclopes,
> Poseidon in a rage, never fear them;
> Those things along the way, you'll never not find them,
> Unless you're aiming high, unless some rare
> Excitement kindles mind and body...
>
> Pray for the road to be long.
> Many summer mornings may you have
> When with what gratitude, what joy
> You'll sail into harbours never seen before.
> Stop off at Phoenician bazaars,
> And find delicious articles for sale,
> Mother of pearl and corals, amber and ebony,
> Perfumes to please and conjure with...
>
> All the time, you'll keep Ithaka in mind.
> Landfall there is all your destiny.
> But don't hurry your step, not one bit.
> Best if it takes you years to make it.
> Be an old man before you reach your island,
> Rich with trophies found along the way,
> Never expecting fortunes back in Ithaka.
>
> Thank Ithaka for the travels you have had.
> Without her you'd never have done them.
> But that's all she has to offer.

---

* Balaklava, on the Black Sea, claims, very implausibly, to be the home port of the Laestrygonians. Sardinia is more plausible.

And if she's poor, Ithaka, she's not mocking you.
Made wise by time, and so experienced,
You'll know by then what Ithakas are for.

* * *

*I*s Theseus so charmless only because no one of Homer's genius dignified and humanized him? Like *"brave Crillon"*, in Henry of Navarre's triumphantly reproachful letter, he was among the *grands absents* at a great victory. In an effort to have him mentioned in despatches, Peisistratus interpolated a line – "Theseus, Pirithous, glorious sons of the gods" – into a list of heroes in the *Odyssey*, but it did little to make Theseus more gallant. Although a son of Zeus, Pirithous was originally a Lapith, one of the pre-Olympian hero-villains, a suitable low-life companion for Theseus's more rackety adventures. He was a principal in the battle between Lapiths and Centaurs fought at his wedding feast after Pirithous's marriage with Hippodameia (not the girl of the same name who made off with Pelops). It was a favourite subject for vase-painting and sculpture, not least on the Parthenon metopes in the British Museum. Pirithous has the attributes of a minor hero, but no more comes to convincing life than his buddy Theseus.

In *Parallel Lives*, Plutarch compared Theseus with Romulus. Both literally foundational figures, neither is easy to warm to. Although officially revered at Rome, Romulus carried the taint not only of fratricide but also of kingship. When that prim hypocrite Octavian took sole power, he considered adopting the title Romulus, but rejected it because it smacked of regality. "Augustus" had elegance without tyrannic, or fratricidal, undertones: like Cain, Romulus killed his brother on the way to supremacy. Being brotherless, fratricide was not available to Octavian. The last western Roman (boy) emperor, deposed in A.D. 476, was called Romulus Augustulus.

Theseus was a composite creation, like the city which enshrined him. Once in charge, his abiding political service to Athens was as a synoecist: he instituted the fusion of disparate Attic communities into a single, dynamic city. The Spartans bucked the urbane trend: they insisted on living in an unwalled enclave in which several villages retained putatively separate identities. Walls, they feared, unmanned their inhabitants.

Theseus conducted door-to-door canvassing in order to persuade four distinct municipalities to become Athens, a name which is itself a plural. Once he had charmed everyone into signing up to his plan, he destroyed the town halls of the old villages and abolished local magistrates. This both precluded second thoughts and deprived councils of anywhere to entertain them.

Theseus's centralization programme gives him almost historical credibility. Other of his more heroic exploits are manifest fables.

Aegeus, his father, has a small, inadvertently comic part in Euripides' *Medea*: he intrudes on the distraught witch-woman as she is about to slaughter her own and Jason's children, in order to punish him for divorcing her. Childless at this stage, Aegeus, king of Athens, has been to Delphi in search of a cure for sterility. Since the fifty sons of Pallas are keen to succeed to his throne, the aging monarch is desperate for an heir for whom Delphi's riddling reply has hardly supplied an accessible formula. Medea abates her rage and promises Aegeus, "...You'll die fulfilled. / You little know what luck today was yours. / I'll cure your childlessness...I've drugs, / I've ways. You'll spill the seed of sons."

In return for a fertilizing potion, Aegeus – who has no idea what horrors Medea proposes to visit on her own children – is unguarded enough to promise that Athens will take her in if she ever needs a home. With this hedge against extradition, Medea has no further reason to abate her butchery. Medea's murder of her children may be "unnatural" (as Jason would have it), but it is not untypical of the gods: Medea's impunity derives less from her mundane deal with Aegeus than from her semi-divine status as a granddaughter of the Sun. Jason's crime was not so much infidelity as sacrilege. Breaking faith with a deity merited the loss of Jason's posterity.

Desperate to father children, Aegeus indemnifies Medea against the consequences of murdering her own. He now tells her what Delphi told him: "Forbear to loose the wineskin's dangling end... / Till you come back home: your own ancestral hearth." Medea has the wit to deduce that "the wineskin's dangling end" is an anatomical metaphor:* Aegeus is not to have sex with anyone until he returns to Athens. However, when the aging man – probably in his late thirties – breaks his journey at Troezen, of which, in Euripides' *Hippolytus*, the mature Theseus is king, King Pittheus persuades him to sleep with his daughter, Aithra. Later the same night, she is also visited by Poseidon.** The god/father will grace the resultant child, Theseus, with divine qualities and three wishes, which he will use with tragic effect.

---

* *Meedea* is ancient Greek for the genitals. Did phonetic proximity, and her personal history, make Medea sound synonymous with sexuality itself? In a lost tragedy of Sophocles, she is the "root-cutter". Apollonius Rhodius has her severing the "titan-sprung" root and concealing it in her "divinely lovely bosom". Jason uproots Medea whose exile she later laments as rootlessness.

** Olympias, mother of Alexander the Great, claimed to have been double-dated (by Philip and Zeus/Ammon). So did the mother of the Spartan king Demaratus. A mythical hero, Astrabacus came to her bed, she said, after her wimpish second husband, King Ariston. Hence her son was sired not by a hitherto sterile man, but by a hero whose name Graves renders as "Sure-Sighted Remedy".

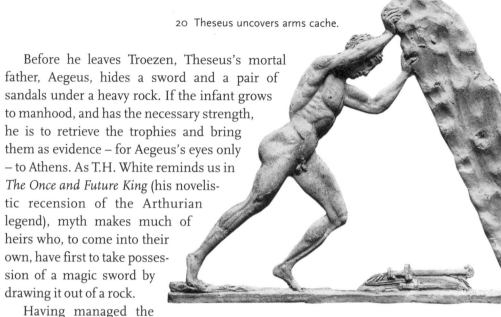

Before he leaves Troezen, Theseus's mortal father, Aegeus, hides a sword and a pair of sandals under a heavy rock. If the infant grows to manhood, and has the necessary strength, he is to retrieve the trophies and bring them as evidence – for Aegeus's eyes only – to Athens. As T.H. White reminds us in *The Once and Future King* (his novelistic recension of the Arthurian legend), myth makes much of heirs who, to come into their own, have first to take possession of a magic sword by drawing it out of a rock.

Having managed the extraction sweetly enough, the adolescent Theseus set off on foot for Athens, although warned that it would be safer to go by sea. A scalp-hunter in need of match practice, he had the ambition to out-Herakles Herakles, the reigning world champion of rough justice. The countryside still harboured a plethora of solitary thugs who – like Thrasymachus (Mr Rash-in-Battle), in Plato's *Republic* – had the philosophy that might was right: if ordinary people prated of justice, equality and humanity, it was because they lacked the nerve to be supermen. Thucydides puts similar arguments in Cleon's mouth. How "logically" to repudiate man's innate violence is *the* moral problem.

Theseus's first bout was with Periphetes, whose mace became his conqueror's hefty attribute (Herakles already had his trade mark in the Nemean lion's skin). Theseus next dealt with Sinis, whose trick was to bend pine trees together, rope his victims' legs to them and then allow them to spring apart. Who is surprised that Theseus did to Sinis what he had done to others?

Plutarch tells the story of Sinis's daughter, Perigoune (the knee-grabber), who ran and prayed to a patch of thorns and wild asparagus to hide her. She swore never to burn either brand of vegetation, but Theseus found her all the same. He treated her gently and she bore him a son, Ioxos, who emigrated to Karia, in what is today south-western Turkey. Its provincial capital is Bodrum, the ancient Halicarnassus.

The tirelessly aetiological Plutarch goes on to say that inhabitants of that part of Asia Minor never burn wild asparagus or thorn bushes. Being a first-century A.D. Boeotian, and a priest at Delphi, Plutarch was at once sophisticated and half in love with the magic of remote antiquity. Aware that myths were adapted, and sometimes flagrantly rigged, for the sake of political advantage, he never quite dismissed them as fairy tales, nor could he resist appending moral conclusions.

Aesop's fables – the most enduring and endearing incitement to literacy in western culture – are noted for pithy morals. The most common characters in the storyteller's folkloric tales are workaday animals or simple-minded rustics. He reminds us, with Kiplingesque realism, that leopards do not change their spots. Marx wanted philosophy to change the world; Aesop promises that most things never will. *Plus ça change* is all his philosophy.

Scholars seem to agree that Aesop lived in the sixth century. He was probably a slave, unlike the grand Athenian writers who followed and often quoted him. In the *Oresteia*, the noble Aeschylus appeals to popular culture with an Aesopian fable about a lion cub that grows up to bite the human hands that fed him (his image of the "heavy ox" that sits on the watchman's tongue in *Agamemnon* is, on the other hand, grandly Pythagorean).

Slave or not, Aesop was free with his tongue, which he employed to amuse and instruct and also, it is said, to plead in the law courts of Samos, where he used the fable of the fox and the fleas to make a case for a rich politician on the grounds that, unlike those who might replace him, he would not need to help himself to the public treasury if acquitted. Being a slave, Aesop must have had remarkable qualities, and prestige, to be allowed to play the advocate even in a democratic forum.

Aesop's talent to amuse is typical of bright, marginal figures who fear that if their wit becomes abrasive they will excite the anger of their audience. Aesop was a joker who has also been accused of revealing the ancient Greeks' lack of compassion: he appears to assume that there is nothing wrong with kicking a man when he is down. His wit was necessarily brief; the underdog, like the stand-up comedian, has to deliver or get off. Today, his fables seem more wry than funny, perhaps because we have heard the best ones before. Their morals, however, often retain their bite. For instance, in the story of the Lion and the Wild Ass, the two agree to hunt together. In the chase, the lion used his strength, the ass his speed. When they had been successful, the lion divided the spoils into three portions. He took the first because he was the king; the second because he was an equal partner in the chase. "As for the third share," he said to the wild ass, "this share will be a greater source of harm to you, believe me, if you do not yield it up to me. And, by the way, get lost!" The timeless moral is: "It is suitable always to calculate your strength, and not to enter into an alliance (or willing coalition?) with people stronger than yourself."

21 Fourteenth-century woodcut Aesop, still moralizing, with assorted props.

It is a tribute to the it'll-always-be-the-same quality of the fables (and of nature, human and animal) that it is so tempting to update them: how many modern applications can be supplied to the story of the Goatherd and the Wild Goats, who refuse to join the peace process, on the grounds that if the Goatherd is willing to sacrifice the interests of his tame friends, he will probably leave them in the lurch too? The fables are timeless because they always have a timely pertinence. One can imagine Israelis and Palestinians making reciprocal rhetorical use of the tale of the wolves who send envoys to the sheep, suggesting they can make lasting peace if the sheep surrender their dogs. In the Middle Ages, Jews renounced the right to bear arms in German cities in exchange for a promise of princely protection.

Then there is the fisherman who is reproached for disturbing the water and making the locals drink muddy water. He replies, "If the river isn't disturbed, I shall die of hunger." We are told, "It is like this in a city-state; the demagogues thrive by throwing the state into discord." Trust a slave who has bettered himself to display Jeevesian contempt for the common people.

Not all morals are conclusively valid. Another fable tells of the farmer and his quarrelling sons. He hands them a bundle of firewood and invites them to break it in half. They can't. He then undoes it and gives each son a stick to break, which is easily achieved. "Stay bound together", he says, like a good proto-Fascist, "and you can be invincible. But if you are divided, you will be easy to defeat." The nice Aesopian moral is: "As long as harmony is maintained, discord is easy to overcome." The twentieth-century rider is: so they voted in a bloc for Fascism (which took its name from the *fasces* – bundled reeds, or rods – carried by the lictors attendant on Roman consuls) and got defeated anyway.

Aesop remains a fundamental figure in western literature, a humble clown attendant on Homer's sovereignty. From La Fontaine to Orwell's *Animal Farm* and James Thurber's fables ("Don't count your boobies before they're hatched", was one of his morals), from Goya to the goofy mythology of Walt

Disney and thence to its antidote, *Shrek*, Aesop's progeny are everywhere. When we first reached Athens, a cinema was advertising a programme of "NTONALNT NTAK", with a decrypting image of Donald Duck alongside.

Aesop proves that one ticket for literary survival is "keep it short" (brevity gets better reviews). As for the man himself, legend says that he was murdered by the priests at Delphi after denouncing their greed. Did success give the storyteller delusions of immunity from the common servile lot?

* * *

*J*ust as different cities worshipped variant aspects of the same deity (echoed by Catholic iconography in which images of the Mother of God take on local colour), so they took different views of the same event: on the Athenian account, the Sciron who was thrown off the Molurian rock by Theseus was a loutish highwayman who made passers-by wash his feet and, as they cowered before him, kicked them into the sea. Theseus therefore had every right to put the boot into him. Megarians, however, regarded Sciron as a local hero descended from Aeacus (a son of Zeus and the nymph Aegina); for them, he was a sheriff who punished brigands. Plutarch – rationalizing as usual – favours the story that Theseus killed Sciron while helping Athens to acquire Eleusis, which then belonged to Megara. Sciron's criminal record put a just face on Athenian expansion: imperialists often vaunt themselves as policemen. The Romans would justify their calling the Mediterranean *"mare nostrum"* by claiming that Pompey the Great gave them title to it by clearing it of pirates.

I first read about Procrustes in Hawthorne's *Tanglewood Tales*. As memorable as they were bowdlerized, his stories were a genteel introduction to a savage mythology. Procrustes was the ugly side of Greek hotel-keeping: affecting to offer travellers a bed, and insisting that they fit it exactly, he stretched the short and shortened the tall. Theseus cut him down to size, but one can still sleep in his beds.

On reaching Athens, Theseus is at first recognized only by the shrewd, and alarmed, Medea, who sees him as a threat to her hold over Aegeus, now suffering from a senile tremor. When the old king invites Theseus to dinner, without recognizing his guest, Medea plans to poison him. Invited to carve the joint, however, Theseus draws the tell-tale sword and reveals his identity. Aegeus's tremor becomes either the reason or the excuse for upsetting Theseus's poisoned wine cup and Medea's merciless plans. When Theseus is presented to the people as their new prince, he is aware that he has not been accepted wholeheartedly. Urgent to prove himself more Athenian than the Athenians, he displays the vigour common to those, such as Napoleon, Disraeli, Stalin, Hitler, Churchill and de Gaulle, who never entirely belonged to societies whose nationalisms they embraced and whose ambitions they articulated, often more belligerently than the natives.

Theseus wins the gratitude of the rural inhabitants of Attica by killing the bull of Marathon. This fire-breathing beast has already accounted for Androgeos, the dauphin of Minos, king of Crete, whose furious grief has led him to demand that, every nine years, the Athenians send seven young men and seven young women to the island as compensatory tribute. They are to be thrust into the labyrinth where the Minotaur – "mixed up creature, miscreant bastard", as Euripides called him – is penned.

While Athenian sources held that they were delivered to their deaths by the heartless Minos, the Cretans claimed that their king was misrepresented: on their account, the maze – devised by Minos's genius-in-residence, the master craftsman Daedalus – was an ahead-of-its-time prison (like Jeremy Bentham's "panopticon"). Secured without locks or bars, the juveniles inside were treated to an amiable regime and a balanced diet, after which – the Cretan version insisted – they were fit to be prizes in the games established by Minos in memory of his dead son. There are, however, hints that at least a few of the Athenians were sacrificed at Androgeos's tomb. The local spin insisted that only one Cretan ever maltreated them: a cruel soldier called Tauros. His name seems to have been devised to lend rational form to the story of the Minotaur[*] and to negate what Cretans regarded as wilful disinformation.

---

[*] In the fourth century A.D. there was a historical colonel called Taurus, who commanded the Praetorian Guard during the reign of Constantius II. He was deputed to knock the Arian bishops' heads together if they failed to achieve doctrinal unity, at the council of Rimini. Julian the Apostate, on assuming the purple, sent him into dishonourable retirement. (For those amused by onomastics, Taurus the bully was trumped by Colonel Buller, curt commander of the British bridge world in the 1930s.)

Aristotle agrees that Cretans were given an undeservedly bad name in Athenian drama. "It is dangerous", Plutarch reminds us, "to attract the hatred of those who know how to talk and whom the Muses favour". Minos was frequently the butt of Athenian playwrights, though Hesiod called him "the most royal of beings" and Homer "the confidant of Zeus". He is almost interchangeable with Rhadamanthys, son of Zeus and Europa and guardian of the laws of the under-world, first drafted by Minos. If they resented the primacy of Cretan civilization, it would please Attic audiences to have its ruler portrayed as both savage and randy (Aigina's Aphaea disappeared when Minos was in hot pursuit).

We have only fragments of Aeschylus's *The Cretan Women*, which is said to have followed the myth of Polyeidos (Mr Many-Formed). Minos was depicted as a loving father who, having lost his son Glaucus in the palace basement, sent the Argive Polyeidos to find him. When he did, the boy was dead. Minos locked Polyeidos in with the dead boy and refused to let him out unless he revived Glaucus. He did this by killing a snake, which was then visited by its mate, with a reviving herb. Polyeidos filched the herb and resurrected Glaucus. Minos was lavishly grateful but – as with Daedalus – reluctant to let go of so clever a visitor. He made the condition that Polyeidos first teach Glaucus the art of divination, which he did. Robert Graves (following the comic poet Apollodorus of Gela, a Sicilian town, the birthplace of Aeschylus, now reeking of a local petrol refin-ery) says that as the departing Polyeidos was on the quayside, he instructed his pupil to spit in his mouth, which returned the gift of divination to its source. The modern Greek demurral, by mouthing "*po, po, po*", is a ritual form of spit-ting. The triple spit has emphatic apotropaic force in Yiddish lore.

It was implicit in the ur-myth that should anyone manage to kill the Minotaur, the cycle of Athenian tribute would be halted. It would be curious if Minos himself had allowed for such a contingency, unless the king was under duress and secretly eager to be disembarrassed of the monster. Had fear of the Minotaur (or of his own wife) pushed the law-giver into making unjust demands of the Athenians?

23 Ayrton's human-all-too-human Minotaur.

When the next season came round for the Minotaur's human diet to be delivered, Theseus made a smart career move by offering to go with the hostages. As a bastard, he was not eligible for selection; by volunteering, he corrected his bend sinister into a badge of righteousness. To Aegeus's question, "Whom shall I send?", Theseus gave Isaiah's answer: "Here am I. Send me."

His ship sailed with black sails. It was agreed that white ones would be hoisted on the homeward leg if he was returning alive (in Simonides' account, the good news was to be signalled by reddish-purple sails, but this smacks of poetic refinement). It is a sweet irony that, like the labyrinth and the Minotaur itself, sails might not have existed if Daedalus had not been exiled in Crete and constrained to conjure them.

Since Plutarch was a dignitary at Delphi, it is not surprising that he reports the oracle to have told Theseus to "take Aphrodite" as a guide. In light of the story that – for whatever pious or prudent reason – Theseus left a statue of Aphrodite on Delos, Plutarch can be suspected of cadging retrospective credit for Delphi once the donation had been made.

The goddess of love was surely responsible for the promptness with which Minos's moon-faced daughter, Ariadne, became infatuated with Theseus as soon as he landed in Crete. Years earlier, the princess's divine mother, Queen Pasiphae, had been no less excited by a fire-breathing white bull soon after it swam ashore on the island. Poseidon had sent the beast to announce his recognition of Minos's authority (over the sea as well as over Crete itself). Thus confirmed on his throne by divine bull, the king was expected to sacrifice the beast to the god. Its potency tempted Minos to keep it alive, for breeding purposes. Annoyed at being cheated, the god gave the king's ambition a sour twist: Minos's hot queen, Pasiphae (whose name means "brilliant all-rounder"), was inflamed by lust and – thanks to the machinations of Daedalus – able to dispose herself to be serviced by the bull. As a result, she gave birth to the Minotaur. From that moment began the decline and fall of the cuckolded Minos. If, as is plausible, the king never regarded the monster with anything but horror, Theseus's exploit in killing it – despite the bad effect on Crete's prestige – was a consummation at least furtively to be wished for. If the Cretan Colonel Bull is a rationalization of the monster, we can imagine Minos to have been a monarch who, like the young King Constantine when faced by the Colonels of the 1967 *coup*, was willing to be rid of a turbulent officer, but lacked the nerve, or muscle, to do it himself.

There is indeed a sub-version of the myth which has Minos openly congratulate Theseus on killing the Minotaur/Tauros. As a reward, the hero is allowed to sail away with the Athenian hostages and, presumably, with Ariadne. On this view, Ariadne's ruse – holding a reel of thread for Theseus to unravel as he

24 In the House of the Vetii, Pompeii. Pander Daedalus introduces Pasiphae to the white bull.

went into the maze, so that he could extract himself again – was less a betrayal of her father than proof of her love for him.

Theseus returned Ariadne's passion long enough only for her to be of use to him: by the time his ship (still flying black sails) had put in at Naxos, he was ready to dump her. Her fate is a multi-choice question. If already pregnant, did she later die of a miscarriage? Some say this happened on Cyprus, where Artemis – goddess of childbirth – was persuaded to turn against her by the jilted Dionysus, touchiest (because least secure) of the gods.

Revert to the Naxiot fork in the tale and the question is, did Ariadne hang herself – a standard tragic death for females, not least Phaedra, who would, on

25 Theseus does for the Minotaur in a Roman mosaic maze.

this count, become Theseus's second suicidal wife – or did she (as in a version
with a seemingly happier ending*) become the bride of Dionysus? This may be
a tactful way of saying that she became an alcoholic. Cloyingly sweet to
modern palates, Naxiot wine was famously *grand cru*.

A genealogical loop asserts Ariadne to be the sister of Deucalion, the
founder of Dodona, who had a son, Amphictyon, the first man to mix wine

---

*The DVD of the first series of *24*, an American TV serial, allows the viewer a choice between its
heroine's death or the happier version, in which she survives. Neither version is truer, since both
are fictions, but the menu advertises the *à la carte* alternatives of a single plot.

26 Ariadne and Theseus: a myth revisited in sixteenth-century style.

with water. Snakes and the Furies were said to drink "unmixed blood", indicating a want of civilized temperance, but also perhaps the symbolic confluence of blood and wine. Diluted wine is standard among ancient Greeks for whom, as for today's, the drunken man is shamefully comic.[*]

Having left Ariadne asleep, Theseus sailed on. His next stop was Delos, where he dedicated to the goddess the small wooden image of Aphrodite carved by Daedalus and left aboard his ship by Ariadne. It seems typical of the hero's recurrent charmlessness that he should unload his lover's gift at the first opportunity. A politer view is that he feared Athenian mockery if he arrived with it and without its donor. Pausanias reports the image, perpetually garlanded, still to be extant on Delos in the second century A.D.: it rested on a square base, instead of on feet.

Theseus is credited with having stayed on Delos long enough to teach its priests the steps of a "crane dance", which mimicked the two-steps-forward-one-to-the-side movement – the knight's move at chess – required to thread the Minotaur's labyrinth. He also instituted athletic contests. Since the olive was sacred on Delos, victors' crowns at the Delian Games were made from palm branches. Theseus was the first man to propose that winners take the palm, as they now do at the Cannes Film Festival.

Among Theseus's misadventures was his failure to replace the black sails on his ship with the white ones previously agreed to signal success. King Aegeus, who was watching out for his son, took him to be dead and threw himself over a cliff into the sea, which thus became Aegean. Was Theseus merely negligent? Having been to Naxos and Delos, not to mention Cyprus, he had scarcely bolted for home. There had been ample time to remember to spread more cheerful canvas; and Freudian reason to forget. His accession to kingship was, in one sense or another, rigged.

At first, Theseus affected ignorance of his father's death. Mourning did not yet become him: he preferred to pour triumphant libations and made complacent sacrifice at Phaleron before suffering himself to become publicly aware of the fatal consequences of his "mistake" (Proust's Duc de Guermantes is equally unwilling to acknowledge the death of his friend Swann until after a social occasion for which he and his wife were already dressed).

* * *

---

[*] On Ios we were warned off a donkey man called Panayotis without a word being said: another islander simply put the thumb of his spread hand to his open mouth and tilted it back.

*T*he ship on which Theseus had travelled was hauled ashore and installed as a museum piece. Over the years, as its timbers rotted, they were replaced. In time, philosophers used it as a test case when discussing whether something was, or was not, the same thing when elements were added or substituted. Did there come a point when one had to say, "This is no longer Theseus's boat?" The same issue arises with regard to restored paintings: how much cosmetic work can be done before it becomes implausible, or improper, to say, "This is (still) a Leonardo da Vinci"?*

There was a similar problem with the True Cross, which – from the time of its "discovery" by Constantine's mother, Helena – was displayed to the Faithful on Easter Sunday. Otherwise, it was in the custody of the bishop of Jerusalem, of whom Gibbon says, "he alone might gratify the curious devotion of the pilgrims by the gift of small pieces, which they enchased in gold or gems...as this gainful branch of commerce must soon have been annihilated, it was found convenient to suppose that the marvellous wood possessed a secret power of vegetation, and that its substance, though continually diminished, still remained entire and unimpaired". The tradition of Dionysus *Dendritis*, the tree-god, persisted in the Christian world; so too did the daedalic habit of encasing *xoana* (wooden gods or sacred relics**) in elaborately worked gold or silver.

If Theseus's boat was constantly renovated, it was in pristine contrast with the rotting trireme which Themistokles' father pointed out to his young son when they were walking along the beach one day. With more prescience than seems plausible, he is supposed to have warned the ambitious boy that the same neglect awaited all those who sought office in democratic societies.

Theseus's political wits were as sharp as his conscience was calloused. When his popularity was at its height, not only did he compress Athens into a single, powerful city, he is also credited with dividing its citizens into three classes: Eupatrids (aristocrats), peasants and artisans. This would come to lend traditional authority to Plato's three-tiered body politic. Theseus is also

---

* John Wisdom (a keen huntsman) once dealt with the philosophical question of definition by allusion to David Garnett's novel *Lady into Fox*. As she changes, her nose grows longer, and "russet". At what exact moment, however, are we right to say, "By Jove, she's no longer a lady, she's a fox!"? More seriously, if genes and organs can be replaced, how legitimately might a murderer claim no longer to be identical with whoever did the bloody deed?

** James Carroll's *Constantine's Sword* details the way in which the cross itself replaced Jesus as the cultic emblem of Christianity. Carroll – an ex-priest – deplores the emphasis on suffering rather than on divine love which this transference came to impose on the Faithful.

said to have favoured majority decisions and to have struck coins, though numismatists have found none minted in Attica before the 570s.

King Gyges, who usurped the throne of rich Lydia from his friend Candaules in the seventh century, is more plausibly said to have originated coinage. Though Alexander the Great was the first to have his head on coins in his own lifetime, it was a clever way for Gyges to legitimize his upstart rule. Since coins were rarely convertible, the scope of their utility defined spheres of influence. Gyges' mythical helmet of invisibility, which enabled him to move and act with impunity, could be read as a metaphor for the power of money to procure results at a distance. Monetary profits are still categorized in the budget as "invisibles".

Most of the measures attributed to Theseus in the synoecistic chapter of his legend are practical and exemplary: concern for detail, and definition, led him to have a sign put up in the Megarid, "You are entering Ionia; you are leaving the Peloponnese"; the converse was emblazoned on the other side. Thanks not least to the lure of oracles, and the pilgrims that trekked to them, there was more tourism in ancient Hellas than its discrete cities suggest. Traders and ambassadors nerved themselves to board ships that, whenever possible, kept the shore in sight. Despite Theseus's police-work, land travel remained more dangerous. Some etymologists derive Theseus from the same root as the word *thesis* (first-class in modern Greek is *protee thesis*). More solemnly, he was the one who set things down, established laws (*thesmoi*) and boundaries.

Theseus's signposting exercise was prompted by more than consideration for tourists: like much modern map-making, it established tendentious "facts" (arbitrary British and French cartography made the Middle East and much of Africa into today's sovereign states). In being so ostentatiously excluded from Ionia, the Megarians were being put literally in their place. This prefigured – unless it was an *ex post facto* justification of – Megara's long experience, in historical times, of Athenian covetousness and jealousy.* This culminated in the "Megarian Decree" of 433, which barred Megarians from the harbours of Athens and her allies. According to Thucydides, the decree not only brought Megara to the point of bankruptcy, but rang alarm bells in Sparta and in Corinth, a city close enough to have greedy eyes for Megarian territory.

---

* The Megarians stood to the Athenians rather as the Scots to the English (the Boeotians more resembled the Irish): as neighbours, they had enough in common to regard each other with appreciative apprehension. The offshore island of Aegina was a similar case; pitilessly ill-used by Athens, she nevertheless fought on her side against Xerxes (and was rewarded by Athenian occupation from 457 onwards). Megara – allied to Sparta during the Peloponnesian War – later allied herself, bravely but disastrously, with Athens against Philip of Macedon.

Corinth has attracted small attention from historians, for whom Sparta remains glamorously austere and tersely paradigmatic. Yet Corinth was rich, elegant – hence Diogenes' ostentatiously boorish residence there? – and adroit in its foreign policy, at least until its destruction by the Romans. The city's links with Syracuse encouraged the Athenians' fatal attempt to conquer Sicily in 415. In the mid-fourth century, the Corinthians sent Timoleon to redeem Syracuse and his own reputation – by ridding their ex-colony of the despotic Dionysius II. Timoleon is one of those second-order figures (Evagoras of Salamis, in Cyprus, is another) who exemplify the cunning and muscle needed to stay, even temporarily, ahead of the Greek game.

Once Theseus had completed his political and territorial housekeeping, he renounced the throne of Athens. In the same spirit, Solon would give up his quasi-dictatorial role after introducing a new constitution. The Delphic oracle sent Theseus a reassuring envoi: "...my father has consigned the fate of many cities / To your citadel. Don't pain yourself with thoughts; / Go away, on ocean's swell, take to the open sea." If this advice was given ahead of the event by the priestess, it was a proleptic vision of Athens' maritime destiny; if after it, the city benefited from a backdated charter for its subsequent imperial adventures. The oracle tended to endorse seagoing excursions, probably because they were often successful: Archilochos was proud of his father's colonization of gold-rich Thasos. "You can't swear that anything won't happen. Never be surprised..." he says, "not even if dolphins change places with wild animals or the booming waves of the sea become more friendly to you than your native heath". In *The Frogs*, Aristophanes recalls how, in Athens' finest hour in 480, the population abandoned their city and Athens' future was "cradled in the sea's embrace as all but an obstinate few took ship to Salamis".

Other Greeks, not least the Spartans, grew weary of Athenians boasting about their finest hour. In something of the same spirit, the British are seen, by foreigners, as excessively concerned with their own war stories. Hellenists such as Patrick Leigh-Fermor, Xan Fielding and Billy Moss, by their exploits in Crete and elsewhere in Greece, contributed a mythic chapter to the history of the Second World War. C.M. Bowra, who had an outstandingly brave record in the First World War, is said to have twitted his fellow-classicist E.R. Dodds (the pacifist author of *The Greeks and the Irrational*, a crucially important revision of Hellenic ideas) by asking, some think wittily, "What did you do in the war, Doddy?"

* * *

heseus's abdication disencumbered Athens of an autocratic tradition and also left the hero free for new adventures, most of which belong to the wilder chapters of myth. The first was to become the ally of Herakles in an expedition against the Amazons. This seems not to have been a success: the Amazons counter-attacked and advanced on Athens. The peace treaty hints that the female regiment had the better of things. Why else were the Amazons offered annual sacrifices at the Theseid? Later, however, their provoked incursion was used to explain, at least to the male population, why women were then disenfranchised at Athens. Though women clearly never had a democratic vote, some Marxist anthropologists argue that there was a primitive Attica in which matriarchy and women's rights prevailed. Tradition did say that, before the reign of King Kekrops, women had equal rights with men.

Although mythology lacked scriptural authority, it had a moralizing, often conservative, force: the unfairness of life was justified by reference to a canon of fabulous instances. Myths might be revised (the Attic theatre made a feature of such recensions), but even ridicule can be a form of piety. On the other hand, open rejection of antique rituals and festivals would amount to abandoning Hellenism itself. Its only orthodoxy lay in keeping up appearances.

Myths were not only stories, they were also parts of speech: Homer supplied a style, or styles, which lasted at least a thousand years. Schools of rhetoric taught the various persuasive devices of his characters. Gibbon quotes one of the emperor's friends as saying that Julian the Apostate switched between "the simple concise" – that is, Laconic – "style of Menelaus, the copiousness of Nestor, whose words descended like the flakes of a winter's snow, or the pathetic and forceful eloquence of Ulysses".

If the most keenly plotted version of Theseus's career is accepted, what time was there in his youth for the boyish adventures with which he is connected, such as going with Jason to Colchis, taking part in the battle between the Centaurs and the Lapiths, and helping Meleager kill the boar? The answer is that myth has no clock.

Theseus appears in extant tragedy in the *Hippolytus* of Euripides (and, in due course, in Racine's *Phèdre*). With dynastic calculation, he had married Phaedra, sister of King Deucalion of Crete, but only after jilting his Amazonian mistress Antiope, who reacted so embarrassingly at the wedding that he took time out to kill her, even though she had borne him a son, Hippolytus.

Phaedra paid the price of the young man's exclusive devotion to Artemis, goddess of hunting. Hippolytus's priggish chastity was repugnant to Aphrodite. While Theseus was absent on business, the scorned goddess made Phaedra conceive a passion for her stepson. As the lovesick queen faded away, she was persuaded by a coaxing servant to reveal her desire to the youth.* After Hippolytus reacted with revulsion, Phaedra tore her clothing and – having left a note accusing him of rape – hanged herself. Queen Jocasta of Thebes killed herself in the same way when she discovered that she had, without knowing it, married her own son, Oedipus. Tragic women lacked swords to fall on.

On Theseus's return, he believed what Phaedra had written ("*Il avait un texte*", Michel Pic remarks, ironically). Theseus first ordered Hippolytus into exile and then, cashing one of three promised wishes, prayed to Poseidon for his own son's death. The four trace-horses on Hippolytus's chariot took fright at an insurgent sea monster; the chariot snagged on an olive tree, hit a rock and overturned, mortally injuring the virgin victim (Hippolytus means "the man who couldn't hold his horses"). Euripides has Theseus realizing too late that his son – who forgives him with his last breath – was innocent: an early case of the danger of answered prayers. Although Theseus is manifestly unfortunate, he is never quite tragic. Phaedra's death recalls Ariadne's, for which Theseus was responsible. And then again, the king's credulity procures the death of his son, as calculation had that of his father. The king's remorse is more pathetic than heroic.

Theseus is supposed to have visited Sparta while the pubescent Helen was living there and to have assisted Pirithous in the nymphet's abduction.** This episode was part of a wild middle-aged rampage, excited, maybe, by the suicide of Phaedra and by Theseus's part in the death of Hippolytus. The mad plan was that he and Pirithous should each get hold of, and marry, daughters of Zeus. That their acquisitive ambition should have Helen as one of its insolent targets indicates her centrality in Greek attitudes to female beauty, in which the suspicion of duplicity is implicit (why else did Zeus swallow his first wife, Metis?).

Menelaus's unfaithful wife symbolizes at once the perfidy of her sex and its potency. Homer always calls Helen the daughter of Zeus, never mentioning her mortal father, Tyndareus, king of Sparta. Theseus and Pirithous's impudent excursion, preceding the Trojan War, illustrates how female beauty, especially Helen's, spells trouble. Her sister Klytemnestra – born of the same egg that Leda*** laid – represents a different, masterful strain of dangerous femininity. Helen is the glory and the bane of Hellas; her very name almost doubles for

---

* Hippolytus's zeal for hunting could be read for a refusal to progress from adolescence to manhood: living in the wild was a rite for young men, but to refuse sex, and marriage, was antisocial.
** One version of the myth says that Theseus raped Helen when she was eight years old. Some hero!
*** As a result of Zeus's flying visit to her in the form of a swan. Yeats made famous poetry of the rape: "her thighs caressed by the dark webs, her nape caught in his bill, / He holds her helpless breast upon his breast. / How can those terrified vague fingers push / The feathered glory from her loosening thighs?"

27 Theseus "raping" a sturdy, sixth-century B.C. Helen, who can't keep her hands off him.

Hellene, yet – as Aeschylus's chorus in *Agamemnon* insists – she brings hell in her train. If Helen is the female as prize, Klytemnestra reaches for prizes which no good Greek woman should seek: political power and the sexual domination of her adulterous consort, Aegisthus.

Helen goes abroad to betray her husband; Klytemnestra betrays hers while he is abroad. Strangely, Klytemnestra pays for her betrayal with her life, and a reputation forever soured, whereas Helen returns to live in resumed matrimony with Menelaus and then, in some versions, goes to enjoy – as a god's daughter should – a blissful afterlife.

Medea – like Pasiphae, a descendant of the Sun – was regarded with similar ambivalence. Did Euripides scandalize his Athenian audiences when he depicted a woman who could kill her own children and then escape all punishment? Witch and goddess, Medea flew first class, by solar chariot (like Elijah and the prophet Muhammad), from Corinth to Athens, where she had booked herself luxurious asylum, leaving Jason – who had jilted her – and his murdered fiancée's father, King Kreon, to endure the pain which audiences were willing to believe they had incurred, and perhaps deserved, by crossing her. Divinities were not to be judged on a human scale, still less were they accountable to human courts.

Medea was saved, at the end of Euripides' play, by a *deus ex machina*, but only because she was herself a quasi-divinity. There is no redemption: Medea is clearly a monster, but she is not a common criminal. What she has done is inhuman, therefore divine: Greek divinities are unpredictable forces, not moral paragons, although Plato came to wish it otherwise.

Once Theseus and Pirithous had snatched Helen, they descended to Hades to abduct Persephone. With a show of *philoxenia*, the king of the underworld invited them to a banquet, at which they were seated in the thrones of Lethe. These places of supposed honour fused with the flesh of whoever sat on them and slowly turned them to stone. Even goddesses were sometimes wise to be careful where they sat: Hera's son Hephaestus, whom she had expelled from Olympus because he was uncomely, left her a clever armchair which embraced her, as she had never embraced her son, so tightly that he had to be recalled to release her.

Theseus would never have escaped his prehensile chair, had not Herakles been sent, coincidentally, by his taskmaster King Eurystheus to steal Hades' three-headed guard-dog, Cerberus. Superman ripped Theseus free (tearing the flesh from his thighs), but could do nothing for the petrified Pirithous. Theseus's buddy was swallowed up in Hades' lowest depths. Minor players rarely have enduring places in heroic stories. Plato's uncle, the oligarchic Critias, is the likely author of a tragedy about Pirithous, of which we have the sixteen (vivid) opening lines. The manuscript, like its unfortunate subject and its putative author, failed to sustain a claim on posterity.

It was neat mythical plotting to have Herakles rescue the man who had taken him as his role model. Meanwhile, Helen had been rescued from her kidnappers – and rapist(s)? – by her brothers, Castor and Polydeuces. Like Helen, the Dioscuri were semi-divine; they too were the children of Zeus. They found their sister in Attica, where her hiding place was revealed by Akademos, a local hero, whose fief remained forever exempt from Spartan depredation.* It was a sweet coincidence that Akademos's stronghold was the place chosen by Plato when he came to found his Academy. No small part of his political philosophy was based on the assumption of the superiority of the Spartan to the Athenian way of life.

After his misadventures with Helen, and in Hades, Theseus was both skinned and skint. Shocked into recovering his wits, but no longer a viable hero, he returned to Athens, hoping to regain the throne. He was, however, spurned by his former constituency. Reduced to beggary, he retired to the Attic village of Gargettos – birthplace of Epicurus – whence he heaped Coriolanian abuse on his one-time subjects. A sea captain, bound for Crete and perhaps aware of Theseus's prestigious exploit on that island, gave him passage as far as Skyros, where he sought help for his restoration from King Lycomedes. But one of his ancient crimes caught up with him: Artemis still resented his

---

* The Spartans were both superstitious and pragmatic in honouring portents. Authorized persons interpreted omens: like oracular weather forecasts, they indicated which way the gods were blowing. The modern oracles Jean-Paul Sartre (to the Left) and Martin Heidegger (to the Right) were both conscript meteorologists.

killing of her acolyte, the Amazon Antiope. The goddess tipped off Lycomedes that Theseus was a lost cause. The king had him pushed off the mountain from whose peak the gullible visitor had been promised an unmissable view of the island. Rupert Brooke too died on (or off) Skyros, in 1915, not "into cleanness leaping" – as his lines described going to war – but on a British hospital ship, of a fever, as Byron had at Missolonghi. Both poets had dubious care from the medical profession. "The doctors have murdered me," Byron said.

A more genial version of Theseus's demise – perhaps devised to avoid offence to Zeus *xenios* (the Zeus of hospitality, who protected strangers) – has him slipping to his death during an after-dinner stroll. There is punning justice in Theseus dying on Skyros: it brings to mind Sciron, the early victim for whose death he wished to atone in later days.

Theseus was neglected after his fall, until belatedly resurrected as *the* Athenian hero. At the battle of Marathon, his shade was said to have rallied the men commanded by Miltiades; angels were seen at Mons in 1914, and a cross in the sky when Constantine defeated Maxentius at the Milvian bridge outside Rome.[*]

Miltiades was the father of Cimon, the admiral who retrieved Theseus's bones from Skyros. The Theseum where the latter had them buried became a place of sanctuary for slaves and poor people, whose champion Theseus was deemed to have been. Theseus was fêted there on the eighth day of the month Pyanepsion, the anniversary of his bringing the original hostages safely home from Crete. Plutarch says that it was sacred because eight is two cubed, and hence signified the stability of Poseidon Asphalios (the untrippable) and Poseidon Gaieochos (the one who holds the earth), an apotropaic name for a god more renowned for shaking it.

Theseus's misfortune is to have no noble role in extant tragedy: he is punished by eternal imprisonment in a prosaic myth which leaves him lapped in heroic achievements, but less than a hero. In the sixth book of the *Aeneid*, when Aeneas goes down to Hades, Theseus is depicted as a criminal with no prospect of remission: "There sits and evermore will sit, / Unhappy Theseus...." In truth, Theseus is to Ariadne as Aeneas was to Dido: a shameful hero, "Stammering and prepared to say many things."

* * *

---

[*] Another heavenly (and timely) cross was seen by Cyril, bishop of fourth-century Jerusalem, when Arianism was being championed by a nervous Constantius II and needed any supernatural favours which divine providence or episcopal fancy could supply. Salutary appearances of the Virgin Mary occurred in the nineteenth century, when Mariolatry was being recruited to enhance papal authority.

*I*n the 1960s, the twice-weekly ferry for Ios left Piraeus at noon. British engineers, no less than scholars and philhellenes, have left their mark on Greece. *Despina* was a renamed, superannuated Channel ferry, built on the Clyde. She was small and old; her first-class cabins were tight and airless. By the time we sailed, mattresses and furniture – unobtainable on the smaller islands – had narrowed the gangways. Before we had quit placid Piraeus, old ladies in black dresses were being neatly sick into grey cardboard boxes.

We passed the white cliffs under the lee of Sounium, where the musing poet carved BYRON on Poseidon's gleaming temple. From such cliffs old Aegeus threw himself into the sea when he saw black sails on his son's ship. *Despina* steered south-east towards Syros; then Paros and wine-growing Naxos. Trussed goats and crew-cut sheep were tethered among the new luggage (mostly bulging, tar-papered parcels, belted with thick string and badged with sealing wax). Chickens dangled, upside down, from peasants' hands, like squawking handbags. A high-hatted priest and two army officers smoked by the rail and lisped in sibilant conclave. *Despina* was scheduled to reach Ios at three or four in the morning before proceeding to populous Santorini. The majority of the passengers would thus be able to disembark at a civilized hour.

Spiro Marinatos had not yet excavated the serried houses of Minoan Santorini (Thera), with their decorative polychrome wall paintings, of which I would later hear a French tourist say, "*On dirait Matisse*". Thera's happiest days preceded its blowing its volcanic top in the middle of the second millennium. The mineral-rich fields and soot-black sand on the beaches were reminders of the ancient catastrophe, when boiling sea filled the crater to leave the harbour and lagoon of today's sickle-shaped island. Did the eruption, and the tidal wave that followed, lead to

28 On second-millennium B.C. Minoan Santorini, kids were still kids.

the Red Sea parting? Was incandescent Thera what the Children of Israel saw as a pillar of fire by night and a pillar of smoke by day?

Minoan civilization was choked, but not suffocated, by the blast: Crete survived the huge seas and the long blackout, but Knossos lost its mastery of the sea. The Phoenicians took their chance; Mycenae cashed in. The Mediterranean is rarely long without the sails of a dominant power.

We were asleep in our cabin when the call came, "Ios, Ios". We went on deck and looked into the night. The ship's lights glistened on toothy rocks on the port side. A red-eyed beacon blinked on its metal tripod at the entry to the harbour. *Despina* turned and slid into the black goal. The breathing glow of cigarettes spotted the purple night: invisible oarsmen smoking as they pulled out to meet the *vapori*.

The anchor was unravelled into Guinness-dark water. Transformed into flat-capped, striped-shirted, collarless porters, the oarsmen swarmed aboard. They grabbed our luggage like amiable pirates. We followed them down a swaying ladder, children in our arms, and were handed into the lighter. On shore, blanketed donkeys with wooden saddles waited for homecoming islanders. Their handlers heaped luggage into turrets on their sad backs. As the single rope was looped around the entire load, parcels and cases seemed to wait in the air, exempt from gravity, until secured.

The only *xenoi* to disembark at Ios, we put up in the Denaxas's narrow hotel on the *plateia* in the harbour. In the morning, we looked up through steep, clear air at the starch-white village: stacked cubes topped by the church tower, a hundred and fifty metres up a zigzag path. The slate steps were outlined by whitewash. Donkeys went and stopped, went and stopped, on their way up, and down. Uneasy ears twitched at the urgency of the donkey men who switched them with twigs, or leaned flat, insistent hands on their neat rumps. "*Ela, ela!*" There were no wheeled vehicles; nor roads on which they could have rolled unimpeded. The hot ancient sky had pelted stone on Ios.

* * *

The Cyclades' zenith of wealth and creativity preceded Minoan civilization. The finest examples date from the third millennium, hard evidence of mythical times: pre-dating Homer by a millennium or two, Cycladic figures are at once unmistakable and anonymous. After Homer, and Hesiod, images of gods and men began to have their names spelt out on vase paintings. In classical sculpture, appearance and attributes announce identity: Herakles has his club and his lion-skin; Zeus his thunderbolt; Athene her aegis and owl; Hermes displays his wand; Aphrodite has her dove and her deep breasts. Cycladic figures are nameless and, apart from the famous "harpists" (of dubious authenticity), lack evident function. Are they mortals or gods? Did they have religious or funeral significance? Some scholars promise that the usually small, always naked, pieces were grave-furniture. Their often slightly crooked legs make it seem that they were intended to be recumbent. Early burial sites in Magna Graecia contain skeletons in much the same crook-kneed posture. Perhaps the intention was to prevent them from walking among the living. One discovery, of three female figures, is alleged to be a rich man's supply of charmers for company on "the other side".

Feminists declare that the larger female figures establish the priority of the Great Mother. Despite the emphatic (some-times cleft) triangulation of the pubis, however, the maidenly images scarcely give a maternal impression, unlike the multi-mammaried grotesques from Anatolia (a splashy and bulbously magnified Roman version can be seen in a mossy fountain in the gardens of the Villa d'Este at Tivoli). The male Cycladic figures, fewer but not rare, have not been recruited to any plausible theology.

Unique in form and attitude, the honeyed inscrutability of Cycladic art remains elusive. Did it pay allegiance to some central Delian cult? The Cyclades are so called for the circle they form around the sacred – once said to be floating – island of Delos: it supposedly dropped anchor only when Leto leaned against a maieutic date-palm to give birth to Apollo and Artemis (the perpetual virgin who became the patroness of midwifery). No mortal woman was suffered to have a child on the same ground where the divine twins were born. Nor was anyone supposed to die on Delos. The Olympic gods, apart from Ares, shunned gore and corpses. In Euripides' *Hippolytus*, Artemis abandons her mortally stricken devotee because god-desses must not be tainted by contact with death.

Geography honoured Delos with its choker of islands. Before reading script, the Greeks read meaning into landscape: a flat rock on the summit of Mount Sipylos in Asia Minor was seen as a bench, where gods might lounge between Olympic flights. This accommodation probably derived from the Persians,

29 Third-millennium B.C. Cycladic eternal female from Amorgos.

who worshipped a heavenly "Zeus", to whom Herodotus says they sacrificed from the mountaintops. Caves too were divinely suggestive: the Greek Zeus was born in the womb-like cave of Dicte on Mount Ida in Crete (mind the slippery steps). Outside Syracuse, a dark hole in the bleak Latomia – the stone-quarries where Athenian prisoners lived, and quickly died, after the disaster of 415 – was called "Dionysius's ear"; it has eerie flanges of stone above it.

Being without freshwater springs and – unlike Naxos, Paros and Amorgos – having no serviceable marble or minerals, Delos might be sacred, but it was short of inhabitants. Its hallowed, but skimpy, soil had to be preserved from pollution by the dying, or the dead. Since intrusion was sacrilege, Delos offered an apt repository for the treasure of the Delian League. This originally voluntary Eastern Mediterranean Treaty Organization was masterminded (and its contributions determined) by Athens, after the defeat, and withdrawal, of the Persians in 479. The funds were later removed to the Acropolis, where they were safer, and more easily appropriated. Perikles offered small apology for using the alliance's subscriptions partially to fund the rebuilding of the temples, not least the Parthenon, burned by the Persians. It was, he said, a patriotic duty for all Hellenes to rehouse Athene. What better destination for some of their cash? Not for nothing would the Parthenon set the style for central banks.

I once reviewed a Canadian novel of which I remember only that it opens with a woman discovered at prayer in a Palladian bank which she had mistaken for a place of worship: God and Mammon rejoice in marbled premises. In pious times, temples doubled for banks as a safe deposit for cash. Peter Green, in *Xenophon's Exile*, tells how, in 394, on his way to war, Xenophon left a fat sum in the keeping of the temple warden of Ephesian Artemis, one Megabyzus. If he survived, the cash would be returned to him; if not, it should be devoted to a suitable memorial. Xenophon did survive and, while he was living near Olympia, Megabyzus came from Ephesus to return it.

Nothing more clearly illustrates the mixture of superstition and shrewd intelligence in even the most sophisticated of Greek states than the Athenians' steady conviction, throughout the ups and downs of the Peloponnesian War, that the condition of the island of Delos was strongly influential on their fortunes. When things went badly, they took elaborate pains to "purify" the island once again, quite as if the gods were as likely to interfere in their war as in Homer's *Iliad*. The question of how "sincerely" they believed in such things is an anachronism: their practice *was* their belief, a matter not of some internal personal "faith", but of communal revalidation and allegiance. Spring-cleaning Delos also reminded anyone who might be inclined to change sides that Athens was still boss in the Aegean.

Perhaps because its early sanctity was overlaid by long use as a wholesale slave market, Delos now seems no more than a flat adjunct to equally flat, if gay, Mykonos. The island's alley of mean lions is all very fine, but the beasts are ranged on pedestals which too easily recall the auctioneers' blocks on which slaves were paraded. A statue of a naked Roman "businessman" – almost certainly a slave-dealer – strikes a heroic pose on the island once sacred to Apollo and Artemis. He recalls the story of Diogenes, who, when captured and put on sale as a slave, was asked what his competence was. He replied, "Giving orders. Ask them who wants to buy himself a master."

* * *

City-states were competitively independent, but they were known to coalesce either voluntarily or under pressure from another city-state strong enough to intimidate its neighbours, but not to prosper without them. Even self-sufficient Sparta, which had enslaved Messenia (whose inhabitants became the put-upon helots), drew closer to her old ally Corinth and others when Athens grew dismayingly powerful. The strategy of the alliance was, however, defined by treaty as what the Spartans endorsed. Other cities might propose, or dissent; Sparta alone disposed.

The most successful unforced synoecism – confederation of cities – was in Rhodos: at the end of the fifth century, a year before Athens' defeat in the Peloponnesian War, the three communities of Ialysus, Camirus and Lindus agreed to form a republic and construct a new capital, Rhodos. It flourished, as a modest democracy, far longer than flamboyant Athens. Soon after the Peloponnesian War, the democratized Rhodians repudiated an alliance with oligarchic Sparta, whose victorious reach overextended its practical grasp, especially overseas. Although pro-Spartan oligarchs had earlier been in control in Rhodos, they yielded, with more or less good grace, to the policy of the majority.

According to Pindar, in his Seventh Olympian, when – after victory over the Titans – the Olympian gods cast lots for all the earthly fiefs, Helios (who was chauffeuring the Sun across the sky) missed out. Then, after the deal, Rhodos rose from the sea, so there was something new available under the sun. The island was allotted to Helios, whose three sons later divided it. Synoecism restored its unity. The Rhodians' energetic fleet kept their trade routes open, but they were never tempted into provocative military action, though they were as adroit as the Venetians in coming to the aid of likely winners: they sent several ships to help Alexander the Great at the siege of Tyre.

During much of the Hellenistic age, which saw the rise of Rome, Rhodos sustained its independence by useful neutrality: it traded with both the Romans and the kingdoms of Asia Minor and Egypt, without being cramped by alliance with any of them. This mercantile ambivalence once again resembled that of Venice in the decades when the Serenissima traded on favourable terms with Constantinople, and then with the Sublime Porte, while formally subscribing to the Roman version of Catholicism. Regarding the Eastern Church as schismatic had supplied a pious licence for ninety-year-old Doge Dandolo's infamous pillage of orthodox Constantinople in 1204. Greed was Venice's true faith.

Like Venice, Rhodos created a famous society without privileging famous men. Corporate discretion trumped the personal hegemonism which, with Perikles, had been the glory of Athens and, with Cleon and Alcibiades, contributed to its downfall. In the end, although the Rhodians took pains not to provoke hostility, the Romans regarded them as an unduly shining example of independent and wealthy democracy, rather as the Soviets did West Berlin in the 1960s. Since Rhodos lacked powerful friends, Rome could be more decisive than Moscow: by making adjacent Delos into a free port, she threatened the island with bankruptcy unless it became the vassal of Rome. However, Rome – and later Venice – adopted maritime laws first enacted by the Rhodians. One of its provisions was that if someone on board was carrying gold or silver, it should be deposited for safe keeping with the captain. Separate compartments for each were found in a sunken Byzantine ship recovered by underwater archaeologists.

*　*　*

The steamer from Piraeus to Ios usually went via Syros, Paros and Naxos. Occasionally, we caught one which went by way of Melos. To a modern eye, it looks to be much like any of the smaller Cyclades, but its name lives, some say in infamy, as a result of Thucydides' account of what took place there in 415.

In the middle of an increasingly desperate war with Sparta, the Athenians challenged Melos's neutrality and demanded its recruitment to their cause. When the Melians rejected Athens' ultimatum, the consequences were draconian: all the adults on the island were put to the sword; women and children were sold into slavery; and the vacant island was handed over to Athenian cleruchs. It was neither the first nor the last occasion in the history of war when such things were done. What makes it memorable, and notorious, is Thucydides' cruelly candid – if wholly fictional – account of the preliminary dialogue between the Athenian commanders and the Melians.

Thucydides has been denounced by some, and congratulated by others, for exposing the degenerate hypocrisy of his own city. The conclusion appears to be that the exemplary democracy of Perikles had declined into a thuggish state no better, and perhaps worse, than oligarchic Sparta, which Brasidas – on Thucydides' account, the most engaging of its commanders – was parading as the saviour of Hellas from Athenian vanity. In fact, Brasidas used exactly the same tactics preliminary to an assault on the city of Acanthus, in Chalcidice, as the Athenians did at Melos. The occasion did not become notorious because, unlike the Melians, the Acanthians yielded to superior force.

Thucydides analyses the back-story with dispassionate clarity: Melos was a Spartan colony which had sought to remain neutral, but was incited to hostility by Athenian attacks on its territory. The force sent to coerce it was substantial (some thirty-eight ships in all) and likely to be irresistible. Before attacking, the Athenian commanders sent delegates whom the Melian leaders allowed to speak only to them, in private. The Athenians insisted that if they had been allowed to speak to the Melians *en masse*, the latter would have been persuaded to surrender. The Melian oligarchs may have been of the same opinion, but the result might also have been their own eviction from power.

Abiding by the Melian leadership's rules, the Athenians did suggest, however, that they make their case, point by point. Instead of replying at length later, the Melians should interrupt them when they had an objection. Dialogue, not a *diktat*, was proposed, and accepted. What is remarkable is less the bluster than the reasonableness of the exchanges. The Melians did not fail to see the logic of the situation: whatever arguments they advanced, the Athenians would be the judges of them; war or slavery would follow. If the Melians were to escape the latter, it had to be with the help of the Spartans, or of the gods, on neither of which the Athenians advised them to rely. There was never any prospect of the Melians' arguments "proving" to the Athenians that they were wrong to intrude on the island. Reason might be a method; it could not be a weapon.

The Athenians did not cloak their action with fine phrases. Their purpose was practical, and the Melians' choice bleak: they either yielded to *force majeure* or embraced their own ruin. "We don't want any trouble in recruiting you to our empire", the Athenians continued, "and we want you to survive for your own good, and for ours."

"And how is it as good for us to be the slaves as for you to be our masters?"

"You'll save yourselves from disaster; and we shall profit from the fact."

The Athenians make no secret of a motive more important to them than the reduction of Melos itself: an admitted part of their purpose is to make an example of the island, in order that their other allies, particularly islanders, be deterred from secession. Hence the Melians' appeal to "fair play" – like the attempt to make the Athenians sympathize with the view that it would be cowardice to give in – is beside the point: "This is no fair fight," the Athenians tell them, "with honour on one side and shame on the other. It's a matter of saving your skins by not resisting people much stronger than you are." This is an almost exact repetition of the fable Hesiod quotes, in *Works and Days*, three centuries before: "Witless the one who challenges a stronger: / Bound to lose, he suffers hurt as well as shame."

Thucydides has been accused of cynicism by insisting that, while there can be justice within a state, between states there is never anything but *rapports de forces* (Palmerston would say that nations do not have friends, only interests). Thucydides' critics have yet to advise us of any paramount power which refrained from acting as it wished because of a notion of a justice which no greater power was available to enforce. The truth may not be pretty, but it stares us in the face just as it did the Melians: morals without muscles are a luxury.

We sympathize with the Melians, not least since we know what their fate is going to be. Yet their purpose was clearly, and understandably, to play for time. Their display of injured innocence is touching, but also disingenuous. Their diplomacy is aimed both to persuade the Athenians to back off and to gain time for the Spartans, or the gods, to come to their help.

The Athenian attitude to the gods pays small tribute to the impartial justice of Zeus: "Our view of the gods, like our experience of mankind, leads to the conclusion that it is a general and inflexible law of nature that men rule where they can." As for the Spartans, how wrong are the Athenians in reminding the islanders that "the Spartans are not, as a rule, exactly venturesome"? They make a feature of "believing that what they choose to do is honourable and what furthers their interests is just."

The Athenians were hardly saying of their enemies anything they denied about themselves. The Melians continued to believe that Spartan self-interest, primed by Dorian solidarity, would bring relief; the Athenians that the Spartans' habitual caution raised the odds against any brave, risky adventure on their part, above all by sea.

The Athenians tell the Melians the unpalatable, but undeniable truth: if they resist, they are betting their lives on an outside chance. Their mistake is capital, not moral: in the real world, as modern diplomats say, they have no practical choice. The Melians' honour is neither in question nor relevant: "There is nothing disgraceful", they are told, "in giving way to the greatest city in Hellas", especially on the reasonable terms which the Athenians will propose for tribute payments. The safe rule, the delegates remind the Melians, is to stand up to equals, to defer to superiors and – a nice wink of metropolitan condescension! – "treat inferiors with moderation".

Having emphasized the harshness of the crisis, the Athenians left the Melian oligarchs to make their decision. When it was delivered, it was brave but, in the event, suicidal: they would defend the liberty the island had enjoyed for seven hundred years. Like the Greeks of 1940, when served with Mussolini's ultimatum, their reply was "*ochi*": no, they would not surrender. The Athenians had assured the Melians that hope of relief by the Spartans was delusory and, despite a gallant defence, the Athenians proved right. The siege was protracted, and featured a brave, temporarily effective sortie by the islanders. However, the Athenians reinforced initial failure and in 415 – aided by treachery – compelled the Melians to unconditional surrender. The Athenians were then as bad as their word: all the threats uttered in polite diplomacy were ruthlessly carried out.

G.E.M. de Ste. Croix offers a convincing defence both of Thucydides' dispassionate clarity and of Athenian conduct. He points out that our view of the dialogue is coloured, very darkly, by knowledge of an outcome from which the Athenians did (and certainly said) all they could to deter the Melians. The shamelessness of which historians have accused them is, on a more plausible reckoning, proof of the urgency with which the islanders were pressed to see sense.

The ultimatum was not pretty, but it did offer the weaker side a genuine alternative to the disastrous decision it took. When the United States gave Saddam Hussein and his henchmen the chance to leave Iraq within forty-eight hours or face the consequences, they were practising a diplomacy no less abrupt, and no more insufferable, than any great power before or since the Athenians sailed to Melos. Moralizing about its exercise has little connection with power (yet philosophers still think they can teach businessmen "ethics"). Moral issues are of a different order from political, economic or military ones. Generals are seldom encouraged to make tactical decisions on a Kantian reckoning: their trade is to do to others what they never consider that anyone should be free to do to them (General Patton, in Franklin Schaffner's film, recommends to his men not to die for their country, but have "the other poor dumb bastard" die for his).

To accuse Thucydides of condemning his own city (whether or not this is considered creditable) is to miss the point: to say, as A. Andrewes does, that they are "represented as more brutal than the abstract argument demands" ignores the fact that the Athenian delegates were being urgently practical. Their "brutality" was intended to bring home to the Melians the starkness of the alternatives. The Athenians played the game according to the rules of the time, and perhaps of all time: "Shock and awe" is no new tactic, though the bangs grow louder and more lethal.

The Athenians have been censured for conduct which – as Thucydides himself points out – is common among dominant powers. It is humbug to lament that the Athenians betrayed democracy by actually doing what they had candidly threatened (one might compare it to the British fleet's ultimatum to, and subsequent bombardment of, the French fleet at Mers-el-Kébir in 1940). Others pass judgment, as if on a tragic hero, by accusing the Athenians of self-destructive *hubris*. The proof, they say, is that the Sicilian expedition ended in failure and led to utter defeat in the war. This argument suggests a tragic "inevitability" which neither God nor History has been consistent in supplying. The Athenians have been stigmatized less because they were exceptionally hubristic (they were not) than because they lost the war. By the same logic, Hitler relied on victory to exempt him from history's judgment.

Small islands, not least in the eastern Mediterranean, continued to have to endure what they lacked the power or the luck to escape. South-east of Rhodos lies Castellorizo, which flourished in the nineteenth and early twentieth centuries, and met with a soft catastrophe almost at the end of the Second World War. Before 1914, when the Ottomans ruled Asia Minor, the island's deep, rectangular harbour was lined with the clippers whose owners and captains oversaw them from the balconies of the tall houses fronting it.

Although Greece favoured the Allies against the Turks in the Great War, Castellorizo was only indirectly involved in the Gallipoli campaign, which nevertheless began her decline. Unlike Melos, Castellorizo was read no peremptory ultimatum. The offer which her shipowners could not refuse was literally pure gold: sovereigns in return for their fleet, which the British needed to help supply the Dardanelles campaign.

In the event, the Gallipoli adventure was a disaster, less ill-conceived than ill-executed. Like the Athenians' Sicilian expedition, the Anglo-French force suffered from divided leadership and lack of accurate intelligence. Had the Athenians succeeded – as they nearly did in a daring night attack – in capturing the heights of Epipolae, which commanded Syracuse, they might have brought off a momentous *coup*. Had the (largely Anzac) Allied troops landed in the right place, with easy access to open ground, instead of on adjacent beaches, facing high and easily defended cliffs, Winston Churchill might have gained enough kudos to become prime minister in 1916, instead of Lloyd George.

It is tempting to argue that, in that case, in power in the 1930s, Churchill would have crushed Hitler early in his career. The playful futility of what-if historical essays is illustrated by the no less plausible possibility that – important with imperial and political responsibility (and in thrall to the Conservative party) – Churchill, like Neville Chamberlain, might have chosen diplomatic caution and the policy of appeasement which, as an irresponsible outcast, he

30 Whatever really happened to Castellorizo?

could afford to denounce. In politics, what are assumed to be constants are often variables.

As it was, the Allies were humiliated at Gallipoli, but not fatally. The Athenians, on the other hand, never recovered from the loss of men and materiel in Sicily. Had commanders on the spot shown the elan necessary, either might have been a master stroke. In both cases, lines of communication were dangerously protracted and the enemy given a chance to regroup. In the case of the Syracusans, their morale was stiffened and their tactics improved under a hastily imported, very competent Spartan general, Gylippus. The Turks, already brave, were similarly organized by excellent German military advisers.

After the Great War, Castellorizo was known as the thirteenth of the Dodecanese. By the Treaty of Versailles, it was mandated to the French, who instituted thrice-weekly seaplane flights to Paris, but gave little incentive to the islanders to invest their windfall sovereigns in tangible (and taxable) assets such as new ships. Nevertheless, the island's economic decline between the wars does not explain today's desolation. The harbour is still there, but without ships. The houses on the waterfront are in ruins. Terraces have moul-dered and collapsed. Fig and almond trees, snagged with brambles, furnish the roofless rooms. Castellorizo is a petty, insular Pompeii.

The final disaster came in 1944, when the British forces were island-hopping towards the Greek mainland. The official story is that the British first liberated the island and then decided to use the excellent harbour as a staging point for the fleet. They persuaded the fifteen thousand islanders that they should be evacuated, since German bombers were likely to make Castellorizo a target. When the war was won, which should not take long, they would be returned to their homes. (When the Spartans wished to dislodge the Plataeans, in 427, Thucydides reports them promising, "Once the war is over, we'll give back everything we took and, till then, hold it all in trust." When their offer was refused, they were every bit as uncompromising as the Athenians at Melos.)

During the last months of the Second World War, Allied troops were bil-leted in the Castellorizans' fine houses, and elsewhere on the island. In 1945, when the inhabitants were finally shipped home, they found their town devas-tated. If, as the British maintained, the Germans had indeed bombed it, they had done so with uncommon, if perverse, accuracy: while not a house was standing, the harbour installations were undamaged.

The unofficial story now is that mutinous Allied squaddies sacked the town. So embarrassing was the damage that it was necessary, and convenient, to blame the Germans. The British offered to transport the homeless islanders to Australia, an ancient form of solution to a modern problem. Many Castellorizans settled in Perth, Western Australia, where their fraternity became known as "Cazzies" (coincidentally, *kasis* is ancient Greek for brother).

Being industrious, and mutually supportive, many Cazzies prospered, but it is still not the Greek style to forget your mother-city. Like the Jews, Greeks are as regularly fractious with each other as they can be solid in the face of out-siders. When the Greeks *are* Jews, the effect is doubled: Primo Levi observed that, at Auschwitz, the thousands of Jews from Thessaloniki never lost faith in each other nor their formidable solidarity.

There is a small, and little advertised, museum in Thessaloniki in the memory of its lost community, but the author of *Z*, Vassili Vassilikis, tells in one of his stories of the promptness with which Jewish property was appropri-ated by its neighbours (the property of the dead attracts similar vultures in Kazantzakis's *Zorba the Greek*). Thessaloniki's elegantly paved and fountained *Plateia Aristotelous* (the philosopher was a native of nearby Stagira), with its delicious bakeries and ample cafés, is the ripped-out heart of Thessaloniki's vanished Jewish quarter.

31 Cosmopolitan 1890s Jews in Thessaloniki, putting on the styles, eastern meets western.

When we went to Castellorizo, there was a small airstrip but no more than a few dozen permanent inhabitants, but – nostalgia being a sentiment at least as old as Odysseus – a number of second-generation Cazzies, having made fortunes in Oz, had returned to rebuild their family homes. We were eating in a little taverna beside the empty harbour when I heard a woman of a certain age talking French with guttural, Levantine fluency. For some reason, I asked her whether she originated from Alexandria.

"Certainly, monsieur."

"I wonder if by any chance you ever met the great Alexandrian poet Cavafy?"

She looked at me with suddenly younger eyes. "*Comme enfant,*" she said, "*je l'ai taquiné dans les rues.*" As a child, she used to tease him in the streets of that once cosmopolitan city. She might as well have told me that she was at school with Sappho.

Gamel Abdul Nasser expelled Greeks and Jews from Alexandria in 1956 in the cause of Arab nationalism. Never an Egyptian city, Greeks and Jews had given it the cosmopolitan vitality celebrated so lushly by Lawrence Durrell in his *Quartet* and, above all, by the man whom Durrell called The Poet of the City: Constantine Cavafy. In the 1960s, on Ios, I met an Englishman who taught at Alexandria University. I told him that I envied him teaching in so exotic a location. He replied that it was now as exotic as Ramsgate.

Castellorizo served as the location for the pleasantly implausible movie *Mediterraneo*. In it, a happy occupying force of Italians passes an idyllic war, in which no shot was fired. On Ios, however, Italians were more disliked than Germans. This was not so on Crete, where the German repression was especially ruthless. Rumour says that, not so long ago, a guileless young German tourist informed some Cretans in the White Mountains that the beauty of their village had been reported to him by his father, who had been there during the war. The villagers murdered him.

* * *

*T*he fate of prosperous islands in the Mediterranean is seldom happy. Too renowned to escape attention and too weak to deter the acquisitive, Rhodos and Castellorizo provide a big and a petty illustration of the dangers of success. Insignificant islands, such as Pholegandros and Sikinos, in the Cyclades, were always more likely to be untroubled, even if, in the sixth century B.C., their modesty did earn them the contempt of the metropolitan Solon.

Solon is usually regarded as one of the founding fathers of democracy. A century and a half before him, however, Archilochos tells of a three-way election on Paros, in which some votes were cast for a mute inglorious candidate called Perikles. The winner was Glaukos, reputedly the fearless commander of the force, including Archilochos, which sailed first to Thasos (the poet observed that the island's silhouette bristled like the back of a randy donkey) and then to war with the Magnesians, against whom Archilochos delivered some scathing lines, imitated by Theognis: "Their dirty deeds, and arrogance, did for the Magnesians.... Cruelty sank the Magnesians, likewise Colophon, Smyrna too. And it's the same with you, Curnos, all the way."

If sea-borne commerce in the Aegean did indeed begin as long ago as 7000 B.C. (as pottery fragments in Etruria suggest), Cycladic prosperity must have lasted for several millennia. Amorgos traded richly with the Near East and Egypt. Melos had unique deposits of obsidian; among other de luxe uses, it supplied blades for daggers which garnished princely graves. The Aegean was more attractive, and lucrative, to traders than jagged mainland Hellas. Prehistoric Greek civilization faced east and south. Dominated by Crete, it was principally insular, at least until the rise of Mycenae well into the second millennium.

Many of the Cycladic islands are mountainous outcrops of marble, Parian the most valued. When we were first on Ios, its inferior local stone furnished tools, bollards, wedges, lids, tables, seats, steps, walls for houses and boundaries. The empty, golden beaches were grizzled with pocked pumice that bobbed in on the clean sea. Did ancient islanders observe, and imitate, the smooth work water did on stone when tides jiggled the loose change of pebbles and rock? Henry Moore's eye is unlikely to have been the first to be alert to the suggestive shaping of natural forms by the fretful elements.

Cycladic figures have a decided, almost unvaried aesthetic: legs, often separated by a groove, never have an open gap between them; arms are rarely distinct from bodies. Yet the figures' controlled proportions scarcely argue that their makers were incapable of larger, or more "realistic", work: it seems more likely that some established canon enjoined modesty.

Were some of the figures intended to amuse? Whatever the piggy-backing double images may have signified to some cult,* can they have failed to be greeted with smiles? Greek divinity was not incompatible with humour: a brazen little old goddess called Baubo flashed Demeter when she was in the dumps while looking for her lost daughter Persephone. The Earth-Mother could not help cracking up when her (neglected?) son, Iacchus, popped out, as if skittishly reborn, from under Baubo's hoisted skirts. Fourth-century sculptures from Priene pre-empt Magritte in depicting Baubo's genitals as her secret face. Ribaldry was not incompatible with Demeter's earthy character: at the Eleusinian mysteries, baskets containing phalluses made of pastry were revealed to initiates, after they had been enchanted by ceremonies honouring the Mother.

Baubo's revealing naughtiness was re-enacted annually – like a trailer – by drolls perched on the parapet of the Kephissos bridge as pilgrims passed to rebirth at Eleusis. Stretching somewhat, Nietzsche makes Baubo into a metaphor for Truth. In his *Joyful Knowledge*, he commends the Greeks for respecting life, in which "it is necessary to remain, bravely, on the surface, to admire drapery, skin, to love appearances, to care for forms, sounds, words, the whole 'Olympia' of appearance! Those Greeks were superficial – in their profundity... and for that reason precisely, artists!" Paul Valéry's glib "*La profondeur de la surface*" is a manifest crib from Nietzsche.

Most Cycladic figures seem to have been intended to be recumbent, though they are often braced upright in museums. The work is blanched and chaste;

---

* In the 1970s I bought a charming, manifestly fake, totemic marble, with one figure humped over another, on the site of ancient Carthage. A fanciful traveller might see a genetic connection with antique Phoenician figures in Carthage's home city.

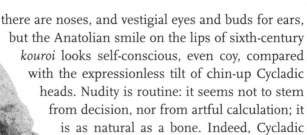

there are noses, and vestigial eyes and buds for ears, but the Anatolian smile on the lips of sixth-century *kouroi* looks self-conscious, even coy, compared with the expressionless tilt of chin-up Cycladic heads. Nudity is routine: it seems not to stem from decision, nor from artful calculation; it is as natural as a bone. Indeed, Cycladic figures are hardly "nudes", since that implies being wilfully unclothed: their unerotic forthrightness belongs to an Eden when clothes were neither put on nor removed.

On Milopota, below where we bought our house, a Frenchman had tried, in the modest 1950s, to found a nudist colony. The bay was then an empty beach and his huts were at the far end, where villagers rarely went. He was tolerated until he made rash promises of marriage to a local girl, and failed to honour them. The islanders made life insupportable for him.

In the 1960s, nudity returned to Ios, but – instigated by the Colonels' Church – locals resented what they proved powerless to prevent. Christianity had made nakedness offensive where – it would be nice to believe – it had once been both innocent and charming. As time went by, and the tourist trade brought thousands to the island's beaches and, more profitably, its bars and clubs, many people on Ios became seriously rich, which they did not find offensive at all.

Western sculpture begins with Cycladic; western writing with Linear-B account slips and tax returns. But whereas Ventris and Chadwick proved that Linear B is certainly Greek, Cycladic art remains detached in aesthetic narrative from all that follows, at least until Brancusi and Modigliani. The Greeks made Daedalus the founder of what they recognized as sculpture, *agalmata*, which never included Cycladic. The scoundrel genius has no separate identity in Homer; even though the adjective "daedalic" and the verb "to daedalize" are not unusual, the essential, artful character of Daedalus seems to derive from them, rather than the other way round.

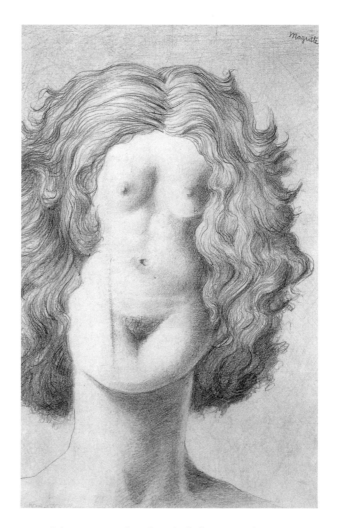

32 Baubo making Demeter smile, in the latter's shrine at Priene.

33 Magritte upgrades Baubo.

As master craftsman, Daedalus was credited with definitive achievements in Greek sculpture: a mortal Prometheus, he too devised lifelike dolls and initiated giving statues open eyes and parted legs and arms that stretched out from the body. He was the first to make three-dimensional images articulate. Yet Socrates – whose father was a stonemason – remarks, in Plato's *Hippias major*, "If Daedalus were alive today, and did the work that made him famous, he would look very foolish in the eyes of our sculptors".

If the statue of Aphrodite deposited on Delos by Theseus was literally daedalic, it was probably in the style of the wooden *xoana* with which archaic Greeks associated divinity. It may indeed have been small and crude, but it was also a novelty: *xoanon* comes from the verb *xeo*, to scrape, or polish. The image may have been tricked out with silver, like the shining icons still paraded by

Greek Orthodox priests, especially at Easter. In art history, pre-Daedalic sculpture was not rehabilitated until the classical categories lost definitive authority. Cycladic work defies aesthetic and anthropological exegesis; in Greek art, it stands alone, although it has affinities with similar pieces found in Anatolia, where the style may have originated.

With Daedalus, art became cunning, and deceptive. Not only the eponymous founder of the Greek style, he was also the archetypal Bohemian, with no fixed address and a criminal record. Prefiguring Caravaggio, Benvenuto Cellini and a whole gallery of rogue geniuses, he was an operator whose skills were so desirable that his conduct could be ignored. One of Daedalus's talents was for bending materials and adapting them to unnatural purposes. His sublime crookery combined art and craftiness.

Daedalus shares Odysseus's dexterity, success with women and deviousness, but was neither uxorious nor nostalgic. Peter Green argues, however, that his flight from Crete was fuelled by a desire to be buried in Attica. This chimes with the claim that he was an Athenian, descended from snaky Erichthonios, and a kinsman of Theseus. Athenian sources depicted Daedalus as a secret agent with a mission to subvert Cretan hegemony.

Philostratus (an amusing Athenian essayist of the third century A.D.) says that portraits of Daedalus emphasized his alert – hence Athenian – expression. Daedalus's elevation to the Attic *Who Was Who* may be a pretty instance of a posteriori naturalization. Whatever his origins, he had to flee from Athens after murdering his sister Polycaste's son, who is variously known as Talos and Perdix (the partridge boy). As apprentice to his uncle, the twelve-year-old nephew proved so precocious that he aroused Daedalus's jealousy.

Robert Graves cites a source claiming that Daedalus was enraged not by his nephew's talent but by his incestuous relationship with Daedalus's sister, Polycaste: an excuse to which the old French expression of incredulity, "*Et ta soeur*", is appropriate. Whether in grief or in shame, Polycaste is said to have hanged herself. The Athenians built her a sanctuary near the Acropolis.

Kenneth McLeish tells us that, having observed how "laboriously archaic potters built up their pots from strips of clay", Perdix proceeded to invent the potter's wheel. As a result, Attic pottery could be made faster and more symmetrical than its competitors. On another occasion, Perdix was toying with a fish's backbone (others say it was the jawbone of a serpent) and used its teeth to saw through a twig.

The flashy Daedalus did not relish being outshone by his brilliant nephew. He took the boy for a stroll on the Acropolis and sent him flying either over the edge or from the roof of Athene's temple: the cue for the victim to be metamorphosed into a partridge. No amount of talent inoculates some artists against the temptation to take credit for other people's ideas: Daedalus did as much with the saw, to which he gave practical use by casting it in bronze.

Caught carrying Perdix's body in a sack, Daedalus had the impudent presence of mind to claim that he was on his way to bury a dead snake, a pious duty enjoined on all Athenians, since their legendary king, Erichthonios, had a serpentine genealogy. Michelangelo would claim that all form was basically serpentine (the wave theory of light is an illustration), though it varied from instance to instance. Taking the same view, Leonardo da Vinci drew attention to the serpentine undulations of everything in nature. The snake is still at the bottom of the Creator's garden.

Daedalus may have been charged with Perdix's murder in front of the Areopagus, and sentenced to exile; he may, alternatively, have absconded (as Socrates – and Oscar Wilde – refused, or neglected, to do). Either way, Daedalus took Talos's toolbox with him and also, at least on some accounts, his own young son, Icarus. He boarded a ship to Crete, which must have been propelled by oars, since – in his personal c.v. – its passenger is credited only subsequently with having invented the sail. Rationalizers claim that it is because, to the gullible, sailing ships appear to fly that we have the story that Daedalus "flew" from Crete. Modern island travel is by "Flying Dolphin" hydrofoil.

The fugitive was received with honour by Minos, to whom he became the court magician and designer. McLeish credits him with inventing "large, flat-bottomed merchant ships" to carry grain. These were forerunners, it sounds, of the "empty ships" which Marcus Samuel commissioned – in Trieste, since no British yard would take the risk – early in the twentieth century, in order to carry crude oil in bulk instead of in the space-consuming barrels by which its production is still measured.

Daedalus anticipated Leonardo da Vinci in applying art to serve the military/industrial complex: he improved the manoeuvrability of warships and designed an underwater ram, in the form of a bird's beak, which reinforced the Cretan fleet's mastery of the seas (as barnacle-proof copper bottoms would give added speed to Britain's "hearts of oak").

Some versions of the myth make Icarus the son of a Cretan woman, Naucrate, from Gortyn where Daedalus relaxed from palace life in Knossos. The late Roman poet Ausonius calls him "the Bird of Gortyn" (a modern might give Naucrate the same title). Minos the philanderer found a kindred spirit in Daedalus, who was also the confidant of Queen Pasiphae. She lamented too loudly that Aphrodite had played her a dirty trick in giving her a husband who failed to want her. If the gods had one characteristic in common with artists, it was dislike of criticism. Aphrodite piqued Pasiphae with insatiable desire for the fire-breathing white bull which Poseidon had sent to confirm Minos's majesty.

Proving no less practical a pander than a shipwright, Daedalus put together the hollow hide, on wheels, in which the queen, anointed with oestrogen, could cower to be pleasured by the bull. Since the latter was of divine provenance, and all female sexual contact with divinities led to pregnancy, the evidence of Pasiphae's adultery soon began to show. As Minos no longer slept with his wife, he knew that he was not the source of her condition. Daedalus was thereupon commissioned to construct a dungeon suite fit for a queen, but out of sight of Minos and her all-seeing father, the Sun. The labyrinthine subterranean nursery was a prison from which Pasiphae could not be delivered until she was herself delivered of her child. Once born, baby Minotaur was penned in the lockless recesses of the palace basement.

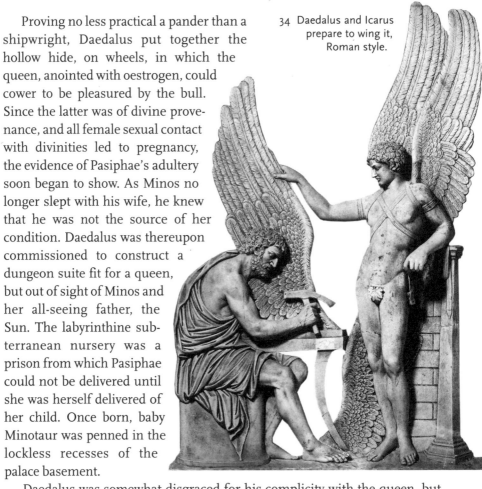

34 Daedalus and Icarus prepare to wing it, Roman style.

Daedalus was somewhat disgraced for his complicity with the queen, but his services remained indispensable to Minos. The king's fear that others might make use of his craftiness kept the artist in pensioned penance: a paradigm of the relationship between money and art. Some credit Daedalus with the creation of the gigantic bronze coastguard (also called Talos) who patrolled the island. Literally hot-blooded, since he had molten metal in his veins, Talos grilled illegal immigrants by clutching them to his breast until they were done for. He eventually leaked to death after having his plug pulled, some say by Medea, when she was super-cargo on the returning *Argo*.

According to Apollodorus, Daedalus once played a joke on Herakles by constructing an image of the hero so realistic that when its model came across it in the gloaming, he attacked it with his club: an early instance of fear of the *doppelgänger*. But then how like is a likeness? The plot of Vladimir Nabokov's novel *Despair* concerns a man who, hoping to start a new life, kills a man whom he takes to be his *doppelgänger*, though in fact his literally dead ringer looks nothing like him.

By a sweet intersection of myths, it was Herakles who relieved Crete of the fire-breathing white bull. It was one of the hero's labours to bring it back to king Eurystheus of Mycenae.

> Herakles chose a sly form of attack:
> His lion-skin, he knew, resisted flame,
> So he advanced by walking front-to-back.
> The bull took one long look and in he came,
> Snorting more fire than put tall Troy to sack:
> To roast a lion was his kind of game.
> Our hero felt the heat and – somersaulted!
> Over the horns, up on its back he vaulted.

After Herakles has corralled the white bull and ridden it back to mainland Greece, there is a fork in the myth: either it was now so docile that it was sacrificed to Hera or it was put to breed among the cattle on the plain of Marathon, where it so recovered its ardour that it terrorized the natives. In the latter version, Minos sent his son Androgeos to recapture the beast. Lacking Herakles' muscle, and guile, the boy was killed. In his rage and grief, Minos blamed the Athenians, from whom he exacted the tribute of boys and girls on which the Minotaur feasted until Theseus embarked on his showboating adventure.

When he was told of Theseus's arrival, Daedalus's duplicity again came into play. Somewhat like his compatriot Alcibiades, his genius lay in mutability. Was he perhaps now as eager to escape Crete as he had once been to find asylum there? Whatever his motive (did he fancy Ariadne?), he tipped off Minos's daughter on how to help Theseus thread the maze and kill the Minotaur.

35 Cowboy Herakles at work.

Once Theseus and Ariadne were safely on their way to Naxos, Daedalus had to make his own escape. Whether he now invented winged flight (for which the daedalian Leonardo also left a blueprint) or whether his skill was limited to spreading sails on the boat(s) in which he and Icarus outstripped their pursuers, he flew, literally or metaphorically, for his life. Although Daedalus took their son, he abandoned his local wife Naucrate (whose name implies naval power). Contrary to pre-flight safety instructions, Icarus melted his waxed wings by soaring too near the Sun, an error reciprocated by the Sun's son, Phaethon, who once flew his chariot too low and scorched the earth.

The layered density of myth, which allows it to be read in variable, and competing, senses is never more suggestive than in the case of Daedalus. Like Odysseus, he not only has *metis*, but also generates sympathy: however badly he behaves, we still hope that he escapes the consequences of his crimes, even when it involves the destruction of his patron and friend, Minos. Michael Ayrton's novel, *The Mazemaker*, is an emulous admirer's empathetic tribute to the artist as ingenious rascal.

If wise, the king might have cut his losses, but like a fool he could not endure them. In vengeful fury, he followed Daedalus to Sicily – that fatal island! – and, although the artist went to ground, devised a ruse for smoking him out: while visiting the court of Cocalus, a local capo, Minos advertised a prize for anyone who could thread the contorted shell of a sea snail. Daedalus had been secreted out of Minos's range, but he was, of course, unable to resist the challenge (prize money is the father of the Muses): he dabbed honey on the shell, having first punctured it with a pin, and inserted an ant with a thread attached to it.

When Cocalus produced the finished article to his guest, Minos knew that only one man could be its author. But he still did not fully know what he was capable of doing. Daedalus had made his mark with Cocalus's daughters, who seduced the Cretan visitor into a pre-dinner bath. Daedalus piped steam into the bathroom and put paid to his benefactor *à la vapeur*.

In an unintentional culinary footnote to this, Athenaeus, the author – at the beginning of the third century A.D. – of the *Deipnosophistai* (The Clever Dicks' Banquet) refers to a cook called Daedalus in a play by the comic poet Philostephanos. The coincidence is the crisper for Athenaeus being a native of the Egyptian city of Naucratis, which sports the same etymology as Icarus's mother.

Once again, Daedalus had got away with murder. A less talented mortal might have been cooked according to the same recipe as his victim, but the quintessential artist was too useful: Daedalus not only constructed a dam to alleviate Sicily's chronic droughts, he also devised a fortress to enable his tyrannical host to live in security with a very small garrison. Ascent to the hilltop eyrie was winding and narrow, somewhat like the sea snail's shell. It gave every advantage to its defenders.

Just as Louis XIV would recall Vauban from civilian retirement, in order to add to his range of ingenious fortifications, so Daedalus was more in demand by his Sicilian master as a military engineer than as an artist. However, he did find time to solve one more teaser. Challenged to duplicate the natural delicacy of a honeycomb, he poured plaster into its cells and then, when it had set hard, funnelled molten bronze into the waxen comb. The bronze cooled and hardened in place of the melted wax: *cire perdue* is a standard process in bronze-casting to this day. Michael Ayrton, who for a bet once matched Daedalus's honeycomb, kept a little fingernail very long, so that he could fret detail into the wax maquettes which he prepared for the Fulham Foundry.

When the plaster was chipped away, and the bronze buffed, Daedalus's factitious golden honeycomb outshone its original. Bees came and settled on it, just as birds were said to have pecked at the *trompe l'oeil* grapes on a mural by Zeuxis, at the end of the fifth century. Zeuxis was a byword for artistic arrogance. Unlike Daedalus, he was rich enough to choose only to give his work away, since he held it beyond price. Daedalus was more the commission-seeking daredevil who, by his charm and craftiness, could get away with anything, whether murder or his nephew's ideas. He could bend rules, just as he bent his materials. He was, however, the patron only of three-dimensional art. He is not credited with decorative skills, unlike those who painted the walls of Minos's palace at Knossos, which were later enhanced by the craftsmen, led by Piet de Jong, employed by Sir Arthur Evans to "restore" their pristine gloss. Many of the panels bear a surprising resemblance to the art nouveau in fashion at the time of their discovery.

A whole nexus of felonious but invaluable intellectuals are latter-day *Daedalidai*, concerned less with their own or anyone else's morals than with opportunities to shine: Daedalic art was characteristically dazzling. The skill of *Daedalidai* is never for its own sake; it seduces and beguiles; it deceives as it shapes, flatters or embellishes the going gods. As art and science converge and overlap, the masters of knowledge and of *techne* – its practical application – become the necessary, but never wholly trusted, servants of any number, or style, of masters. Daedalus is the forerunner both of Leonardo and of Dr Strangelove, a character based on Edward Teller, the "father of the H-bomb".

It was, however, Teller's quondam boss, J. Robert Oppenheim, who relived Daedalus's privileged, distrusted role at Los Alamos, when he was crucial to the development of the atomic bomb, but suspected of playing a double game with Communist Russia. The A-bomb has something in common with the Daedalian technology which made Talos the hot shield of Crete.

Daedalus was a master of mimesis. The highest form of imitation supplants its original: by giving his work mobility, he made the medium the message and its messenger. Plato has been much derided for his expulsion of artists from the ideal *politeia*, but his apprehensions were not empty. He himself was an instance of what he found suspicious: the Socratic dialogues furnish us with a philosopher so realistic, who speaks so plausibly, that it requires an effort not to take Socrates to be the very person for whom Plato's art substituted a literary *eidolon*.

* * *

*A*fter a few days in the hotel in the harbour of Ios, we rented a *spiti* (cottage) from Nikos Plakeotis. There was a plank bed with a straw-filled "mattress", no running water and no electricity. Our sole luxury was a deckchair. There was a sacking-curtained earth-closet across the field from the well. The *spiti* was of whitened plaster over unmortared stone; floor and roof (resting on a bamboo trellis) were rammed earth. Yellow daisies and black-eyed, blood-banded poppies sprang from the fertile roof. Next to them, a small fig-tree displayed green-nailed buds. Nature lived on the floor above us.

When we had a violent nocturnal storm, rain lanced through the roof. Some kind goddess umbrellaed our children: not a drop fell in the corners where they slept. Niko's father came by in the morning while we were bailing out. "*Megalee phortouna stee nykhta*," he said: big storm in the night. *Phortouna* – the modern Greek for storm – sounds like a Latinate *meiosis*: the Roman goddess Fortuna was Luck, the source of worldly success. In the same ingratiating spirit, Athenians called the irascible Black Sea "Euxine" (nice to strangers). Language means and does not mean what it says.

As weeks passed, Dionysus posted his signature on Niko's cottage: an arthritic grapevine felt for, gripped and began to mount the wire lattice over the terrace: its summer leaves would shade the hot table where I sat typing my novel, *Lindmann*. It was tempting, in that remote spring, to imagine Ios to be somewhat as it was in classical times. Yet not even the sky was the same: modern dawn's rosy fingers are chemically dyed, Homer's unalloyed. The fifth-century population of Ios may well have exceeded ten thousand; it was now two hundred. The ancient city has yet to be fully excavated or, as they say, "published" by scholars. It was, however, sometimes pillaged by local rogue archaeologists, who knew where to look. Almost forty years ago I bought what was promised to be an authentic proto-Cycladic figure. The British Museum declared it fake, but I still have it, and a vestigial belief that some inglorious pre-daedalian made it.

When we first went to Ios, there was a rusting sign at the harbour advertising the way to "HOMER'S TUM"; maybe he, or one of him, is buried there: some authorities maintain that he was a corporation of rhapsodes. Their work was compiled into a single authorized version when the repertoire was edited in the eighth century B.C. Paul Zanker says that, in the fourth century, Ios issued splendid silver coins, bearing a head of Homer. With his flowing hair, the poet could easily have been taken for an image of Zeus (which had probably been hijacked by the die-cutter). However, there is an authenticating oracle, allegedly given to Homer, which says, "There is an island, Ios, your mother's fatherland, which will welcome you when dead". Samuel Butler wrote a mischievously straightfaced scholarly article proving, from internal evidence, that the *Odyssey* was written by a woman. Today he might be taken seriously. Whatever sex the poet was, he or she could indeed be buried on Ios.

* * *

*A*s schoolboys, we came late to Homer: his archaic Greek was too difficult for beginners and unsuitable for imitation. Even his matter required adroit interpretation before it chimed with official Carthusian morality. The *Iliad* is an encomium on an insubordinate, self-centred hero: Achilles' own vanity was his sole commander. A bad loser in his quarrel with the C.-in-C., Agamemnon, over whose bed the captive Briseis should sleep in, Achilles went and sulked in his tent. What made Briseis desirable was less her innate charms than that Agamemnon had pulled rank in order to procure her beauty for himself. René Girard has argued that desire is a function of emulation: men come to want what they observe other men to be wanting (Oedipus saw Jocasta as a *prize*, never as his mother). Achilles' determination to be the first among men made his possession of Briseis a matter of honour. When frustrated, he withdrew his labour.

His secession led to many deaths, in particular that of his lover, Patroklos, to whom Achilles had lent

36 Patroklos bandaged by a tender Achilles on a fifth-century B.C. vase from Magna Graecia.

his armour. The Trojan hero Hector imagined that he was fighting the Achaean champion. In some sense, the arms *were* the man: when Patroklos was defeated (by Apollo) and despoiled of Achilles' shield and armour, Achilles' divine mother, Thetis, persuaded Hephaestus, armourer of the gods, to design a new set. Only then could Achilles rise again.

Patroklos was older than Achilles, who did not, therefore, send a boy to do a man's job when Patroklos went into battle. Were they physical lovers? McLeish says that Achilles, like all the offspring of sea creatures (Thetis was a sea nymph), was bisexual and "slept alternate nights with Briseis and Patroklos". Modern myth is more chaste: Butch Cassidy and the Sundance Kid were bosom buddies without exchanging so much as a kiss.

Achilles returned to battle less for patriotic reasons than to avenge his friend. He not only killed Hector but, contrary to the rules of chivalry (which often led to the exchange of compliments as well as inflammatory insults, and always to respect for the dead), demeaned his corpse by dragging it behind his chariot in the dust, three times, around the high-walled city. Rage, pride and guilt/shame banished *sophrosyne* (moderation). The Greek "national" cause was of negligible significance to its greatest hero, nor did Homer ever proclaim it.

The first poet to blare the patriotic note, in the seventh century, was Tyrtaeus, the Spartan Sousa. His marching songs promoted selflessness above individualism. Personal ambition was suspect in Sparta (those who broke ranks or protocol achieved the fame of obloquy). To avoid tyranny, its constitution was elaborate with checks and balances; hereditary dual kingship supplied the throne(s) with the brake and accelerator of mutually wary dyarchs. The Roman consulship, though annual, was not dissimilar.

Achilles was both a supreme example (of *arete*, manly virtue) and an awful warning (of the dangers of impetuous vanity). His lack of *sophrosyne* was not compensated by the mood swings which led him, briefly, to pity King Priam: his tears are salted with conceit. His ghost, however, did not spare Priam's grandchildren.

Alexander the Great was a gross parody of the mythical hero. Never reluctant to fight, he sought to emulate Achilles by becoming greater in fame even than his model. His first landfall in Darius's realm was at the Hellespont, where – like his hero – he flung the first spear to bite Asiatic soil. With the *Iliad* under his pillow – a suitable vade mecum for a natural-born killer – he set out to stage a remake of the Trojan War. Persia doubled for Troy, Darius for Priam; his own (marginally Greek) Macedonians served for Myrmidons. Alexander had no redemptive ambition, nor had his companions anything in common with the chorus of elders in Aeschylus's *Agamemnon*, who announced,

37 Alexander on the way to ride in triumph through Persepolis.

38 Burton the Great (in Robert Rossen's 1956 *Alexander the Great*).

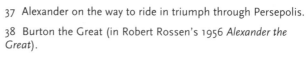

"I never want to sack a city". Hell-bent for booty and glory, Alexander could never sack enough cities, and was often first over their walls. His treatment of those with whom he picked his quarrels was rarely magnanimous: if he was gallant towards the Persian royal ladies (he is even said to have slept with Darius's mother, if that was gallantry), there was condescension in his grace. He was notably sadistic when balked. After the siege of Tyre, he crucified two thousand of its brave defenders; and after that of

Gaza, the city's staunch and resourceful commander (a eunuch called Batis) was dragged behind a chariot, in imitation of Achilles' treatment of Hector. However, Hector was dead when his body was abused; Batis was alive. We have to believe that Alexander was not primed for such barbarity – imitated gleefully by today's motorized terrorists – by the annotated volumes of Homer with which his ex-tutor Aristotle had supplied him.

Throughout antiquity, the *Iliad* was a manual of war as well as an inspiration. As late as the fourth century A.D., Julian the Apostate disposed his forces – once more against the Persians – in accordance with the tactics advanced by Nestor: the bravest soldiers were divided between the front ranks and the rear, where they could police those who might be minded to turn and run.

Julian's respect for Homer was of a piece with his attitude to the Homeric pantheon and his tolerance for all gods, including that of the Jews. He earned the long hatred of Christianity not because he persecuted Christians but because he rejected their persecution of others. Bitter experience of Christian charity – at the hands of the sons of the great Constantine – turned him from membership of the Church to a votary of the Olympians. Had he reigned for longer than two years, instead of dying of wounds while still in his early thirties, who knows what inevitable course history might then have taken?

There was another attempt, in the first half of the fifteenth century, wilfully to restore paganism, in the now ruined Byzantine city of Mistra, whose stepped ruins rise on the hill behind Sparta, which is topped by a Venetian fort. The Neoplatonist Gemistos Plethon proposed a theurgical programme: a version of "white magic" which, according to Egyptian devotees, conjured beneficent spirits with a view to miracle-working. The ghosts of today's Mistra are piously Christian and Byzantine.

As for Julian, in seeking to reverse the progress of theological (and practical) history, the emperor insisted that the public schools under his aegis teach the great classical authors and the ancient religion which underpinned them. Christian youth would, he thought, thereby be compelled either to revert to paganism or to forgo erudition and remain forever in the B-stream.

In response, Gibbon tells us, Apollinaris "produced...Christian imitations of Homer (a sacred history in xxiv books), Pindar, Euripides, and Menander; and Sozomen is satisfied that they equalled, or excelled, the originals". Sozomen was a stylish fifth-century A.D. pedant in Constantinople who promulgated the validity of secular material in Christian culture. The issue of whether state schools should tolerate, or sponsor, religious particularism continues to vex both French and American education.

* * *

*A*chilles died on Trojan soil; Alexander would also die prematurely, in Babylon: another mimetic touch. His crowded hours too had been glorious, if killing was glory. On the shield he fashioned for Achilles' Big Fight, Hephaestus depicted peace and war in adjacent panels. It would be nice to believe that peace was advertised with more enthusiasm than war, but manliness could be proved only in battle. The bookish Dr Johnson remarked, in the Homeric tradition, that no one who had not "been for a soldier" was ever quite sure of his virility. Virtue was a battle honour. When writing his own epitaph, Aeschylus did not mention his more than ninety plays or the prizes they won; he chose to be remembered only for having fought at Marathon (he may also have been at Salamis). He preferred that his courage, rather than his art, survive him, or that people should think he did.

Yet the Greeks were regularly aware of the scandal of war, especially between themselves. Jean Giraudoux's play *La Guerre de Troie n'aura pas lieu* was a modern attempt, about the time of Munich, to emphasize the folly of war and (ironically maybe) to staunch its epic source in western culture. Of course, the playwright's Trojan War *did* take place. Giraudoux later became a minister in the Vichy government. Pacificism too can have dirty hands.

Thucydides' account of the negotiations, in 421, which almost put an end to the Peloponnesian War (and did procure an uneasy truce in the so-called Peace of Nikias) is full of presumably sincere attempts to abate internecine killing. Greeks almost as often felt shame at killing other Greeks as they found occasions to do so. Their treaties provided for negotiation rather than war, but "gods and heroes" would, it seemed, keep determining them on renewed combat.

The only plausible, and practical, solution to the habit of mutual slaughter was pressed by fourth-century orators such as Isocrates and Aeschines: for all Hellenes to combine against *the* barbarian enemy, Persia, as they had – with the exception of Thebes and most of Thessaly – when Xerxes invaded in 480. Their once brave coalition was repeated only in shame, after Alexander of Macedon conscripted the Greek cities, which his father had crushed at Chaeronea, to fall in with his pan-Hellenic coalition. The great Athenian orator, Demosthenes (384–322) – who was said to have enhanced his diction by rehearsing with pebbles in his mouth – was always held up as an example of brave resistance to Macedonian *force majeure*. He compared the Athenians' inept reactions to Philip of Macedon's aggressive expansionism to those of a barbarian boxer, who – lacking the wit for more artful self-defence – always puts his hands where he was last hit. Winston Churchill's pre-war Philippics warned, in similarly patriotic periods, of Hitler's expanding lust for conquest:

the British should arm themselves and be, as they now say, proactive rather than merely react to the German menace.

Demosthenes tried to rally Athens to an enterprising policy for which it no longer had the clout. His rhetoric was as much an obituary of the city-state as that of Perikles over the Athenian dead in the first year of the Peloponnesian War had been an encomium. By denouncing Philip, and – after Alexander's death – by calling, yet again, for the Athenians to rise against the repressive Macedonians, Demosthenes was as anachronistic as he was stalwart. During the war, Churchill spoke of Britain fighting on, "if necessary alone", but she was never as bereft of resources as fourth-century Athens.

Translated into a modern Englishman, Demosthenes would almost certainly rail against involvement in Europe. The Athenian *demos*, so often accused of vacillation, remained astonishingly, perhaps foolishly, loyal to him, despite the bitter fruit of his policies. They may have been keener to applaud than to march, but they agreed to surrender the orator to the infuriated Macedonians only when he was clearly inciting them to suicidal resistance.

The influence of the tragic theatre on Attic oratory cannot be precisely assessed, but a certain osmosis is manifest: Demosthenes was an *actor*, metaphorically, in the way that Solon, two centuries earlier, disdained to be (though the latter was not above pretending to go mad when it came to advocating the annexation of Salamis).

As theatre became a part of democratic life, its style and vocabulary infected political performance. Demosthenes was the tragic messenger as practical politician; his great enemy, Isocrates, had actually been a *tritagonistes* (a bit player). We are promised that part of the decorum expected in public debate was that speakers not interrupt each other: when Greek contradicted Greek, it was, so it is nice to suppose, only after waiting until the other had finished. Here again there is a theatrical tradition to wait for another actor to finish his speech (and give you your cue) before saying the next line. In tragedy, the semblance of interruption could, of course, be catered for by a broken, shared line, in a passage of stichomythia. Today's politicians are conscious performers for the camera: the medium alters their vocabulary and pretties their appearance. The media of radio and television tend to encourage speakers to cut in on each other, which echoes the "realism" of method acting, in which spontaneity, or its appearance, trumps antique courtesy. Since "news" is now a twenty-four-hour turn-on, modern politicians are also theatrical messengers, but they seek always to make the news seem good, or themselves heroic, in clean shirts.

* * *

39 Ingres's Oedipus, the Man Who Would be King, quizzes the Sphinx.

*M*iasma – the pollution that follows ill-doing – was regarded seriously by classical Greeks. It lingers on as what is taken to be hereditary bad luck (that of the Kennedys, for example, whose founding father, Joseph, was a bad man). Christians internalized miasma as bad conscience, to be purged – Mother Church promised – by confession. Bad blood leads to bad acts: Sophocles' Oedipus pollutes his kingdom with wholly involuntary transgressions. In ritual pollution there are never mitigating circumstances. In the Old Testament, when Uzzah steadies the Ark of the Covenant as it is falling into the ditch, he is struck dead. Reasonable intentions never excuse breaching irrational taboos.

On his travels, Oedipus kills an arrogant and aggressive stranger, for what Greeks would have thought forgivable reasons. Laius, in his chariot, crosses Oedipus, on foot, on the road outside Thebes. When Oedipus refuses to give way, Laius yields to chariot rage and orders his men to push Oedipus off the road. In the ensuing fight, both escort and Laius are killed. Oedipus proceeds to Thebes, solves the riddle of the Sphinx and is crowned king alongside Laius's widow, Jocasta. For all his intelligence, he has no way of knowing that Laius was his father nor that his widow, the queen of Thebes, is actually the mother from whom – on oracular advice that the baby would kill its father – he was separated at birth. The infant was meant to be exposed, but the menial deputed to dump him was too soft-hearted to leave him to die.

That Oedipus is neither a wilful parricide nor consciously committing incest cannot allay the miasma he has incurred and which, because of his now royal position, has infected Thebes. The notion of "original sin" is not uniquely Christian: Oedipus was tainted before his birth because, in at least some versions of the myth, his father, Laius, was the first (mortal) pederast.* Miasma both was and was not a solemn preoccupation in classical times. The great Athenian Eupatrid (aristocratic) family of the Alcmaeonids, to which Perikles partially belonged, on his mother's side, was said, by its enemies, to be indelibly tainted by sacrilege. In the seventh century, the would-be tyrant Cylon's supporters were killed after being promised immunity if they would quit the altar where they had taken refuge. Since it happened during his watch, the Alcmaeonid archon Megacles was held responsible. This did not prevent his descendants from being among the most distinguished, and richest, in Athens.

It might seem, therefore, that miasma and the *agos* (black mark) which went with it were not taken seriously in practice. However, the charge against the Alcmaeonids gave their enemies an abiding and, in some respects, an irrefutable excuse for pointing the finger at them. Prejudice was allayed by conspicuous service, philanthropy or good fortune, but it could be revived if things went badly. The plague at Athens which, against all rational expectation, lamed the city during the first three years of the Peloponnesian War took place while Perikles was still in charge. A historian as sophisticated as Thucydides might not read the plague as evidence that Perikles was indeed infectiously polluted, but it is not surprising that the Spartans put it about that he was, nor that some Athenians feared they were right.

---

* Is it true that "the Greeks" had no notion of the impropriety of at least certain forms of homo-eroticism? Orators denounced opponents for taking the "female", passive role (or for oral sex). Taking money for sexual services disqualified citizens from public office, and entailed an element of unpurgeable *agos*, or pollution. (In the Victorian age, when it was still reprehensible, masturbation was termed "self-pollution". Today, football referees are accused of being given to it.) The rituals of proper pederasty between full-blooded citizens suggest that, formally, it was a matter of love not lust (which slave boys could serve).

The Jews are today's bearers of the taint of miasma (the mythical equivalents of the Alcmaeonids were the Atreidae). Their alleged cry, at the time of Jesus' trial, "His blood be on our heads and on the heads of our children" (eagerly rehearsed in Mel Gibson's film of the Passion) supplies a perpetual death warrant to anti-Semites. Yet Jewish genius has informed (the Nazis said "infected") western civilization. Post-Holocaust Europe is supposedly proof against such ideas, but Arab newspapers and websites advertise them in their most vicious form. Egyptian television recently ran a forty-part serialization of the notoriously forged *Protocols of the Elders of Zion*. English politicians have used the term "something of the night" to describe the fatal flaw even of putative, "incidentally" Jewish, colleagues.

Thucydides says that the *Nosema* fell on Athens like an army. As random as it was lethal, the plague stimulated contempt for sacred and profane law, just as moral and social decency was shattered by the *stasis* on Corcyra. The *Nosema* was regarded as an "alien intruder" from Ethiopia "beyond Egypt". The introduction (in which Proust's doctor father had a once honoured part) of the "racist" *cordon sanitaire* against cholera in the nineteenth century was regarded as a reasonable form of defence against alien infection. Immigrants can still be denounced as a "plague". Hurricanes such as Katrina are given female names, like angry Furies.

* * *

*T*he *Iliad* ennobles contradictions which run through western literature. Greeks and Trojans are presented in diametrical opposition: one must, and will, destroy the other. Yet they worship the same gods, of whom Hera hates and Zeus loves the Trojans. There was a Trojan shrine of Athene which, as long as it stayed intact, guaranteed that the city would remain inviolate. At Athene's own suggestion, Odysseus and Diomedes set about stealing the goddess's Palladium from a shrine in the heart of the besieged city, so as to clear the way for Troy's capture. Helen, the daughter of Zeus, was also a kind of common property: both Greeks and Trojans felt that she belonged to them, though neither regarded her with affection. Later, barbarians refused to believe the story of the Trojan War: they found it incredible that men should go to war just because of a faithless woman. Herodotus, however, tells of many earlier fights over abducted princesses: wars and alliances could have the same source.

So closely related were Troy and the Achaeans that the *casus belli* was a breach of common rules. Paris's "sin" was not so much his theft of Menelaus's wife as that he abused the norms of Zeus *xenios*: guest-friendship among nobles involved reciprocal obligations. In the Mediterranean world, whoever displaces himself to visit another – with no matter how many followers or expensive presents – is in the postulant role. And however richly a guest is entertained, there is always a sliver of humble pie on his plate. Perhaps because it was from Sparta that Paris removed Helen, the Spartans became the least open-handed of hosts: when Philip of Macedon asked whether he should visit them "as a friend or an enemy", they had the laconic wit to reply: "Neither".

Greek grandees of different cities often had relationships close enough to be suspect in time of war. Perikles feared that his guest-friend Archidamus, one of the Spartan kings, who was in command of the invasion of Attica, might exempt the Athenian leader's estates from devastation,* and so excite the anger or suspicion of Perikles' unfortunate rural neighbours. In peace-time, mutual friends, known as *proxenoi*, would supply diplomatic services to foreigners from cities where they themselves enjoyed visitors' privileges.

Ancient life was always dangerous, and often short, or shortened, but within the city it was literally civilized: weapons were not carried in public, proprieties – even of gesture – were honoured, and vulgarity despised. The control of anger was constantly enjoined, which argues that explosions of rage were not uncommon. Following this line, I once suggested that eye-gouging and testicle-twisting were part of the "fun and games" at Olympia. A learned correspondent reminded me that such things were expressly forbidden by the rules, and hence could never have taken place. But how often are laws enacted against crimes which are never committed?

According to Herodotus, in the council of war before the battle of Salamis, Themistokles broke protocol in his urgent determination to bend the allies to his will. Adeimantus, the son of the commander of the Corinthian contingent told him, "Themistokles, in the races, the man who starts before the signal is whipped."

"Yes," replied the Athenian, "but those who start late win no prizes."

* * *

The *Iliad*'s advertised theme is the *menis* (anger) of Achilles, which almost brings disaster on the Argives. The 1950s catchphrase "the blue meanies" encapsulates, as it inadvertently puns on, the sulky rage to which Achilles yielded. The nuances of the range of Greek terms usually translated

---

* In 1939, the RAF refrained from bombing certain targets in the Ruhr because, said Neville Chamberlain, they were "private property". Such refinements were definitively abandoned by "Bomber" Harris, for whom no German target was a priori illicit.

40 A sixth-century B.C. black-figure Ajax totes the dead Achilles to his pyre. Has he nabbed the hero's helmet, which he will lose to Odysseus?

as "anger" are a matter for scholars, but uncontrolled passion was always a menace both to civil and to military order: *orge* impelled Achilles to break ranks in order to indulge his furious resentment.

Having redeemed himself by killing Hector, Achilles became an emblematic hero. But, in accordance with the oracle which offered the choice between a short, glorious life and a long, ignominious one, he was soon killed by an accurate arrow from the bow of the caddish Paris. Unlike Trojans or Persians, Greek noblemen were never archers, though Odysseus drew a strong bow when he got home. Crete – where no "Hoplite Revolution" modernized warfare – was renowned for its bowmen. The bow was less noble when hunting than the spear.

Achilles' death was followed by a competition between the surviving Greek brass for his equipment, not least the shield fashioned by Hephaestus. Aias, otherwise Ajax,* son of Telamon, was the likeliest candidate, not only in his own eyes. However, the wily Odysseus culled the votes, and the arms. The mortified Aias went mad and slaughtered a herd of sheep and oxen, under the delusion that he was killing Agamemnon and Menelaus, who had failed, as he saw it, to show him respect.

Not to receive their due affronted both heroes and gods. Aias's folly began in vanity, when he denied his patroness Athene any part in his prowess. Her hurt feelings tripped Aias's fall. When the hero came to his senses, and realized what a lunatic he had been, shame obliged him to suicide. His halfbrother Teucer (whose bastardy is underlined by his being an archer) returned from Mysia – a place associated with feebleness and effeminacy – to take uneasy charge of the fortunes of Aias's woman, Tecmessa, and their infant son. Proverbially, to be "*Muson leia*" (Mysian fodder) was to be "prey to all".

---

* Two of three British ships which cornered the German pocket battleship *Graf Spee* in the south Atlantic in 1940 were the destroyers HMS *Achilles* and HMS *Ajax*: companions-in-arms again!

It may be that Teucer was off on a plundering trip, but isn't there a touch of Sophoclean genius in presaging Teucer's Mysian impotence when it comes to redeeming his family's fortunes?

After his half-brother and leader's impious death, Teucer's own position is perilous: the Greeks vent on him the rage they feel at Aias's destruction of their flocks and cattle (his insults against Odysseus and the warlords seem to have caused markedly less general offence). Since Teucer is a bastard (and Tecmessa a captive princess reduced to slavery), the survivors' prospects are doubtful. Teucer knows that he can no more rely on his father Telamon's understanding than could Aias himself: he guesses that part of the hero's motive for suicide was dread of his sire's reaction to his disgrace.

Few minor figures in the heroic age are more touching than Teucer. Without powerful allies or happy hopes, he displays exemplary dignity. When Odysseus, in a late surge of decency, offers to help bury Aias's body, Teucer's refusal is courteous but unyielding. Agamemnon relents only in allowing Aias's body to be buried, in a wooden coffin, as befits a suicide and a civilian, rather than cremated like a warrior. Aias's lonely tomb was on Cape Rhoeteum, in the Troad. In the classical era, it was marked by a famous statue, catalogued by Strabo, impersonating Arete (manly virtue), with her hair cropped in ritual mourning. Arete could be shown to respect what arrogant Athene did not.

The loss of Sophocles' *Teukros*, his sequel to *Aias*, both robs Teucer of his place centre stage and denies us what is likely to have been an exception to the Aristotelian "rule" that tragedies should detail the *hamartia* (generally trans-lated as tragic flaw) which brings down their heroes. What did Teucer ever do "wrong"? When he returns to Salamis, the heaviest charge against him, advanced by the grief-maddened Telamon, is of having failed Aias by being absent when he might have restrained his brother. What rational or ritual cal-culus makes this a *hamartia*?

Telamon was as prone to crazed rage as his son: he had been convicted, in his youth, by his father Aeacus of the same crime with which he now charged Teucer. All the same, Telamon's grief is manifest in extant fragments of Sophocles' play: "...so, my son, it was vanity, / The pleasure when I heard your praises, / Imagined you alive. The Fury, in her darkness, / Made of my delight a dirty trick."

The Roman dramatist Pacuvius wrote an adaptation of Sophocles' *Teucer*. Cicero cites a fragment in his *De Oratore*, in which the innocent bastard son is abused by Telamon for daring to come home to Salamis "without *him*". Royal rage yields to bombastic self-pity as Telamon goes on, "*cum aetate exacta indigem / liberum lacerasti, orbasti, extinxti....*" Accused of having "savaged, bereaved and crushed" an old man already "drained by age", Teucer is then banished, for having failed to insist that Aias be given the arms of Achilles (a case which Teucer had negligible chances of pressing), and also for not having repatriated Aias's bones or his "widow" Tecmessa and their son, Eurysaces (for whom, in the *Aias*, Teucer shows honourable concern). The exiled scapegoat finally finds refuge in Cyprus, where he has the small consolation of founding a deutero-Salamis.

Teucer's literary reward was to become a byword for an unfairly abused son who never yields to bitterness. In Sophocles' lost play, he is said to have defended himself movingly and robustly when indicted for constructive fratricide by an Odysseus, who – reverting to his true, unreliable colours – loads onto Teucer the guilt more evident in himself.

However, the suggestion that a bastard might be complicit in the death of his true-born brother has an abiding plausibility: Edmund, in *King Lear*, embodies the sinister duplicity unfairly imputed to Teucer. "Now God stand up for bastards!" he cries. No deity of any consequence did so for Teucer. His redemption was left to Roman literature, which took an admiring view of his phlegmatic fatalism. Cicero cites – though he, like Ovid, scarcely lived up to – the exiled bastard's "*patria est ubicumque est bene*" (My fatherland is wherever things go well). Horace makes Teucer a spokesman of his own philosophy of *carpe diem*, when he has him say, on the eve of leaving Salamis for ever, "*Cras ingens iterabimus aequor*" (Tomorrow we'll venture again on the boundless sea). Even though, in the *Aeneid*, the original Teucer is not the Greek archer but a legendary king of Troy, there is nice irony in Virgil using "*Teucri*" as his term for the Trojans who, in their exile, take ship for Italy and found Rome.

In the *Aias* cycle, Sophocles appears to have broken a number of Aristotle's *ex post facto* "rules" for tragedy. Teucer's only manifest *hamartia* is illegitimacy. He gives no sign of the *hubris* that is often said to be punished by divine visitation. Kenneth McLeish, in his monograph on Aristotle's *Poetics*, pointed out that Christian moralists elaborated the notion of *hamartia* so that it seemed to prefigure un-Greek concepts both of sin and of possible redemption. *Hamartia*, McLeish insisted, means more "error" than moral delinquency: he compares it to a "dropped stitch" which – social no less than moral – damages stability and leads to disaster until repaired, by whatever terrible means.

Aias also breaks the alleged embargo on showing bloodshed on the stage. The traditional view has been that Greek audiences were too refined to enjoy theatrical gore. In fact, although "Golden Age" Greeks never favoured gladiatorial shows, their altars and festivals reeked of sacrificial – albeit, in historical times, rarely human – blood. Normally, Greeks killed only domestic, edible (and docile) animals on their altars. Treaties were more solemn when sealed with the blood of fully grown victims. Dogs were sometimes sacrificed to underworld gods and to Artemis in her role as midwife. The Macedonians

41 Klytemnestra can't look. Aeschylus describes Iphigeneia as gagged, "that she might not speak ill-omened words". Here, in Pompeii, she looks voluble.

marched to war between the severed halves of a dog. In 480, Xerxes' army set out between two halves of a slaughtered man, whose father, Pythius the Lydian, with four sons already serving with the Great King, asked that one be left to him. So he was. Fish supplied luxurious supplements to ancient diets, but were never sacrificed (though Pausanias says that they were "sacred to Hermes" – slippery customers both – at Pharae in Achaea).

The reluctance to depict bloodshed on the stage may owe something to a wish to keep sacrificial ritual and theatrical declamation – whether or not they had a common source – in piously distinct places. Ill-motivated sacrifices, in particular Agamemnon's of his daughter, had tragic consequences. Since human blood polluted where it fell, ancient audiences might well have been seriously horrified by the staging of what many could have taken for the real thing. Panic was caused when Aeschylus's gift for *opsis* (spectacle) led him to begin *Eumenides* – the third of the *Oresteia* trilogy – with the dog-faced Furies actually on stage, drooling with bloody thirst. Should we assume that Athenians distinguished easily between real and theatrical gore?

The Romans, who relished the theatre of real blood in the arena, were less disposed to squeamishness: Seneca's tragedies are wilfully close to Grand Guignol, from which the modern horror film derives: he gave the people what they continue to come for.

With a study-bound scholar's distaste for *opsis*, Aristotle read drama solely as text. Modern appreciation of classical literature has been stirred by recognition of the enlivening role of the performer: both in theatre and in verse, action and gesture have become part of the vocabulary of translation.

Although often depicted on vases, bloodshed did nearly always take place off-stage. It was then reported, usually by nameless, characterless messengers. Their protracted bulletins supplied nettlesome material for schoolboy unseens. The messenger could also be quizzed in elliptic stichomythia – enigmatic, ritual-based exchanges of single-line dialogue – of which A.E. Housman's "Fragment of a Greek tragedy" offers a parodic epitome:

> Alcmaeon: I journeyed hither a Boeotian road.
> Chorus: Sailing on horseback or with feet for oars?
> Alcmaeon: Plying by turns my partnership of legs.
> Chorus: Beneath a shining or a raining Zeus?
> Alcmaeon: Mud's sister, not himself, adorns my shoes.

The punctuation of sonorous garrulity by the ritualized staccato of stichomythia was surely a form of wit that provoked applause, if not laughter, in a tragic audience. Whatever the ritual sources of tragic *données*, displays of virtuosity in dialogue are unlikely to have owed much to any tradition but that of the stage and of poetic flyting in knockabout revels.

In the *Iliad*, Nestor – with his sententious counsel – is the regally verbose precursor of the tragic messenger: the rhapsodes' narrator is deconstructed, in Attic theatre, into an anonymous tale-bearer. His comic equivalent is the stand-up comedian to whom funny things happen on his way to the theatre.

* * *

*T*he *hubris* which tragic heroes are often said to display is not only, in the cant phrase, "overweening pride", but also the idiot violence which it generates. In daily life, violence was most regularly visited on slaves. If few Greeks had a conscience about the institution of slavery as such, more – Epicurus for outstanding instance – advocated the humane treatment of those in their power.

Karl Popper in *The Open Society and Its Enemies* insists that there was a strong movement in favour of "equalitarianism". He cites Hippias, as quoted by Plato: "...we are all kinsmen and friends and fellow-citizens, if not by conventional law, then by nature". In similar spirit, Euripides said, "Man's law of nature is equality". Gorgias's disciple, Alcidamas offered, "God has made no man a slave".

However, when Popper concludes that it is "one of the greatest triumphs of Athenian democracy that it treated slaves humanely and came very close to abolishing slavery", one wonders if the brutalized miners at Laurium ever got wind of this. In the first century B.C., Diodorus Siculus describes appalling cruelty in the mines of Spain and Egypt which led miners to prefer death. Since every Athenian hoplite took a slave body servant to war with him, it is unlikely that male citizens would ever have voted for liberation, which would have obliged them to carry their own kit.

It remains true that Euripides was accusingly alert to the anguish of *The Trojan Women*, who fell from high places into the power of alien enemies. If, like many writers, he drew part of his fame from the stylish insolence of his heterodoxy, he also wanted to win prizes, and did. As David Hare's and Tom Stoppard's plays illustrate, it is possible to strike daring attitudes without embarrassing one's chances of comfortable renown. Siding with the underdog cannot wholly have outraged the Athenian public, although Euripides is said, in his last years, to have absconded to Macedonia, "embittered by unpopularity". It is not unknown for theatrical personalities to regard mere fame as a slight.

Aristophanes probably exacerbated Euripides' grievances, though his parodic jeers, in *The Frogs*, are savagely flattering. He did also accuse the playwright's mother of selling vegetables. Tradition says that Euripides acquired an estate and vineyards on Salamis. A pot fragment incised "Euripides" was recently found there, in a cave which was perhaps his *noli me tangere* retreat. It is unlikely that his grapes were not culled by servile labour. If the civilized view was that slaves should never be punished in hot anger, they could expect rough treatment from kings and tyrants. However, even the Great King of Persia was embargoed, if only by custom, from putting a citizen to death for a first offence, though no one was likely to chide, let alone sanction, him for explosions of temper.

Politics was a war of words, but weapons were rarely drawn, or worn, inside the city. The same was true in republican Rome, despite the notorious exceptions of the Gracchi and the Catilinarian "revolution", during which Cicero put on armour to emphasize how seriously he took the situation, and himself. Greek heralds were traditionally "sacred", though the Spartans threw Persian "ambassadors" down a well after they had demanded to be given earth and water, as tokens of submission. Diplomacy is still conducted in neutralized environments. When Nikita Khrushchev hammered the desk with his shoe, in the UN General Assembly, he was showing that he was not bound by diplomatic niceties.

Whatever the rules, violence could always break out within a family or society. Perikles' associate, Ephialtes – no relation of the homonymous Phocaean who sold the pass at Thermopylae and may be the reason why *ephialtes* is modern Greek for "nightmare" – was murdered by political enemies in 461, but the Athenian constitution was not least a means of keeping anger within polite bounds. "Polite" derives, in fact, from the Latin *polire*, to polish, but *polites* was also Greek for a citizen.

No one was more aware of the thin crust of civility than Thucydides when he described the *stasis* on Corcyra in the 420s. Similar savagery recurred – to Aristotle's horror – at Argos in 370 and, two millennia later, both in the Greece liberated from the Turks (its first president, Capodistria, was soon assassinated) and in the civil war of the 1940s, of which Nicholas Gage's *Eleni* provides a bitter reminder.

* * *

Over the centuries, Greek cities adopted all manner of political systems, from kingship to tyranny, oligarchy to democracy, and back again; Plato supplies a ladder of how one form leads to another, in an order descending to democracy and mob rule. Improvisation and coercion (never incompatible) were more common than preconceived dogma. Athens and other democracies might maintain the unique virtue of their pliable constitution and its robust tolerances, but they had nothing approaching a formal two-party system. Indeed, around 508, Cleisthenes devised, in ostracism, an abrupt means of "beheading" political opposition without bloodshed. It was also a crowd-pleasing measure – the first use of the plebiscite – likely to win applause from the *demos*. Democracy sublimated, but never abolished, social divisions that might lead to disruption or to civil war.

Ostracism was a process available only once a year. It combined innovative (and entertaining) social engineering – by reducing the danger of *coups d'état* and *stasis* – with an antique recipe: the eviction of the scapegoat, in this case the people's choice. The process could be capricious, and sometimes unjust: fable says that Aristeides, a hero of Marathon, was ostracized only because people tired of hearing him called "The Just" (the evidence is one recorded vox pop.). In fact, there was more to be said against his conservative policies; and much was, by Themistokles, who had good reason to regard his rival as a dangerous reactionary who preferred horses to ships. The two were reconciled, after a fashion, in the lead-up to Salamis. Since all hands were needed on deck, Aristeides was recalled from exile. Six hundred years after the event, Plutarch was so biased against Themistokles (as he also was against Herodotus) that he inflated Aristeides' pedestrian part in the victory.

Ostracism was an inverted election: whoever got the most votes was the loser and had to leave Athens for ten years, although his property was secure in his absence and he seems to have incurred no abiding odium. The result could be dramatically, even comically, unexpected. That heroes such as Xanthippus (the father of Perikles), the great admiral Cimon and Themistokles himself were, at different times, voted the weakest link seems to advertise the institutional ingratitude of democracy.

In practice, however, ostracism was a device to make sure that new policies could be put into practice without obstruction. The capacity for swift reactions – which Perikles claimed to be typical of Athens – could require the quick dropping of one pilot and the urgent assumption of another: Aristeides' ostracism, in 482, cleared the decks for Themistokles' shipbuilding programme, which was justified two years later at Salamis.

After the battle, not even Plutarch could deny Themistokles his glory: Herodotus records that the great man was cheered by the assembled Hellenes for a full twenty-four hours when he did a walkabout at the subsequent Olympic Games. Yet nothing failed Themistokles like success. Aristeides' political comeback was due less to democratic indecision than to a changed military situation: after Salamis, ships were irrelevant to dealing with the large army, led by an excellent general in Mardonius, which was left behind in Greece by Xerxes after his defeat at sea in 480. The vindication of Themistokles' maritime policy had the effect of making him redundant after Salamis, especially when he refused to carry the war to Persia itself. In similar fashion, the same people who cheered Winston Churchill in May 1945 voted his party out of office later in the same year. For Themistokles, however, disgrace followed eclipse. In 471, he was himself ostracized. He went to live in

Argos, Sparta's sullen Peloponnesian enemy. Unlike Aristeides, he never returned to Athens. In 468, he was condemned to death *in absentia*, by his countrymen, on a charge of "Medising". The Spartans always feared his influence and probably took their chance to supply, or fabricate, incriminating evidence, as Odysseus had against Palamedes.

Themistokles responded to the perhaps false accusation by making it true: he went into service with the new King of Kings, Artaxerxes, who had been his admiring enemy during Xerxes' invasion of Greece and whose loyal satrap he became for the remaining nine years of his life. In a bizarre peripeteia, both Themistokles, the victor of Salamis, and Pausanias, the Spartan king who destroyed the Persians at Plataea, found asylum with the enemy whom they had, between them, forever evicted from Hellas. It was, however, true that Pausanias's family had guest-friendships in Asia.

When Themistokles died, in 459, rumour said that shame had driven him to suicide. Whether or not he had a bad conscience, the Athenians did: his body was repatriated and buried near the walls of the Piraeus, whose construction owed much to him. The gesture was more than a posthumous apology: the bones of heroes were potent fetishes. Who would want Themistokles' body to lie in Persian soil, lending psychic force to the Mede?

Themistokles had *metis* to match Odysseus's. Duplicity is perhaps vital to a democratic politician: if he has a long-term policy, he can realize it only by remaining popular at election times, which came at least once a year in classical Athens. After Marathon, in 490, the young Themistokles feared, rightly, that the Persians would come back, in force. He was convinced that it was urgently important to increase Athenian naval power, but in public he had the wit not to be unduly – or even duly – alarmist. Knowing that voters would prefer the prospect of short-term profit to having their minds concentrated – perhaps paralysed – by fear of the Great King, Themistokles found a providential target in Aegina, an offshore island which had the temerity, and firepower, to resist Athenian hegemony, even in the Saronic gulf. It was easier to argue for constructing ships to tackle a manageable local difficulty than to persuade the *demos* to arm the city against a distant, but much greater, menace.* Themistokles achieved the latter while advocating only the former. The fleet he had been authorized to raise to subdue the Aeginetans was maintained to

---

*The routine problem of democratic politicians remains that of how to further unglamorous long-term objectives while seeming to offer immediate vote-getting gratification. The cant of the Welfare State enables modern English politicians to raise taxes in the undeniable name of Health and Education, whose demands it is heretical to challenge. In fact, all taxation goes into the so-called General Fund, which allows governments discretion to allocate it wherever they choose.

fight on the crucial day of Salamis. The Aeginetans then went into battle alongside the Athenians and claimed to have been the first to engage the Persians. Herodotus tells of an Aeginetan captain, Polycritus, racing Themistokles' trireme and yelling over to him, "Who said Aegina was pro-Persian?" Clearly, Themistokles had used that charge as a way of winning votes for his rearmament policy.

His greatest political *coup* had taken place back in 483, when the wretched slaves in the state mines at Laurium hit an astonishingly rich seam of silver. Aristeides proposed that the bumper profits be divided among the citizens. It would be as if every one of them had as good as won the lottery. Themistokles urged that the unexpected bonus be spent on the "wooden wall" which the Delphic oracle, gnomic as always, had declared to be Athens' best defence.

How did he find the eloquence to make, and win, his case? The critical question was, what exactly did the Pythian priestess mean? It is a reminder of the communal reverence for the oracle that ancient political issues were rarely *only* political. At this stage in Athenian history – whatever the cynicism which prevailed later – doing the right thing was also a matter of obeying the gods who had clearly favoured the Athenians at Marathon.

Aristeides and his conservative friends insisted that, since the Acropolis, when first fortified, had had wooden palisades, Delphi was saying that they should be restored. The gods – themselves first represented by wooden images – would reward such pious hopes; the Persian cloud would disperse and the Athenian voters could enjoy the silver lining.

Who would have backed any politician to persuade the Athenians, or any other electorate, to renounce a private fortune for the public good? A modern

43 On the Erectheum on the Acropolis, Athenians, toffs and *thetes*, all pull together.

44 Per Ardua ad Astra.

Chancellor might contrive not to have to give them the choice, but Athens had no "government" as such. The decision was put directly to the people. Themistokles' rare eloquence convinced the *demos* to donate its windfall to the common purse. His vast shipbuilding programme was undertaken like a communal liturgy. Putting public safety before private wealth, the Athenians proved that they were not selfish "idiots" (the Platonic corporate state was not entirely alien to them).

Piraeus was fortified; Athens' fleet was ready in time to meet and destroy the Persians, just as the Spitfire was, just, to win the Battle of Britain in 1940 (the Spitfire, however, was built more in spite of public opinion than with the electorate's self-denying endorsement). Who can doubt that, during the 480s and 470s, Themistokles was anything but wholehearted in opposition to the Mede? With the unfairness of Greek politicians down the ages, his detractors maintained that he was always disposed to duplicity. They instance the trick he worked on Xerxes in the tense hours before Salamis: anxious lest the Persians fail to attack the allied fleet while it was still cohesive, he sent a trusted slave – his children's tutor, Sicinnus – to pose as a renegade from the Greek camp. Herodotus says that Sicinnus delivered a personal message from his master to Xerxes, warning the Great King not to let the Greeks escape.

The intention was to incite Xerxes to advance his cumbrous ships into the narrow waters where the superior seamanship, and heavier ships, of the Hellenes would count for more than Persian numbers. To lend plausibility to Themistokles' message, as Sicinnus was delivering it, it so happened that

Xerxes caught sight of a detachment of Corinthian ships quitting their stations and heading for home.

In their desire for all the credit, the Athenians later made out that the dodgy Corinthians turned back and joined in the battle only when the Greeks were already winning. However, in his *Greco-Persian Wars*, Peter Green makes a forceful case for the Corinthian "flight" to have been a preconceived feint: it allowed the returning ships to take the Persians in the flank.

Since the Greek gift of sending Sicinnus with a deceptive message had proved so successful, Themistokles' *metis* was widely enjoyed. Only when his stock had fallen did his enemies insinuate that he had played a double game whereby, if the Persians lost, he would be a hero to the Greeks, but if Xerxes were victorious, he would be well placed to make a separate peace and claim his reward. Whom should we believe? It is true that Themistokles was imbued with the Achillean urge to dominate, and to sulk if balked. He was certainly little inclined to abide by the judgment of the Athenian jury, in the Socratic style, when condemned to death; but this does little to prove that he had from the first intended to keep in with the Great King, for whose defeat he argued, and fought, so furiously.

* * *

The practice of ostracism fell into abeyance after 417, when Hyperbolus, a much less significant political fixer (despised by Thucydides) was exiled as the result of a stitch-up contrived by the two intended alternatives for the drop, the usually irreconcilable Alcibiades and Nikias. Their cynically, and briefly, united clout contrived that their supporters made a mockery of a vote which had been called to give one or the other a clear field in dealing with Sicily, and Syracuse in particular: Alcibiades favoured the big stick, Nikias the carrot of bribery. Hyperbolus, whose name itself suggests an exaggerated reputation, has probably been maligned by history. He was not merely the fall guy squeezed between two more charismatic figures. He had commanded a trireme and was a skilled speaker with serious political pretensions. Glamour and wealth enabled Alcibiades to seduce part of Hyperbolus's constituency, just as Nikias's solid military reputation kept the careful voters on his side. Hyperbolus's bellicose populism alarmed Aristophanes, whose derision has helped to confirm him as a butt. Having gone into exile on Samos, his bad luck continued: he was murdered by oligarchs in 411.

The supposed joke of framing Hyperbolus was a good one, but it could not be cracked again. The voters had drawn their own attention to the clumsiness, and now the frivolity, of ostracism. René Girard might see the "sacrifice" of a stooge as a travesty of the crucifixion: by his innocence, no less than his insignificance, the victimized Hyperbolus drew attention to the emptiness of the process. Much worse, by their brief complicity, Nikias (who opposed the Sicilian expedition) and Alcibiades (who championed it) contrived to be left in joint, but never united, command.

Without there being any clear relation between them, the practice of ostracism and the great period of Attic theatre almost coincided. The catastrophic defeat of Athens at the end of the fifth century put paid to the purgative dignity of both tragedy and ostracism. Life got too real, and political issues too fraught, for local solutions. Did Athenian democracy fail because of its politicians' ineptitude? The city-state lacked microphones and the communications machinery that might have allowed it, rather than autocracy, to mobilize larger units. To honour majority government, voters had to meet in one place and be able to hear the orators. The massed subjects of the Great King or of Alexander the Great met only to hear their orders.

Athenians victorious in the annual elections obtained the offices for which they had been candidates (including that of General), but they did not form cohesive "governments". The nearest translation of what we mean by a political party is "*hoi peri* (those around) X". In the same style, the French still cluster "*autour de*" some great man. The Athenian constitution gave office-holders – especially the elected strategoi (generals) – powers and duties; but it provided for nothing at all like a permanent civil service. The treasury might be filled or become empty, but there was no ongoing concern for "the economy". When Xenophon wrote his treatise *Oikonomikos* (literally, house-regulation), it was – as suited a country gentleman – about estate management.

When Athens was flush, Perikles commissioned the Parthenon; when she was short of cash, he and his successors dunned the subject allies, taxed trade or relied on *leitourgiai*. "Liturgies" were more or less spontaneous gifts from public-spirited *pentekosiomedimnoi*: five-hundred-bushel men whose land had the fattest yield. They were expected to make conspicuous contributions to the public good, especially ships. As State Treasurers, they had the right, and perhaps the pleasure, of challenging each other for generous donations. The tradition of volunteering ships continued in modern times. Shipowners from Syros and Chios honoured it in the war against the Turks in the 1820s. Warships were still being donated to the Greek navy by individual millionaires until very recently. In the ancient process known as *antidosis*, a rich man unwilling to perform a so-called "liturgy" could propose the exchange of his fortune for that of a man he claimed to be even richer.

45 The Parthenon, where the Athenians' treasure was.

This kind of challenging playfulness extended, on one famous occasion, even to warfare. In 425, the civilian Cleon attacked the competence of the generals – including the historian Thucydides and the experienced Nikias – with such ferocious rhetoric that the latter resigned. The *demos* then appointed Cleon to use his loud mouth in command of Athenian forces on Sphacteria, where a crack Spartan force had been isolated, but not yet forced to surrender. Against even popular expectation, Cleon succeeded where the military men had failed. As if in some Aristophanic peripeteia, his triumph went to its author's head, which – to Thucydides' delight – he lost in a later campaign against Brasidas.

In crucial matters concerning peace and war, the whole citizen body was called upon to vote. Decisiveness was sometimes lamed by compromise: in 415, in order to reconcile contentious opinions, three ill-assorted generals were appointed for the Sicilian expedition, presided over by the same Nikias who had opposed the enterprise and was also in doubtful health. Like Louis-Napoleon at the battle of Sedan, Nikias suffered from kidney stones. Whereas the French defeat was the direct result of Napoleon III's foolhardy adventurism, Nikias was innocent of anything but an excess of superstitious caution and the wish for a compromise peace. If he lacked genius, he had had long, locally successful, military experience.

Plato's contempt for a republic in which *peitho* – the goddess of persuasion (and hence of rhetoric) – had so much power was strengthened by the irresponsible influence of wild words on Athenian history. Inconsistency is a common charge against open societies. On the other hand, Plato's own professorial expedition to Sicily in 387 was no advertisement for preconceptions.*

The Athenian assembly was guilty of many misjudgments, not least the venial, but ultimately fatal, mistake of reinforcing failure in Sicily. In truth, the Assembly was answering what appeared to be an urgent appeal from Nikias, the commander in the field. It has been argued that Nikias asked for more than he thought he could possibly be granted, in the hope that the Athenians at home would baulk at the expense and summon the entire expedition to return. On this argument, the last thing he wanted was the loyal support he received and which he eventually squandered. Even so, the fresh troops very nearly succeeded in the night attack on Epipolae, which failed only through want of adequate rehearsal and resolute leadership. Hindsight has now made fools of the *demos*, but readers of Thucydides know that the decisive battle in

---

* Leszek Kolakowski, the Polish ex-Marxist philosopher, wrote a book *In Praise of Inconsistency*. Having lived under the inflexible caprices of ideology, Kolakowski insists on the merits of mutability as against the rigidity of a pseudo-logical "line". Mankind's "crooked timber" cannot long be ruled by Party lines.

the Great Harbour of Syracuse was a cruelly close-run thing. Who rereads it and does not hope that this time the Athenians will break the Syracusan chain and the siege have a happy outcome (even though the Athenians were manifest imperialist aggressors)?

* * *

On other occasions, the *demos* deserved credit for wise second thoughts: for example, when it reversed its own harshness after the suppression of the Mytilenean rebellion of 427. With Perikles recently dead, the demagogic Cleon was approaching the height of his loud influence. He proposed that the whole population of Mytilene be put to death, even those who had had no part in the rebellion. After he won the first vote, a trireme was despatched with a grim warrant to that effect.

The *demos* slept badly that night. The following day, Thucydides says, "there was a sudden change of feeling...people thought how cruel it was not only to destroy the guilty, but the entire population". Since what we would call "the polls" (our cyber-polis) indicated a change of heart, a new debate was called for. As he reports them, Cleon's speech and Diodotus's reply exemplify Thucydides' dramatizing genius. He renders brutally plausible the view of a demagogue for whom, elsewhere, he cannot conceal his contempt. Cleaving to ruthlessness, Cleon dismantles the conceit which encourages the Athenians to believe that they are "widely loved and admired by those whom they have subjugated".

In blunt rehearsal of the hypocrisy implicit in democratic imperialism,* Cleon tells his audience,

> What you fail to see is that your empire is a tyranny lording it over subjects who don't like it and who are always plotting against you. You will not make them obedient by damaging your own interests in order to please them. Leadership depends on superior strength, not your subjects' goodwill. The worst thing you can do is to decree measures and then not stand by them. We should accept that a city is better off with bad laws, provided they remain immutable, than with good laws that are always being tampered with. Lack of learning, backed by firm common sense, is more fruitful than clever ideas that spin out of control.... States are better run by ordinary people than by intellectuals.

---

* Christianity supplied a long excuse for righteous massacres of the heathen, or of those with improper versions of Christ's message or substance. The Gospel of Democracy now promises peace on earth, impersonally policed by market forces and the institutional wisdom of the United Nations, the European Union, and so on.

(This and other passages from Thucydides are based on, though not wholly faithful to, Rex Warner's elegant, dated translation.)

How "authentic" are the speeches which the historian puts in the mouths of various of his contemporaries? He himself claims only to encapsulate the general drift and tone of their arguments. Although exhortations to the troops (on both sides) may have been less elegantly composed than he reports, ancient orators, certainly in the later fifth century, had to prepare performances of a high quality in order to dominate an audience. The speech that Perikles delivered over the Athenian dead took place early in the war, but it is difficult, after the event, and the result, not to see it as an epitaph on the democracy itself (and on the Olympian's own leadership of it). If Thucydides died before Athens was utterly crushed, he lived long enough to see that his city was defeated. Perikles is allowed by Thucydides to take the moral high ground and to vaunt Athens as an incomparable paragon of all that is best in Hellas. In doing so, the speaker – in Nicole Loraux's phrase – "invents Athens": a posteriori, he makes a case for a supremacy which is its own apology: the Athenians deserve to succeed because they are so successful. In saying so, Perikles pats his audience on the head and himself on the back.

Thucydides' report is probably close to the truth here: Perikles' speech may well have been put about in written form. Thucydidean irony is implicit only in the direct cut from Perikles' fine words to the unforeseen plague which did so much to wreck his policy: *logo men*, Athens was invincible, *ergo de...*

Cleon's rough candour, in the Mytilenean debate, exposes the unlovely aspect of a city that had basked in the envious admiration of all Hellenes. With Perikles no longer at its head, Cleon's view of Athens is ingloriously crude. Perikles had died, in 429, probably of the plague which rumour accused him, as a miasma-carrying semi-Alcmaeonid, of bringing on the city. The contagion is more likely to have resulted from the Olympian's dubious policy of abandoning the countryside and concentrating everyone inside the city walls, where insanitary conditions (due not least to lack of Roman-style drainage) soon prevailed.

46 Perikles, Olympian warrior, with his lid up.

Perikles has often been praised for his foresight, as opposed to the short-termism of so many democratic politicians. Having assumed war with Sparta to be inevitable, he did a good deal to hasten it. He took, and was able to impose, the view that it would be folly to march out and confront the Spartans in a land battle. The Athenians' command of the sea rendered them, in his view, invincible in the long run. Meanwhile, he withdrew from the Attic countryside, which was left for the Spartans to ravage during their annual incursions. The intelligence of Perikles' policy led him to ignore its psychological consequences. Not only did Athenian farmers have to watch, impotently, as their lands were pillaged, houses burned and olive trees (notoriously slow to grow) cut to the ground; the Athenian infantry was also demoralized by their general's assumption that his men stood no chance against Spartans. Later events showed that Perikles' pessimism on those grounds was not entirely warranted.

Deconstructing the noble gloss of Perikles' Funeral Oration, Cleon does not advertise an envied centre of art, enterprise and culture, but bangs home his unblinking policy of self-interest. Cleon stood to Perikles as Mrs Thatcher to "Winston", as she always called him. Periklean Athens was a function of success, especially in the Persian wars, which crowned the city's fame and warranted her leadership of free communities united against the resurgence of Persian power. Some of these cities were freer than others, and none so free as Athens, which collected (and assessed) the tribute that the majority had to pay in lieu of ships and men: Chios and Samos at first supplied the latter, but lost their exemption for misbehaving. Athenian hegemony was based on the security she promised. Until the collapse of the Soviet empire, the Americans were similarly respected by those who were protected by their nuclear might. By the time of Cleon's speech in 427, few of Athens' allies retained any illusions about her altruism. Sparta, not Persia, was now the preoccupation of Athens and they had been forced to go along with her: St George, as it were, had become a dragon.

The quotient of sincerity, or truth, in Perikles' and Cleon's speeches is not very different, but times have changed. Cleon's Athens has the same problem with morals as Eliza Doolittle's father: she can't afford them. Hence he warns his audience, "...if you are going to give the same punishment to those forced to revolt by enemy coercion and to those who do so of their own accord...everyone will revolt at the slightest opportunity, if success means freedom and failure has no calamitous consequences." If an imperial power admits rebellion to be understandable, it concedes that it was wrong to hold power in the first place. "The only alternative is to surrender power, so that you can indulge in philanthropy."

Modern British political rhetoric has echoes of Thucydides/Cleon's remarks. Where the British once idealized the exportation of their "justice" (a nice name for imperial clout), they have now fallen back on the narcissism of claiming that their National Health Service is The Envy of the World. In all eyes but his own, Narcissus may well have been, as Michel Pic has suggested, *"un garçon sans qualités aimables sauf dans sa propre vision"*.

Thucydides' unsentimental reading of man as a political animal inclines some Hellenists to prefer Herodotus, who, even at a time of Hellenic triumph and optimism, cast an amiable eye on barbarian and Greek alike. Others find it hard to see in his good-natured, ragbag narrative any coherent assessment of human prospects. Herodotus writes in the unshadowed high noon of Hellenic self-confidence; Thucydides in the twilight of Athens. Herodotus has the expansiveness of his own curiosity; Thucydides draws gloomy conclusions. When the latter praises Themistokles' exceptional genius for intelligent pre-science, one suspects that the historian is composing his own apologia.

Herodotus has a generosity of interest (and credulity) which Thucydides, an Athenian watching Athens in the toils of a terrible war, cannot match: like a doctor with a stricken patient, the latter seeks to draw scientific conclusions from a case that is breaking his heart. In Cleon's speech, Thucydides allows the contradictions of empire to be brought out by his personal enemy, a populist who recognizes that his decisive constituency is his home audience. Statesmen may imagine that their standing is confirmed by world opinion, but what election was ever won by offering a new deal, or the taxpayers' treasure, to foreigners? Nixon, Gorbachev and George Bush Sr. hoped to convert their acclaim by aliens into a hedge against dwindling support at home. All were disappointed.

Today's European Union has not resolved the contradictions of a system where nationally elected politicians seek to regulate a transnational organization whose executive includes no elected officials. National leaders who fail to satisfy the home electorate that they have prevailed in community negotiations risk eviction from domestic office. Idealists seek to argue, from the existence of a World Court, and of the United Nations, that supranational legislatures could create a worldwide "parliament" in which universal laws could be passed by incontrovertible "democratic" vote. In practice, it is impossible to imagine (but not to conceive) such a system compelling a major power to honour its decision. Aesop's fable of the lion and the donkey cannot be voted into irrelevance.

In the case of the Delian League, Athens grew increasingly brusque with whoever interfered with her interests. Glad to export democracy to weaken her enemies, she was unwilling to yield to a majority of its allies. Athenian *thetes*, while they were lowly voters at home, paraded as strutting imperialists abroad. Karl Marx would lament that the British proletariat was lost to The Revolution for a similar reason: miserable toilers in those dark, satanic mills, they could pride themselves on being lords and masters of the empire. Cleon's words might have made bad propaganda for Athens if broadcast through Hellas. As it was, his words carried only as far as his voice. Such chauvinism had its last shout (perhaps) in Adolf Hitler, who appealed to no audience but Germans.

Cleon's opponent in the debate over the fate of Mytilene was a more reasonable figure. Diodotus was probably primed by the Mytilenean delegation, not a few of whom – while immune as long as the debate proceeded – faced execution if Cleon's Draconian motion were to be confirmed. Diodotus spoke in the tones of classic liberalism. As *peitho* might advise, his remarks were not without appeal to Athenian self-interest. For the purposes of advocacy, justice was relativized to conform to *raison d'état*. A generation later, Plato would argue that justice had no meaning outside a well-run state: an *état de raison* must "nationalize" justice. In a logical (totalitarian) society, justice is what serves the interests of the state. Democracy involves, and embraces, compromise; in logic, there can be no compromise.

Diodotus maintained only that the guilt of the islanders, even if heinous, did not entail that they should die, unless it was to the advantage of his audience. He recommends measured retribution not on the merits of the Mytileneans but for the good of Athens. Later, and consistently, he points out,

> If Cleon's method is adopted, every city will make much more thorough preparations for revolt, and will hold out to the very end, since whether it surrenders early or late, the consequences will be the same....
>
> As things are, in all the cities the democratic element is friendly to you...but if you kill the democratic party on Mytilene, which never took part in the revolt and who, as soon as they got arms, voluntarily surrendered the city to you, you will be guilty of executing those who rallied to you and you'll be doing precisely what would best suit the reactionaries.

The next day, the assembly voted, narrowly, to reverse itself. A second trireme was sent to countermand the first. The crew rowed so urgently with the good – or at least better – news that it managed a dead heat with the earlier one. The reprieve was delivered just in time.* The leaders of the revolt were, nevertheless, put to death, as were the thousand or so ringleaders who had already been arrested and taken to Athens. The fortifications of Mytilene were destroyed and most of the island, apart from loyal Methymmna, distributed to

---

* Some two decades ago, when he was editor of the *New Statesman*, Bruce Page proposed that, despite all the savage evidence to the contrary, there was a small bias in history in favour of the good guys, if only because men will strive harder to do what is humane than what is not. He gave the urgency of the second crew on the way to Mytilene as a key, and sweet, example.

Athenian cleruchs (imported settlers who retained full voting and property rights in Attica). Some may have been previously licensed absentee landlords who threatened trouble if magnanimity deprived them of their prospect of easy pickings.* The Athenians also helped themselves to the mainland towns (in Anatolia), previously under Mytilene's control. Since Mytileneans now became Athenian subjects, Cleon did not wholly lose his case: any future rebellion would, by definition, be treason.

* * *

*D*id Athenians, one wonders, ever make a slip of the tongue which elided Cleon with Kreon, the luckless king of Thebes who, in Sophocles' *Antigone*, often expresses Cleontic opinions? Thucydides' hatred of Cleon, albeit a compatriot, is as unconcealed as his admiration for Brasidas, the Spartan general whose genius contributed to the historian's own disgrace as an Athenian general during the campaign of 424 and 423 in the Thracian Chalcidice. Thucydides' account of his own performance is tersely third-personal:

> ...Thucydides with his (few) ships sailed into Eion just after Brasidas had captured Amphipolis.... If the ships had not arrived so quickly to relieve it, Eion (the port of Amphipolis) would have fallen to him by dawn.
> After this, Thucydides organized the defence of Eion to keep it from immediate attack by Brasidas...[who] suddenly sailed down the river (Strymon) to Eion in the hope of seizing the headland...and so commanding access. This attack was supported by land forces, but both were beaten off....

Thucydides' unselfish dryness does not conceal a conviction that he did as well, with his limited forces, as could be expected of him. The question remains why he was not on watch when Brasidas arrived. In any event, he never received another command. Disgrace left him free to be the historian of Athens' slowly descending fortunes for the remaining twenty years of his exiled life. When he credits Brasidas – who was himself to die in 422, while still campaigning in Thrace – with exceptional qualities, not least speedy improvisation and some eloquence (he was, Thucydides says, not a bad

---

* In today's Northern Ireland, the Ulster Unionists are the descendants of Protestant cleruchs whose militant loyalty to the mother country (and their own ascendancy) warrants opposition to all attempts at generosity to, or disengagement from, the indigenous islanders, whose resentment is equally implacable.

speaker, for a Spartan), the historian can be forgiven for implying that his own performance was unduly criticized when he had been worsted by a general of genius.

Brasidas was clearly a remarkable man. Advertising the justice of the Spartan cause as the liberation of Hellas from Athenian oppression, he depicted Sparta's reluctance to embark on maritime adventures as a form of self-denial (the Melians – abandoned in their hour of need – could be excused for taking a different view), never of fear of Athenian naval supremacy. In fact, Brasidas had first made his name as a trireme commander. However calculated his affectations of disinterestedness, he told provincial audiences what they wanted to hear and was received as a deliverer, or potential protector, in many cities which had once favoured, or had been intimidated by, the Athenians.

Seemingly without the prejudices or fears of the Spartan old guard, he won the confidence of local levies with inspiring leadership and was sincere enough, in talking of liberation, to favour the freeing of helots to serve in the army. Seven hundred "*Brasideioi*" (helots who had been on active service) were indeed freed. However, when a large party of such *neodamodeis* (emancipated veterans) returned to Sparta, they proved to be an alarmingly insolent pres-ence. On an occasion in 424, when Sparta announced its wish to free the bravest helot auxiliaries, two thousand who presented themselves were taken away and killed. The highly conservative Secret Police considered slaves with a good opinion of themselves as a danger to society.

There was mordant irony in the fact that a man who, in Thucydides' view, was the best of the Spartans should have died, of wounds, after a campaign against an army commanded by the man whom he considered the worst of Athenians. Cleon's force had, however, already been routed and its general killed (to the straight-faced glee of the cashiered Thucydides).

As a career officer, Brasidas combined patriotism with personal integrity. Unlike other Spartan commanders – from the regent Pausanias (who died in 470) to Lysander, killed in battle in 395, when possibly on the verge of mount-ing some kind of *coup* – Brasidas was not corrupted by success nor lured by opportunities for personal enrichment. However, he might not have disagreed with Lysander's reformist ambition to make the Spartan kingship elective. As Donald Kagan emphasizes, Lysander was of the *déclassé* fraternity known as *mothakes*, some of whom were the bastards of full Spartan citizens and Helot mothers, while others came from Spartiate families who had fallen on hard times and could not, as it were, afford their officers' mess bills. Gylippus – who did so much to engineer the Syracusan victory over Athens – was another such, though he lacked the genius which made Lysander's radical ideas so alarming to conservative Spartans.

Brasidas had no chip on his shoulder, but he was capable of intellectual no less than of military initiative. As his enemy, the Spartan general charmed Thucydides as few Athenians did: although Alcibiades was not to be denied aristocratic glamour, he was only every other inch a gentleman. Yet Brasidas was as ruthless as any Cleon when it came to bullying Acanthus. The latter was a colony of Andros with a docile tradition: an earlier generation of Acanthians had been equally pliant when wooed by Xerxes on his way to Salamis, and put on Persian trousers to prove it (a sign of wealth among Persians was to have several pairs).

Thucydides' admiration for Brasidas resembled that of General Montgomery for the German Field-Marshal Erwin Rommel in 1942. In contrast with Thucydides' respect for Brasidas, "Monty" praised "The Desert Fox" because his own Eighth Army had defeated his rival's Afrika Korps. Unlike Xenophon, who lived to see Athens defeated, Thucydides was never an admirer of Sparta: he was, no doubt, as shocked by Alcibiades' self-interested defection, in 415, as he was dismayed by the increasing recklessness of Athenian policy. His loyalty was not to conservatism, but to the evanescent Athens depicted in Perikles' Funeral Oration. Thomas Hobbes, the author of *Leviathan*, was the first translator of Thucydides directly from Greek into English (in the seventeenth century). His idealization of the sovereign ruler, to whose command his subjects defer in their own interest, may well owe something to the idealized vision of Perikles which is projected by an uncritical reading of his part in the Golden Age of Athenian hegemony, when, as is so often quoted, his city was in theory a democracy but, in fact, was ruled by one man. Recent revisionists take a less gilded view of him, as did his fellow-citizens when they grew disillusioned by his strategy.

As the plague took its toll, Perikles was no longer the flawless Olympian. Life in the city resembled the bestial chaos which Hobbes considered typical of a state without a universally accepted leader. Thucydides' account of the pitiless civil war in Corcyra (traditionally known as *stasis*) must also have impressed Hobbes, for whom the English Civil War was a haunting actuality, with the result that, for him, order took precedence over supposed "rights". The *philosophe* Joseph Joubert remarked shrewdly, in 1793, and hence in the light of the French Revolution, that civil wars are more murderous than any others because it is more tolerable to have one's enemy a contemporary than to have him as a neighbour: *"c'est qu'on ne veut pas risquer de garder la vengeance si près de soi"*.

It is slightly surprising that Hobbes's belief in benevolent autocracy was unaffected by Perikles' fall from seeming infallibility. He had led Athens into a war he claimed that it would certainly win, in the long run, only to see the citizens decimated by disease at its very outset. When the Olympian proved as mortal as the next man, by dying of the plague, his memory had been soured among those who had depended on him.

As the fate of Miltiades had shown after Marathon, one day's hero could be the next day's pariah. In 490 Miltiades was the man of the year, but his fame hardly survived it. Having embarked on a greedy and ill-starred voyage of conquest against Paros, he was wounded in the unsuccessful assault, and, while dying of gangrene, was accused of embezzlement (by Xanthippus, the father of Perikles), convicted and fined fifty talents. Miltiades' supposed helmet (in the Olympia museum) is a businesslike bronze affair. By contrast, a bust of Perikles portrays him with his visor up, giving it the appearance of a cocked hat.

* * *

Nearly all political, and aesthetic, theories about the Greeks have been a posteriori. The fifth century was marked by Athenian military and commercial ascendancy, and by its celebration in art and architecture. How many citizens spent time in abstract questioning of policies which were tailored to their advantage? Until power was lost, philosophy was a subject more for derision than for respect: when he wrote *Clouds*, Aristophanes hoped to win prizes and applause by his mockery of Socrates. Plato probably took the dramatist too seriously in blaming him for the philosopher's unpopularity: Socrates' condemnation took place a quarter of a century after *Clouds* had failed to enchant the public. Aristophanes was the ancient counterpart of a journalist such as the *Daily Telegraph*'s Peter Simple: a reactionary satirist, smarter and more outrageous than the common man, but reflecting, and pandering to, his prejudices. How else would he have got the laughs and the applause for which he touted? Like Euripides, Aristophanes presaged the modern proverb which says that "movies are not written, they are rewritten", by going back and reworking texts which did not win the prizes he craved.

The trial of Socrates, in 399, was often regarded as a pagan rehearsal for that of Jesus (without the mumbo-jumbo, as one classicist put it, quietly). Both involved the tragic conviction of a righteous man, which brought disgrace on those who conspired to condemn him. Pontius Pilate became the emblem of Roman indifference and "the Jews",* holus-bolus, were forever stained by

---

* Berel Lang's essay, "On the 'the' in 'the Jews'", in *Those who Forget the Past*, is a dry analysis of the almost imperceptible verbal slippage which leads to the sustained stigmatization of all Jews.

47 Socrates having the last word in David's version of Plato's *Phaedo*.

their allegedly unanimous hostility to Jesus, a Jewish preacher whose popularity among the common people (almost all of them Jews) was said to threaten established authority, Roman and Jewish alike. At His very brief trial, Jesus offered no defence other than His innocence. He made no speech and there was no jury; He was sentenced to a scapegoat's death by a weary provincial governor who, no doubt, wished that he had never been posted to Jerusalem. Anatole France's *The Procurator of Judaea* depicts Pilate, in retirement, being asked about an obscure troublemaker called Jesus. The old man has difficulty in recalling Him.

The case of Socrates was different. He did not deny the authority of the court, nor was he deprived of a fair hearing. Plato's account, in *The Apology*, depicts Meletus and Anytus, Socrates' accusers, as unsubtle political zealots, but their case was not empty: Socrates *had*, for a time, been friendly with Plato's clever uncle, Critias, the disgraced leader of the oligarchic faction, known as the Thirty Tyrants, which brought a Spartan-sponsored reign of terror to defeated Athens in 404. During that time, however, Socrates had refused to implement a dictatorial order to arrest an innocent citizen.

Earlier, in 406, when president of the assembly after the victory of Arginusae, which was marred by the admirals' failure to pick up drowning crewmen, he alone voted against the illegal decision of the *demos* to try (in effect, to lynch) all the commanders at once. In short, he honoured the dictum of a twentieth-century French Socrates, Alain: "*Résistance et obéissance, voilà les deux vertus du citoyen. Par l'obéissance, il assure l'ordre; par la résistance, il assure la liberté.*"

Having also done his duty as a soldier, notably at the siege of Potidaea, Socrates was not contrite, self-important or even very serious in his own defence. However, he certainly did not concede the justice of the charge of introducing "new gods". If his *daimonion* (personal conscience) seemed like an unlicensed guardian angel, both Pythagoreans and Orphics believed in such things. Routine Greek for pushing your luck was "putting your *daimon* to the test". As for corrupting the young, the accusation referred less to sexual misconduct (though it did suggest it) than to the inculcation of a cult of self-regard. The late Alcibiades – still as notorious as he was once handsome – was the precocious instance, though he had needed little instruction.

Would Socrates ever have been sentenced to death had he not exasperated a jury by no means predisposed to treat him harshly? It was not uncommon in Athenian courts for convicted men to be invited to suggest a mitigated sentence. Contrition helped: courts still attach significance to "remorse". Had Socrates shown it, if only out of politeness, he might have been applauded. Instead, invited to propose an alternative to the prosecutors' demand for the death penalty, he suggested that he be pensioned with free meals for life, quite as if he were an Olympic victor who had brought fresh laurels to the city. His flippancy was that of a *performer*, not of a chastened defendant: treating the court like a theatre, he put on the wrong show. He may have expected to have the jurors (the *demos* in judicial guise) grant him the last laugh, but – insulted by his refusal to take things seriously – they condemned him to die by a larger majority than had found him guilty.

The theatre had been institutionalized as a public spectacle in Athens by Peisistratus, who dignified his tyranny with civic festivals. Whatever its source, in rustic dances, the dithyramb or religious ritual, it soon became a central aspect of Athenian culture. The great tragedians transcended the limits of what Peisistratus or the originators of the form had in mind. Using the theatre for a range of purposes its pioneers can never have envisaged, mature tragedy put the audience to the question, about morals, the gods and the city. The very architecture of the ancient theatre was a social innovation: in what earlier civilization, however noble its public buildings, could a whole (male) population sit in full sight of each other, in one place, applauding, laughing or weeping at an instructive, essentially *critical* performance?

Pandora's box never had such disconcerting contents. In looking at the play, the citizens were incited to look at themselves. The examined life, so ardently advocated by Socrates, was a feature of the city long before he staged his own question-and-answer form of street theatre. Tragedians were traditionally said to "teach" their choruses; their instruction culminated in the performance itself, in which the lesson was passed on to the audience. Athens could boast that it was the schoolroom of Greece.

Learning from the way in which playwrights (not excluding comic writers) based their work on myth, and on current politics and politicians, Socrates/Plato recycled previous, and contemporary, philosophies as the basis for dialogues in which their original authors were treated with more or less respect: Protagoras was in the first category, Thrasymachus in the second.

By the end of the fifth century, Athens had become a theatricalized society, just as today's art, politics and opinions cannot be divorced from the media by which they are publicized. Can anything similar be said about Judaea at the time of Jesus' trial and crucifixion?

Socrates' fate at the hands of the Athenian *demos* has been used as an argument against democracy, quite as if the freedom of speech which he enjoyed would be better secured by authoritarian states. The appropriation of the term "Democratic" by the totalitarian states of the ex-Soviet bloc, and by tyrannies that still pretend to higher principles than "bourgeois" states, proves the disingenuousness of those who argue that society is to be perfected by dispensing with free elections.

Having made ill-timed fun of the Athenian jurors, Socrates accepted their unamused sentence with honourable resignation. Set in the condemned cell, Plato's *Phaedo* is a postscript with the solemnity of a requiem, though even its text has a wry coda in Socrates' quip – as he takes his fatal medicine – that he "owes a cock to Asclepius", the "Always-Gentle" hero-god of healing. There is allusive theatricality here: the notion of drinking hemlock as if it were a cure for life is of a piece with Sophocles' dictum, "call no man happy (healthy?) till he is dead". When Socrates considers the possibility of immortality (of which Plato makes more than his master), he is not propounding a gospel – as Christians would like to think that Jesus did – but describing the logic of mortality: either death is the end, in which case there is nothing to fear "beyond" it, or there is something else, in which case it will be interesting to see what it is. The alleviation of fear (including – why not? – his own) is more pressing than notions of divine justice. In this, Socrates is the predecessor more of Epicurus than of Jesus.

* * *

*G*ood taste was a matter of practice, not of theory, in ancient Hellas. Criticism was not a separate genre: it was implicit in one poem being better than, or ridiculing, another. The culmination of such antagonism was that between Callimachus, a knotty professorial epigrammatist, and his alleged friend, and possible one-time pupil, Apollonius Rhodius (*c.* 295–215), whose *Argonautica* was a consciously archaizing attempt to retrieve the epic stretch of Homer. The venom with which Callimachus abused his colleague (both pursued higher studies at the *Mouseion* of Ptolemaic Alexandria) had nothing of the knockabout, satirical zest with which Aristophanes teased (and flattered) Euripides and Aeschylus in *The Frogs*. Callimachus was a pioneer of *odium academicum*, the dry scorn with which men with the same tastes and specialities rake each other. The scholar and poet A.E. Housman (1859–1936) prepared abusive comments about other classicists and left the names blank until the next victim of his contempt broke cover with a publication which deserved (as which did not?) his premeditated vilification.

Like Philip Larkin, an English poet of similarly aggressive refinement, Callimachus earned his bread as a don and librarian (in the great library of Alexandria). Unlike Larkin, he seems to have kept his critical scorn short: "*mega biblion, mega kakon*" (big book, big crap) was his comment on Apollonius Rhodius's *Argonautica*. While he may have displayed similar brevity in his densely textured (and teasingly allusive) poems, legend credits Callimachus with eight hundred "books", which hardly suggests systematic reluctance to put stylus to papyrus. Unlike earlier poets, he is on record as having written prose with equal zest. Tradition holds that Apollonius was so mortified by Callimachus's assault that he retired to Rhodos. His revenge was that, like *The Lord of the Rings*, his epic, despite the pundits, proved irresistible to common readers.

A recent poll alleged that Tolkien's fabricated fustian was among the first two or three "favourite books" of the British public. If so, it is probably because an Oscar-winning trio of movies has served to advertise a dusty confection without any deep root in British myth (unlike even Tennyson's *Idylls of the King*). Fame promoted Tolkien into seeming to be a national treasure whose title at least it would be shameful to deny having read. In the case of Apollonius, the myth of Jason was indeed fundamental to Greek group-memory, though not in the archaic form he gave it. The epic's instantly aged tone allowed it to become the reproduction literary furniture whose bogus antiquity was warranted by the age of the myth of the *Argo* itself (it is already available to Homer). Sea stories always work.

Callimachus also rewrote myth, but in a modern form, terse, allusive and designed "for the happy few". One can easily imagine him circulating clever

48 Jason and all-star crew on "tight-thwarted Argo".

pages among his friends as Cavafy did in the same city two millennia later. Callimachus's spite towards Apollonius was not pretty, but nor was it empty: T.S. Eliot's attack on Gilbert Murray's translations of Euripides had something of the same righteous indignation at the turning of trim ancient texts into sanctimonious Edwardian tushery. Eliot's *The Family Reunion* and *The Cocktail Party* were based on the Orestes and the Alcestis myths respectively.

Criticism no less abrupt than that of Callimachus was practised by the drama judges at the Great Dionysia. Fifth-century Athens knew neither journalists nor professors. First, second and third (last) places were handed out summarily and without appeal by ten judges, drawn by lot, one from each tribe. Sophocles, who wrote one hundred and twenty plays, was distinguished by never coming lower than second.

No one formulated rules for Tragedy until Aristotle, by whose time the great age of Attic theatre was done. In creative eras, the best criticism of art is better art. Despite having all two hundred and fifty of the great tragedians' plays available to him, Aristotle's "laws" for drama constituted, as did Plato's *Republic* for antique Sparta, an essay in prescriptive nostalgia.

In its dominant years, Athenian democracy was defended as a successful practice, not as a moral principle. Disgruntled pamphleteers, such as the – possibly quite young – man known as "the Old Oligarch", denounced its opportunism, though even he had to admit that, if theoretically deplorable, Athenian democracy worked pretty well in practice. Xenophon has been accused of being the pseudonymous author, but chronology makes this implausible. Xenophon and Caesar were the first, exemplary writers of their respective languages to be studied in our traditional classical education. Both appeared to be trim models of unaffected clarity. But if their prose promised modesty, in life both generals were far from self-effacing. The style was not the man himself in either case.

The Athenians' capacity to innovate without precedent, and to press policies which flew in the face of tradition (as Themistokles did in the years before Salamis) looked like irresponsible flightiness to those who confused inflexible social, military and religious habits with responsible government and respect for the gods. Before becoming a principle, democracy was a device to abate disruptive anarchy.

After Athens' humiliation in the Peloponnesian War, the vagaries of popular voters could be blamed for the defeat. Plato was made to seem reasonable when he advocated aristocracy in his blueprint for an ideal, immutably stable city-state. So great was his distaste for the proles of the Piraeus, who had pulled together at Salamis and supplied the engine-power for the Athenian empire, that he advocated a polis with no maritime outlet (the democratic tradition of seagoing Greeks was sustained, in 1967, by the refusal of the navy to support the Colonels' *coup d'état*). Plato's blueprint implied contempt for the Athens where *parrhesia* (free speech) had given him a freedom not to be found in his scheme for a closed and landlocked small town society of never more than 5,040 citizens.

Plato's rich uncle Critias's attempt, in 404/403, to impose a narrow oligarchy proved so unpopular, and its rule so inept, that even the Spartans, who – at the instigation of Lysander – had sponsored the *coup*, became embarrassed. On the other hand, if more than small fragments of the tragedies of

49 Lady Democracy (voteless herself) crowns the People with power.

Critias had survived, their quality might disturb us. His literary criticism had the acumen, and animus, often to be found among intelligent, resentful elitists. After a brief reign of terror, Critias was more or less expunged from the city's history. He was killed while seeking to put down Thrasybulus's democratic counter-*coup* in 403; his plays were similarly, perhaps unjustly, binned.

The Colonels who tried to put Greece right in 1967 were of the same reactionary stamp as Critias, though none was a writer or intellectual of his class. They paraded themselves in line with the myth of the simple soldier, but their simplicity, when not murderous, was vainglorious. Papadopoulos (nicknamed "Papa Dop" in honour of his affinity with "Papa Doc" Duvalier, the tyrant of Haiti) led Greece into political pariahdom. In 1974, when Turkey was provoked to invade Cyprus, he was powerless to react and his regime collapsed.

During the Colonels' tyranny in the European state with the longest, most illustrious literary tradition, the only reading allowed in the cells of distinguished men whom they bullied, and in many cases tortured, had been Papadopoulos's own so-called "Creed". A modern version of Aristophanes' *Lysistrata* was banned by the Colonels' censors because, although written two and a half millennia before, it mocked their rule so accurately. Art, said Ezra Pound, is news that stays news.

Compared in the very early days of their *anastasis* (which can mean both "uprising" and "resurrection") with Cromwell's no-nonsense Major-Generals, the Colonels lacked the vision, but shared the ambition, of the great and vindictive Lysander, an adroit tactician who – with the aid of Persian money – clinched Sparta's victory in the Peloponnesian War. When enforcing the terms of surrender, he took pleasure in burning a number of Athenian triremes, to the sound of flutes, on the precise anniversary of Athens' triumph at Salamis. In 1940, the Germans made the French sign the "armistice" in the same railway coach in which Foch had dictated the French terms in 1918.

In 403, Lysander proceeded to threaten the sclerotic Spartan establishment with reform. When he was alleged to be planning to make the dyarchy open to annual election, Pausanias – one of the two Spartan kings – took calm fright: he marched to Athens, where Lysander had his headquarters, removed the troublemaker from his proconsular eminence and negotiated a democratic restoration. Pausanias punctured Lysander's pretensions without depriving Sparta of his services. When the impatient general was killed leading a blitz on Boeotia in 395, his reforming ideas died with him. A quarter of a century later, at Leuctra, the dwindling ranks of true-born Spartans, constrained by traditional, time-worn tactics and pinched numerically by endogamic exclusiveness, were cut to pieces by Epaminondas and the Theban phalanx. The young Philip of Macedon, whose greatness was yet to be earned, was in exile in Thebes soon after Leuctra and applied the tactical lessons of the battle when destroying Greek independence at Chaeronea in 338. His son Alexander led an uncompromising campaign against Thebes itself in 335. As for King Pausanias, after dismissing Lysander, he enrolled the redemocratized, but still chastened, Athenians in an alliance to counter increasing Persian intrusion in Greek affairs. Persia was the objective winner (because Sparta's banker) in the Peloponnesian War, in which – as if in some dramatic competition – Sparta came second and Athens a sad third.

* * *

*A*mong the first acts of the post-war Athenian democracy was a law bidding the citizens *mee mnesikakein*: not to remember bad things. There is learned doubt about what *exactly* was being embargoed by the measure, but none over its general purpose: except in a few flagrant cases, bygones were decreed to be bygones. The amnesty was not merely a genial recommendation: the wound in Athenian social cohesion was deep and poisonous and needed prompt first aid. The new law was a bar against reverting to public hatreds now formally deemed to be settled once and for all. In the same spirit, the wilful forgetting of old enmities is at the source of the European Union.

The Megarians had tried, by similar measures, to abate their *stasis* in 424, but their oligarchs reneged and murdered many democrats. Even at Athens, there were limits to forgiving and forgetting: the reliable Xenophon observes that Socrates' friendships with both Alcibiades and Critias prejudiced jurors against him.

By the law *mee mnesikakein*, the Athenians were not attempting to legislate about people's private *feelings* (always a futile endeavour), but to allay the divisive consequences of their public manifestation. The new law allowed exiled Athenians to recover their property (as oligarchic exiles had been, when they, like Aristeides, came home to join up before Salamis); it also probably denied prosecutors the right to blacken witnesses, or bring charges, on account of misdeeds committed under Critias's aegis. Because, "incidentally", it also barred fortune hunters from bringing suit to dispossess passive supporters of Critias's oligarchs, the measure was, to some degree, favourable to landowners. In this it was in line with "*nomois tois archaiois*" (what the Romans called "*mos maiorum*", the traditional custom): Solon, and even the legendary Drako, had inaugurated similar measures. Drako lives on, adjectivally, for having been "Draconian", but little is known of him except that he ordained the death penalty for intentional homicide and for pilfering agricultural produce and equipment, about which Hesiod had complained furiously.

Whatever the inevitable infringements, the law *mee mnesikakein* testified to democratic magnanimity – even Plato paid tribute to it – almost without parallel in other societies. After Cannae in 214, however, Marcus Terentius Varro, who survived the disaster for which his rashness was partly responsible, led the surviving legionaries back to Rome. Fearful of a court martial, he was greeted by the Senate – composed almost entirely of his political enemies – not with recriminations but with ritual congratulations that, despite the disaster, he had not "despaired of the Republic". In modern times, on the restoration of the French republic, in 1945, General de Gaulle sought to mitigate the bloody "*épuration*" (against Vichyites and Germanizers) by promoting the reconciling myth that (almost) all Frenchmen had rallied to the Resistance, although many of the hard core of fighters had – especially in the *années les plus noires* – been foreign-born (often Jewish refugees and Spanish Republicans).

Plato's attempts to implement his own political curriculum in practice ended in tragicomic humiliation. He went to Sicily first in 387, at the invitation of Dion, a well-connected and well-heeled admirer, to make a philosopher-king of the latter's brother-in-law, Dionysius I, who had inherited the tyranny of Syracuse. The process of graduation took too long for the impatient ruler, and for his supporters, who expected prompter and more profitable proof of their leader's education. Faced with choice between the moral high ground (and higher mathematics) as against kingship, Dionysius chose the lower road. Dion was exiled, Plato dismissed.

In 367, Plato tried again, with Dionysius II, with no more success. After his first failure as *éminence grise*, Plato was for a brief time sold into slavery, before being ransomed by admirers. On returning to Athens in the 380s, he founded the Academy, where his theories were never again embarrassed by being measured against reality. Forgery or not, Plato's *Seventh Letter* offers a plausible apologia for his Sicilian experiences, in which he gives the impression that the union of wisdom and power was nearly realized. If, as is probable, Plato's later letters are forgeries, they are the first in that enlightening category of ancient pseudo-autobiography to which Thornton Wilder, Rex Warner, Robert Graves, Peter Green and Marguerite Yourcenar have since contributed.

Plato did indeed seek to reconcile the Greeks in southern Italy. Unity might have saved them from the mutual hostilities from which neither he (with words) nor Pyrrhus (with force) could redeem them. The Peloponnesian War had the side effect of increasing the fractionalization of the cities in Magna Graecia. To do him justice, Plato did indeed seek to reconcile the Greeks.

Plato's last book, *The Laws* – in which Socrates is replaced as interlocutor by an anonymous Athenian – shows signs of his having discovered, from harsh practice, that man cannot be defined and dragooned into virtue. *The Laws'* provisions make rueful concessions to the mundane intractability of human beings and admit the possibility that, over the years, legislators too may have to learn from experience. Despite these reluctant concessions to the limits of human malleability, Plato was less a convert to Popper's Open Society than resigned to easing the loopholes in his citizens' patriotic straitjackets. It does seem, however, that life under *The Laws* was not to be entirely uniform and unsmiling: if scarcely happy-clappy, the older Plato did suggest that men were fashioned as the toys of the gods. One of their duties was to delight them with singing and dancing. Effacing Socrates from *The Laws* suggests a failure of the nerve which had once sanctioned Plato to remake his master in his own tendentious image. The choice of a Cretan as a Nothing-If-Not-Critical lawgiver indicates the dignity which Crete's antiquity conferred. Its myth fortified Plato's reason.

At the same time, Crete was a byword for duplicity: one of Zeno's teasing conundrums was based on the mainland proverb "All Cretans are liars". Zeno's kicker was: "What if it's a Cretan who says this?" In that case, if what he says is true, the fact that a Cretan has said it falsifies the generalization; but if it is a lie, the premiss equally cannot be true. The "evidence" for Cretan untrustworthiness is said to have been that some Cretans claimed that Zeus was born on Mount Ida, others on Mount Dicte.

The Laws lacks the variety of interlocutors whose objections give *The Republic* an ebullience absent from the summing-up of the wiser-but-older Plato. *The Republic* begins with a polite dialogue about the definition of justice. The sudden irruption of the irascible Thrasymachus, with his brazen definition of Justice as "the will of the stronger", is so dramatic, and his views so cogently expressed, that Plato is as hard-pressed to refute his insolence as Dostoyevsky was to confound his own creation, the Grand Inquisitor, in *The Brothers Karamazov*.

The Laws verges on a sententious monologue spoken in the voice of disenchanted experience. If Plato was inhibited from thrusting dry, statist sentiments into Socrates' mouth, was it because the nobility of his dead master had been crowned by obedience to the laws of democratic Athens? Socrates' refusal to go into exile – an accepted, and not dishonourable, method of self-reprieve – was a gesture of insolent piety: by not allowing the poison cup to pass from him, he condemned the Athenians to swallow the hemlock of their own shame. By the same token, staying to die was also an acknowledgment that he could not imagine life anywhere but in his own state.

How misleading is it to use terms such as "state" or "government" in relation to the ancient *polis*? Such usage risks being anachronistic, but is hard to avoid. It is certainly the case that some ancient societies were more "statist" than others. Sparta, with its *krypteia* (young terror-squads, whose initiation included the systematic intimidation and repression of helots, on whom Sparta formally declared war every year, in order to justify their murder), was the prototype of the police state, in which repression, of men and ideas (as well as art), is a fundamental element. Athens never institutionalized terror and hence never laid the ground for the "culture of delation" which afflicted imperial Rome. An accuser in Athens had to bring his case personally and answer for the consequences of an acquittal.

Socrates' refusal to leave Athens may have had several motives. For the ancients, exile was a living death, from which there could – as Orestes exemplified – be redemption only through rituals of purification and of rebirth, often in another land (Teucer was a lesser example). In the Heroic Age, displacement was a spur to conquest and the creation of new kingdoms, but for Socrates – as for Oscar Wilde – exile would deprive him not only of his preferred stage, but also of a knowing audience. How much more splendid it was to drain the hemlock as if it were a cocktail and in the sweet company of friends whom he could chide for looking sad! One can imagine his silent toast to his grieving entourage, "To democracy!" The actor, the martyr and the joker could scarcely have contrived a more ironic exit, even though the symptoms of hemlock poisoning are crueller than Plato depicts in the *Phaedo*. It sentimentalizes ancient Hellas to suggest that it was unusually humane. One of its ways of punishing criminals was to cover them in hot ash, a literal case of incineration.

Despite Plato's elderly retreat from confidence that a perfect recipe could be devised for human society, philosophers continued to suppose that the world could be improved by the imposition of ideal states of affairs. Democracy has rarely been a logical (still less a logician's) answer to humanity's unruliness. Only the greatest did not disdain it: Spinoza was the noblest, John Locke the most influential, of those for whom other people were not as naturally despicable as they were for Plato and his admirers. Social theorists can be divided into Procrusteans and Prometheans: the former top and tail man in order to fit him for the ideal furniture in which they propose to bed him, while the latter propose to bless mankind at large with freedom and responsibility for its own destiny, however unpredictable.

Tyrants have regularly cherished, and been cherished by, didactic theorists. Anaxagoras of Clazomenae (on the gulf of Smyrna) was a favourite of Perikles; his idea that *nous*, mind or intelligence, was the ruling principle of the universe suited the vanity of the architect of Athenian hegemony. Perikles was, however, unable to save Anaxagoras from the consequences of his more materialistic, and hence blasphemous, speculations. Since the philosopher was a metic (resident alien), there was no appeal against his banishment when he dared to suggest, to the outrage of unsophisticated Athenians – as superstitious as they might claim to be rational – that the sun was a large stone "about the size of the Peloponnese". His eviction was also a reminder to the Eupatrid Perikles that there were limits to his claim on the allegiance of what would now be called "the ordinary Athenian".

Philosophers continue to be drawn to the powerful: alternating between clown and savant, they rejoice, like the Fool and the Oracle, in being granted freer speech than others. Voltaire preened himself on speaking frankly to Frederick the Great, but no more liberalized Prussia than Plato educated Dionysius II of Syracuse. Aristotle was supposed to teach *sophrosyne* to Alexander the Great, and Seneca stoic virtue to Nero; the only marked differ-

50 Voltaire seated, Frederick
the Great, his pupil, on his feet?
A likely story.

ence between them was that Aristotle
survived his pupil, just, whereas Nero
killed his master. When Heidegger
realized (if he truly did) that he had
been duped by Hitler, or by the construction he put on him, and resigned
the rectorate of Freiburg University, in
order to return to pure thought, some
of his subtle colleagues dared to ask
him, "Back from Syracuse?"

Plato – always more moralist than
politician – idealized the city-state
when it was, in practice, already out-
moded. Although the Athenian empire
revived, in more modest form, after the
Peloponnesian War, defeat had fatally
weakened the city. Victory soon did the
same for Sparta. Refusing to widen the franchise to include more than the traditional ruling elite, the Spartans flattered themselves into demographic
bankruptcy (Plato's "ideal state" would be equally doomed by its static roll of citizens). Sparta's defeat at Leuctra gave the rest of the Hellenes one more
opportunity to unite, or at least to federate. Might they then have deterred Philip
II of Macedon from picking them off, piecemeal, a few decades later? In the
event, Epaminondas's genius served only to license the petulant ambitions of
lesser cities. Within five years, in order to abate the anarchy in the Peloponnese,
he had to return to the charge, against a motley alliance of Athenians, Spartans
and others, at the battle of Mantinea, where he was killed in the moment of
triumph. As he lay dying from a spear wound, he admitted to regretting never
having had any children, but then, he consoled himself, his victories were his
children. They did not live long: Thebes' brief dominance was followed by
eclipse at the hand of Philip II of Macedon (382–336), whose son, Alexander,
brought its utter destruction.

Epaminondas's decisive innovation had been his thickening of the phalanx
to form a solid mass of foot soldiers, up to fifty ranks deep, bristling with pikes.
Its morale was sustained by the tradition of the Theban Sacred Band, an elite
formation composed of pairs of male lovers who, it was said, fought for each

other with passionate dedication. A chaste version of the Theban bonding ritual persists in the "buddy system" in the US army and in two-man "partnerships" in the police. The linguistic curiosity of the "dual" case in Greek conjugations is a combination of our "we" and "you", which implies that two people are paired in some action or condition. No modern European language echoes this suggestion that two people doing something was a category so specific (and so common) that it merited its own grammatical case.

The disciplined, heavily weighted impact of the Thebans broke with tactical convention. Philip of Macedon and then his son, Alexander the Great, improved on Epaminondas by arming his phalanx with *sarissas* (pikes) eighteen feet long, in order to drill the first hole in an enemy line while remaining out of range of its shorter arms. The Companion Cavalry – the equivalent of Hitler's panzers – could then smash into the flanks of the stalled and disconcerted foe. As the chess manuals put it, "A pinned piece is a paralysed piece."

* * *

While Demosthenes played the patriotic part, he was supported, almost to the end, by a majority of the Athenian *demos*. Its susceptibility to sentiment went back at least as far as the Milesian Aristagoras's request for help from the Athenians in the ill-fated rebellion of 499. He had appealed first to Sparta, but was rejected by King Cleomenes. Herodotus remarks, "it is easier to impose on a crowd of 30,000 than on an individual".

Demosthenes' great rivals, Aeschines and Isocrates, called for a Strong Man who would dissolve interstate differences by recruiting all Hellenes in common hostility to Persia. If he can be accused of being a kind of proto-Fascist, Isocrates was scarcely a populist. Like the late Enoch Powell (a Nietzschean Hellenist), he had the detachment – and high-hattedness – of the academic who takes a prophetic overview of events. Love of power inclines the intelligent to parade on the side of History, by which they mean the probable winners. The logical mind, craving inevitabilities, is tempted to argue for the unarguable. Those who predict, and conspire with, the Course of History echo the oracular voice which advised the Greeks to yield to Xerxes.

But might not Athens (and Sparta) have done better if they had associated themselves freely with Macedonia from the outset? If Aeschines and Isocrates advocated what they lacked the nerve to challenge, Demosthenes' prescience – with regard to Philip's territorial ambitions – did not extend to the realization that no single city-state, however resolute, could sustain confrontation with the populous, militaristic and efficiently led Macedon, whose forces had no need to cross the sea, where the Athenians might still hope to confound them.

The English Channel, no less than Churchillian grit, and rhetoric, deterred the panzers in 1940. On the other hand, had Britain been defeated after Dunkirk, who today would regard Churchill as other than a proud, anachronistic fool who had missed history's bus?

Only after the death of Alexander in 323, when Demosthenes tried yet again to rouse Athens to resist Antipater, the implacable Macedonian *Gauleiter* of Greece, did the Athenians finally abandon quixotry and vote to surrender Demosthenes. He fled to the island of Calaureia and there committed suicide. Half a millennium later, Pausanias the travel-writer said that Demosthenes illustrated the fate of anyone who "devotes himself to his country's welfare and trusts the people." The truth is less that the *demos* betrayed Demosthenes than that it was consistently persuaded by fine phrases (and obsolete patriotism) until forced to accept that the clock could not be put back to the great days of empire and Periklean rhetoric. Yet it is true that Athenian democracy died with Demosthenes, whose name stood for the power of the people.

The emperor Augustus is said, in later life, to have come upon one of his grandsons reading the works of Cicero, at whose murder the emperor, as Octavian, had connived. Commending the boy's taste, Augustus said that Cicero had been a great patriot. Cicero's speeches against Mark Antony, traditionally known as "Philippics" had sealed his fate. The great Roman orator was like Demosthenes in seeking to preserve a style of life which also underwrote his style of rhetoric. Masters of language rarely promote a society in which advocacy ceases to be a moving force. Cicero and Demosthenes favoured republics which, however regrettably, were obsolete.

Two Persian wars, during which Athens and Sparta refused to yield to the Great King's ultimatum, had offered a glorious example but set a delusive precedent: the Macedonians were scarcely barbarians, did not come from overseas, needed no whipping to make them fight and were never overextended. In their own eyes, they asked for little more than recognition that they were the *de facto* champions of the Hellenes. Although in outlandish accents, they could claim to be as good Greeks as any. Even today, Thessaloniki claims to be the "second capital" of Greece. Its citizens resent the suggestion that Macedonia is not as Greek as Attica. Athenians are unconvinced. Yet when the hinterland of ancient Macedonia detached itself from disintegrating Yugoslavia and proclaimed itself an independent republic, metropolitan Greeks were indignant: the province of Macedonia, and certainly its name, belonged – they now said – to Greece.

Greek fractiousness was its social weakness and its artistic strength: while her cities lacked the desire, or the economy, to create enduring and cohesive empires, local pride and a parade of festivals fostered the Muses in myriad corners of Hellas. Division sponsored diffusion. Attic drama spoke for a common culture, but in competing tones: the choruses, it has been claimed, hark back to more harmonious, tribal times. The great tragedies, however, had transcendental appeal: they could be heard in countless provincial theatres, from Miletus to Syracuse. It is said that when the Athenians were defeated and rounded up after their comprehensive defeat by the Syracusans, their captors reprieved only those who could recite verses from Euripides. In Polanski's film, *The Pianist*, a Jewish musician is similarly spared by a German officer. Aeschylus probably staged *The Persians* in the Syracusan theatre, which overlooks the Great Harbour. The Messenger's tale, of how the Athenians trapped the Persian fleet at Salamis and slaughtered its sailors like tunny in the *matanza*, had a savage echo, fifty-nine years after its premiere, in the Syracusans' destruction of Nikias's ships, and men.

Athens never excited the centripetal urge which impelled ambitious provincials to converge on imperial Rome. Roman talents might originate elsewhere – Lucan, Seneca and Martial were born in Spain – but the road to fame, and to power, led to the Seven Hills. Where else did a Latin-speaking littérateur ever make a famous name for himself? (Ausonius lived in what is today Bordeaux, but that was during the last years of the by then decentralized western Roman empire.)

When Plato called his Athens the "town hall of Wisdom", it was a boast rather than a fact: sophists were to be found in many other cities. If the lustre of fifth-century Athens drew orators to the agora, it was as much for cash as for kudos. The democratic zeal for litigation fostered logographoi, speechwriters who also gave paid opinions, like modern barristers with their metered partisanship. Antiphon, 480–411, a native Athenian, was one of the earliest, and most able.

It is tempting to read Antiphon's name as a description of his profession: *anti* means "instead of", and -phon suggests *phone*, a voice. What better advertisement for someone who spoke for others? While Demosthenes improved his diction by putting pebbles in his mouth, Antiphon preferred other people to put gold. One of the brains behind the eventually disastrous oligarchic *coup d'état* in 411, Antiphon failed, or refused, to flee with the extremists (who wanted to introduce a tyranny by committee) and stood trial for treason. Perhaps he had never meant to go as far as the other conspirators (he belonged to a moderate element among them), but it is probable that he fancied his chances with a jury. He had written textbooks on how to convince, or confuse, them. He failed in his own case and was executed. Like the mythical characters who planned to outsmart the gods, he suffered a fatal peripeteia.

In the fourth century, legal consultancy attracted foreigners, such as Deinarchus of Corinth. Disqualified from active politics, their advocacy was at a premium. The intelligent *metic* lived by his wits, which – like the Jew's in Christendom – were sharpened by outsiderdom. In fourth-century Athens, Deinarchus was a latter-day parody of Demosthenes: facile and witty, he lacked an innate place in the metropolis he amused and provoked. An improbable accent can license effrontery, but its licence always has limits: George Bernard Shaw played the anglicized Oirish wag to long applause, Oscar Wilde to shorter.

Greek cities and islands produced innumerable poets, philosophers and historians who preferred to remain the first men in their village, or city-state, rather than become the second, or lower, in Athens. Asia Minor, southern Italy and Sicily had communities to which their citizens were no less proud to belong than to Athens or Sparta, Thebes or Corinth. Croton was an aggressive collector of Olympic laurels (and has been accused of paying transfer fees to promising athletes who took up residence there). Sappho made Lesbos famous, and killed herself, they say, by throwing herself off a cliff, for love of a man. A millennium later, Hypatia – that conclusive symbol of Greek female genius – never left Alexandria, where she was killed (in A.D. 415) by a Christian mob. The only class of women ever likely to travel voluntarily were courtesans: Corinth was their golden magnet.

How much did the radiant diffusion of Hellenism owe to polytheism? A multiplicity of gods, and cults, was honoured in local lore and swarmed in everyday language and superstition; hence Thales' "The world is full of gods". Polytheism did not contrast with, or oppose, other notions about the nature of the gods, or God, until Greeks came into contact with Zoroastrians, Jews, and then with Christians, whose inelastic monotheism appeared incomprehensibly uncivilized: if the Greeks would tolerate it as one cult among many, why would it not tolerate them? The Athenians' altar to "the unknown god" betokened both hospitality for a deity without a character and a prize for Pauline rhetoric.

Paul was several things, but scarcely a single-minded Greek. As Jew, Roman citizen and a son of Hellenistic Tarsus, in Cilicia, his tripartite nature was neatly reconciled in his conception of a Triune deity dominated by Jesus. Since he had no native allegiance to the Olympian gods, what was the art, or livelihood, of the silversmiths of Ephesus to him? Their guild specialized in images of an Artemis akin to Egyptian Isis. Her great temple was a ranked Wonder of the Ancient World. St Jerome said that the "Diana" honoured there was not the huntress famously favoured by Hippolytus, but Artemis, the many-breasted, whose affinity was with the Anatolian Great Mother.

Only one disjointed column is still standing of the Virgin Goddess's shrine. When I last saw it, there was a stork's nest on the top. Alexander the Great offered to rebuild it but was refused because "it was not fitting that a god

51 Diana of the Ephesians,
in her great days.

make offerings to the gods" (the real problem was that he wanted his name, big, on the credits). Tradition says that the temple was burnt down by Herostratus because he was unable to create anything as marvellous. Nihilist wreckers continue to destroy or deface works. Duchamp's mustachioed Mona Lisa is the wittiest instance. Since ideological wreckers – Copts, Nazis, Taliban, Puritans, Iconoclasts, and so on – honour moral imperatives, their vandalism is more thorough, and complacent.

Polytheism describes a state of affairs rather than a theology. The Greeks worshipped both the ubiquitous Olympians and local divinities who, like petty wines, were never exported to a wider market. The Great God Pan lived in Arcadia, though he had shrines on the Acropolis and in a cave at Vari, on the coastal side of Mount Hymettus.

There were, however, regional versions and variations of the Olympians: Athene had her central bastion, and showiest image, in the Parthenon, but there was also a Spartan Athene, whose tutelage covered only the *polis* of Sparta. All the Olympians put on their uniforms when visiting Lacedaemon: like royalty at ceremonial parades, the entire roster of gods was depicted in military kit in Spartan iconography.

Centres of cult were visited by pagan pilgrims no less than Lourdes or Santiago or Rome came to be by Roman Catholics, but there was no single central authority in Greek religion: no Jerusalem, Rome or Mecca affected to be the headquarters of divine power. While Delphi was the call centre for information about Apollo's take on things, cloud-capped Olympus was a vertiginous Versailles, where Zeus's convocation of the principal deities kept them under luxurious surveillance of the kind to which the Sun King later obliged the French *noblesse*. Inaccessibility made Olympus the cloud-wreathed doorstep of heaven, but no human was ever going to make it there.

Kinship, and the nexus of relations it involved (in particular the guarantee of citizenship), did nothing to dispose Greeks to make a life elsewhere than in their own communities, unless disgrace or necessity propelled them into exile. The unusual poverty of the Attic soil had made it unappealing to the

Dorian invaders, who – at the expense of the indigenous tenants – made the fertile Peloponnese their own. Athenians claimed to be born from their own soil, but its limited fertility impelled surplus citizens to seek new opportunities, if not new identities, across the sea: hence Asiatic Ionia.

In his Funeral Oration, Perikles makes a virtue of the individual initiative of the busy Athenians. However, what he values in their competitive rivalries is their cumulative contribution to general prosperity. Until the Greeks lost control of their own political fate, personal happiness was never the admitted purpose of *polis* life. Our word "idiot" derives from the Attic *idiotes*, a citizen who lives only for himself, of whom Perikles said, "He has no right to be here".

The primacy of personal achievement seems heroized in Achilles and his fatal ambition – which *was* his character – to excel all others. Yet the defeated and the also-rans testified to his excellence. Who can excel in isolation, except, perhaps, an artist? So much has been written about Greek art that it is assumed that the Greeks accorded similar respect to those responsible for making it. Yet the emblematic artisan god Hephaestus was also a figure of fun: lame cuckold, gauche in company – he ejaculated prematurely while seeking to breach the disgusted Athene's virginity – and at home in the shadows, he was a crepuscular habitué of forges and the armourer of those more suited to daylight (and limelight) than himself. He made Achilles' shield and armour, but was too gimpy to figure in heroic battle.

Among quasi-mortals, Daedalus was as much defined by murderous envy (of his nephew) and duplicitous treachery (against his patron, King Minos) as by the ingenuity of his artefacts. Pheidias, who followed the same trade as Daedalus, although never accused of murder, was charged with embezzling gold allotted for his statue of Athene in Perikles' Parthenon. Since he was paid no more than the masons who worked alongside him, Pheidias might have been forgiven a gilded perk or two. However, he confounded his accusers by unbuckling the gold – which they had presumed integral to the image – and weighing it before their eyes. Not an ounce was missing.

Later, a charge of sacrilege drove him from Athens: he was accused of putting "men among the gods", when he embellished the Acropolis with the frieze depicting the great Panathenaic process (it has also been suggested that it might be a kind of cursive calendar, parading the principal festivals of the Athenian year). Like Anaxagoras, he was a scapegoat for his unassailable patron, Perikles, whose use of public funds, and disdain for popular credulities, could not be questioned with the same directness. Pheidias fled to Olympia, where the Eleans commissioned him to make their gigantic chryselephantine statue of Zeus. In due time, it would be rated among the Seven

Wonders of the World by Hellenistic Alexandrian scholars, who made a fetish of catalogues and rankings. Societies in decline finger the beads of their heritage, as if the process of ranking established their pundits' aesthetic superiority (though rarely their artistic achievements).

When the exiled Pheidias had finished his masterpiece at Olympia, his Elean patrons found reason to put him to death. Whatever the precise charge, there was a foretaste of Herostratus in the Eleans' ensuring that Pheidias never excelled himself elsewhere. The artist is always threatened by the possessive gratitude of his patrons. Why else put him under contract?

* * *

*T*he principal and universally respected institutions of the Greek world were the Games, which probably had their origins in funeral celebrations for heroes. In the *Iliad*, Achilles celebrates the most famous of such events for his dead companion, Patroklos. The poem ends with the Trojans' Games for Hector's funeral: grief and celebration are common to both sides.

From 776, the Olympic Games became a quadrennial, pan-Hellenic attraction. It is often held that the Greek craving for unity was symbolized by the traditional truce, allowing contestants at war with each other to compete in sporting immunity, as the Germans and British did when they played soccer in no man's land at Christmas 1914. The Olympic truce could also give an opportunity to hostile diplomats to indulge in horse-trading, some of it possibly literal: chariot races were the showiest advertisement for the victors' cities and must have led to sell-offs. Mutinous Mytileneans lobbied for aid against Athens at the Olympiad of 428. In 420, the Eleans, who were supposedly the umpires of propriety, played politics with the Games by asserting that the Spartans, who were at that time isolated even from their allies, had violated the sacred truce. The Olympic court (conducted by the Eleans) imposed a fine, of which they offered to rescind half, if the Spartans would give back the city of Lepreum to them. The Spartans declined to be humiliated and were barred from the Games.

As Donald Kagan points out, the Eleans would never have dared to defy Sparta in this way, had they not been sure, at the time, that other Peloponnesian democracies and, most importantly, Athens would back their judgment and defend their city.

Kagan recalls that Lichas, barred from competing as a Spartan, donated his chariot team to the Boeotians. When it was victorious, Lichas himself placed the winner's crown on the Theban charioteer. When the Eleans sent officials to whip Lichas off the track, the Spartans did not, at that stage of their military and diplimatic fortunes, have the power to respond as forcefully as they might have wished. They took the same line recommended by L.B. Mayer, the one-time tyrant of MGM studios, when a friend complained of being unjustly used. "Do what I do: turn the other cheek. Turn the other cheek and bide your time." The Spartans did just that.

Greek chronology was calibrated by Olympiads until Theodosius I put an end to the Games by his edict of, it is sometimes said, 13th November 393. The confidence with which historians date events in antiquity suggests more assurance about precise days, months and years than anyone had the means of recording at the time.

As Pamela-Jane Shaw has pointed out, the genius of ancient astronomers did not extend to a generally agreed calendar. When, at the end of the sixth century, Darius built a bridge and crossed the Danube to march against the Scythians, he called together the Ionian tyrants deputed to guard it and showed them a leather strap, in which he had tied sixty knots. They were told to undo one knot each day. If the Great King had not returned when the last knot was untied, they were free to go home. Clearly, he could not nominate a date two months ahead on any common diary.

There were local "calendars" as there were local cults, but no universally recognized chronology until Timaios, in the third century B.C., standardised the reckoning by Olympiads. For more than a thousand years, men from all over the Greek world came to Olympia, and elsewhere, to compete – with increasing professionalism – for laurel (or olive) wreaths. More palpable rewards included pensions for life from thrilled compatriots, enhanced marriage prospects and, occasionally, new gateways punched in city walls for the entrance of victors dressed in purple and drawn by white horses (the ceremony of a Roman triumph took a similar form).

The size and antiquity of the temples, and of the sacred enclosure adjacent to the stadium, are solid evidence of the abiding religious dimension of the Olympic and other athletic festivals. Etymologically speaking, religions bind people together; practically, they give them common reasons to despise, and sometimes to destroy or enslave, those outside their knot. The athletic events at Olympia began – at least in the case of the foot-race – in ritual, but they became blatantly commercialized. The Games drew contestants and tourists from all over the Mediterranean. A rich city such as Syracuse claimed as many Olympic crowns as any in mainland Hellas: its most famous tyrant, Dionysius I, could afford the best horses for the chariot race, which brought kudos to the owner of the winning team, not to the jockey. Alcibiades flaunted his personal fortune by entering seven teams, including the winners, in the same year.

52 In a version by Pierre Puget, a lion champs on ex-champion Milon.

As for individual athletes, no one ever equalled Milon of Croton, on the east coast of Calabria. In the sixth century B.C., he outdid even the great British oarsman Steve Redgrave's five successive Gold Medals, by winning six consecutive wrestling victories at Olympia, over a period of twenty years. Milon repeated the performance at the almost equally prestigious Pythian Games at Delphi. It was a superhuman span of achievement, in a savagely demanding event, at a period when the average expectation of life was no more than forty years (during the siege of Troy, Nestor had been a garrulous – if beefy – senior elder statesman at, very possibly, little past that age). In historical times, however, the members of the Spartan *gerousia* (Council of Elders) had to be over sixty.

Milon's successes were famous even among non-Hellenes, who were barred, by their origins, from competing against him. After Democedes had been hired as physician to the great Darius, he requested permission to leave the capital, Susa, to return to Croton, where he planned to marry Milon's daughter. Socially this trumped even his privileged position at the Persian court, earned by curing Darius's wife, Atossa, of an abscess on her breast.

There was a rueful conclusion to the great champion's career. After he had passed his prime, the vanity of age impelled Milon to prise apart a tree, but it snapped back and trapped him in the cleft. Hungry wolves devoured the serial winner who was reputed once to have carried a live heifer across the stadium above his head, killed it with one blow of his fist, and then eaten it in a single day.

Milon may have been a historical figure, but his strength, and appetite, derived from imitation of Herakles: tradition promised that the hero – never renowned for his manners – once devoured a whole steer, raw. To eat uncooked flesh was tantamount to barbarism, but uncontrolled appetites, and showing off, marked the champion. Herakles and Milon were heroes who never lacked stomach for the fight.

It is difficult not to see Milon as the precursor of the professional wrestling star, flexing his oiled flesh and flashing his bouncer's implacable smile. Milon's home town Croton was a city with a bully-boy reputation. It was responsible, in 510, for the destruction of its Calabrian neighbour, Sybaris. Sybarites remain a byword for luxury and *la dolce vita*. Cocks were forbidden within the city limits, because they crowed and woke people up too soon. Deploring the early call of the cock became a standard trope for versifiers: Antipater of Thessaloniki was still sighing about it in the first century A.D.

The Sybarites were, in many respects, Greeks like any others: for all their hedonism, they too lived by the sword. But if the Crotoniats could claim to have been spurred to war by dissident Sybarites, why did they treat the once happy city with vindictive malice? It was as if other people's pleasure was an insult to them. By the time that Petronius wrote his picaresque Satyrica, in the first century A.D., Croton was a prosperous but unlovely Roman city which, so the novelist said, was notorious for unscrupulous fortune hunters. The modern city – dominated by a huge, unlovely Norman castle – has an air of surly prosperity: it offers not even a counterfeit smile of welcome. You sense a place with a cocksure want of conscience. Of insouciant Sybaris, now literally submerged, there remains no obvious trace. Its colony, however, was Paestum. Made uninhabitable by malaria, its ruins still display three of the great temples of Hellas.

* * *

*A*s founder of the Olympic Games, Herakles was notorious both for gluttony and for sexual voracity. He was often demented by rage, especially when provoked by his stepmother Hera, for whom his birth was squalling proof of Zeus's infidelity. She sent snakes to nab him in his cradle. After the infant had strangled them, she pursued him with the malice she dared not visit on his father. Yet she was the involuntary source of his eventual divinity: as a suckling, he had been set to the goddess's breast, from which he drew the milk of immortality before she thrust him away. There is a version of the myth – rendered plausible by her early temple at Olympia – which holds that Hera and Herakles were once husband and wife. Whatever their relationship, she was such a shrew that, on one manic occasion, he fired an arrow into her right breast. The goddess could not die of her wound but suffered keenly from it, as Aphrodite did when she leaked divine ichor from an arrow wound after tripping unwisely into the Trojan War.

Immortality supplied no anaesthetic: hence the wounded centaur Chiron's prayer to be allowed to die, after battling for the Olympian team against the

Lapiths. His decease left a place among the immortals for Herakles, the son of Zeus by the mortal Alcmene, who was in agony from being fitted with the caustic shirt of Nessus. Zeus's thunderbolt seared him from the torment of his mortal flesh and he was assumed into heaven.

Herakles seems the incarnation of man's capacity to achieve the superhuman. Yet there is ambiguity even in his name, which can be interpreted either as "Glory of Hera" or as "Glory from Hera", or both. Ambivalence makes him both a man's man and, in comedy and folklore, an effeminate clown. Similar slightly derisive veneration follows David Beckham, the football star, whose decision to sport a hairslide was deemed unmanly by his pink-faced manager.

It is typical of the cruel comedy of Herakles' life that the lethal shirt, misguidedly given to him by his loving wife, is always described as a *"peplos"*. The story seems steeped in tragic irony, but the comedy remains that – in Greek ears – the word *peplos* meant more a woman's shift (or a winding-sheet) than a man's costume, which was usually a *chiton*.

The most popular of Greek heroes was also the most travestied. He is often depicted in female clothes and sometimes portrayed on vases as fully bearded while sucking on Hera's divine breast: a bristling baby. The athlete, sexual or otherwise, may be revered, but deference generates mockery. Aeschylus famously said, "Learning comes through suffering", but so did comedy:

53 Cranach the Elder's Herakles petted by Omphale, queen of Lydia. She bought him at a slave auction and later cross-dressed, and slept, with him.

54 Arnie. California, here I come.

today's Greeks often greet pain, not least in animals and in children, with curious, if not cruel, laughter.

Ancient Greeks gloried in competition, both in athletics and in the arts. To become mythical was a dangerous eminence. Myth was full of awful warnings about the danger of challenging the gods. Marsyas, the great flute player, was flayed alive by Apollo, whose skills he had claimed to surpass. The Olympians drew the line between themselves and presumptuous mortals by exemplary punishment: the days when men and gods dined, and revelled, on equal terms were ended when the randy Ixion, whom Zeus entertained as a kindred spirit, went too far and made a play for Hera, after which he was bound to a fiery wheel which spun through the night sky, advertising the limits of Olympian tolerance. The distinction between human and divine competence later became logical: by definition, the divinity *cannot* now be surpassed.

Yet even mythological victims retained a kind of glory: they became part of the language of Hellas. Who looked at a spider's web without thinking of Arachne? To die dramatically was to live on in men's minds. The fifth-century philosopher Empedocles jumped into the crater of Mount Etna in order to seem never to have died at all. Since the story became current, it seems that he failed. Metaphorically, however, he succeeded: his name lives on. Diogenes remained perverse to the end, by dying as wilfully as he had lived: he chose to hold his breath until he expired.

By contrast, the great mathematician Archimedes was merely murdered, in 212 or 211, while working on his triangles in the sandy beach at Syracuse, by a Roman centurion who didn't know, or care, who he was. Archimedes' last words are said to have been, "Don't mess up my triangles". The composer Anton von Webern was shot and killed by an American soldier at the end of World War II because (like "Saki", H.H. Munro, in the trenches) of a cigarette unwisely lit at the wrong moment. Plutarch tells us that, though adept at inventing weapons of war, as a good Greek, Archimedes regarded such banausic achievement as of no interest. J. Robert Oppenheim betrayed something of the same spirit in feeling that, by yoking pure theory to impure purposes, the physicists who worked on the atom bomb had supped with the devil.

Greek drama – by which is meant plays written by Athenians[*] – peaked in a system in which prizes promoted excellence. However, triumph over the Persians seems to have primed a surge of inventive – and assertive – confidence which deserted Athens after defeat in the Peloponnesian War. Dramas continued to be written in the fourth century and beyond: the New Comedy became lively and much more realistic than that of Aristophanes, but the summer had gone out of the year, and after it Melpomene, the Muse of Tragedy, lost her bloom. Entertainment alone remained, which has the bitch-goddess Success for a Muse.

Poetry was not an exclusively metropolitan activity. Even shepherds engaged in ritual exchanges, often of teasing insults: Theocritus, a Syracusan who lived in Alexandria in the early third century, confected pastoral verses which elaborated the artful flyting of Sicilian peasants. Faced with their knotty rustic texts, it is easy to forget that Theocritus's verses were meant to amuse a sophisticated audience and were performed to music.

Virgil's eclogues glossed Theocritus's already glossy productions (pastoral sublimated the cruelty of slavery, as comedy did). Horace was a supple follower of Archilochos, Virgil of Homer. Greek and Latin models form the bridge between antiquity and Christian Europe. Western culture and religion are palimpsests: under-paint and under-writing bleed through the surface. Repetition, revision and even revulsion thicken and subvert the original myths and images. Chapman translated Homer, and Christopher Logue is improving him; Dryden and Cecil Day-Lewis Englished Virgil. The good translator is less traitor than double agent: he delivers the old thing in a new way. North made Plutarch an English gentleman and Shakespeare made him a sourcebook. *A Funny Thing Happened on the way to the Forum* begins with Menander, is retailed by Plautus and becomes a musical in New York, and then an English sitcom with Frankie Howerd. Woody Allen's films *Mighty Aphrodite* and *Melinda and Melinda* play on ancient tragedy *and* comedy.

Modern artists, such as Giorgio de Chirico, Picasso, Anthony Caro, Henry Moore, Michael Ayrton and countless epigoni, embellish, revitalize and vul-

---

[*] Aristotle's sniping pedantry led him to claim that the word "drama" derived from the Dorian *dran* (to act). The Attic equivalent was *prattein*. So? He added that not even comedy was an autochthonous Attic product, but originated in Boeotia. Is that why Aristophanes made a butt of the rustic Boeotian accent?

garize ancient themes. Even misunderstanding bears fruit: Freud's bourgeois Oedipus has no kingdom, and little connection with Sophocles, or even with Shelley's "Swell-Foot the Tyrant". The Freudian postulate of universal incestuous urges rescribed antique fears of miasma in order to unravel the guilts of modern analysands.

Great predecessors intimidate, and exasperate, even as they inspire: how many glorious monuments foster a furtive Herostratus, aching to destroy what he cannot create? Even Alexander the Great's burning of Cyrus the Great's capital, Persepolis, might be of this order: what cannot be matched can always be burned. Hitler (and Count Ciano) bombed with pleasure. Criticism too has its squadrons of hatchet men eager to do down what they can never match.

The classic trinity of Attic tragedians cast so heavy a shadow that no subsequent Greek playwrights shone as they did. The weight of precedent becomes crushing: Byron said he never read Shakespeare for fear of seeming derivative, yet his Venetian play *Marino Faliero* is manifest pastiche. "Free verse" was an early modern attempt to break step with the metrical tramp of tradition. "Bloody Mozart", said Kingsley Amis's lucky Jim Dixon: what else is there to say about those who have "said it all"?

The Mediterranean has long been a favourite setting for Anglo-Saxon attitudinizing and fancy-dress parades: from Byron to T.E. Lawrence, swish robes have their fans. Some English writers are never more at home than when abroad: only then do they come out in their true colours. Norman Douglas's *Old Calabria* – his dawdling account of a prolonged trek through the shank of southern Italy that once was Magna Graecia – seems to depict the peregrinations of a curious and solitary Englishman among colourful Latin natives (and scoundrelly Albanian immigrants). How many of his readers at home, in what Byron called "the tight little island", guessed from *Old Calabria* that Douglas was of the same mind, and appetite, as Strato in choosing a twelve-year-old boy as a travelling and sleeping companion?

Like Douglas, the Arnoldian curriculum was guardedly selective: more attention was paid to grammatical niceties than to the unchristian morals of pagan ancients. Schoolboys were sooner introduced to war than to love: the first Platonic dialogue in our curriculum was *Laches*, in which the eponymous protagonist, seconded by Nikias (whose sorry end must have been known to Plato's readers), offered his analysis of the concept of courage. There was cruel irony in their recruitment to the topic: although Laches was a successful general during the Athenians' preliminary involvement in Sicily in 427 (at the urgent invitation of Leontini, now the site of a pungent refinery for Libyan oil), his superior Nikias was, of course, to be the far-from-inspiring commander of the calamitous armada of 415. Understandably perhaps, their generalizations were regarded by cold-wartime schoolmasters as more salutary than Plato's *Symposium*, the story of a philosophical piss-up which takes for granted the charms, if not the superiority, of same-sex love ("The Real Thing", as camp theatricals used to call it).

As for Socrates' suggestion that the priestess Diotima* was a better authority on heterosexual love than anyone else, what sort of preparation was that for Christian marriage? No wonder that ancient eroticism was, for centuries, locked on a high shelf. That sort of thing was what abroad, and after school, was for. Yet it would be a sentimental error – hallowed by tendentious romantics such as Shelley – to imagine antiquity unguarded in sexual matters: Strato was wickedly outrageous, even for the Greek Anthology, but he too conceded that it was crossing the line to make passes at boys under twelve.

In Greek laws against personal assault, the charge of *hubris* covered sexual attacks on citizens. Slaves had to take their chances – meagre if they were attractive – of avoiding unwanted attention, but even they were protected, if not by law then by civilized custom: a gentleman was expected to control his behaviour towards them, at least when observed by his own class.

Nikias, the C.-in-C. of the Sicilian expedition, a rich and civilized man, derived his wealth, in large part, from mining rights and the leasing to others of slaves who were worked to death underground in hellish conditions. Household slaves were better treated, because more highly valued and trained. In general, however, as Aldo Schiavoni puts it, "the entire realm of labour was enclosed in a shell of ethical and cognitive indifference...nothing that happened there fell within the purview of reason and sensitivity". The banausic life was regarded as obscene. No ancient could have honoured (or understood) Camus's injunction, "*Il faut imaginer Sisyphe heureux*".

In ancient Rome, slaves such as Cicero's *amanuensis* Tiro (who lived to be a hundred years old) could become the intimate friends of their masters, and were often freed by them, if only in their wills. Yet no one ever repealed the *senatus consultum Silanianum*, whereby if a master was killed by one of his slaves, all the slaves in his household had also to be put to death. It was invoked after the murder of the senator Pedanius Secundus in A.D. 61. Although – in a rare show of outraged solidarity – the Roman plebs rioted at the decision, the sentence was carried out on hundreds of Pedanius's slaves, including women and children. Delation was a duty among slaves, which later made slaves of senators, who were expected to tell the emperor of any plot which might threaten him. Ovid's failure to be a sneak led to his elegantly, and lengthily, lamented exile.

---

* With pre-Victorian reticence, Lemprière calls her "a woman of great literary eminence [who] gave lectures on philosophy".

55 When Greek
met younger Greek.

The temptation to derive a licence for homoeroticism from the Greeks is a generalization from limited precedents. How many modern moralists give slavery a retrospective nod because the Greeks saw nothing wrong in it? In any case, the Athenians never regarded homoeroticism as a durable life-style; they disqualified adult passive lovers from politics and never regarded same-sex liaisons as anything like marriages. Even between the *erastes* (mature lover) and the *eromenos* (his juvenile beloved) there were quasi-ritual limits. The essence of the relationship was that it was, in principle at least, inhibited. The *erastes* had to impress by his mature wit and wisdom, and the *eromenos* proved his quality by taking as much and giving as little as possible. The convention of intercrural sex, by which the lover procured relief without penetration, allowed the pleasure of the older without requiring the disgrace of the younger man. Xenophon's *Symposium* insists that a well brought-up *eromenos* was expected to regard his adult *erastes* with coldness. Paedophilia had no acknowledged open season: only authorized persons were allowed in school grounds out of respectable hours. Severe laws were enacted against men who prowled boys' dormitories at night. Sex was hardly less ritualized than warfare, with which it shared a vocabulary.

The gods were not blessed with moral scruples, nor did their bad behaviour bring punitive consequences, unless they acted *ultra vires*, as when Hephaestus tried to have sex with Athene. When Zeus, in the form of a swooping eagle, abducted Ganymede (whose name means "rejoicing in his own sexiness") from Troy, where his father was king, the boy quite literally went up in the world: he became the divine golden bowl-bearer on Mount Olympus.

Kenneth McLeish reminds us that Goethe followed Zeus in watering down Ganymede's role. Ignoring the homosexual aspect, he wrote a poem in which the boy's literal rapture by Zeus leads to his being "engulfed in and united with the Divine". Like Zeus, Goethe is said to have been intimate with both female and male lovers. An odd statue in the Vatican museum shows Ganymede as a big lad and Zeus as a small eagle very unlikely to be able to lift him. By contrast, a mosaic in the Roman villa at Bignor has an eagle bigger than its Ganymede, who looks unappetizingly mature for a catamite.

Jealous as usual, Hera did not look kindly on the new domestic help, not least because the boy had supplanted her daughter, Hebe. Zeus was sufficiently irritated, Graves says, to put Ganymede among the stars, as Aquarius the water-carrier. One can imagine Zeus saying to Hera, "Happier now?"

* * *

The distrust, and repression, of women in antiquity has had all manner of interpretations. Treachery is the mark both of Eve and of Helen: bad women abound in the mythologies of Greeks and Jews, though the latter had Deborah to match Delilah. Greek women (like Muslim) won marks for meekness: Perikles advised Athenian females to abate their griefs over the war dead. Perhaps he feared a peace movement of the kind which the mothers of the *desaparecidos* organized in the Junta's Argentina.

56 Achilles' way to treat an Amazon lady.

Mythologically, the strength and daring of the Amazons were somewhat admired, but more generally feared. It has been argued, and at length, that female deities dominated palaeolithic and neolithic society. Some Cycladic figures are read as bird-goddesses: the stork, for instance, who Nanny used to say left babies under gooseberry bushes, was the bringer of spring. Caves, such as the one in which Zeus was born, were the wombs of the Mother Goddess. The moon, so Anne Baring and Jules Cashford maintain, was

> the central image of the sacred to...early people because, in its dual rhythm of constancy and change...its perpetual return to its own beginnings, it unified what had apparently been broken asunder...the moon, in all mythologies up to the Iron Age, was regarded as one of the supreme images of the Goddess, the unifying Mother of All.

The cycles of the moon chimed with the ancient lack of any faith in Progress: that things continued to turn over, in seasonal regularity, was to have a life as good as free Greeks and Romans could well imagine. Even Plato's ideal state could, logically, have no better future to look forward to: perfection is, by definition, hopeless.

It is tempting to speculate whether the recurrent cycles of the moon influenced the evolution of language: fulfilled expectation leads to the utility of the future tense. In similar fashion, families and group activities (harvesting, hunting and war) sponsor the plural. The first person singular fits the case of those driven by heroic desire for distinction.

The copious scholarly interpretation of pottery and sculpture, which supplies a "text" (a weave of material), echoes the taking of omens from entrails. Seeking evidence for their notion of the pre-eminence of the Magna Mater, Baring and Cashford see the lionesses over the entrance gate at Mycenae as the familiars of the Great Goddess, on whose central pillar they plant their paws. If true, this lends underlying force, and irony, to the drama which mythology and, more particularly, Aeschylus sited in the city. Elektra is a pivotal figure here, the daughter who, by becoming, like Athene, "strong for the father", is at once a symbol of female loyalty and – on a feminist reading – the betrayer of her mother and the primacy of her sex.

The mysterious grandeur of Klytemnestra draws on the divinity under whose emblem, we are promised, Agamemnon marched out to war. The sacrifice of Elektra's sister, Iphigeneia, was necessary to procure the favourable wind which would blow the Greek fleet to Troy. The innocent female has to be slaughtered to take the men to their war.

In the ancient world women not infrequently stand for peace and men for war. In Aristophanes' *Lysistrata*, Athenian wives go on a sex strike, refusing their favours to their men until the war is brought to an end. Would the plot have amused its audience if Greek men were as happy (or happier) having sex with each other as with women? *Lysistrata* is hardly a documentary, but the lack of recourse to same-sex sex in order to break the female strike suggests that "homosexuality" was, at the least, not plot-threatening. Or was that a male-bonded part of the joke? In any case, the play must have drawn uneasy laughter from an Athenian audience that, in the midst of the Peloponnesian War, had good reason to fear that the women were right.

Greeks and Romans might depict females as feeble men, scarcely better than child-bearing children (Aeschylus calls them the furrow in which the seed is set), yet they were also – most memorably in tragedy – somehow more adult and sometimes, like Medea, more powerful than the men who abused, enslaved and murdered them. At the junction of Roman myth and history, the

Sabine women who, after their rape, have borne children to the Romans run imploringly between the ranks of the Romans and Sabines, as they are about to resume battle, and procure their peaceful fusion.

The dread of women is, in part, the dread that what they represent is a lost, paradisal, matriarchal time when war was unthinkable. Eve, like Pandora, is accused of bringing trouble to mankind because, in some vestigial way, she is the source of what man has bloodied. The suspicions loaded on females are the projection of male bloody-mindedness. Like the penalized Phrynichus, she reminds men of the gory shambles for which the male sex is responsible. Euripides' caustic genius lies in his insistence on the enforced innocence of the defeated and defiled.

The celebration of the Mysteries at Eleusis, of which nothing could be revealed in public, were in honour of Kore/Persephone and of Demeter, the Mother Goddess who at least kept a seat among the Olympians after the reshuffle which put Zeus at their head. The rite was one of purification and rebirth. What could be reborn annually, like Persephone herself, could also prime the Orphic hope of eternal rebirth, at least for "baptized" initiates.

"Veneration" has a female etymology (from the Latin Venus) which hints at prolonged male apprehension of what they still somehow fear: the primal power of the sex they have devalued. In his Funeral Oration, Perikles licensed the mothers and widows of the fallen to weep only in private, and then briefly. He himself remained resolutely phlegmatic over the death of his own legitimate children in the plague, but did finally break down at the loss of the last. Only then did he ask that his son – also a Perikles – by Aspasia be admitted to full citizenship. As we shall see, this turned out to be another answered prayer with cruelly ironic consequences.

An excess of loud lamentation publicized the pain, not the glory, of war. Spartan women traditionally said goodbye to the warriors with the admonition that they should come back "with their shields or on them": mothers and wives had to endorse the male ethos and deny their own instincts. In the First World War, patriotic women distributed white feathers to men whom they suspected of malingering, thus proving what men they were.

René Girard interprets war as a mimetic male response to the bloody creativity of women, symbolized by the flux of menstruation, which modern slang degrades into "the curse". Warriors kill each other in a bloody parody of life-giving childbirth: women bring life, men death. The glorification of fertility has been interpreted, at length, by anthropologists as typical of female-dominated societies with matrilineal succession, and female deities. When the warrior cult trumped peaceful agriculture (gardening is still a favourite female province), spear-bearing kings favoured killer gods and matriarchy was supplanted by the reign of strong men: the incursive Dorians brought phallocratic Zeus in their bloody wake. Modern business promotes women into men's offices and encourages in them the unisex ruthlessness of those who hire and fire. Women are now said to fuck men, a usage without sense in ancient Greek metaphor (although the Amazons, to fill their ranks, did recruit males as unenfranchised semen donors).

* * *

*T*he long fear of what women are doing when men cannot see them can be, and has been, read in a number of ways. Zeus's first wife was not Hera but *Metis*, goddess of cunning intelligence. She was such a headache that he dared not let her out of his sight and swallowed her so that he could always be sure where she was. He then had a famous headache himself, which turned out to be an ectopic pregnancy, cured only when his cranium was trepanned (with an axe) and the "motherless" Athene released. Since her defining quality was virginity (and owlish wit), she was immune to seduction: her heart belonged irredeemably to daddy. Freudians see Athene's aegis as a sublimation of her intimidatingly immaculate genitals (by the same token, Medusa's head is a displacement upwards of her *aischra**). Aphrodite, by contrast, was deep-breasted and well-hipped, though, curiously enough, while nude male statues displayed pubic hair, female never did. Aphrodite was promiscuous, touchy and delightful, but not markedly clever: outwitted by her husband, she and Ares, not the brightest of the gods, were trapped in bed together, under a golden net. The sight provoked more laughter than disapproval. Sexual morality became a divine hang-up only with the advent of a full-time professional clergy with a repressive warrant.

When Zeus swallowed his wife's cult and style into his own, it was not out of character: he came of cannibal stock. His father, Kronos, took family planning to the point of breakfasting on his own newborn children: a prophecy had foretold that one of them would unseat him. Families were sources more of power than of affection (Hesiod warns of how long a man may have to work to leave enough to avoid quarrels among several sons). Oracles were grim with warnings of what children would do to their parents; and myth made sour comedy of the latter's attempts to sidestep fate, without incurring the miasma

---

* The female genitals – "That Obscure Object of Desire" in Luis Buñuel's film – excite dread and appetite. The mystery of the female is that what is concealed has no form. In *Basic Instinct*, Sharon Stone fascinates her interrogators by hiding *nothing* under her skirt. Nothing is seen as a rare form of something.

of killing their own progeny. Exposure was a favourite means, which – in the case of Oedipus, among others – allowed oracles to have the last, tragic laugh; easier laughs were procured by comic plots which could also be sprung by the rediscovery of long-lost kin.

The gods were less squeamish: immortals could neither bequeath nor inherit, only usurp. In deposing his father, Ouranos (the Sky-God), Kronos castrated him with an adamantine sickle. The last spurt of Ouranos's sperm fell into the sea, and from the froth came Aphrodite (*aphros* meant foam). Kronos's wife Rhea "suffered terrible grief", Hesiod says, as her babies were consumed by their father, who feared a filial *coup* similar to his own. When Zeus was born, she handed over a stone, wrapped in swaddling clothes, for her husband/brother to swallow. Anthropologists claim that this was a "thunder-stone", a foretaste of Zeus the thunderer. The godling was secreted in the womb-like cave of Psikhro, high above today's many windmills on the Cretan plain of Lasithi. His cries were drowned by the babysitting Curetes, who clashed spears on their shields in what one scholar identified as a "bee dance". Fed on honey supplied by Melisseus, the bee-man, baby Zeus grew up with divine speed (the third-century poet Aratos, of Sicyon, whose *Phaenomena* made him, for a while, almost as famous as Homer, says that Zeus matured within a year). The Curetes accompanied Herakles to Olympia when he founded the Games, in which they were also-rans.

As a youth, Zeus contrived to become his father's cup-bearer. In haste to consume Zeus's older siblings, Kronos had gobbled them whole. Hence, after draining a concoction of nectar mixed with emetics, the cannibal father vomited up Zeus's five brothers and sisters intact (the Zeus-stone became, it was said, the sacred *omphalos* at Delphi). With Kronos forced into retirement, Zeus's siblings made common cause with their younger – but always senior – brother in repressing a counter-*coup* by the Titans and kindred semi-deities left over from the previous reign.

Rhea earned small gratitude for her maternal grace. Whether her son banished his parents to Hades or, more filially, sent them off to preside over some distant Eden, Rhea remains a feminist icon: the all-loving Great Mother, treacherously displaced by the spiteful male. By the fluke of a wholly English anagram, Rhea can be reshuffled into Hera, the goddess who became Zeus's hard-done-by wife. Was Hera older than her husband and, in "fact", a revision of the Great Mother? Certainly she had a (wooden) temple at Olympia before her husband's edifice overshadowed it. Zeus's eviction of Kronos warned him against allowing anyone ever to be in a position to depose him. Polytheism did not rule out autocracy: the Olympians might be a consortium of divinities, but Zeus – the original voice of thunder – meant to stay on top.

*D*emocratic politicians had much less stable leases. In Athens, the generals were eligible for re-selection, but not the *archontes* (who, after 487, were chosen by lot). The latter were venerable magistrates, headed by the *archon basileus*, a vestige of the ancient kings of Athens who may once have impersonated the *eniautos daimon*, the "spirit of the year" which had to be renewed each spring, by the death of one king and the rise of another. Jane Harrison, the Cambridge classicist (1850–1928), saw (however fancifully) the *eniautos daimon* fluttering in the corners of Greek iconography as a vestige of chthonic deities whose "delicate magic of life", in D.H. Lawrence's phrase, had been buried by the Olympian gods.

The autocratic Perikles became "Olympian" because of his military record: in his youth, he led many Athenian expeditions either to support colonies or to plunder tempting targets. The new, improved Parthenon was an advertisement of what his policies had done for Athens. I have never found it quite as marvellous as I expected when we first climbed the hot steps towards the Propylaea and bought fresh orange juice for ten drachmae.* The lonely Doric temple at Bassae, in Arcadia, is far more evocative.

In the fifth century, the Parthenon was at once temple, treasury and ostentatious proof of Athens' hegemony. It was guaranteed to exasperate the Spartans, who had contributed most to the decisive land victory at Plataea, a year after Salamis. Mary Beard compares Pheidias's relationship with Perikles to that of Albert Speer with Hitler. According to "Putzi" Hanfstaengl (Hitler's pianist), the Führer compared himself to Perikles "storming the Areopagus". We are promised that he had read about the Athenian leader in a volume entitled *Historische Charakterbilder* by one A.W. Grube. Beard also suspects the Spartans who defended the pass, and Greek liberty, at Thermopylae of having been "brainwashed" and "suicidal". Everything is something like everything else if you defy Euclid and stretch a point.

In about A.D. 600, the Parthenon was converted to the Church of the Virgin Mary. Its Christian phase lasted longer than its pagan pride. After the Turks conquered Greece, the church doubled as mosque and ammunition dump. When the Venetians scored a direct hit, in 1687, they shattered and scattered a unique monument, but failed to dislodge the Ottoman *Tourkocratia*. It was almost another century and a half before Byron and other selfless philhellenes helped the Greeks – keener on cash than on nostalgia – to create an

---

* A unit of currency based, etymologically, on the amount a man could squeeze in his fist. Hence making money "hand over fist"?

independent modern state, its vanity still overhung by the crippled shadow of the Parthenon.

Greeks have been steadily haunted by heroic pasts: they always believed in better yesterdays, and dubious tomorrows. Constantine Cavafy was never more Greek than when he advised against lying awake, worrying about what might happen tomorrow. It will almost certainly not happen, he promised. Something much worse will.

Like the Jews, Greeks looked back at a primal flood (dated by the Parian Marble – a third century B.C. engraved gazeteer – at the equivalent of 1531 B.C.), which only their own Noah, Deucalion, was privileged to survive. He was tipped off by Prometheus about the flood which would swamp the Bronze Men, a mythical generation of pre-Olympian potentates, of whom Tantalus was first the ornament and then the shame. In the days when men and gods often sat down to table together, Tantalus – Zeus's bastard by a Titaness called Dione – had had dining rights with the gods. In the hope of feasting his Olympian guests on something more delicious even than their own ambrosia (of which he had stolen a taste), he diced his son, Pelops, and served him in a stew.

Perhaps Tantalus had not heard that Lycaon had already tried a similar recipe on Zeus and been turned into a wolf for his inhumanity. Prefiguring Freud's Wolf Man, Lycaon "civilised Arcadia and instituted the rule of Zeus Lycaeus; but angered Zeus by sacrificing a boy to him" (Graves). Is this another instance of a Greek gift that embarrassed a reformed recipient? When Tantalus had the Pelopian *plat de résistance* put on the table, all the gods except Demeter gagged at the sight and smell, but the Earth-Mother – distracted by anxiety over her missing daughter, Persephone – made a prompt meal of the shoulder.

On Zeus's orders, Pelops was reconstituted by Hermes, whose duties included escorting the dead to Hades. Even Zeus could not resuscitate a man without a dispensation from Clotho, the Spinner, one of the three sister Fates, *Moirai*, who Hesiod says were Zeus's daughters by his second wife Themis, the judge of fair measure. Clotho spun out the mortal coil. With her fiat, Hermes reheated the disjointed prince in the same pot in which he was stewed and so returned him to life. Repetition as a means of reversal is now routine in electronic control systems. Demeter supplied a prosthetic ivory shoulder to replace what she had already consumed. The renovated Pelops went on to do great things. The Peloponnese – said to be shaped like a shoulder-blade – became his island after he won Princess Hippodameia (the horse tamer), his prize in a winner-takes-all chariot race with her father, King Oenomaus of Pisa, the first roaring-drunk driver. His Pisa was a towerless hamlet near Olympia, where – in recorded time – the chariot race would be the sport of tyrants and of flash young men, Alcibiades the flashiest.

Like many heroes, Pelops had to be as devious as he was brave: he fixed the race by suborning the king's charioteer Myrtilus. In return for a promise of first go at the virgin princess, the latter substituted a wax plug for a vital axle bolt. When its heated acceleration melted the wax, a wheel came off Oenomaus's chariot. The king was killed in the crash. Treachery succeeded treachery when Pelops dumped the randy charioteer into the ocean before he could claim his reward: a quick exit is often the price of being a minor character (in *Of Gods and Men*, I made a film script of the episode).

Contests between suitors for the daughters of kings were common in myth. The Trojan War is only the supreme example of the genre. Love and war abrogate the rules of civility and honour. Helen alone remains fair as her suitors' armies fight it out in sight of the Scaean gate (it opens to the south in today's layered ruins). Helen – whom the chorus in Aeschylus call "Hell for men" – is duplicity incarnate: as the movie title put it, "The Girl Can't Help It".* She watches the battle alongside Priam, the wise old king who has the nobility not to blame his "daughter-in-law" for the ruin she is fated to bring on his city. Fathered on her mother, Leda, by Zeus himself, her beauty both victimizes others and is itself a victim: *eros* tears the fabric of friendship (between Paris and Menelaus) and destroys the honour of those who cannot resist infatuation, with all its implicit emptiness. Helen is real neither to herself nor to others. Her want of substance makes plausible the version of her c.v. that says that she never went to Troy, but was secreted in Egypt for the full ten years, while her lifelike shadow patronized the war.

During this time, back in Ithaka, symbolizing the virtue Helen lacks, Odysseus's wife Penelope resists the suitors that besiege her. Their impatient greed parodies the traditional contest for royal brides. Their importunities frustrated for twenty years by Penelope's promise to take her pick once she has finished the needlework (on her father-in-law Laertes' funeral shroud), which she unpicks, with furtive virtue, every night, the suitors are nailed when Odysseus returns.

Helen's mortal father was King Tyndareus of Sparta who, when she reached the right age, announced a pan-Hellenic competition for her hand. In the first half of the sixth century, Stesichorus – the *nom de plume* of one Teisias, who lived in Sicily – suggested that Tyndareus made the error of sacrificing to a number of gods, but (thus repeating Hippolytus's mistake) not to Aphrodite.

---

* The showbiz Helen was a dumb blonde played by Jayne Mansfield.

Affronted vanity led the goddess to turn his daughters, Helen, Klytemnestra and Timandra (who evidently never dated the A-list), into flagrant adulteresses.

When Helen's suitors arrive for the championship of which she is the prize, her (mortal) father makes them swear that if anyone ever abducts her, after her marriage, all will band together to retrieve her. The seeds of the Trojan War are set before she is even engaged to Menelaus. The image of seeding is particularly apt if the original Helen was a fertility goddess: if she made things grow bigger, the phallus was not the least of them. There is irony in the competition for a Helen who (if we buy this version) never went to Troy, since she was won in the first place by a prince who either did not dare or did not deign to enter the lists in person: Menelaus was represented by his big brother, Agamemnon, the king blessed by fortune with golden Mycenae and – since he was married to Klytemnestra – already Tyndareus's son-in-law.

Tyndareus's tactlessness towards Aphrodite also typified his attitude to mortals; having called together the Hellenic *jeunesse dorée* to compete for her hand, he announced that a deal had already been made for Helen to marry a man who never appeared on the start-line. Agamemnon had brought an offer which no dynast could refuse: the Atreidae and Tyndareus's own royal house would now share control of the Peloponnese. Achilles would have been seeded above even Menelaus, but he either disdained or feared to be a candidate. He was living "among the women" on Skyros, where his mother, Thetis, having heard from the oracle that her son would live either a long and obscure or a short and glorious life, hoped he would remain in unwarlike drag and speaking – like some brawny Tootsie – in female tones.

Modern meta-Marxists, unwilling to believe that the Greek alliance would have sailed to Troy solely to redeem the honour of a shameless woman, have argued that the "crusade" to redeem Helen must "really" have had a mercantile purpose. After all, the Athenians eventually lost their fleet in much the same region, at Aegospotami, in a vain effort, in 405, to keep open the trade routes to the wheat fields of southern Russia. The unromantic view sounds more hard-nosed, but it leans unduly on a dubious economic model. What evidence is there that the Trojans impeded Greek shipping in the Dardanelles? They may have taxed it, perhaps to the piratic point of confiscation, but could the indignation of this or that city, or shipowner, have mobilized the massive fleet enumerated in Homer's sonorous catalogue?

Paris's action was an undoubted crime: by breaching the rules of guest-friendship, he sullied not only Helen's honour but – more dangerously – that of the Atreidae. To fight a war to redeem a faithless wife may have seemed absurd to barbarians; for Greeks, not to have fought it would have been effeminate. Paris's breach of faith was tantamount to an offence against religion, a word

with no exact Greek equivalent. In Latin, its root meaning is "bounden duty": for Greeks and Romans, it was a matter less of – as modern cant puts it – deeply held "personal" beliefs (almost always taken from a specific and preconceived menu of doctrines) than of abiding by communally observed forms. Oaths kept things together; their breach tore Hellas and Troy apart.

The Greek fleet did not come, for the most part, from cities with commercial interest in the destruction of Troy. Achilles and Odysseus had no "patriotic" inclination to turn up at all. While Achilles hid among the women, Odysseus faked madness: what pressing economic reason did the king of a small island on the *west* of Greece have in fighting for the right of tax-free passage through the Dardanelles? When cornered and culled by Palamedes, Odysseus was obliged to keep his word because he had sworn he would, not because Ithaka's vital interests were at stake. George Thomson's claim that he was a feudal-style "vassal" of Agamemnon and owed military service in return for his fiefdom is a Marxist notion as plausible as it is an over-schematic anachronism.

Plato, in the *Phaedo*, described the myriad of Greek cities as being "grouped like frogs around a pond" (the Mediterranean and Black Sea coasts), but some frogs were a lot further from Troy than others. Ithaka neither needed grain, nor sought spoils, from so far away. Like Swift's Big-Endians, men fight, and die, for reasons which later seem absurd. Archaic Greeks are more likely to have gone to Troy because Tyndareus made Helen's suitors, and their families, swear an oath than to protect common economic interests. Economic "realism" never fully explains reality.

* * *

For better and for worse, the alliance of Helen and Menelaus was made on the hinge of mythical and historical time, during which Herodotus makes it clear that bride-contests continued to be held. In the early sixth century, Agariste – daughter of Cleisthenes, the unmythical tyrant of Sicyon (adjacent to Corinth on the north shore of the Peloponnese) – was the prize in a competition whose final event, after the gymnastics, was between the odds-on favourite, rich and famous Hippocleides, and Megacles, another well-heeled Athenian of the famously tainted Alcmaeonid family. The play-off involved singing and after-dinner speaking.

Hippocleides did not put enough water with his wine* and, in premature triumph, revealed himself to be heels-over-head in love with Agariste, the Bride-to-Beat-Them-All, by prancing acrobatically on the table, in an overenthusiastic Spartan routine. He went over the top when he stood on his hands and exhibited *ta aischra* (his shameful/ugly parts, otherwise known as *aidoia*) to the company: the shamefulness of the genitals did not begin with Christianity, which did not inhibit the twentieth-century (Communist) poet Yiannis Ritsos from writing, in his *Ismene*, a monologue featuring Antigone's unrebellious sister, "Oh, my sister decided everything with 'must' or 'mustn't'; / As if she was the herald of that future religion / Dividing the world: between what now is and what's to be, / Bisected the body and junked what lies below the belt."

The ancient opposite of *aischra* was *kallista* (most beautiful); Hippocleides' folly lay in showing how ugly he was, not how improper. Freud, a fervent Hellenist, followed Greek precedent when he assumed the ugliness of human genitalia, though Yahweh too admonished the young not to look upon the nakedness of the father: Noah's sons ceased to respect him after seeing him in a naked and drunken sprawl. Herodotus says that the Spartan king Cleomenes, notorious for going mad, began his decline when negotiating with the Scythians with whom he acquired the habit of taking wine without water. The Spartans used "Scythian fashion" to mean drinking wine "neat".

Since Hippocleides' display was enough to disqualify him, Agariste was awarded to Megacles. She later gave birth to the more famous Cleisthenes, who limited his acrobatics to setting the Athenian constitution on its head: he organized the democratic scheme which endured through his city's most glorious years. His grandfather – Cleisthenes the Sicyonian tyrant, who probably belonged to a pre-Dorian tribe – so hated neighbouring and Dorian Argos that he banned the *Iliad* from local recitals because Homer praised the Argives (Plato would ban Homer because the poet depicted the gods as immoral as well as immortal).

---

* Meleager wrote a charming little elegiac epigram in which he declares that the newborn Bacchus, fresh from the fire of Zeus's thunderbolt, was washed in water by the nymphs. Hence Bacchus (wine) is most amiable when mixed with water (the medium of the nymphs). Without it, you are swallowing fire.

It was no accident that both the finalists for Agariste's hand should be Athenians. Athens was the ally Sicyon needed against Argos. Love and war were never alien in dynastic calculation: the Dorian Peloponnesians would indeed be ranged against the Ionian Athenians (although the Spartans shared Cleisthenes' hatred of Argos). In the Peloponnesian War, Argos rallied, albeit ineffectively, to Athens. Its Homeric king was Diomedes (godlike cunning), but his diminished city resembled Thebes – a no less fertile mythological locus – in making decisions of fatal stupidity at key moments.

* * *

*H*aving been consigned to Hades, Tantalus was eternally frustrated in famished efforts to eat what seemed to be just in front him: as he leant forward, the food receded. With a wink at the legend of Damocles, a fanciful variant story has Tantalus at table with a huge rock suspended over his head. Fear deprives him of the capacity to swallow. Either way, he was transformed first into a figure of anguish and then into a figure of speech.

After their disgusting experience *chez* Tantalus, the gods ceased to dine with mortals. What could have inspired the half-Titan to offer a menu so self-destructively misconceived? His transgressive hospitality leaves a suspicion that an earlier race of anthropophagous deities were only too happy to trade rain for human veal. The Phoenicians' Baal, with whom the Jews' Yahweh had a famous duel, was a historic instance: the Phoenicians' colonists, the Carthaginians, regularly sacrificed infants (Flaubert's *Salammbô* dwells verbosely on the details). Could the habit of exposing unwanted infants, which some Hellenists have tried to rationalize as a form of post-birth control, have had its origins in placatory offerings to carnivorous gods? The Spartans threw unhealthy infants into a cleft in the earth, which recalls the pig sacrifices of the *Thesmophoria*. Fanciful anthropologists have read the Jewish habit of circumcision as a vestigial tribute to a god who once craved more than titbits. Did Yahweh revert to his old appetites when he zapped the first-born of Egypt?

Tantalus's crime, like Lycaon's, may have been to offer a menu *à l'ancienne*. René Girard has argued that repressed recipes for human sacrifice underlay much of what was encoded in political and liturgical ritual: all religions have dead men in their cargo. Animal blood was a late substitute for human, as the ram's was for Isaac's when Abraham was about to honour God's command by cutting his own son's throat.

Underworld gods never abated their appetite for blood: spilled life replenished theirs. In book XI of the *Odyssey*, the hero gains access to Hades only after filling a trench with fresh sacrificial blood in order to enliven the anaemic shades. In historical antiquity, selected domestic animals supplied surrogates for human beings, but myth constantly reverts to the bad old days, and ways. The carnivorous *Homo sapiens* is the descendant of *Homo necans*, for whom human sacrifice was, and – as terrorism proves – remains, a binding ceremony. When Artemis demanded Iphigeneia's blood as the price of a fair wind to Troy, Agamemnon's compliance was a prime instance of public duty discounting private sentiment. Aeschylus's chorus describes the scene:

> Father, priest, king, he prayed the prayers,
> Commanded attendants to swing her up,
> Like a goat, over the altar,
> Face down,
> A gag on her lovely lips
> In case she spoke ill-omened words,
> And cursed the royal house.
>
> Gagged, bound, silent,
> Saffron dress slipping to the ground,
> She cast piteous looks, arrows of grief,
> At the ministers of sacrifice.
> She knew them each by name.
> In her father's halls, she had sung to them
> In a pure, virgin, voice....

As with Abraham, so with Agamemnon, in some versions: in one, a hind was substituted by a squeamish Artemis for the innocent girl (as a ram was for Isaac). Iphigeneia was then spirited away to Tauris in the Crimea where – according to Stesichorus – she was immortalized. Dark elements, however, break through: in Tauris, some say, she was "forced to preside over human sacrifices". Among them was going to be her brother Orestes, with whom she managed to flee the scene.

The story of Iphigeneia serves to bear out Girard's conviction that human sacrifice is always behind the arras of myth, which both covers and draws attention to it. Iphigeneia's connection with such sacrifice is ambiguous: the victim becomes an executioner and, when immortalized by the goddess who demanded her death, becomes the object of a cult to which (Herodotus says) "the Taurians sacrifice shipwrecked men and captured Greeks". Among anthropological curiosities, the "turning" of Iphigeneia from innocent victim to demanding quasi-deity is a paradigm of the scapegoat mechanism: the sacrifice of an innocent victim is compensated by repeated enactments of *auto-da-fé*.

The original "injustice" may be an aetiological afterthought, a "plot-point" to warrant the regular practice of sacrificial killing: for the Aztecs, the demanding thirst of their gods required incessant wars so that it could be slaked with the blood of prisoners. The sincerity of the killers' "faith" is irrelevant: the Aztecs certainly cowed subject tribes by devotion to a religion which excused (and required) "state terrorism", but which came first – *raison d'état* or credulity – defies definitive answer. As for how so bestial a "civilization" could raise such sublime monuments and create Tenochtitlan, whose canals and gardens were said by Cortés's chroniclers to be "richer and more beautiful than Venice", the Greeks (and their gods) would hardly have understood the problem. Bloodshed procured beauty and confirmed majesty. Ancient Hellenes not infrequently slaughtered prisoners (as Achilles did at Patroklos's funeral games). Captives were also sold into slavery, along with their women and children. It could be argued that the institution of slavery substituted penal servitude for the death penalty. Throughout the history of war, high officials were more often ransomed, or exchanged, than ill used (in the Hundred Years War, such commerce was one of the purposes of fighting). The rank and file either died or could be put to hard labour. Even the current Geneva Convention allows for private soldiers to be assigned non-belligerent work; Officers and Gentlemen are spared such banausic degradation.

* * *

*A*fter being alerted by Zeus to the imminent deluge, Deucalion built a large chest, in which he and his wife Pyrrha spent nine days. When it grounded after the flood, in depopulated Thessaly, Hermes brought word for the couple to "throw their mother's bones over their shoulders", a gesture still practised, *in parvo*, by salt-spillers at superstitious tables. Since husband and wife had different mothers, they interpreted the order to refer to Mother Earth. Reading a heap of rocks, left by the flood, for nature's bone-yard, they followed Zeus's instructions. A new generation sprang from the stones, composed of men and women to whom – Zeus may have hoped – human sacrifice would be abhorrent.

After Deucalion had planted the oracle at Dodona, it was believed that the divine tree delivered Zeus's coded messages. Speaking doves were also rumoured to live in the branches. One of them warned off a woodman who was about to take his axe to the sacred timbers. The mythical Mopsus, who could understand birdsong, was a local resident. Birds – with their privileged access to the upper air – were plausible intermediaries with high-living gods

58 If you've got it, flaunt it. Gold oak-leaf cluster from a high-ranking Macedonian's tomb.

(and, in the case of Athene's familiar, the owl, retained divine charisma). In Aeschylus's *Agamemnon*, the priest-seer Kalchas takes the behaviour of eagles as a sign, literally from heaven. Aristophanes' *The Birds* was not a mere larky flight of fantasy, nor was Cloud-Cuckoo-Land entirely a joke: Aristophanes was harking back to divinities that flew higher than Olympus.

In Boeotia, oak trees were designated as suitable material for divine images by a critical crow, which was encouraged to make accessible choices by previous set-dressing in which lumps of boiled meat were appended to appropriate branches. When the bird had "spoken", the axe was applied with the assumption of divine approval. Inanimate nature often had a voice (and a soul) in myth. Before Jason sailed to Colchis with his company of heroic oarsmen, in search of the golden fleece, the crafty Athene inserted a branch from Zeus's oak tree at Dodona in the keel of the *Argo*. The vessel was then able to put in a wise word when Jason's pilot got lost.* What could be better placed to give inspired advice when a helmsman had to be replaced than a chip off Zeus's own block? George, the automatic pilot, has a rural family tree with *Gee-orgos*, the earth-worker, at its root. Stanley Kubrick's HAL, the sensitive computer in *2001*, is a modern mutation of Jason's talkative keel.

---

* In poem 4 Catullus's "garrulous" *phaselus* resembled *Argo* in having a versified voice of its own.

Ancient steersmen were liable to mishap: on his way from Troy to the foundation of Rome, Aeneas lost Palinurus, who fell asleep, and overboard, off the Calabrian cape which bears his name. No stranger to fallibility, Cyril Connolly made the drowned pilot his talisman: his book *Palinurus* put a literary wreath on his unquiet grave: *soma, sema*; tomb and tome.

According to one version of the Daedalus story, his son Icarus did not fall from the sky, but drowned while steering his skiff near the (still enticing) island of Ikareia. The rationalizers who claim that Daedalus never literally flew from Crete, but invented the sailing boat which, in coastguards' eyes, seemed to fly across the seas, also argue that, since he was said to have steered by the stars, mythical embroiderers came to depict the trickster as scaling the sky. The Hollywood/Jewish take on the Icarus story is by Mel Brooks: "If God had meant us to fly, He would have given us tickets".

A local variant, promoted by today's Icarians, is that his son lacked the ambition which led Daedalus to crave the company and favour of the powerful, in order to display his genius. When his boat capsized, Icarus swam ashore and made sure that his father did not find him. The local tourist board in Aghios Kirykos maintains that Icarus was so happy on his eponymous island that he lived a long, obscure and untalented life there. Since Daedalus was a restless fugitive for whom not even genius was enough (why else did he steal his clever nephew's ideas?), it would be a pretty irony if his inept son did indeed turn out to be a contented dullard.

59 Breughel's ploughman ignores low-flying Icarus.

Pieter Breughel preferred the aeronautic myth: he depicted Icarus's fatal splashdown in the strait which bears his name. An indifferent Dutch-looking ploughman is too busy aligning his furrow even to look up at a myth in the making. Icarus, the original high-flyer, retains a certain charisma. When we first went to Crete, and wanted to change our airline tickets, I was directed to IKAROS TRAVEL in the main street of Heraklion.

Knossos is an amazing site, and its back-story haunts the imagination, but the ground itself does not feel, as Byron said of Marathon, "hallowed" (would he say as much today as the jets from Venizelos airport scream low overhead?). The little frequented Minoan palace at Kato Zacro, at the eastern end of Crete, had a vestige of the old magic: I scratched the ground where we were picnicking and discovered a fragile bowl, which did not, I have to confess, survive being unearthed.

There is something stonily complacent about the palace of Knossos. Daedalus and his sly activities seem to have soured the place. Or did his departure rob it of its magic as well as its magician? Tripods conjured by Daedalus were said to be capable of three-legged races on their own. The Pythian priestess at Delphi was enstooled on a magic tripod (some Christian apologist claimed that the sacred nature of the tripod in ancient furniture was the triune prefiguration of the Trinity).

The Pythian crone chewed intoxicating laurel leaves and inhaled vapours arising from a cleft in her cavernous sanctum. Like some antique Miss Havisham, she was an old woman in girlish clothes. As she inhaled the god, her excitement was as incoherent as it seemed spontaneous. The counsel recommended to routine visitors was the Apolline line: *Meden agan* (Don't overdo it) and *Gnothi seauton* (Take a close look at yourself). Ancient sources attribute these two cracker mottoes to Solon, one of the original Seven Wise Men, who was wise enough to disclaim the first place among them. A couple of centuries later, Delphi declared Socrates "the wisest of the Greeks". With his notorious *eironeia* (less irony than mock modesty[*]), he attributed the compliment to his prudence in claiming to know nothing. How, some ask, did he know that he didn't? And what about that slave boy in Plato's *Meno* to whom Socrates proved that, in fact, he knew more than he knew?

As her fame increased, and visitors grew more illustrious, the Pythia's ravings were edited into intelligible, but cryptic, hexameters. The compositions of her secretariat grew more worldly, and elusive, as geopolitics impinged on the local and the sacred. Delphi's claim to be the navel of the world impressed barbarians as well as Hellenes. Herodotus says that Croesus

---

[*] Invited to review a philosophy book by C.E.M. Joad, a catchpenny contemporary, Bertrand Russell responded, "Modesty forbids".

several times sacrificed many hecatombs of beasts at the shrine.

It was natural that he, and the oracle itself, presumed that this would procure him preferential treatment from the Olympians. As every schoolboy used to know, Croesus was assured that if he crossed the Halys and attacked Persia he would "destroy a great empire". Vanity (and the favours he expected to have purchased from the god) inhibited him from suspecting that the destruction would be his own. Had he followed the Apolline precept of *Gnothi seauton*, he might have had second thoughts. But then he would not have been Croesus. "Character is (determines) fate", said Heracleitus, whose condensed, oracular Greek could just as well be interpreted to mean "Fate determines character".

Delphi's prediction to Croesus came to seem like veiled prescience, but its clairvoyance was a trick of language: heads the priestess was right, tails she was bound to be right again. If Croesus went into a zero-sum war with Cyrus the Great, reason ordained that one great empire was indeed certain to be destroyed. Logic and divination were secret cousins. As predictions became more elaborate, and more politically sensitive, the Delphic editorial board mediated between the impressive – but incoherent – ramblings of the priestess and the hopes of the postulant. The richer he was, the likelier they were to tell him what he wanted to hear: God and the big battalions are old allies.

Late in the sixth century, the Spartans were outraged to discover that the Eupatrid Athenian clan of the Alcmaeonids had bribed the priestess repeatedly to tell them to "liberate Athens", without mentioning that this meant promoting the political career of Cleisthenes after the collapse of the Peisistratids. King Cleomenes of Sparta had duly marched, in 510, to get rid of Hippias and clear the way, so Cleisthenes hoped, for his election.

Two years later, the conservative Isagoras was voted in as Athens' annual King Archon. Cleisthenes was no better a loser than Peisistratus's surviving son, Hippias (he had defected to the Persians, whose help he solicited to restore him). Cleisthenes now played the popular card by proposing, in Aristotle's words, "to give away the state to the *demos*". In response, Isagoras called on the Spartan king again to restore order in the reactionary interest, a task much more to his taste.

The *demos* rallied to Cleisthenes. Cleomenes' second visit proved a catastrophe. When he tried to abrogate even Solon's proto-democratic laws, he and his troops, along with *hoi peri* Isagoras, were blockaded on the Acropolis by the inflamed populace. They were eventually released to return, ignominiously, to Sparta, taking Isagoras with them (his followers were not so lucky). It is hardly surprising that the Spartans wondered how they had been lured, against their own cautious interests, into the Athenian hornets' nest. It was plausible, and convenient, and probably right, to accuse the Alcmaeonids of fixing the oracle. Sparta's tendency to superstitious credulity was, however, in no way abated by evidence that Apollo was on the take.

When Xerxes, the Persian King of Kings, invaded Greece in 480, his agents charmed, paid or intimidated the priestess into advising the Hellenes to yield. The nearest big city, Thebes, had already sided with the Persians. Theban leaders – from Oedipus and Pentheus until, but not including, Epaminondas – had a genius for disastrous decisions. While Delphi went public with a call for collaboration with Xerxes, it hedged its bet by surreptitious encouragement to Athenian and Spartan resistance.

Oracular ambiguity presaged the word games that logicians came to play. In his philosophical sports report of Achilles' race with the tortoise, Zeno the Eleatic seemed to prove, against all empirical odds, that the swift-footed Achilles could never catch a slower adversary. Since he had always to get to the point which the latter had just left, Achilles was always behind the tortoise, albeit less and less. The routine way for common sense to be redeemed (and Achilles declared the winner) is to argue that, although the distance of the race seems infinitely divisible, the track is in fact finite and Achilles will reach the tape ahead of the tortoise. The argument may be empirically valid, but it leaves logicians uneasy. In the Antalya museum, a statue of Apollo has the god's foot resting on a tortoise, as if to allow Achilles to make a winning dash for the line.

Zeno's arrow was also said to be unable to reach its target. Consider its flight as represented by a series of dotted lines, as it might be in a comic book, and it is always possible to imagine inserting one more line – one more place where the arrow might be – before it gets to its mark. As for actual arrows having the ability to reach their mark, an epigram of Callimachus has Menoetas of Lyctus dedicating his bow to the god with the words: "The bow of horn I give you, and the quiver, / To Serapis. The arrows are lodged in the men of Hesperis."

Zeno's paradoxical style was more impressive when applied to physical objects: after the fifth-century philosopher Democritus invented (that is, postulated) the atom, which he defined as the uncuttably smallest fragment of matter, modern physicists did indeed show – as Zeno might have guessed – that it could be split into infinitely smaller, and more potent, elements.

Oracles mystified by opaque declarations and sly wording: St Paul's "through a glass darkly" was all their method. Philosophers came to assume the same vatic style. While dispensing with divine sanction, they employed heightened and elusive language and – in the case of gurus such as Parmenides (Zeno's master), Empedocles, Heracleitus and Pythagoras –

affected quasi-oracular inspiration. Obscurity became the mark of the Masters. By saying and not saying what they meant, they gave generations of clerks opportunities to explain and elaborate their thinking. Pierre Hadot, for recent example, has conjured a fat, very interesting book, *Le Voile d'Isis*, from a single apophthegm of Heracleitus (number 69 in the canon): *He physis philei kruptesthai* (Nature loves to hide herself).

The notion of "meaning", as something to be teased from a text, like a trout from its stream, begins with reading omens. The archaic natural world was itself a three-dimensional text which had to be conned and interpreted. Human intelligence found significance in what might be shown, but was not said openly: Zeus's voice was thunder. Gods spoke, no less than moved, in a mysterious way. The Christian sermon affects to unpack the cryptic words of God's book, which is sufficiently deep, and obscure, for new conclusions – all of them tinted with ultimate truth – to be drawn perpetually from its deconstruction.

It is no surprise that Pindar, a native of Thebes, had a close relationship to the Pythian hierarchy. Born in 518, he combined clever flattery with Delphic intricacy. His speciality was epinician odes, the verbal fanfares commissioned by victors at the Olympic and other games. Pindar's tailored odes had something in common with that green blazer which is available to the winner of the US Masters golf championship almost as soon as he sinks the clinching putt. As if in apology to the Muse for his professionalism, Pindar ravelled his verses with an abstruseness that only Callimachus would match two hundred years later. His rented genius never went out of style: more than a century after the poet's death, when Alexander the Great was in a pitiless rage with the Thebans, whom he had crushed after their misguided rising against Macedonia, he gave the curtly prosaic epinician order for their entire city to be razed to the ground, but tipped his hat to poetry by ordering Pindar's house to be spared.

It was in the Greek interest for Delphi to retain its supranational repute. Since her office was both to gratify and to restrain barbarian potentates, the Pythia had to walk as delicately as the biblical King Agag when he picked his way between a rock and a hard place. Centuries later, that Christian oracle the Vatican had to adopt a similar gait. At the end of the Middle Ages, the purchasing of indulgences was as much an affront to Martin Luther as Delphic venality was to the Spartans. Papal pliancy, in allowing cash and clout to procure celestial preference, was in line with antique practice, and fiscal prudence. Sophisticated visitors came to Rome, as to Delphi, to pay homage which might yield practical dividends *ex cathedra*. The Pope's weighty Latin, like the Pythian's opaque sententiousness or Dodona's take-home leaves from the sacred tree, compensated pilgrims for their investment or displayed diplomatic *sophrosyne* in the face of military or economic *force majeure*. For notorious example, in October 1364 the Pope refused to sanction the arranged marriage of Edward III's fifth son, Edmund Langley, Earl of Cambridge, to Margaret daughter of Louis de Male, the most valuable heiress in Europe. Urban V denied what he might otherwise have allowed, in order to avoid the encirclement of the French. Margaret was later married to Charles V's brother, Philip, Duke of Burgundy, to whom she was even more closely related by blood than she was to Langley. Holy places and money-changers have rarely been strangers for very long.

The dosage of Delphic duplicity varied according to the importance of the suppliant and the narrowness of the odds. Just as Christendom would be, the Greek world was scissored by rivalries and hatred. Its barbarian neighbours, aggressive and superstitious, added vexatious variables to an already unstable equation. Forthright evasiveness was the Pythian priestess's enduring way of baffling, and entertaining, her clients. As Cavafy tells it, the defeat of easy expectation continued to be part of her duplicitous game:

> It didn't bother Nero when he heard
> The verdict of the Delphic oracle:
> "Seventy-three's a dangerous age."
> He had plenty of time to have his fun.
> Thirty is all he is. There's a long way
> To go on the lease the god has given....
>
> That's Nero's view. Meanwhile in Spain,
> Galba recruits, and trains, a secret army.
> He's getting on. Seventy-three years old.

In the slicker hotels in modern Delphi, naive visitors can still get a surprise: on the steep flank of Mount Parnassus, when you enter the lift at ground level and press the button for what would normally be a higher floor, it goes down. Did not the priestess draw surreptitious knowledge from the depths in order to serve the will of those above?

The wise snake slithers through the mythology of the eastern Mediterranean. Jane Harrison saw the Olympians as a fraternity of impostors, living on the secret wisdom of earthier gods whom they had repressed. The most impressive of the sixth-century terracottas in the Acropolis museum are of larger-than-life snakes (Mexican myth deified the Plumed Serpent). Familiar with the underworld, snakes were fundamental, chthonic forces: like

60 The snake that Apollo scotched at Delphi.

the Devil and Professor Moriarty, they had enviable powers, not least seeing in the dark. The clairvoyant Tiresias acquired *entrée* behind the scenes, both sexual and temporal, after killing a pair of coupling snakes. Belonging to no specific sex and to no specific time, the blind seer could then see it all.

Like clients of the oracle, modern celebrities sometimes turn to psychics to decide on the right career move. Credulity rules, and venality is its courtier: the advice given to the late Peter Sellers was inflected by his agent's surreptitious telephone calls to the star's stargazer. Newspapers still sell on the strength of plausible horoscopes: the elastication of language can make every glove fit. Modern oracles can be as sagely corrupt as Delphi: economic tipsters and financial journalists lean thumbs on the scales and profit from their own prophecies.

Even disinterested forecasts tend to validate themselves by prompting the very movements in the market which they have predicted, although Karl Popper pointed out that Monday's prediction that the stock market will rise on Wednesday will almost certainly refute itself: if believed, its publication on Monday ensures that prices will rise on Tuesday. "Markets go up and down," the cynics say, "but not necessarily in that order."

God and Mammon share the world to come: brokers, like oracles, deal in futures. As Philostratus put it, in the third century A.D., "...the gods perceive things in the future, ordinary people things in the present, but the wise perceive things about to happen". And if fools think they do, fortune-tellers (and fund managers) make their fortunes.

* * *

On the hinge of the sixth and fifth centuries, Heracleitus of Ephesus was the first secular oracle: he did and did not wish to be taken for a spokesman of the supreme deity who "wishes and does not wish to be known as Zeus". Two and a half millennia after Heracleitus, Wittgenstein's *Tractatus* echoed the Ephesian's trenchant obscurity. For Wittgenstein, philosophy was not an academic subject but a spiritual exercise: in his seminars, he distinguished between "tourists", impelled by idle curiosity, and true disciples. Only initiates were equipped to receive the Word and climb to wisdom up a ladder which they were then advised to throw down. Heracleitus's aphoristic style made similar demands that his listeners be complicit with its author.

The Master's followers and exegetes train for entry to a semi-sacerdotal fraternity. Difficulty of access lends cachet to discipleship: Pythagoras (who quit Samos for Croton in the middle of the sixth century) created a secret society, with probationers and initiates who had their own argot and passwords and a jealous allegiance to the Master; so did Zeno and Epicurus. Deviation entailed excommunication from the inner circle, a recurrent phenomenon in coteries: Freud excommunicated Jung, Stalin ice-axed Trotsky; Camus was dumped by Sartre, Friedrich Waisman by Wittgenstein.

Pythagoras was as interested in the diet of his philosophical freemasonry as in the square on the hypotenuse. He is said, by Aristoxenos (a snide fourth-century writer from Tarentum), to have introduced weights and measures, presumably in the days when he was a political power in mercantile Croton (from which he and his followers were evicted in 510). Contemporary with the Buddha, he too was a vegetarian and argued for the migration of souls: a duck, he might have agreed, could be somebody's mother. Pythagoras refrained from eating even kidney beans: their form reminded him of human embryos (or testicles).

Imitation of the Master's life-(and death-)style is a feature of philosophical *ascesis*, the intellectual exercises from which Christian asceticism (and *Imitatio Christi*) derived. Pythagoras's prestige was a product of his analysis of the fundamental harmonies of the world, and of how to remain in tune with them. A pioneer of applied mathematics, he made number the language of creation: his god (and Plato's) encrypted genetic formulae mathematically. Galileo worked on the same principle: his world was a book written in the unspeakable notation of mathematics. Later European philosophers turned words themselves into things which could yield cryptic, circumstantial truths: Hegel, Heidegger and Derrida broke language into pieces in order to derive "knowledge" from its entrails. The alleged universality of their intelligence sometimes founders by being based on untranslatable puns and *jeux de mots*.

Pythagoras's social ideas were somehow validated by his innovative numeracy. Yet there was, in truth, no logical connection between it and his dietetic and other doctrines. In much the same way, Bertrand Russell's (and A.N. Whitehead's) *Principia Mathematica* – a work so long and so difficult that Russell considered that only six people had ever read and understood it – provided the warrant of his general wisdom and lent lustre to moral and political ideas which he, or anyone, could as well have advanced without possessing the least mathematical genius.

Two centuries after Pythagoras, Epicurus began the modest tradition of cultivating one's garden. Voltaire endorsed it in *Candide* and exemplified it, without marked modesty, in his *château* at Verney. The modern cult of gardens, both real and televised, is a mutation of the Epicurean recipe for secluded contentment. Privileging friendship above passion, Epicurus embraced at least some slaves and women in his circle, of which the Bloomsbury group was a twentieth-century remake: elitism and egalitarianism marked both. Leonard Bast, the culture-loving oik who comes to a bookish end in E.M. Forster's *Howard's End*, exemplifies the charm and danger of emancipation from a lower class.

Never the sensualist that rumour made him, Epicurus was undogmatic, but sceptical, concerning the existence of the gods: even if there were any, he doubted that they would bother themselves with mortals. His views came to pique Christian zealots: he encouraged people to be happier on earth than was likely to be good for their eternal souls.

The Roman poet Lucretius began his *De rerum natura* – the greatest of all didactic poems – with the phrase "*Primum Graius homo*" (First of all, a Greek man...), a tribute to Epicurus's pioneering liberation of man from the fear of death and dread of the gods (scholars have preferred Virgil's evangelical imperialism to Lucretius's sonorous sincerity). Peter Green, with untypical animus, excoriates Epicureans for being proto-Stalinists, with a cult of the Great Leader and a rigid Party line from which members deviated at their peril. There is abiding charm, all the same, in Lucretius's vision of the world's natural variety being constituted from a limited palette of elements just as our vocabulary from the rearrangement of the few letters which form it.

* * *

Christianity has made the distinction between B.C. and A.D. – first codified by Dionysius Exiguus, a Scythian monk (or abbot) resident in Constantinople in the sixth century A.D. – the hinge on which the world's prospects turned, but there is a case for regarding the sixth century B.C. as cardinal: new ideas seem at that time to have blown into the Greek consciousness from many directions. In *Black Athena*, Martin Bernal insists that Hellenic culture itself originated elsewhere, in particular, Africa, from which much of it was siphoned and relabelled. He sees this process as beginning as early as 2000 B.C. His argument, based on linguistic evidence too specialized for amateur evaluation, has excited furious criticism, and voluminous retorts.

Since tradition puts Buddha's prime in the middle of the first millennium B.C., new influences (of various kinds) were undoubtedly generated, and soon went on their travels – as had Dionysus – from at least that early. Theological and linguistico-cultural transitions, and smuggling, clearly infected Hellas with ideas from elsewhere. Nevertheless, what is most remarkable in Greece belongs to the Greeks: the resource, and urge, to change themselves, and renew their arts, by experiment and criticism. Where else in the ancient world enjoyed free speech, and the witty use of it, in both politics and art?

Herodotus says that Thales of Miletus – with Solon, one of the original sixth-century list of Seven Sages – established his reputation by predicting the solar eclipse of, probably, 28th May 585. Since Thales had a theory that the world floated on water, his prediction cannot have owed much to his cosmology. The same eclipse brought peace between the Medes and Persians, who were later spoken of (by the Greeks) in one breath. At that time they were engaged in a war which had already lasted five years. Herodotus says that the eclipse occurred as they were engaging in another battle. Alarmed by what they took for an omen, they agreed to a reconciliation clinched by a royal marriage, a traditional way of binding both sides to their oaths. For added security, the contracting partners made shallow cuts in their arms, and licked each other's wounds (as in modern Bosnia). Those who do not trust each other often practise blood brotherhood. Hollywood bears hug; Judas kissed.

Thales left no written texts, but several theories are attributed to him, not least that water is the primal stuff (*arche*) of life. As for philosophy, it began, he said, in *thavma*, usually translated as "wonder" or "amazement" (in view of the number of students who once had to know this, it is a nice coincidence that Thales' father was called Exam-yes). In fact, *thavma* carries overtones of magic or trickery: like the gods it is full of, nature deceives as well as enchants.

However airy Thales' theories, the first meaning of *theorein* is to look, and then to consult an oracle. The oracle of the Milesians, at Didyma, was second only to Delphi. As in Hierapolis (today's Pammukale), a comatose priestess delivered Apollo's verdicts, George Thomson says, after inhaling "aqueous (sulphuretted?) gases". Does the primacy of water in Thales' "science" owe something to its locally magic powers? His ideas were, however, distinguished by close attention to nature. Plato, in the *Theaetetus*, tells of a Thracian serving girl who burst out laughing when she saw Thales walking along, nose in the air, so eager to construe the meaning of the stars that he fell into a well. More than two millennia later, Jean-Jacques Rousseau expressed his doubt whether man could ever know the truth by asking, "Are we doomed to die shackled to the head of a well in which the truth has concealed itself?" When we first lived on Ios all our water came from a well

61 Pompeian Plato at high table with fellow-dons.

which seemed reluctant to have it drawn. Spoilt by the facility of taps, we had to learn the last-minute twitch of the rope which tilted the too buoyant bucket for that first cool gulp.

Thales was a literal no less than a philosophical speculator: he made a fortune by securing a monopoly in olive-pressing. As Heracleitus would say, gold – like water – passes from one place to another and, like science itself, with no respect for man-made boundaries. Water too was a common (valuable) currency.

Thales' keynote observation, "The world is full of gods", was less theory than commonplace: language itself was god-ridden. When men spoke of Ares, it was not a metaphorical way of speaking about war; it *was* speaking about it: Alcaeus talks of warriors "mingling Ares with each other". The world became prosaic after the "invention" of history, on the hinge of the fifth century.

As for gods visiting the world of men, the myth of Baucis and Philemon exemplified that one never knew at what improbable moment gods might knock on the door. In the peasants' world, any unexpected visitor might be a "thief in the night". When Zeus and Hermes rapped at the humble peasants' door, the two gods – travelling incognito – were touched by the old couple's generous *philoxenia*. On departing, the divinities rewarded their hosts with a jug of inexhaustible wine (which prim Nathaniel Hawthorne turned into milk). Thales avoided scandalizing the pious, or the gods themselves, by questioning the existence of divinities. His physics discounted – but never denied – their practical interference in the world. Old gods never die; they become terms of speech. The village blacksmith in Ios had HEPHAISTOS on his doorpost, as if still franchised by the god of metalwork.

Like Bertrand Russell, Thales used his sage reputation to advance what he took to be dispassionate political views: he advocated federation to the Greek cities of Asia Minor, but they lacked his impartiality. Thales was taken to be a reader of sexual as well as of cosmic prospects: asked when a man should marry, he replied, "Young men not yet, old men not at all." Bertrand Russell did not take either of these hints.

* * *

Oracular and scriptural exegesis was the first form of literary criticism: close reading, and legal glosses, begin with scrutinizing the contract between man and god, not least when there is good reason – or pressing desire – to ignore its obvious meaning (what else are casuists and lawyers for?). In the decade between Darius's defeat at Marathon, in 490, and Xerxes' vengeful invasion, the Delphic oracle advised the Athenians to trust to their "wooden walls". This tersely reported instruction was by no means all the priestess had the wind to say. In fact, as Herodotus recalls, her text was plumped with florid, intimidating verbiage:

> Pallas (Athene) cannot appease Olympian Zeus,
> Begging him with fine phrases and smart advice.
> I tell you this again, in adamantine confidence.
> When all else is captured, so much as Cecrops holds
> And the recesses of god-haunted Cithaeron,
> The wall Zeus gives to Trito-born (Athene) is of wood,
> The one thing to keep you and your kin secure.
> Stay not for coming horsemen, and the march
> Of land-based hordes. Do not sit back: retreat,

Show them your back. One day you'll turn and fight.
Divine Salamis, you shall destroy the sons of women,
Either when Demeter sows or when she reaps.

A verbose message to send to a city on the verge of annihilation! Read in the light of later events, it appears less cryptic than its shortened form suggests. The last line is significantly imprecise about the timing of the big battle: autumn or spring. That the venue is stipulated as Salamis is either prescient or – more plausibly – smacks of a posteriori interpolation.

When the message was relayed to Athens, the conservatives, led by Aristeides, argued that Apollo was demanding that the Acropolis be fortified in archaic style: the bastion was originally reinforced like a laager, with wooden palisades. Obedience to the gods was more virtuous, and less risky, than innovation. Piety was not Aristeides' only motive: he and the rest of the aristocratic officer-class wanted Athens to invest its treasure in land forces, over which they could expect to exercise command. Aristeides' pugnacious younger opponent, Themistokles, was convinced that the terrestrial option would be disastrous. Still only in his forties during the *entre deux guerres*, Themistokles too was of ancient family, but his non-Athenian (Karian) mother led him to be regarded by Aristeides and his friends as "not one of us".

When the Colonels staged their *coup* in 1967, Eleni Vlachou, the Athenian newspaper owner, deplored their action less on political than on social grounds: they were, she said, "*agnostoi*" (unknowns). In the long run, this (and their incompetence) precipitated their fall: the rich and famous, whose interests they seemed to serve, had no links of friendship with the reactionary "revolutionaries". When the latter lost control of the ship of state, the old conservative class abandoned them without a sigh and called on one of their own – Konstantine Karamanlis, who had been in Parisian exile for eleven years – to take the tiller. When he received their summons, his first words are said to have been, "What kept you so long?" In accordance with *mee mnesikakein* (Karamanlis had good reason to wish people to forget the "Lambrakis affair", the basis of Costa-Gavras's memorable film, *Z*), he rechristened – some said whitewashed – his party "*Nea Demokratia*" (New Democracy). Like Solon, he was both patriot and a friend of the possessing class. When he had restored stability, he was again removed from power by those who remembered, and traded on, the miasma of Lambrakis's assassination. Their leader was Andreas Papandreou, to whose Socialist Party – led by Andreas's father, Giorgos – Lambrakis had belonged. Karamanlis was left to ruminate, as Themistokles' father had warned his son, on the ingratitude of democrats.

As for Themistokles in the 480s, fearing a charge of *asebeia* (sacrilege: literally, not-reverence), he dared not dismiss Apollo's words; instead, he reinterpreted them. By "wooden wall", he argued, the clever oracle was alluding to new ships on which Athenian salvation depended. Apollo, he concluded, was recommending a maritime policy. It also happened to be Themistokles' own. The debate was close-run, as the war would be, but Themistokles won the vote.

Did his ingenious interpretation* – which graced oracular verbosity with wit, and the Athenians with the brains to appreciate it – lead the voters to give the tense proceedings a theatrical twist? If the great days of tragedy were still to come, Athenians already appreciated *coups de théâtre*. The Athenians were flattered by Themistokles' confidence that they would follow his argument against the obvious reading, but they did not do so for frivolous reasons: if his wit enabled them to act against what Delphi proposed, while affecting to honour it, they would never have done so had they not approved his strategy. Mixed motives, and logics, are the heart of Greek morals; divinities, politics and art operated *ola mazee*, all together, as the (no less fractious) modern Greeks so often say.

In buying Themistokles' argument, the *demos* anticipated the palaeological principle of "*difficilior potius*". When ancient texts became rare and/or flawed, or miscopied, the business (and pride) of scholars was to reconstitute "corrupt" passages: those distorted by casual copyists or defaced by the accidents of time or the *parti pris* of moralists. The rule of *difficilior potius* advises preferring the more difficult reading in a variety of manuscripts (or conjectures). Lazy scribes were deemed more likely to have banalized a subtle manuscript than to have intruded inadvertent strokes of genius.

In the hands of scholars such as the Scaligers, Wilamowitz-Moellendorff and A.E. Housman, textual emendation was a sublime form of invisible mending: lacunae were filled with coherent wit, clever sense stitched back into ravaged material. Housman used the same test for having found the right reading as he did for recognizing poetry: the hairs on his neck bristled at the discovery of The Real Thing.** Housman never, of course, argued for horripila-

---

* Themistokles' reading was not unprecedented: in an earlier Delphic pronouncement the island of Siphnos is advised to "beware of a wooden ambush and a red herald". Since all ships were painted red at the time, the nautical reference is unmistakable.
** This whimsical method, advocated by a scholar known to take no prisoners, infuriated F.R. Leavis, for whom literature needed the hard test of the common pursuit of good taste, marshalled by him.

62 Cnidos: Delphi decreed "As you were", and so it still is.

tion as a conclusive method of textual emendation: his hunches had to be sustained by scholarly argument. Nevertheless, a theory can (and often does)
precede the reasons that make it respectable as much in science as in scholarship; but intimate conviction has to be susceptible to public scrutiny and
sustained (if only later) by rational argument and evidence.

Although textual criticism and re-evaluations can be said to derive from
oracular interpretation, it is fanciful to insist, as anti-science polemicists do,
for whatever "spiritual" reasons, that scientific theories come from similar
erratic sources. Our oracles are to be read not in *Nature* but in *The Economist*
and in Treasury forecasts which weigh imponderables on Delphic scales.

The Pythian priestess could also be brief. When Cnidos (a thriving city in
Asia Minor – now offering spectacular, unfenced ruins – whose inhabitants
claimed descent from Sparta) planned literally to cut itself off from Lycia by
slicing a canal through the peninsula which separated it from the Karian/Lycian
mainland, the workmen had so many injuries – especially to their eyes,
Herodotus says – that the Cnidians asked the oracle what was impeding
progress. The Pythian's reply was indeed pithy: "Don't fence off the isthmus; and
don't dig. / Zeus would have made an island, if he'd wanted to." The Cnidians
abandoned their attempt to isolate themselves and surrendered to the Lycians.

In the fifth century A.D., after all pagan oracles were closed by imperial, Christian edict, the Church became the only voice of God. When the oracular role was digested by the Roman popes, their responses to vexing questions had, like Delphi's, to be alert to diplomatic pressures. In the words of a member of his Curia, one of the medieval popes was "resolved to be the lord and master of the world's game". He did it by becoming both player and referee, the role of the "a-political" down the ages. (That "a" in a-political is a vestige of the Greek "alpha privative" which negates the positive terms which follow it.)

Constantine the Great was the first to exact all the advantage in the world from the heavenly gift of infallibility. After the secular western Roman Empire collapsed, the popes combined mundane imperium (hence that triple crown) with mystic *réclame*. They derived their warrant from Jesus' remark, "Render unto Caesar the things that are Caesar's and unto God the things that are God's". Faced with a provocative dilemma, Jesus had the Delphic agility to put laurels on both its horns.

Some three centuries later, His reply was held to give an irrefutable nod to the convergence of Caesar and God in the person of the later Roman emperors. When the Roman Sovereign Pontiffs were called on to mediate between conflicting temporal powers in their segment of Christendom, their temporal domains and consequent worldliness (and the challenges to it), led quite fortuitously to the dis/integration of western society and made space for secularism (in French, *intégrisme* is used of Muslim fundamentalism). In the Greek world, the Byzantine emperors continued to combine spiritual and temporal power in their single theocratic persons. The consequence was social sclerosis.

* * *

*E*very observation about Greece leads backwards and forwards. Linear narration never embraces the whole intricate story. As in tragedy, whatever moment is chosen to begin, something has always happened before it (in tragedy, it is somebody's death). The official version hides things which vocabulary and dramatic form will reveal. What Zeus said was law, but he himself was not quite in at the creation, nor had he been its creator. Parricide, usurper, lecher and father of gods and men, he had had to defeat, repress or assimilate previous deities. He could neither countermand Fate (hence his need to ask a favour of the Fate Clotho, in the case of Pelops) nor contradict logic. Since Clotho doubled as a goddess of birth, and of rebirth (a common mimetic process in initiation ceremonies), her sanction was needed to procure the reconstitution of Pelops. Justice belonged to Zeus, but he still had to compromise with inescapable limiting forces.

St John's "In the beginning was the word" (*logos*) is a pagan sentiment: a fragment of Heracleitus's lost book *On Nature* begins, "Of this *logos* that is always true, people remain ignorant, both before and after hearing it". Heracleitus's "gospel" allowed the first principle to be ubiquitous, but – like Spinoza – made god and nature indistinguishable: they were different ways of speaking of the same primal fire. By saying that divine fire "wished and did not wish to be called Zeus", Heracleitus implied that the primordial stuff of creation* preceded Zeus. Zoroaster proclaimed fire as synonymous with his god, Mazda, after whom light bulbs were named.

The social conditions of Ionian Greeks – the nervous autonomy of their splendid, vulnerable cities – made inflexibility inadequate to human expression, and needs. Heracleitus's dictum *"Panta rei"* is always translated as "everything is in a state of flux", but "everything is on the run" is not a silly gloss: Ionians never had a settled life. Experience taught them to think as they were obliged to live, daringly. Where Thales had postulated water as the essential – no less unstable – ingredient of the world, Heracleitus substituted fire. By concluding that "War is the king and father of all things", he made fire-power the determinant, restless force in the world. The history of the West does little to refute him.

On the cusp between the Greek and the Persian/Egyptian spheres of influence, imagery and eloquence, the secular use of language was crucial to the survival, and the diplomacy, of the Ionians. Like the Phoenicians, they learned to be as duplicitous as their exposed condition required: it was in their part of the world that a Greek gift that was not a gift (*doron adoron*) undid the Trojans. Asia's Ionians had to be linguistically agile in order to say and not say what they really meant. Political necessity and geographic ambiguity (were they in Hellas or in Asia?) sponsored the rift between ritual conservatism – in which formulaic repetition was a religious duty – and *parrhesia*, the free speech on which Ionians and their blood brothers, the Athenians, prided themselves. Asiatic Ionia was to Attica, and its Ionian cities to Athens, as New England was to England.

Textual criticism became the literary continuation of political outspokenness. Our knowledge of ancient authors is a complex weave of original sources, quotations and commentaries. The dissection of Greek literature, by

---

* Heidegger made this nameless element exemplify "Being". His respect for pre-Socratic philosophy was due to the way in which a godless language seemed to speak through it. Language "thought" as science could not (and as Heidegger sometimes would not).

scholars and scholiasts, not only made it accessible but turned criticism into part of what it criticized: commentary thickened into the intricate banding which sustained the text. Descartes said, "The ivy cannot grow taller than the tree", but it can: Christian sermons are an extension of pagan close reading; in both, as in the Talmud, exegesis becomes more compendious, and haughtier, than its sources.

Free use of language loosened the Greek tongue to speak of "justice" abstracted from its supposed Olympian enforcer. Philosophers came to postulate a world order without unpredictable or dicey divinities. The new thinkers were advised to speak softly, to avoid charges of atheism by the uneducated majority, but – by a kind of moral atomism – their theories differentiated ideas into their component parts and sponsored scientific logic. Without Zeus's authority, Aristotle codified logical rules which not even Zeus could negate. Even now, God's omnipotence is expressed in what limits it: the logic of His own putative creation.

In Zeus's case, *Moira* (usually translated as Fate, but carrying implications of fair apportionment and hence of justice) prevented him from exceeding his discretionary bounds. Man is a free agent, but not all-powerful; gods are all-powerful, but not free agents. The game of theology is still played with formal pieces: how else can God be "forgiven" for Auschwitz? There is only so much that His self-imposed contract with man allows Him to do. Blame *Moira*.

Language mastered myth, but reason never killed it; it put it to work. Pindar talks of "tricking out myth with fancy elaborations". As the dramatists proved, myth was fun to play with, and elastic enough to stretch in various ways. It may fade, but it never dies, even when people cease to "believe" in it. Claude Lévi-Strauss claims that no version of myth is more "authentic" than another: for him, Freud's tendentious reading of the Oedipus myth is no less valid than Sophocles'. Even when no longer central, myth evolves and metastasizes. Like Lewis Carroll's Cheshire cat, it may lose its claws, but its smile lingers on.

A good deal of classical scholarship has contributed to, if not supplanted, the mythology of the ancient world. The sweetness and light of Romantic and Victorian fancy and the last century's plethora of anthropologico-Marxist, meta-Freudian, Jungian and (post-)structuralist re-visions have compiled or postulated a new ancient world which now seems truer than the dry material which more inhibited scholars glossed and explicated. How many scholarly readings of his religion, society and states of mind would an ancient Greek *redivivus* recognize as an undistorting mirror image of the world of Solon or Plato, Alcibiades or Alexander? What we mean by "ancient Greece" now includes much modern material.

The process of deconstructing its solemnities culminated in the so-called enigmas found in the Greek Anthology. For instance: "I killed my brother, and me my brother killed, but put it down to dad; / Our mother, after we died, the pair of us we killed." The answer is that "I" am Eteocles and my brother is Polyneices, the children of Oedipus and Jocasta. The brothers were doomed by their father's incest. And after their mutual slaughter, their mother committed suicide. Post-classical larkiness collapses tragedy into a riddle, which – as a solemn, initiatory quiz – contributed to an aspect of its original form. When the house-slave says, in *Agamemnon*, "The dead the living kill", Klytemnestra replies, "A riddle, but I can guess its meaning."

* * *

*I*rreverence, like superstition, was a long habit with the Greeks. Money, charm and wit were needed to furnish it with impunity. Alcibiades was the most flagrant instance of a man who seemed able to flout all the rules and remain charismatic. Unlike the sophists – rootless intellectuals who lived on their wits – Alcibiades (an Athenian with a Spartan name) was a major political player who did not hesitate to play both sides against the middle, which was always his favourite place on the public stage. Alcibiades almost won the Peloponnesian War for each side in turn, and very nearly got away with treachery to both. He was murdered by the Persians, in 404, probably at the joint instigation of the victorious Spartan general Lysander and of pro-Spartan Athenians who feared that Alcibiades' inexhaustible, two-faced effrontery might yet redeem the empire he had betrayed.

Back in 415, he sought sanctuary in Sparta after jumping ship on his way back from Sicily to face trial in Athens for *asebeia*. He earned his black broth (the unpalatable Spartan speciality) by giving his hosts excellent tactical advice: to send an experienced general to organize Syracusan resistance to the Athenian force, of which he had recently been a commander, and to fortify Dekeleia, inside Attica itself, in order to give fugitive Athenian slaves a place of refuge. The Spartans sent Gylippus to do the first job, and soon undertook the second.

There was irony in Greece's slave owners *par excellence* offering sanctuary to escapees. By 413, twenty thousand of them, mostly miners, had taken the bait (in cruel practice they were sold on, mainly to the Boeotians). Half a century earlier, the Spartans had panicked, at the revolt of their Messenian helots (who had fortified themselves on Mount Ithome), and begged Athens for aid. The aristocratic Cimon marched south with a force that was later sent packing, lest it exploit Sparta's weakness. If Athenians and Spartans differed in almost all regards, they were – *pace* Karl Popper – united in dread of servile insurrections. Long before the Spartans took Alcibiades' advice and established the "asylum" at Dekeleia, the Athenians had used the same tactic. Once Cleon had captured Sphacteria in 427, the Athenians fortified Pylos, which was near enough to the estates of Sparta's grandees to furnish a dangerous lure to fugitive helots. Whether, in the event, these escapees were any better treated by the Athenians than those who repaired to Dekeleia (and were sold on into slavery in Boeotia) is a moot point.

For all his facile versatility, Alcibiades found that Sparta, which disdained the soft arts (and fresh fish) of the Athenians, supplied a dull diet: a kind of porridge was its mortifying speciality. The visitor amused himself by seducing the wife of King Agis. When her husband took an unsmiling view of the liberty, Alcibiades packed his bags (or, more probably, had someone do it for him). The story is that the adulterers were caught because the earth moved, literally, during their lovemaking and they ran into the street to avoid being crushed by falling masonry.

However Agis saw it, it must have occurred to Alcibiades that he was playing Paris to King Agis's Menelaus. Agis's wife did not elope (or was given no chance to do so), but who knows if she imitated the belatedly repentant Helen of Spartan hagiography, who was still worshipped locally as a goddess?

Herodotus tells of a woman of Sparta who was very ugly as a child. Her nurse carried the baby daily to Helen's shrine, and prayed the goddess to alleviate its ugliness. One day, a woman appeared and stroked its head and declared that it would become the most beautiful woman in Sparta. She did, and was married to a prominent man. The Spartan king Ariston – childless after two marriages – coveted her, and gained her by a trick. She gave birth, before term, to a son, Demaratus. When he was king, Demaratus was suspected of not being of royal blood, but behaved very like Ariston when it came to grabbing the woman he wanted. He eventually disgraced himself by defecting to the Persians, whom he patronized rather as Guy Burgess did the Russians, when he turned his coat but continued to wear his Old Etonian tie.

Ten years after his Spartan dalliance, Alcibiades had not changed his ways. By then an exile in Persia, he almost certainly seduced a Persian official's wife. The barbarian was as unamused as Agis had been, but Alcibiades had no more coats to turn or places to run to. Did he manage a wry smile at having contrived himself so sexy and unforgettable an exit? Theatrical and handsome, he was the corrupt, irresistible and egotistic issue not only of Perikles' wardship, but also of the Achillean tradition. He was not far from Troy when he was murdered.

63 Alcibiades "at home in Sparta". But not for long.

Alcibiades grew up rich and irresistibly seductive. His only sexual rebuff, so he said, was by Socrates, who resolutely refused his advances. The ugliest man in Athens[*] had the moral finesse to decline a favour which few other men or women ever resisted. A master of the high life and of cutting corners, Alcibiades' genius lay in seeing life as a game (in this lies his modernity). Egotism banished patriotic cant; mutability disdained abiding partiality. His tactical vision was unclouded by parochial piety. The readiness with which he changed sides, and immediately saw matters from the perspective of those whom he had just been doing his best to destroy, made him a chess player to whom it mattered little whether he played with the black or with the white pieces: he cared only to be a grand master. During the Peloponnesian War, he came as close as a man well may to sitting simultaneously on both sides of the board. Provided he had the upper hand, he hardly cared which prevailed. Sincerity never touched him; stylishness was all. A man for whom only his own standards of vanity were high enough to be of concern, Alcibiades was a unique ancient Greek dandy.

His self-reliance mocked the state – *any* state – in which he happened to be; its loyalties and its morals might be exploited; but they were never respected. Being an Athenian with Spartan connections, he was immune to local fidelities. Plutarch's "chameleon", *mutatis mutandis* was all his style. He was perhaps[**] the one man who, in different circumstances, could have emulated Alexander the Great and united Greece in a predatory confederation against Persia. But could he ever have bothered to engineer anything so grandiose, or so collaborative? Alexander was energized to the point of fanaticism by doubts

---

[*] Socrates' image changed with time. As he came to impersonate the virtues of Athenian *paideia*, sculptors graced his *papposilenic* features with philosophic finesse. Alcibiades paid the price for his egotism by hardly being portrayed in Athens or anywhere else: Narcissus, however beautiful, leaves his self-image only on water. The epitome of the golden boy, Alcibiades was, by Attic standards, a remarkably big landowner. Yet his estate was only seventy acres, which suggests income from other sources as well.

[**] The use of "perhaps" by scholars (of whom I do not affect to be one) merits a monograph: what *ballon d'essai* has not been tethered to respectability by its affectations of tentativeness?

about his worth (like many obsessive achievers he was short); Alcibiades was made frivolous by his confidence in his own qualities.

Alcibiades was a strategic dilettante who enjoyed proposing schemes to those with nothing better to do than execute them. What could be more flattering than to have your strategy adopted without dirtying your hands? Like Byron, for whom seduction presented no problem, Alcibiades was never disposed to take men or women as seriously as they took themselves. He deceived others so easily because he never had to deceive himself. Even when he paid homage to the enchantingly ugly Socrates, there was narcissism in it: imagine, he implied, someone as pretty as I am being turned down by the Silenus-faced son of a bloody midwife.

Alcibiades embarrasses historians because, alone of Greeks in the Age of Perikles, he seems not quite to belong to his times, or to his city. What Thucydides regarded as the most significant of all wars appears to have been perceived as a sport by Alcibiades. Although, when in Athenian colours, he was an exacting collector of tribute debts (he racked a hundred talents from Halicarnassus), he was a *condottiere* who never needed money; applause and access to the top tables, and beds, were reward enough. His readiness to side with whoever gave him the best welcome made a joke of patriotism, not only between Greeks, but also between Hellas and Persia. He made a point of cultivating the satrap Tissaphernes, whose principal consultant he became after he fell out with the Spartans. He was then cynical, and self-seeking, enough to recommend that Persia dispense its financial favours to both Sparta and Athens, so that they should exhaust each other. It can be argued, and no doubt was, by Alcibiades, that the immediate result was that Tissaphernes reduced his subventions to Sparta and that, in truth, Alcibiades was being true, in his fashion, to the Athenian interest, once it had again become his own.

As Alcibiades saw it, war was a game whose participants lacked the wit to see what they had in common. The egotist is at once above the battle and a cool judge of the right move. Alcibiades embarrassed, impressed and alarmed the Athenians by being right more often than was good for him, or for them. As for Sparta, he served its cause no more loyally, but no less effectively, than that of the Athenians. Irreverence was his charm and his nemesis. It had made him the prime suspect in the affair that came to be known as the Profanation of the Mysteries.

This took place in 415, on the eve of the departure to Sicily of the expedition which Alcibiades himself had urged the Athenians to undertake, despite conservative misgivings. He appealed, as had Themistokles, to the gambling boldness of the *demos*. Alcibiades' arguments for his Big Idea combined audacity with shrewdness: if Syracuse could be forced into their camp, the chronic problem of the Athenians' grain supply would be solved. As it was, much of their city's vital imports had to come from the "bread basket" of the Black Sea coast. Transports were liable to interception by whatever ships – Spartan or Persian or hired by either – were prowling the Aegean or the Hellespont.

If Alcibiades saw himself as a second Themistokles, his Aristeides was Nikias, a similarly unimaginative, honourable and rich conservative, though he was not quite out of the top drawer: he was mocked because his father made oil-lamps (he may well have owned the factory). Invited to choose between Nikias's caution and Alcibiades' daring, the *demos* elected to prefer both. The alternatives were appointed joint commanders of an amphibious force which represented a huge – in the event, disastrous – investment both in manpower and in treasure. Nikias was as wary as Alcibiades was forceful: urgent only for compromise, he had been the diplomatic engineer of a treaty in 421 which had procured what turned out to be a brief outbreak of peace between Athens and Sparta. His money gave him almost as much influence as Alcibiades, but none of his flair.

The pragmatic merit of Athenian democracy was that it could supply trenchant decisions. Faced with choices, in policy and leadership, the people had first to decide, and then to honour their decisions: the voters were also the soldiers and sailors whom they committed to war. In the case of the Sicilian expedition, the *demos* put simultaneous trust in one man who advocated and in another who deplored it. Accelerator and brake were applied at the same time.

To make things worse, in the hope of making them better, a third general was drafted to supply a safety belt. Lamachus was a brave, experienced officer, but he had neither the strategic authority to overrule nor the social grace to reconcile his colleagues. Had Alcibiades been able to use all his energy and charm, not only with his fellow-commanders, but also with the troops, the expedition might have changed the flow of history: with Sicily conquered, or cowed, Athens would have been an abiding and unifying presence in southern Italy. She might then have done better than Pyrrhus in resisting, or forestalling, the expansion of Rome. Athens would, however, have had to recruit the whole of Hellas: only with a cohesion which they never achieved might the Hellenes have mustered the demographic resources to take lasting control of the Mediterranean, as the Romans would. In the early years of the Republic, the Romans too fought with their neighbours. Other Italians were at first subdued by force. Later, they were wooed by associate (and finally full) citizenship. All had the common goal of repelling or repressing the incursive Greeks and, later, the Carthaginians. This rewarding cause meant that, after Hannibal's defeat, the legions were rarely short of recruits.

Having committed themselves, the Athenians devoted more men and treasure to the fleet than even Alcibiades had expected. Hope and doubt combined to double the stakes. And then, just before the ships were due to sail, the city woke to find that a number of the ithyphallic images of Hermes, which were posted at the doors of most houses, had had their phalli wilfully snapped off. Whether or not they were responsible, such sacrilege might seem like a lark to Alcibiades and his set. To the less sophisticated, it was an affront to the gods. It was as if the phallic message, "Keep it up", had been impiously sabotaged. Who, then, had deliberately wished bad luck on the expedition? Since bad omens were the last thing that its principal advocate would want to bring on so risky a venture, why did Alcibiades and his friends become instant suspects? Such was the golden boy's reputation for outrageousness, and for indifference to popular beliefs, that the superstitious Nikias and his friends found willing ears for rumours implicating their political enemy. If innocent, Alcibiades had every reason to suspect Nikias of hiring *agents provocateurs* to damage the herms so that he could attribute the outrage to a well-known iconoclast (Xenophon described the young Alcibiades asking precociously cheeky questions of his guardian, Perikles).

A commission of inquiry was appointed, but since the departure of the fleet was imminent, it decided to pursue its inquiries in Alcibiades' absence. Pending a verdict, he retained his joint command. The Athenians were splitting their bets; and halving their chances. Unless indeed responsible for the outrage, Nikias had sound reason to regard Alcibiades less as a colleague than as an impious playboy. As for the latter, unless *he* was guilty, how should he perceive his fellow-general except as a devious hypocrite? Lamachus lacked the clout decisively to oppose, or support, either of his colleagues.

By their impetuous indecision, the Athenians helped to procure the disaster which the mutilation of the herms seemed, both then and in retrospect, to have presaged and deserved. The expedition sailed with the commanders, whose cohesion was always fragile, scarcely on speaking terms. The irony is that Hermes was the god of communication: people spoke to him and, it was said, he spoke back. In sacrifices, he was offered the tongue.

Soon after the fleet had reached Sicily, and found things little disposed to quick success, the commission arraigned Alcibiades, in his absence, on a charge not of damaging the herms – which is likely to have been engineered by Andocides, the leader of an ultra-conservative rural faction, in order to frame the urbane Alcibiades – but of a secondary, still capital, offence of having guyed the Eleusinian mysteries. A Roman socialite of similar aristocratic insolence, Publius Clodius – the rabble-rousing playboy brother of Catullus's Clodia – would be accused, some four centuries later, of desecrating the rites of the Bona Dea by dressing in drag and pretending to be one of the girls.

Since those who supported Alcibiades were the keenest to sail with him, public opinion at home (another form of nemesis) had been vested in senior citizens to whom his appeal was, to say the least, limited. The small-minded Andocides seems unlikely to have been in cahoots with the cosmopolitan Nikias. The latter had financial interests in Sicily and friends in Syracuse, who might be bribed to betray the city. Peter Green has suggested that Nikias's dithering, once the Athenians had landed in Sicily, was the function of a vain hope that he might anticipate the tactics of Philip of Macedon, who preferred to buy his enemies rather than to fight them. Philip's favourite form of siege warfare was to suborn a faction into opening the gates. He once remarked that he could always capture a city, provided there was a path wide enough for a donkey, its panniers loaded with gold, to be despatched to its gates.

After Alcibiades' conviction, a sacred ship – sailing on the gods' business – was sent with a warrant to arrest and escort the accused home. One did not have to be Alcibiades to conclude that discretion was the better part of patriotism, but who other than Alcibiades could have responded with such speed and elan? Having consented to go quietly when the warrant was served, he knew that if he was to save his neck he must never complete the homeward journey. For whatever reason – the casualness of the officers sent to arrest him or the exercise of his own rich charm – he was allowed to follow the sacred ship in his own. Since the convoy hugged the coast, in the habitual style of Greek mariners, Alcibiades soon found (or bought) an opportunity to jump ship on the coast of southern Italy. From there, he found easy passage to the one city where he could hope to receive an enthusiastic, if surprised, welcome: Sparta.

It is hard to excuse the Achillean egotism which impelled an Athenian general to put his intelligence at the service of the Spartans, but Alcibiades must have seen himself as matching betrayal with betrayal. However louche his morals, he would have had to be very drunk (which is possible) and very stupid (which is unlikely) to have been guilty as charged. His enemies, however, would not have been out of character if, possessed by envy and small-mindedness (typical of rural politicians), they sacrificed an expedition for which they had no stomach in order to destroy the one man who might have made it a success.

Alcibiades fascinates ancient writers, but not artists: like Venice's doge Marin Falier, his portrait was not in demand. Paul Cartledge has kindly informed me that there is a "wonderful late Roman mosaic" which depicts him, "back home" in Sparta. I doubt if its subject would think it a good likeness.

* * *

*T*he Athenian expeditionary force was left under the listless command of the last man who wanted to be on it. Before his death in 414, Lamachus did his best to generate the impetus for prompt action, but when a night attack on the crucial heights of Epipolae failed, by a small but fatal margin, the Athenians lost the initiative. Despite the arrival of reinforcements, they never regained it. Like the British at Gallipoli, they missed their early and only opportunity. What might have been a brilliant stroke turned into a protracted disaster. Had the Delphic oracle employed the same double-talking priestess who gulled Croesus, she might have told the Athenians, "If you send enough men and ships to Sicily, you will destroy a great armada".

Afflicted by pessimism and kidney trouble, Nikias resembled Louis-Napoleon at Sedan: gallantry led him to cling to command of a dispirited army which he might have served better by resigning. His superstitious reaction to an eclipse of the moon led him to postpone the retreat which, even *in extremis*, might have saved a considerable number of his men. After a disorderly scuttle, he was captured by the Syracusans and executed, just as he had hoped that Alcibiades would be. Those Athenians who had not been killed already, either in the futile battle to break out of the Great Harbour of Syracuse – which the Syracusans had blockaded with ships linked by a massive chain – or in the panic retreat across country, were herded into a suburban quarry where they died a parched death. It is now a touristic park, called the "*Latomia del Paradiso*".

Magnanimity was rarely a mark of ancient victors. The Syracusans' willingness to spare Athenian prisoners who could sing Euripides to them had an added irony in view of the fact that the city's magnificent theatre, which – if you stand tall on the top tier – overlooks the Great Harbour where the Athenians went down to defeat, had housed an early production of at least one of Aeschylus's plays: the Syracusans had almost certainly staged his *Persae* in which the triumph of Salamis was celebrated. The description of the Persian fleet's humiliation now applied to the Athenians, whose victory was described by the messenger in *Persae*:

> ...Ship after ship capsized;
> The sea was swamped with wreckage, corpses,
> The beaches, dunes, all piggy-backed with dead.
> Our ships broke ranks, tried one by one
> To slip the line. The Greeks, like fishermen
> With a haul of tunny netted and trapped,
> Stabbed, gaffed with snapped-off oars
> And broken spars, smashed, smashed, till all the sea

64 Today's "*Latomia del Paradiso*" in starker times.

Was one vast salty soup of shrieks and cries.
At last black night came down and hid the scene.
Disaster on disaster. I could take ten days,
And not tell all. Be sure of this: never before
Have so many thousands died on a single day.

In 480, as Xerxes was advancing into mainland Greece on the way to Salamis, Syracuse too had struck a great blow for Hellas: legend says that on the same day that Leonidas and his three hundred (minus one on sick leave with an eye infection and another involuntary absentee, who later hanged himself for shame) died at Thermopylae, Gelon the tyrant of Syracuse brought off an against-all-the-odds victory over the Carthaginians at Himera. Although it greatly outgrew its mother-city, Carthage was originally a Phoenician colony; hence Syracuse and Athens were both engaged, Greeks against barbarians, West against East, simultaneously: "*Même combat*", as the French say of coincidental allies.

There was a legendary umbilical tie between Syracuse and the Greek mainland. The river Alpheius – Coleridge's Alph the sacred river – was said to run from its source in the western Peloponnese, past the site of the Olympic

Games and under the Mediterranean, before bubbling up, fresh and magical, in the papyrus-fringed fountain of Arethusa on Ortygia, the promontory overlooking the Great Harbour of Syracuse. It has since been polluted with salt water as the result of an earthquake.

An anonymous epigrammatist in the Greek Anthology makes scabrous use of the legend that the Alpheius was "in love" with the famous fountain: "Keep away from Alpheius's mouth. He loves Arethusa's breast, / Plunging head first into the salty sea." The Greeks derided not only *cinaedi* (males who allowed themselves to be penetrated, often for money), but also those who enjoyed oral sex with men or women. Callimachus said, "I hate a lover who puts himself about. Catch me drinking / From a fountain. Everything that everybody does makes me throw up."

With its narrow front on the landward side, and its fine, sheltered harbour, Syracuse lent geographic encouragement to tyrants: its citadel was easy to defend – Daedalus-style – and, in view of its fertile hinterland, a competent ruler could hope to deliver the material success which reconciled the citizens to autocracy. Gelon was only one of a succession of Syracusan militaristic despots, but he resembled the popularly elected Themistokles in having the wit to add Odyssean *metis* to valour. He had needed both. His situation seemed desperate when the Carthaginians decided to crush him before he could present an even greater threat to their local hegemony. Gelon's chance came when his men captured a courier from Selinus whose despatches promised to reinforce the Carthaginian general, Hamilcar, with a squadron of cavalry. Gelon was outnumbered, but decided to attack the Carthaginians, although they were in a well-defended position, before their force grew stronger still.

Armed with secret intelligence, the Syracusan was able to plan a master stroke. He cloaked a squadron of his own cavalry to resemble the Selinuntine contingent and had them ride up, at first light, to the gates of Hamilcar's camp at Himera. When the disguised Syracusans called on the sleepy guards to open up, they did so.

In his vivid and closely argued account, Peter Green guesses that Gelon's men must also have been primed with the password. This may be a more elaborate excuse than necessary for the folly of Hamilcar's dozy squaddies. At all events, the Syracusan cavalry entered the camp, torched it, massacred the disorganized Carthaginians and, to cap their triumph, skewered Hamilcar before roasting him on the great fire which he had already had prepared for a holocaust of sheep and oxen.

Gelon and his Syracusans had won a victory decisive for the future of the Hellenes in Sicily. His descendants' victory over Nikias was no less decisive in making sure that the Athenians would never again dominate on the island.

Achillean egotism once more ruptured Greek unity: the cities, like the hero of the *Iliad*, always dreamed of their individual fame, which implied (and relished) the subjection of fellow-Hellenes. It is nice to read high-minded lamentations about violence, especially in tragedy (*Bia*, brute force, is a loutish enforcer in Aeschylus's *Prometheus Bound*), as conscientious objection to its use, but in practice it was rarely renounced, still less tempered by chivalry.

News of the fate of the Sicilian expedition, in which it had invested so much, was slow to reach Athens. Legend says that a traveller who had left his ship to have a shave in a barber's shop in the Piraeus happened to mention, as if it were common knowledge, that the Athenian fleet had been destroyed in the great harbour of Syracuse. The other customers dragged him out of his chair and, after he tried to run away, lynched him. It was a savagely prosaic instance of the crossover between theatrical tragedy and historic disaster. The messenger in Aeschylus's *Persae*, who brought news of the catastrophe at Salamis to Atossa, the Persian queen mother, was treated with more decorum.

Xenophon and Plato were only the most articulate of those who wished that Athens could be more like Sparta. We hear nothing of Spartans who admired Athens (unless jealousy is a warrant of admiration), but few lacked an appetite for the handsome silver *tetradrachm* or for the two-drachma *stater*, the reserve currency of the Athenian empire. The official Spartan coinage consisted only of non-negotiable iron bars. This used to be paraded as evidence of indifference to flashier forms of lucre, though Alcaeus quotes Aristomenes (a legendary Messenian hero in the eighth-century war against Sparta) as saying "shrewdly" that at Sparta "Money is the man, and no poor man is good or honourable". There was no shortage of wealth (based on the ownership of land) in classical Sparta; but it was not to be flaunted on parade. The Spartan education deprived the cadet warrior class of any domestic comfort, including warm clothing. The majority of recruits had to come from privileged homes, but they were denied the joy of them. If they wanted to raid the larder, it had to be somebody else's, and they had to endure the consequences if caught. The male sex's business was war, and war alone. Spartan self-denial was a tactical not a moral practice. If only for reasons of continuity, Spartan women could inherit and hold property.

Athenian enterprise and individuality might be alien to the official Spartan ethos, but one Spartan king after another, and their great general Lysander, was tempted by quasi-treasonous offshore opportunities. Out of range of supervision, Spartan kings and generals were rarely averse to golden opportunities. While on campaign against the Thessalians, in the 470s, Demaratus's enemy, King Leotychides, allowed himself to be bought off by the enemy. After being caught red-handed "sitting in his tent on a glove full of coins" (it was a

Persian gauntlet or possibly sleeve; certainly more commodious than the usual translation makes it sound), he was banished and his house destroyed.

Homer's Menelaus was the loud-mouthed king of a Mycenaean Sparta not yet subject to the austere Dorian regime which Lycurgus, that snappy (eighth-century?) wolf of a drill-sergeant, would impose on a previously arts-loving state. Paris's disrespect for his host mobilized, and united, the Achaeans. Sexual morals were neither here nor there; nor even, according to one view, was Helen herself: in his *Helena*, Euripides follows Stesichorus in making play with the myth that Paris abducted only an *eidolon*, a facsimile, as it were, a pin-up of Menelaus's queen. This echoed the trick devised by Zeus when he substituted a cloud for his wife Hera's body when she was forcefully proposi-tioned by Ixion, the Titan who got above himself.

In Euripides' take on the story, the flesh-and-blood Helen spent the ten years of the Trojan War hanging out in Egypt, whither her victorious husband – doubtless hoarse from a decade of loud war-crying – came, after seven more errant years, to collect her. Euripides does not quite have her say, "What kept you?", but *Helena* is so close to comedy that it questions Aristotle's (a posteri-ori) distinction between theatrical genres. Helen was the prototype of unreliable wives: the seventh-century poet Semonides of Amorgos supplied a bestiary of them, descended from various animals; in his jaundiced view, only the bee-like woman was a blessing to her husband.

* * *

While Trojans and Achaeans were fighting their zero-sum battle, the Olympian gods presided, contentiously, over both sides. Divine godfa-thers and godmothers favoured their heroes, or kin, and plotted the ruin of individual enemies, but not even Zeus could procure a victory for the Trojans, whose supporter he was (Hera wore the Greek colours and, as it were, the trousers).

The war was both ruthless and ritualized: when champions stepped forward, the Myrmidons and other extras abated their anonymous mutual slaughter to become a single audience for the main event, as Spartans and Argives did at the so-called Battle of the Champions (in 545), where the Spartan victory was evidence less of their superior prowess than of their smart (and apparently) convincing reinterpretation of the rules, which allowed them to claim the day on the "last man standing" principle; even though two Argives were still alive, they walked off the field, leaving one Spartan to claim victory.

In one of the *Iliad*'s great set pieces, Paris's peerless, uxorious brother Hector takes leave of his wife, Andromache, and of their infant son, Astyanax ("City-Lord", though he will die before he grows up). It is affecting to see Hector as a

65 Said to be Leonidas,
apparently on a good day.

civilized patriot, but he was no more disinclined to shed
blood than any other Homeric hero. Putting a brave face
on his prospects before the final bout with Achilles,
Hector prefigures Leonidas, the Spartan king who, in
480, defended Thermopylae knowing that he and his
three hundred Spartiates had been outflanked and must
die. Leonidas drew inspiration from his ancestor and role
model, Herakles, who died not far from where the
Spartans made their stand. The durability of what George
Seferis called "The Greek style" survives in Constantine
Cavafy's 1910 poem, *Thermopylae*:

> Honour to those who during their lives
> Stand firm and guard Thermopylae,
> Never flinching from their duty...
>
> And greater honour is owed to those
> Who foresee – and many do foresee –
> How Ephialtes will come in the end,
> And the Medes will eventually break through.

Only Greek and Hebrew literature sustain such cross-millennial continuities
of reference, respect and ruefulness.

Greek wars were often between people who knew each other well. Hatred
can be deeper for being fratricidal: there is sour evidence in Eteocles' speech
before going to battle, and death, against his equally doomed brother
Polyneices, in Aeschylus's *Seven Against Thebes*:

> From the moment he slipped from his mother's dark womb
> Through all his childhood, his growing up,
> Till the beard of manhood thickened on his chin,
> Not once did Justice say yes to him. And now
> He plots rape on Thebes. If Justice stands by,
> Says yes to this madness, she denies her name.
> So I believe.
> I'll face the man myself.
> Prince against prince, brother against brother,
> Enemy against enemy – who has more right than I?

In 480, Xerxes paused – on his way (so he hoped) to teach the Greeks a lesson – in order to make sacrifice at the ruins of Troy. It was as if he proposed to avenge its defeat as well as that of his father Darius, at Marathon ten years earlier. By implication, he was also casting himself as a central character in an ongoing Greek saga. There was, after all, nothing barbarian about Homer's Trojans. To speak of "the theatre of war" is a cliché with some truth in it: impersonation and rhetoric are part of both. Battles have audiences, and soldiers perform.

In the *Iliad*, the overarching community of heroic values is exemplified in the pity which the previously vindictive Achilles displays to Hector's old father, King Priam, when he comes to beg for the corpse which the Greek hero has mutilated and defiled. All passion spent, for a moment at least, the two of them consider life from a shared perspective, and are equally moved by it.

Art, said Turgenev, is one of the four things that unite men. Homer reconciles Priam and Achilles in a harmony both humane and poetic: the two men suit, and speak, Greek hexameters. If it is true that a lost Hittite epic also covered the Trojan War, one wonders whether its metrical scheme accommodated the same heroes, or its vocabulary accorded them the same qualities.

The ambivalence of the *Iliad* sets literary seed for Aeschylus's *Persae*, which – granted its Athenian partisanship – looks at the 480/479 war from a standpoint which recognizes the mortal frailty of both winners and losers. In the same tradition, Racine's play, *Alexandre le Grand*, makes a hero of the defeated Porus, the gallant Indian prince whom, in a rare spasm of sportsmanship, Alexander recruited as friend and satrap. The Trojans had been treated to no such *megalopsychia* on the part of the Greeks: once defeated, their city was razed, their women and children enslaved. Alexander usually followed the Homeric model. Much was made, in the Age of Imperialism, of the great man's chivalry towards Persian ladies of quality. Caesar extended the same courtesy (if that is what it was) to Cleopatra, and Titus, the slaughterer of the Jews, to the beautiful Jewess Berenice.

Although defeated, the Trojans were never disgraced. And when Aeneas takes his old father Anchises on his shoulders into exile, it is in the Greek tradition of going west, to found a new city. When Phocaea – a Greek city in Asia Minor – was besieged by the Persians in 540, most of the inhabitants decided to emigrate to southern Italy. There they established themselves in Elea, which became a prosperous, and philosophical, city. The Phocaeans were already famous colonizers: the French credit them with the founding of Marseille and of Nice (I first travelled to the latter city in a charabanc which bore the name *Phocéen Car*). Themistokles threatened to follow the Phocaeans when, before Salamis, he warned his vacillating Peloponnesian allies that unless they stood

66 Aeneas on the run: loses Troy, founds Rome.

firm with Athens, he would abandon Greece and decamp, with the entire Attic population, to Italy, or beyond, in order to build a new city in a safer spot.

To those defeated in war, flight was the only alternative to death or – if female or under age – to slavery. Aeneas was the most conspicuously successful ancient refugee. His enforced tour of the Mediterranean ended in Rome, which was fated to become a second, greater Troy. Aeneas's descendants would have the last word in the Trojan War when Sulla returned with an invincible army and, in 85 B.C., subjugated the empire of King Mithridates of Pontus. Mithridates should not be seen as an avenger of the outsiders against Rome (as Freud saw Hannibal), least of all was he the champion of *to hellenikon*. During his rebellion, he attacked and pillaged the island of Delos, which – with its lavish theatrical festivals – was a radiant, and accessible, beacon of Greco-Roman culture in the eastern Mediterranean (the largest, literal beacon was, of course, the Pharos of Alexandria).

Almost three hundred years before Sulla marched in, the wealth of the Fertile Crescent had lured Alexander to remedy Macedonia's near-bankruptcy by what affected to be a remake of the Trojan War. In practice, it was a pan-Hellenic coalition of the fairly willing, bent on raiding the Persian treasury.

The subsequent Hellenization of "Asia" meant that it developed into an even more tempting target for Roman generals, who rarely bothered to cook up myth-historical, still less moral, reasons for profitable depredations. Alexander's more or less honest attempt to concoct a homogeneous "nation" from disparate ingredients did not abate the now endemic instability of the region. The mass wedding at Susa, of Macedonians with Persian and oriental women, was publicized by the conqueror's propaganda machine as a practical symbol of the union of Greeks and Persians, but there was no reciprocal delivery of female Macedonians to Persian bridegrooms. The mass marriage was more like a cross between the showboating affairs mounted by the Reverend Moon and the baby factories set up by the SS in Hitler's Germany. Alexander hoped to be supplied with something like the Ottoman corps of Janissaries, whose sole allegiance (and hopes of preferment) would centre on him.

The imposition of an alien ruling class and culture contributed to the abiding tendency of the indigenous population to identify themselves by "race" and religion, rather than by any national allegiance. The Jews were exceptional in overestimating their potency, which led them into a series of rebellions. That of the Maccabees, against the Greco-Syrian king Antiochus Epiphanes, in 168, was unique in being other than disastrous. As so often, Jews were divided: this time, about the virtues of the victory of a Hellenizing faction, with its tendency to unorthodox open-mindedness. Modern Zionism excites similar hostility from Jewish traditionalists, as did the "reformist" followers of Jesus. Pauline Christianity responded by vilifying "the Jews" (by which it meant the Orthodox), who were accused of refusing the chance to join the big battalions when they were confronted with the Truth that could have made them free, not least of centuries of Christian persecution.

Jewish obstinacy was regularly accused of being responsible for failure to embrace Christianity. In A.D. 640, John Philoponus, a Syrian patriarch, had a conversation with the conqueror of Alexandria, Emir Amrou ben al-As, who was trying to make sense of the doctrine of the Trinity. Philoponus insisted that the Trinity failed to be mentioned in the Pentateuch (which was sacred to Muslims as well as Jews and Christians), not because it was not disclosed to Moses, who – as Muslims did not doubt – had had very long conversations with God at the summit of Sinai, but because it would have been unwise for him to publicize it: the people were still tempted by polytheism and might have been confused by so subtle a doctrine. The Emir was not convinced.

67 Alexander defeats Darius in round two, at the Issus, before final victory at Gaugamela.

According to Cicero, Chrysippus the Stoic read allegories of Stoicism into Hesiod and Homer, to whom it was as foreign as the Trinity to Judaism. Ritual and textual overlap is the badge of all our tribes: Hellenistic effusiveness embellished the language and iconography of Christianity in a way forbidden to the Jews, from whose number Jesus never excepted Himself. Christ Pantokrator came to be addressed with the verbal and literal prostration first required by Persian kings, and then appropriated by Alexander the Great and his successors.

Yahweh was no democrat, but there was a midrash according to which a Rabbinic assembly proceeded with its agenda before He arrived, and voted a law which He had intended to quash. He laughed and said, "My children have outvoted me". What element of the Christian God ever cracked that kind of a smile?

To debate Alexander's high purpose in attacking Persia begs the question of whether he had one. The justification of wars and conquests often come after the events: noble cause follows murderous effect. While canvassing the consequences of Alexander's appropriation of the Persian Empire, in terms of cities founded and thrones filled, it is easy to ignore the simultaneous orientalization of Hellenistic thought and morals.

By confounding *to hellenikon* – the Greek style – with Persian manners, and vice versa, a legacy of amalgamation *and* duplicity descended on the Levant and on Hellas: the art of war blended into the art of the deal; both were a matter of business, not of national salvation nor of the defence of liberty, as the Greeks could claim, and with cause, when Xerxes invaded in 480. What freedom was there to defend in the Hellenistic world? *Tyche* (good luck, the traders' justification) rather than *Dike* (old-style justice) became the dominant deity until the Roman emperors superimposed their own sun-godly cult. Fortuna, the romanized *Tyche*, continued to be a much solicited deity.

For Romans (as for classical Greeks) Asiatic morals were "effeminate" – what else could you expect of people who wore trousers? – and their style of limited warfare likewise. When Hannibal almost annihilated the Roman army at Cannae, he allowed his troops to rest in Hellenized Capua (which welcomed them with open gates) instead of marching at once on Rome. The Carthaginians, for all their ferocity, conducted their campaigns in the Hellenistic spirit: a defeated enemy was assumed to be ready to bargain for terms. Whatever his sworn hatred of the Romans, Hannibal could not easily imagine that they would elect to go on with a war that was clearly lost, and then win it.

The soldiers involved in Hellenistic wars were usually hired; though the best might be willing to give honest measure, few were inclined to die gallant deaths in battles once they seemed lost. Mercenaries might, as Housman put it in the fanciful epitaph he coined for them, save "the sum of things for pay", but not if they could help it. In line with the theatricalization of life, military men were as much performers as patriots. The other great mercenaries were actors and musicians. At the Apollonia festival on Delos, in the third century B.C., two "cyclic flautists" were paid 700 drachmae each. The wages of a skilled artisan remained the same two drachmae *per diem* that Pheidias was paid when working on the Parthenon. Spartans marched into battle to the sound of flutes, and long-jumpers at the Olympic Games jumped to the same tune. Skilled flautists are still rarely unemployed.

Even fervent Jews were lured into expressing themselves in the Hellenic style: the prophet Ezekiel wrote a "Greek" tragedy on the subject of the Exodus (with "six maidens" as the chorus). The topic might seem beside the point for Greek audiences, but there is evidence of a Jewish theatre in what is now Benghazi. Hellenistic culture impinged on Jewish manners in other ways which horrified the orthodox: so strong was the lure of going to the gym and exercising naked, in the Greek fashion, that young Jewish men took to wearing false foreskins in order to assimilate with the dominant culture. African lawyers still wear "British" wigs.

Similarity is a form of difference. Greeks became more like barbarians, and vice versa. The new, factitious, homogeneity was administrative and cultural. *Proskynesis* was an un-Greek form of crawling which was exacted by

Alexander's surviving legates and generals, the so-called *diadochoi*, when they mounted the thrones of the kingdoms they carved from Alexander's empire. Democratic scepticism found small expression in their showy, literate, but servile capitals. Philosophy declined into a form of attitudinizing, like today's journalism. Medicine, being a vital service, was freer to make new discoveries or claims; its practitioners might advise a despot, but they seldom threatened him. In the same spirit, while it might be dangerous to have new *political* ideas, philosophies of personal conduct – stoicism and Epicureanism, like today's diets and exercise programmes – gave individuals a sense of independence which, like the practice of medicine, was politically neutral. Although the medical theories of, for instance, the Pythagorean Alkmaion, applied terms such as *isonomia* (equal rights, balance) and *monarchia* (undue domination) to the human body, such usage was strictly metaphorical. Even St Paul incites his correspondents to imitate the athlete, by running a good race, rather than by offering a challenge to society. Christianity was a mutation of Judaism without the nationalism: by enrolling the Gentiles, St Paul encouraged Christians to bypass the irredeemable earthly life and to dwell, spiritually, in the world to come. The oppressive social system which controlled the Fertile Crescent helped to elevate any hope of individual freedom from the mundane to the spiritual level.

The riches of the East flashed temptation to the Romans not least because the successor kingdoms were the unstable result of a land-grabbing race by Alexander's generals. Which of their great capital cities, from Pergamum to Alexandria, symbolized the robustness of a state of loyal citizens, rooted in their soil and united in defence of their commonwealth? Hellenistic monuments – such as the great Altar of Zeus at Pergamum – never stood, as had the Parthenon, for the pride of a nation.

68 Pergamene Hellenistic version of giant Alcyoneus (the Mighty Ass), whom Herakles did for.

They established only the eminence of rulers who taxed and conscripted their subjects without being elected by them or even belonging to the same race. The Ptolemies, for showy instance, might affect Egyptian ways, especially when they adopted incest, which kept power (and property) in the family, but their culture and their city, Alexandria, remained almost exclusively Greek. The first Ptolemy, one of Alexander's generals, had been quick off the mark in acquiring the personal fiefdom which, of all the recently conquered Persian Empire, had the best prospects of defence, on account of its unusual inaccessibility. He and his successors remained in power until Cleopatra fell to Octavian, and Egypt with it. The last of the Ptolemies was the first member of the dynasty actually to speak the local language. When he became *princeps*, the emperor Augustus learnt a lesson from Ptolemy and made sure that only his personal legate (a knight, not a senator) governed a potentially autonomous province on which Rome depended for much of its wheat.

In Hellenistic societies, rhetoric distorted logic, style content, flattery truth. Telling the truth might once have been a Persian virtue, but it was unlikely to be rewarded under the Seleucids or Demetrios Poliorketes, whom – in 307 – the Athenians thought it wise to worship more openly than the gods, since he brought more palpable benefits, not least the city's liberation from another Demetrios, of Phaleron, who began as a law-giving saviour and ended as a paranoid dictator.

* * *

*G*reeks were curious, if nervous, travellers. The sixth-century philosopher Anaximander of Miletus is credited with making the first – largely speculative – map of the inhabited world. He assumed (as Alexander would) that the earth was surrounded by the great stream of ocean; myth shaped his vision of reality, just as the a priori assumption that the earth was the centre of the solar system was regarded as incontestable by the Aristotelian cardinal Bellarmine, who showed Galileo the instruments of torture as an argument for terrestrial centrality.

The Milesians were at once conscious of their superiority (because of the wealth and culture of their city) and apprehensive of the Persians (for the same reasons). It is hardly surprising that the barbarian Other alarmed and fascinated the first Ionian historians. Hecataeus of Miletus and his alleged pupil, Herodotus, who was born in Halicarnassus, doubled as travel-writers, map-makers and, no doubt, prospectors. Although they did not fail to bring home tall tales, travel did broaden their minds, and their vocabularies: if early historians still took myths for some kind of reality, observation abated their chauvinism.

"The Greeks", Hecataeus remarked, "say a lot of stuff, and it seems to me that it's also ridiculous." Yet he also asserts as a fact that the mythical Cadmus had Phoenicians among those whom he settled in Boeotia. They (or their descendants) later emigrated to Athens, where they were admitted to limited citizenship: they kept their own temples and forms of worship. This tale probably explained the practices of some extant (or at least remembered) sect, but it also hints at how rationalization can refer credibility, of a kind, back onto myth: Jews, some say, are forbidden to eat pork because pig-meat goes off rapidly in hot climates, as do shellfish. All this may be true, but there is no evidence that the Holy One, Blessed be He, ever meant to fortify His divinity by doubling as a hygiene inspector.

Travellers acquired cosmopolitanism as they observed diversity. In 494, after the disastrous failure of Miletus's rebellion against the Persians, Hecataeus was chosen as Milesian ambassador to mend fences with the Mede: he was known to have been sceptical of the prospects of successful secession and perhaps predisposed to compromise. Drawing on what credit this gave him with the Persians, he asked them why, even after its surrender, they continued to be so suspicious of Miletus. Darius the Great's half-brother Artaphernes replied, sensibly enough, that he feared that the Milesians would always bear a grudge for their sufferings.

"If suffering makes us suspect," Hecataeus reasoned, "fair treatment will make the Ionian cities loyal to the Persians." It was a pretty argument, which subsequent events did little to validate. However, Hecataeus could see what would be agreeable for both sides in the peace process, and especially for his own: advocacy masked partiality with reason, which always affects to be neutral. Reason is a method, not a theory.

Miletus was *obliged* to be a reasonable place: it straddled the fault-line of the Greek and the Persian world, conscious of the dialectic which grated two civilizations against each other like the plates of the earthquake zone on which they stood. Its surviving ruins prove that Miletus was a great city with a fine seafront prospect. Its culture was precocious, and inventive; but its location perilous. As the Athenians recognized to their shame, Miletus was deserted first by its allies, who left it to be sacked by the angry Persians, and later by the sea, which receded from its port and left the city literally high and dry. There are still green signs, at least in spring, of the fat valley in which it stood, but Miletus's citizens cut down the fine trees in the surrounding hills, which supplied shade, sponsored a temperate climate, and had held back the erosion which eventually choked the harbour.

Hecataeus was an early example of critical neutrality: appreciating both sides of racial and religious borders, and arguments, he sought common ground on which to reconcile them in the unifying narratives of history and geography. In a region where no single culture could maintain unchallenged hegemony, neutrality and partisanship grew on adjacent stems. "Where?", "How?" and "Why?" were Hecataeus's questions. As for "When" (would the Greeks be free?), he left that question to inflammatory poets such as Callinus.

In seeking common ground, diplomats adapted the elucidating logic of early Greek scientists. For example, Anaximander was well placed to discover, or at least postulate, what might be true for all men. Friction with Persia made life nervy in Asia Minor; but the clash generated illuminating sparks. So did that between Greeks and native tribes in Calabria and between Phoenicians and others in Sicily. Philosophy originated more copiously in Ionian Asia Minor, and in the cities of Greek settlements in southern Italy, than on the mainland.

Philosophers sought unities even in antagonism: the Sicilian Empedocles (492–432) was prolific of ideas, including that of repeated cycles in world history: Love (*philia*) replaced Strife (*neikos*), he claimed, only for the latter to reclaim its dominance in due course. The world breathed in and out, as it were, coming together in *philia* and diverging into *neikos*. The Stoics incorporated the same notion in their idea of the world's eternal return to its original state. The modern economists' theory of the trade cycle, and its inevitable heating up and slowing down, its spasms of free trade and protectionism, of militaristic partiality and international compacts, is a rescription of Empedoclean moral philosophy in terms of money and power.

Reason was the fruit of *neikos* no less than of *philia*. Persia had the wealth to underwrite its vanity; the Ionian Greeks the wit, and energy, to challenge it. Both sides had reason to admire, and fear, the other. The *logos* became a transcendental means of scrutinizing what all had in common: physiology, physics and gold (Thales was an adroit speculator: gold, like his primal substance water, flows across frontiers). Medicine was first practised (somewhat) scientifically on what Cicero would call "the civilized fringe of the barbarian world". Hippocrates of Cos (469–399) is credited with a code of medical practice which even today requires doctors not to discriminate between patients, but to try to alleviate the suffering of all, rich or poor, friend or foe.

The influence of Hippocrates was more salutary than his medical ideas. Giants can have clay shoulders too: John Locke's theory of "the blank slate" was basic to the emergence of modern democratic theory. Plausible at the time, and nobly fruitful, the Lockean conception of the mind as a *tabula rasa* is without scientific merit. Over the centuries, Hippocrates' notion of "four humours" governing the body more impeded than advanced medical science, yet his ethical contribution to humanity remains indelible. He was probably a more effective physician in specific cases than his theories suggest: it is said that he staunched the plague in Athens in 430, by fumigating the city, though this may be one of those *post hoc ergo propter hoc* coincidences which serve to bolster reputations.

Medicine, like justice, was ideally blind: the mythical Tiresias was an example to both. The blind consultant viewed the human condition from a dispassionate, unworldly standpoint. Like Phineus, king of Thrace, Tiresias lost his sight because he happened upon Athene as she bathed. St Augustine glosses this to mean that Tiresias saw only the goddess's *xoanon* (image) "bathing itself", a primly implausible view.

The Delphic oracle called memory "the face of the blind"; the mother of the Muses sponsored the inner life of the creator. Homer's blindness was assumed to have enriched his imagination. The seer's in/sight was deflected from fugitive outward appearances onto in/visible reality. The atomist philosopher Democritus – an amiable materialist who was hardly a mystic – is said to have blinded himself in order to avoid being distracted by the outside world. The unveiling of *physis* (nature) became an iconic goal of impudent philosophers: "*Physis* likes to hide herself", said Heracleitus. The hermetic prison cell has been a haven for thinkers, from Boethius to Bertrand Russell and Gramsci. Plato's cave flickered with delusive shadows, from which he affected to deliver the inmates in order for them to see the light of his Ideas. Others took total darkness for the sanctuary of abiding truths. A few embraced blindness, others had it thrust upon them, among them Stesichorus, a nickname meaning "The Choir-Master". He lived in Himera, in Sicily, where Gelon would annihilate Hamilcar's Carthaginians a century later. The story is that, in his own (lost) epic, Stesichorus was morally blind enough to endorse Homer's view of Helen of Troy as a flighty woman, and was literally blinded in consequence. By stripping Helen of divine attributes, the poet had denuded and demeaned her. He recovered his sight, and restored the goddess's modesty, by composing a retraction, the *Palinode*, of which only as much survives as Socrates quotes in Plato's *Phaedrus*.

Stesichorus's rewriting of Helen cleared her for redemption and for the divine honours due to the immaculate daughter of Zeus and loyal wife of godlike Menelaus (once honours begin to be heaped, the recipients' humanity is buried under their titles). If Helen's divinity appears difficult to reconcile with the mundane Helen's conjugal treachery and shameless egotism, the common factor is an ability to bewitch and enchant. Power is divine: one woman's capacity to mobilize so many men to fight on her behalf was evidence of superhuman provenance. The polar archetypes of bitch and Madonna (although no one accused Helen of sustained virginity) are present in Mediterranean attitudes to women long before Roman Catholicism depicts them as impersonated in the immaculate Mother of God and the penitent Magdalene.

In *Oedipus Rex*, Sophocles portrays the self-blinded king as a complacent tyrant who ends in lonely despair and exile. Yet in *Oedipus at Colonus*, the man who blinded himself (with his wife's brooch) at the end of the previous play is transformed into what Wittgenstein might call a *deep* sage, to whose painful wisdom others defer. Blindness to his own guilt has been sublimated into the symbol of his insight: the ex-king becomes the spiritual double of Tiresias, who first exposed his miasma. The blind outcast is reborn as someone who has seen it all.

René Girard takes a different view of Oedipus's metamorphosis: he argues that by taking the scapegoat's burden on himself and exiling himself from Thebes like a criminal, and by taking the plague with him, Oedipus worked a healing redemption which led to his being regarded as the vessel of supernatural powers. A tyrant who was earlier tainted by incest and parricide becomes the shaman who has drained evil from the city. His prestige recovered and enhanced, Oedipus rises higher than before. As an unknown young stranger, he solved the riddle of the Sphinx and lifted its blight from the city; as an old man, he is again a source of salvation. He has acquired the learning which, according to Aeschylus, comes through suffering. The scapegoat who magics the blight away from the city prefigures the Christian saints whose miracles still have to be certified before their sainthood can be confirmed by the Vatican.

* * *

Although the contradiction between the common culture of the Hellenes and their pandemic contentiousness may have cost them the leadership of the ancient world, it also engendered their genius: trial by jury, philosophy and drama alike derive from hypothetic and adversarial dialogue. All are varieties of mutual examination unknown, perhaps literally unthinkable, in any previous or contemporary society. Just as Daedalus gave statuary articulation – the movement of its limbs – so it is nice to think that the Greek language, more articulate than its sources, gave rise to intellectual life.

Democracy can never be consistent or logical: it thrives on the uses of division. The Persians had many qualities, and exquisite artefacts; their king demanded, and his courtiers told, the truth; their cities were no less magnificent than Athens in its prime. Their script was elegant, and influenced Greek, but what could be said in it that was not hedged by the Great King's expectations? The truth he demanded was his truth; Greek truth was impertinent. *Parrhesia* could mean nothing but treason in Persia. Cyrus the Great once said to the Spartan envoy, Lacrines (who had dared to warn him not to meddle with the Greek cities of Asia Minor), that he had never been afraid of "men who have a special meeting place in the centre of their city where they swear this and that and cheat each other". What such men called free exchange he considered to be vulgar haggling. The Persians, Herodotus says, "never buy in open trading...and have not a single market-place in the whole country".

The shame that attached to trading and bargaining (even in societies, including Athens, where they were vital to prosperity) may account for the curious habit of the Phoenicians – notorious for their mercantile character – in leaving merchandise on the beach at their ports of call and returning later to see whether their price had been met.

If the mutual suspicions of Greeks were politically schismatic, they were a cultural blessing: reason, applied to life, is a way of working towards – even bargaining for – agreement, not of supplying truths. There was a not dissimilar split in ancient Israel, where the stand-off between prophets and kings was fortuitously fertile: division primed literary variety and sharpened both dialogue and moral subtleties. The justice of monotheism – which entailed direct and unquestioning obedience to the Law of God – is distinct from the *Dike* of which Zeus was the custodian. The *meaning* of G-d's law may be disputed, but it is not limited, as Zeus's authority was, by other forces. Disputation over legal nuances became habitual among Jews, although drama did not.

Polytheism involved a variety of gods with clashing claims on mankind: in Euripides' *Hippolytus*, the partiality of the hero for his favourite goddess, Artemis, ignites Aphrodite's murderous indignation. This particular brand of conflictual drama could make no sense to Jews, among whose orthodox communitarians both freely composed literature and dialogue (not least with fellow-Jews of less rigorous orthodoxy) continue to be regarded with dismay.

Because it often promotes innovation, art tends to heresy. Choice (*hairesis*) characterizes open societies, but is seen as a source of error in authoritarian states. Plato's banishment of the poets is echoed in the totalitarian habit of cramping artists in an official aesthetic programme. Islam follows Judaism in forbidding representational visual imagery. The Stalinist programme of "Socialist Realism" defined the only politically correct images to be unambiguous reflections of the Party line.

As Pheidias discovered, when accused of putting man among the gods in his Parthenon frieze and on the shield of his new chryselephantine statue of Athene, there are always politico-theological limits to tolerance, which can even be said, by those who crave the moral whip, to be "repressive" or – more commonly – "decadent". Good art cannot exclude the possibility of bad, but when only one kind of art is allowed to be good, it isn't.

The *agora* – whose origins, Jean-Pierre Vernant suggests, lie in the space created by the circle of warriors in conclave – and the theatre supplied architectural correlatives of free speech. They were constants in almost all Greek cities. On the steep flank of modest and lovely Priene, not far from Miletus, the council chamber is incised, like a small theatre, in the side of a hill overlooking a green valley. You sense the affinity between politics and drama: the same tiered structure might as well house them both.

The synagogue too has its theatrical element: Jesus first announced his genius by astonishing the rabbis with his precocious arguments. The palace never promoted dissentient views, nor has the established Christian Church. Once the Pope had become both the Vicar of Christ and a sublime Caesar, it was not out of character that – although not until the nineteenth century – the successor of St Peter should declare what was implicit in his sovereign pontificate: his own *ex cathedra* infallibility.

To have an index of forbidden books, and ideas, is common to dictatorial regimes, as is its ascription to the will of a Higher Power. The Greek Colonels who banned Aristophanes in 1967 were the proponents of a Greece of Christian Greeks. There is no room for frivolity in closed societies: quite "logically" Plato banned "loud laughter" in his *politeia*. Ribaldry takes, and promotes, liberties. By a sweet coincidence, Plato had a virtual contemporary of the same name who was a comic dramatist. Among his plays was one called *Sophists*.

In the ur-myth of Gaia and Ouranos, space had to be cleared between the heaving deities' undifferentiated bodies before their progeny had space to breathe. As long as the two were clamped together in mutual gratification, nothing could be born of their airless copulation. Plato's image, in the *Symposium*, of lovers as severed halves craving their lost unity, is as amusing as might be expected of its proposer, Aristophanes, but sexual solipsism has no issue. However Edenic, mutual absorption leaves neither wish nor space for generation.

Women and men were both candidates for Plato's highest social class, the Guardians. What seems like an enlightened elevation of womanhood is also a denial of female otherness. Women in Platonic relationships were components of a higher Civil Service in which asexuality was a condition of entry (as it would be in the Christian heaven).

For Plato, human fecundity itself was suspect: ripeness was too much. Perfection lay in what did not change, including the number of citizens. The

69 The theatre of local politics: Priene council chamber.

repression of artists is of a piece with Plato's fears of disruption, of the unforeseen, of new generations with new ideas. The Good has no future. The
Platonic preference for a landlocked site is symbolic of dread of political sea
change: more independent of central command, sailors are disposed to
democracy. Freud – a citizen of landlocked Vienna – associates the sea with the
female, its unfathomable claims and indefinable desires.

The crew of the battleship *Potemkin*, canonized by Eisenstein's Soviet film,
lit the fuse of revolution in 1905. In 1921, the crews of the fleet anchored at
Kronstadt revolted against the Bolshevik dictatorship and were vindictively
repressed by the Red Army under Leon Trotsky. Dissent was now condemned
as counter-revolutionary terror. Sailors cannot be regimented as landsmen
are. During the Second World War, the German navy generally honoured the
laws of the sea, for instance in never interfering with neutral navigational
lights and in showing at least some humanity to its victims. The latter cannot
be said of the *Wehrmacht*.

* * *

*I*t has become a winsome commonplace that books write their authors; and read their readers. Wars, in particular, are how they are reported: our response to bloodshed is mediated by the way in which it is presented. The crucifixion of Jesus stands for, and obscures, all human suffering. If we could have footage, as the TV companies say, of Alexander's mass crucifixion of those two thousand brave defenders of Tyre, the debate about his putative great-heartedness would be abbreviated. Homer turned a Bronze Age slugfest into an enduring epic. The Muse could immortalize louts, as long as their names scanned. The Trojan War was the first to be fought in hexameters and, for all the "realism" which Michael Schmidt ascribes to Homer, the *Iliad* lent it a cruel glamour which was challenged by Thucydides' prosaic history of the Peloponnesian War. The medium *does* shape the message: ancient warfare – if photographed as close-up, and as eagerly, as modern – would be seen to be at least as brutal as any campaign which, through the presence of cameras, becomes unacceptable to those "back home".

The Russian novel was said, by Belinsky, to have "emerged from under Gogol's Overcoat"; Aeschylus admitted that tragedy was Homer recycled. But then Homer himself was said, by Diodorus Siculus, to have appropriated some of the better lines – composed in a variety of styles – by Daphne, the daughter of Tiresias, when she was employed as a copywriter for the Delphic oracle. The sources may be manifold, but Attic drama transcends its plural provenance. Tragedy's uniqueness lies not in affinity with liturgy or folklore, but in how it differs from them. Ritual repeats, drama innovates. Ezra Pound's "Make It New" was the aesthetic fashion in fifth-century Attic theatre. Tradition says that the great tragedians took leading parts in their own work (Sophocles specialized in female roles), but lavishly paid professional thespians were the rule in the Hellenistic era. The original sixth-century Thespis was said, by Horace, to have toured Attica with a roadshow: the word *skene* (our scene) was first used for the awning on a wagon. Later, grander touring companies favoured revivals. Visitors to the Hellenistic Apollonia on Delos were like opera fans: they liked to know what they were paying to see and hear (with its often forgotten musical accompaniment, tragedy *was* operatic). Like actors, scene painters were at a premium: on third-century Delos, one of their surviving bills was for a fat 2,500 drachmai.

Even in the Golden Age, drama had in some respects to entertain, but it was less a diversion than part of the evolution of democracy's self-conscious scrutiny both of its roots in myth and of the means by which the city's future could be disentangled from its knotty past and liberated, intellectually and socially, from constricting deference to its own antiquity. Tragedy seems to pay tribute to a heroic past, but it also untrammels the writer, and the audience,

70 The paths of glory on an Alexander sarcophagus, now in Istanbul.

from excessive credulity. The progress of Greek poetry, down to George Seferis and Yiannis Ritsos, in the twentieth century, has been one of aggressive respect for the tradition. In "Here Be Light", Ritsos rebels (as only a Greek Communist could) by parodying the ponderous and allusive imagery which weighs on modern Greek literature. In the surrealistic tones of high culture, he calls, in *Short Songs*, for less of it: "On these marble slabs, no vile rust grabs hold, / No chain clamps a Greek foot, no shackle binds the wind. / Here be light, here the shore – golden, milk-blue tongues; / On the rocks, stags like axes chop fetters into food."

The great playwrights craved applause, but part of what the people admired was their daring in deconstructing tradition. After the eclipse of imperial Athens, new plays continued to be written, but without the social context which made Aeschylus and his contemporaries significant. The mental medicine which had stimulated a city in its prime was diluted to a placebo.

Even at the zenith of Athens' intellectual vanity, it could be dangerous to make a drama too new: Euripides wrote *Bacchae* in Macedonian exile after having given myth one iconoclastic twist too many. He could not resist provoking those whose praise he solicited. The public likes being *slightly* shocked, but draws abrupt lines. Success had previously made the allegedly misanthropic Euripides a wine-grower flush enough to offer drinks all round the *demos* when he won first prize with his (revised) *Hippolytus*. Those who bait the bourgeois rarely fail to take pleasure in honours and rewards: even Henrik Ibsen was notoriously addicted to honours; David Hare is a knight; Tom Stoppard has no laurels left to collect. Only Harold Pinter hoards his scowl.

In a recent lecture, Dr Peter Jones gave a convincing account of the revisions made to *Hippolytus* after Euripides' first version had flopped. Urgent

both to succeed and to scandalize (a combination which often makes for theatrical boldness), he refined his original Phaedra from a lustful harridan to an exemplary wife, shocked by her own passion for Hippolytus; and Hippolytus from an innocent youth to the priggish incarnation of repressed desire. The artist discovers new ground, and truths, by stylish aversion from the obvious and the trite.

In his lifetime, Euripides – though widely quoted – was never as much revered as Aeschylus and Sophocles; but after his death, he too was venerated: Sophocles, who was older, but survived his rival, dressed the chorus of one of his last plays in black when he heard of Euripides' death. Would he have made so public a display of mourning if Euripides was not admired even by the society he had quit? Oscar Wilde's plays are frequently revived by the English, who drove him into exile.

Sophocles shared Wilde's taste for young men, but suffered no comparable stigma. Schoolboys used to be told the moral tale of how, when in his seventies, the playwright was asked if he still desired women, to which he replied that he did not, and that it was like being delivered from a wild beast. What we were not told was that, even in old age, Sophocles was renowned as a persistent *coureur* of young men (notably a pretty waiter).

Attic theatre in the Golden Age was not yet show business, but it could be show-politics: the *choregos*, who funded the production, often had ambition for public office. Both Perikles and

72 Sophocles.
Rehearsals not going so well?

224

Themistokles had experience as impresarios (*choregoi*). In the same way as the owners of the victorious *équipe* in the chariot race were rated as winners at the Olympic Games, the sponsor of winning plays gained as much personal kudos and celebrity as the writer and performers. Producers still go on stage to collect the culminating Oscar for "Best Picture", quite as if they themselves were artists.

Although tragedians found canonical subject matter in myth, their take on it was inflected by personal attitudes and topical reference. The *recyclage* of ancient themes was a long habit in France. Racine and Corneille raided Plutarch more often than the Attic tragedians, but their epigoni often ennobled verbiage with classical trappings. André Gide wrote *Le Prométhée mal enchaîné* in 1899, *Le Roi Candaule* (on the Gyges theme) in 1901 and *Oedipe* thirty years later. In 1929, Jean Giraudoux mocked this antiquarian fetish in his *Amphitryon 38*, so called since it was the umpteenth time the theme had been addressed, but he was not inhibited, a decade later, from staging *La Guerre de Troie n'aura pas lieu*.

In 1944, Jean-Paul Sartre's *Les Mouches* – his recension of Euripides' *Orestes* – allowed him to make a plague of archaic flies stand for the Nazi occupation of France. If the Germans were symbolized by the infestation, Sartre's duplicity not only eluded their censorship but also allowed him to be among the *collabo*-Nazi *gratin* at the first-night party, which took place on the eve of the allies' invasion of Normandy. He was later able to represent himself as an active member of the Resistance. *Polyeidos* "Poulou" came in many forms.

Jean Anouilh's *Antigone* came from a less *engagé* hand but also made a point against the occupying Germans: King Kreon stood for the fascistic dictator before whom Antigone/Marianne refuses to bow, even though she must die for her defiance. Anouilh also mined the classics in *Medea* and *Eurydice* (Point of Departure).

Duplicity (in the Daedalus style) has long enabled artists to rise, and shine, in dangerous climates. Molière was an obsequious iconoclast at the court of Louis XIV. Bertholt Brecht deceived first the un-American Activities Committee in the US, then East German Communist censors. Dmitri Shostakovich, it is said, grovelled *ironically* to the Communist *apparat*, while composing against its grain. Daedalian Boris Pasternak survived Stalin; but Ikareian Osip Mandelstam did not. Celebrity enabled the painter of *Guernica*, albeit an extremely nervous Communist, to live unscathed in occupied Paris. Fame may be the spur; it can also supply a celebrity's *laissez-passer*.

* * *

*T*he Attic dramatists' progressively sceptical attitude to the gods emerges from – but is of a piece with – Homer's unintimidated vision. In contrast with other Middle Eastern epics – Gilgamesh, for obvious instance – Homer's gods may take sides in the war, but there are no cosmological consequences to its outcome. Greeks and Trojans are equally human, and pathetic. Heroes and villains win or lose, suffer or triumph, but the same Hades awaits them all.

As partisan spectators, the gods cheer on their favourites from above the fray, but their own paramountcy is never at risk. Only rarely are immortals caught in crossfire. Unwise Aphrodite is the only divinity to be wounded and beats a painful retreat. Love had clearly strayed from her domain. However, since she licensed Paris to abduct Helen, and so set the war in train, her battlefield scar was not unmerited.

Despite divine sponsorship and kit (after he has been re-equipped by Hephaestus), Achilles remains a mortal who has chosen a brief and glorious rather than a long and uneventful life. His divine mother, Thetis, does what she can to help him, but divinity itself is not in her gift. Achilles must honour the Heracleitan dictum that character determines fate (and vice versa?): to choose a short life, and immortal glory, *is* his character/fate. "*La gloire*", said Balzac, "*est le soleil des morts*". Once dead, and among the shades, Achilles thought he had made a bad bargain, but – as Cavafy might say – that is what it was to be Achilles.

Name/character and destiny fused long before Heracleitus made a *mot* of the fact. Minor figures are branded by their names to advertise their fates: Dolon, the spy whom Odysseus and Diomedes unmask, has a name which puns on *dolos*, a trick: when duped by a promise of immunity, he is Tricky Dick tricked.

* * *

*A*lmost the only character whom Homer treats with gleeful heartlessness is Thersites, the sole common soldier with a speaking part (there are no Ancient Pistols in the *Iliad*). Said to be *ametroepes* – translated as "blabbing" by Robert Fitzgerald, but surely implying "cannot measure his words", hence unworthy of epic stature – Thersites appears only in Book Two, as a barrack-room lawyer, yelling at Agamemnon:

Hey, son of Atreus, what's your problem then?
Your ships are stuffed with brass, you're not short
Of crumpet up at G.H.Q. – much thanks
Us Achaeans get – each time a city's sacked.
Want gold as well, do you? Kicked back by Troy's
Old dads who've come to ransom bloody sons
That me or some poor squaddie's gone and nabbed?
New tail? Old story: you spot the prettiest
And stick "reserved" on her! It's not accept-
able to be their king and knock the lads:
He calls us bloody girls, not men. Know what:
Let's sail for home! The general can stop
And have a smashing time in Troy. Forget
What all of us have done for him; or not.
This here's the bloke that calls Achilles crap –
Who's twice the man he is – and nicks his bird.
But he's not sore, Achilles, is he now?
The day he is, my lord, you're bloody through.

Homer gives (brief) voice to anti-war sentiments, but he also mocks the protester's deformed physique, as if it confirmed his warped character. Lameness often stands for crippled personality: Hephaestus is the divine, Shakespeare's Richard III a mortal instance. By contrast, being left with only one eye supplies glamour: Philip of Macedon, Antigonos the one-eyed, Lord Nelson and General Moshe Dayan are fighting examples. In the 1950s, Hathaway shirts were advertised by a Man of Distinction with an eye-patch. As the Cyclops proves, to be *born* with but one eye, and that set in a funny place, is not so good; and to have only one between three of you, like the Graiae, grey old crones, who also shared one tooth, is even worse.

When Agamemnon seems not to know what to say to Thersites, Odysseus pulls rank with a few contemptuous words and then whacks the lowlife across the shoulders with his swagger stick. Thersites' mates, the Myrmidons, have been murmuring agreement with their ugly comrade, but Odysseus's cutting condescension makes them laugh at the rebel's tears. Officer-like qualities have restored order.

Odysseus acts as Agamemnon's legate, although – as Sophocles shows in *Aias* – he was never an unconditional adherent of the Atreidae. Can it be that when Odysseus slaps down Thersites, he does so, in part, because the lout expresses the same nostalgic wish which dominates the hero's own secret thoughts? Certainly, Odysseus had no appetite for the war in the first place.

In some respects, he was an indispensable, if princely, version of Thersites: neither wanted to come to Troy and neither got anything out of it. Like the Abbé Sieyès during the French Revolution, Odysseus's proudest boast had to be that he survived.

The Messenger in Aeschylus's *Agamemnon* is something of an anonymous Thersites: "...Cramped quarters, / Crowded decks, thin blankets, thinner rations: / Who wouldn't complain?... We slept huddled on the marshes under a weeping sky / Clothes rotted on our bodies. We lived with lice. / In winter the birds fell frozen from the sky, / And then the summer heat...."

After his thumping, Thersites never speaks, nor is he mentioned again in the extant text. In the apocrypha, he gets killed, in the aftermath of the war, when he accuses Achilles of unnatural desire for the corpse of Penthesilea, queen of the Amazons, with whom – in more sentimental accounts – the hero fell in love at the moment of slaying her.

Thersites has Iago's talent for plausible insinuation, but small guile in its employment. Thersites' flaw was less insolence than inability to resist cheeking his betters and questioning their motives, too accurately for his own good (in a modern-dress version, he could be a television journalist: his advocacy of peace makes Pax-man a plausible Latinate nickname for him). In the *Aethiopis* – a lost sequel to the *Iliad* by Arctinus of Miletus* – Thersites gouged Penthesilea's eyes out before incurring Achilles' lethal fury. According to other sources, however, he was by no means the lowlife Homer depicts, but a patrician cousin of godlike Diomedes. In the *Iliad*, his loud agitation for a quiet life leads him to be reduced to the ranks. Elsewhere in the poem, Homer makes one concession to the feelings of the poor bloody infantry, when he refers to battle as *"ergon"*, a job of work.

Was Achilles' only true love Patroklos, as gay pietists would like? When it came to women, the hero seems to have been attracted particularly to the doomed or the unobtainable. One myth has him, or his shade, in a happy after-life with Helen, whom he might have had long before the war, had he shown up as a candidate for her hand at the time when she was awarded to Menelaus. In type she resembled Achilles: both were inescapably glamorous superstars. Locked in celebrity, they had no peers but each other. Only when Achilles was a child, and hidden among the women by his mother Thetis – in the empty hope that he would not elect to be conscripted to fame – did he speak a girlish, unheroic language and absent himself from the limelight.

---

* Our knowledge of such books derives from quotations and summaries in Homeric manuscripts. The fetish for footnotes and concordances began early among scholars and scholiasts.

73 Dante Gabriel Rossetti's Helen, Spartan goddess.

74 Marilyn, celluloid goddess.

Helen was marked as a beauty from birth; the darling of her mortal family, the emblem of divine election, she was never seen as a woman who could be free to be other than what others made of, and saw in, her. Transcending Simone de Beauvoir's *"on ne naît pas femme, on le devient"*, Helen was born a woman, and became a myth. She can plausibly be said never to have been more, or less, than an image. Larger than life but less substantial, models and movie stars are of the same genre: their inflated, bloodless screen persona is ageless and more assiduously maintained – by publicists and photographers – than the perishable reality. What we mean by Marilyn Monroe is that girl with her skirt blowing up on the subway grill, or with the ever-young lips (to which President Mitterrand could compare Mrs Thatcher's) in Andy Warhol's lithograph; never the drugged, sorry woman who died alone.* Helen too was something of an actress: taken to see the Wooden Horse, she mimicked the voices of the hidden warriors' wives, trying to tease those inside into blowing their cover.

---

*"Marilyn" (Monroe) was the projection of what men imagined they desired. Movie stars exercise the same larger-than-life allure as magnified Norma Jean. The celluloid sacrifice of intrinsic personality, in pursuit of stardom, makes discontented goddesses of Hollywood's queens and, when it deserts them, leaves them "not knowing who they are". Their shadows outshine the stars.

The story of Achilles and Helen reconciled in love (before or after the end of their earthly leases) is sweet with insight and pathos: as Michel Pic once remarked, *"Au bout de longues années, ce n'est que les anciens ennemis qui s'embrassent"*.

* * *

*H*owever many rhapsodes may (or may not) have come together to contribute to the corpus stamped with Homer's name, the second great reservoir of Greek literary données – Hesiod's *Theogony* and *Works and Days* – was undoubtedly the work of a single, identifiable poet: we know where Hesiod lived and what kind of life he had. Although he had never been there, he reads as a spiritual exile from easygoing Aeolian Cyme, on the shore of Asia Minor, whence his father had fled – before Hesiod was born (around 700) – to go and live at Ascra, in the Boeotian hills. Like George Seferis almost three millennia later, the poet sprang from the fretful, fruitful collision of Asia and Europe.

Seferis was evicted from Smyrna (now Izmir, in Turkey) during the forcible "exchange of populations" between Greece and Turkey after the débâcle of 1922. He writes, in his notebooks, of returning to his family house, decades later, and hearing the same creak as he opened the gate that he had heard, as a boy, when it last closed behind him.

Hesiod describes his adopted native heath as "bad in winter, suffocating in summer, no good at any time". How often are peasants uncomplaining friends of the earth? Hesiod was not a man to look on the bright side. *Works and Days* is a grumbling georgic in which he warns his brother, Perses, against subverting the venal Boeotian justices and doing him out of his due inheritance. Exile and return are recurrent themes in Greek literature (Romans were more reluctant civilian travellers: for Catullus, at least, there was no place like Sirmio). Odysseus is a key figure in Seferis's *Mythistorima*, with its rustic's epigraph from Rimbaud: *"Si j'ai du goût, ce n'est guères / Que pour la terre et les pierres"*. It is tempting to mistranslate this (for Hesiod, as it were) as, "If I like anything, it isn't wars, only the earth and the stones".

Homer and Hesiod stand together, and poles apart, at the source of European poetry, though we get glimpses of the Hesiodic world of the peasant through the "windows" of Homer's similes, which – like the rural scenes glimpsed through the pillars or casements of Renaissance paintings – remind us of an unheroic, or unholy, world elsewhere. The battles of the gods in Hesiod's *Theogony* may be titanic, but they are never moving: without humanity, they articulate a cosmic struggle which lacks pathos.

75 Flaxman's Hesiod takes a break.

Farmer Hesiod was more solitary, and sedentary, than the corps of rhapsodes who did the rounds of campfires, singing for their suppers. If Homer is a group-name for the composers and performers of the Homeric corpus, Hesiod never enrolled in such company: he was, he tells us, tending his sheep when he happened on the Muses dancing round the "violet-dark spring and the altar of Zeus" on Mount Helicon (John Fowles's *Journals* has a fine description of its poetic aura). Hesiod heard the Muses' trilling laughter and sublime song, as they disappeared in a thick cloud on the summit, after nominating him the poet of "what will be and what has been" (Moses too mountaineered to contact the divine).

Homer the Realist never affected the prophetic role which some readers admire in poets. Hesiod's pretensions helped him to be ranked, surprisingly to modern critical opinion, as the equal of Homer. The *Iliad* and *Odyssey* have become fundamental to European literature, while Hesiod has dwindled into an archaic curiosity. Archilochos's fame too was, at one time, almost equal to Homer's, partly due to his metrical innovations, though also to the ferocity of his scorn, but a paucity of manuscripts damaged the circulation of his genius.

Although owing an obvious debt to Homer (and the incantatory mode), Hesiod probably either dictated or wrote down his verses. If so, he was not only the first Greek poet to speak in the first person (Archilochos was a hot second), but also the first to distinguish himself from the Homeridae, for whom a protracted blend of improvisation and recitation was a common style (and a paying proposition). Hesiod's *Theogony* is a hexametrical *Who's Who* of the gods: it established genealogies, folkloric or fanciful, on which later writers relied; unless – like Heracleitus – they made a show of scorning it as the work of a witless rustic.

The *Theogony* is a mini-epic of competing divinities. Some – such as the fundamental figures of Earth and Sky, and their titanic offspring – are pre-Olympian, and set to be conquered by Zeus and his more or less opportunist allies. The poem is also a genealogical grammar: it spells out ingeniously fanciful divine kinships, and at the same time gazettes images and metaphors (for instance that sleep is the brother of death, a conceit appropriated by Byron) on which European imaginations have descanted ever since. If only because he supplied the terms by which various nuances – of feeling, passion, and in nature itself – could henceforth be itemized, Hesiod made conceivable the split in Greek thinking which separated the mythical from the rational. Two wedges – "scientific" logic and the rise of *isonomia* in a *polis* based on public law – would split intelligent men from the superstitious masses who continued to fetishize oracles and put faith in personalized supernatural forces.

Hesiod's vocabulary and distinctions were never wholly superseded. The shades of his epic supplied shades of meaning in post-mythic legal and logical argument. Philosophers might disparage Hesiod's callowness, but the arts are still presided over by the Muses he invented, and inventoried. An academic journal is still entitled *Klio*, after his Muse of History (the patroness of *kleos*, fame).

With the rise of law, kinship became a matter less of heroic affinities than of human continuities and entitlement. In the mythic version, Oedipus's crime was incest and parricide, but the logico-legal anomaly was that the confusion of generations made nonsense of orderly succession. Miasma might dwindle in significance; property certainly did not. And how could any law of inheritance, or the institution of marriage, make sense of a father who was his own children's brother?

Said to have been formulated by Solon, Attic inheritance law was heartlessly favourable to male heirs. If a man died without children, his property reverted to his kin in strict order: the father, the brothers and their children, the sisters and their children, paternal cousins and their children, maternal cousins and their children. If a man had children, the property was divided by the sons, on condition that they kept their sisters until marriage and gave them a (modest) dowry. If a man had only daughters, they could inherit, but were compelled to marry his next-of-kin, beginning with his brothers. The inheritance passed to their sons as soon as they came of age.

If an heiress was already married, she could be obliged to divorce her husband in order to marry the next-of-kin, who had to divorce his wife. In Sparta, by contrast, women were notoriously rich, and owned as much as 40 per cent of the land. Adultery was an outrage in Athens (a husband could kill his wife's lover, if caught in the act, without penalty); in Sparta, women could please themselves (they might even have several husbands): promiscuity was no scandal.* Economic circumstances, not sentiment, determined the laws of marriage and of succession. Heracleitus was notoriously condescending to the extravagance of Hesiodic fancy: "The Master of the majority is Hesiod. They take him to know the greatest number of things. And this a man who doesn't understand what Night and Day are. The fact is, they are one thing." If Heracleitus's scorn marks the breach between rambling poetic mythology and terse Ionian "science", the breach was also a bridge: Clémence Ramnoux argued that it is naive to regard Heracleitus's words as calmly dismissive. Since Hesiod had supplied the ladder which Heracleitus had climbed to obtain his overview, the *Theogony* encapsulated what lay at the centre of later sophistication, and furnished its lexicon. Sneering at Hesiod was Heracleitus's way of announcing – as Ramnoux put it – "*une conscience tout fraîchement débarrassée de ses terreurs infantiles*".

Although Heracleitus publicly discounted the divine grandees and dark forces in the family album of the *Theogony*, several of the names of the children of Night were adopted, in pre-Socratic texts, as the poles of contrasting opposites: what began in sacred poetry ended in a secularizing index. Heracleitus's oracular style honours what he affected to disparage: his forked assertion that there was a power that "did and did not wish to be called Zeus" denies and asserts the force of Hesiod's mythology. Nietzsche claimed that all philosophy concealed another: every opinion has a secret codicil, and every statement was also a mask.

Philosophers have a long habit of discounting ideas which have more tenacity than they care to admit: A.J. Ayer's reduction of ethics to nothing more than an amalgam of irrational exclamations of approval, or disapproval, may have served to excuse his personal habits, but did not inhibit him from

---

* In twelfth-century Aquitaine, before the Catholic Church exerted its authority there (as it had in northern France), the laws of succession and property were similarly favourable to women. They could inherit property and rule over it like feudal lords. Men were often absent at war, and were likely to die at a younger age than women. In her *Eleanor of Aquitaine*, Alison Weir goes on to say that Aquitanian noblewomen "were renowned for their elegance in dress...and females of all classes were notorious for their lax attitude towards morality.... A wife's adultery was not punished, as elsewhere, by imprisonment or execution".

taking moral positions. Wittgenstein said that the challenge in philosophy was to "say the new thing in the old language". Heracleitus found it easier to mock the Boeotian know-all than to free himself from the terms Hesiod had devised. Seen in the light of a certain logic, Night and Day are indeed a seamless continuum, but logic itself is a tool that serves only the wide-awake: dreams and night-fears are proof against it.

The great divide between the Hesiodic and the pre-Socratic world-views was the consequence more of Pythagorean than of Heracleitan philosophy. Pythagoras did not put mythology down in so many words; but because his account of the world was mathematical, and because the Hesiodic pantheon and bestiary could not be translated into numbers, he and his followers left them behind. Although it had its own rites and fetishes, Pythagoreanism was not in showy competition with the old gods: distinct in tone and – more significantly – in notation from traditional religion, it never directly challenged the traditions from which, especially in the case of its off-shoot Orphism, it derived.

Hesiod's *Works and Days* is more insistently personal than the *Theogony*. It is a ragbag: part rural calendar, part cry of fraternal rage against Perses, the brother who was seeking to dispossess its author. At first sight, it reads as though the poet lacked the clout which Perses seems to have acquired with the Boeotian magistrates, but Peter Green has argued, with his usual forceful erudition, for the view that Hesiod was displaying his ability to run rhetorical rings around his brother in order to deter him from making a fool of himself in court. The ancient poets wrote to be performed, not to be read, and their words could be like bullets. Archilochos is notorious for having literally mortified the objects of his rage: Lycambes and his daughters (one of whom, Neobule, he had promised, briefly, to the bastard poet) were driven to suicide by his memorable derision. Michael Ayrton portrayed the sublime lout with superb boldness.

Works and Days foreshadows both the bantering, aggrieved satire, which Romans elected to boast was "entirely our own", and the agricultural manuals produced by the prosaic Xenophon and, in the Roman world, by Varro and Virgil. With traces of charm amid the bile, its folksy side is exemplified by Hesiod's term for the snail: the "house-porter".

Elsewhere, Hesiod has the lineaments of a Boeotian Polonius: "Don't be known as a man of many guests, nor yet of none; seek not the company of scoundrels nor scorn propriety. Never say ill of a man on account of his damnable, soul-destroying poverty; the Blessed Ones give and the Blessed Ones take away, and always will. The tongue's best treasure is its reticence. Its greatest charm? Restraint! Speak ill, and you'll hear worse, of yourself. Stand your round when in company; in sharing, more people have fun, and fewer pay the price."

Such voluble crabbiness amounts to doleful comedy. Of English poets, Hesiod most resembles John Clare: both were lumbered with the miseries of rural life, but had accurate sympathy for those with no choice but to live it. There are few darling buds in Hesiod's year.

In the section on domestic life, Hesiod parades the usual prejudices against women. Even when emphasizing the benefits of a good wife, he harps on how rarely one finds her. The dread of cuckoldry, or of too independent a female, disposes him to prefer a virgin bride, raised locally, who can be taught good ways. The hints for conjugal life go straight to the point: "When your private parts are mottled with semen...don't allow them to be seen in the fire light". Was this advice a scabrous joke, or did it owe something to superstition? Hestia, the goddess of the hearth, was a virgin protectress, in front of whom a certain modesty might be expected. Comedy of a kind comes from dread.

As a frowning friend of the earth, Hesiod warns against pissing in rivers and especially against fouling springs. Superstition and prudent hygiene are inseparable: he is keen on frequent washing, but warns against doing so in the same water as a woman: "grim penalties" may follow. The separation of Gents and Ladies is by no means a function of modern plumbing or of Christian prudery. Dread of the female pudenda is an early part of the male desire for them. Was the abuse of women in classical Greece a symptom of bad conscience at their social and economic relegation? *En bon Marxiste*, George Thomson was convinced that females had enjoyed equality (at the least) in a Golden Age of primitive communism before the differentiation of private property.

Little in *Works and Days* carries a flavour of the Arcadian rusticity in which later bucolic poets chose to revel, if seldom to work: Horace's Sabine farm was his pleasure, but how often did he plough the fields or scatter the good seed on the land? As the realistic registrar of Boeotian country life, Hesiod had a hard row to hoe. Bad times were always just around the corner. So – more significantly – was the rise of the city-state, whose dominant class lived on the wealth of the countryside, but concentrated its ambition on an urban culture with happier days than any rural calendar could offer.

Works and Days stands near the beginning of European literature, but its routines, like the superstitions of the *Theogony*, belong to a way of life on whose labour the world would continue to depend, but of whose population and religion the city-dweller became increasingly disdainful. The lament of the peasant over his hard life was, in *Works and Days*, largely to do with the battle with nature, but the poet's own brother moved to dispossess him by urbane means. Perses' questionable use of the courts presages the "legal" impoverishment of the peasantry which, in Attica, led to the eviction of share-cropping peasants and their final recourse to selling themselves into slavery. Solon was brought in to remedy the resulting, and deepening, social crisis. The brevity of Hesiod's two mini-epics hints at an audience with more urgent things to do than to listen to the old, old stories. The *Theogony* – less a drama than a prolonged dramatis personae – betrays an almost involuntary impatience with the mantic affectations abbreviated in it. As for *Works and Days*, it combines the countryman's diary, a catalogue of woes and a foretaste of the hickish comedy which came to play rusticity for laughs: Aristophanes' comic Boeotian yokel is Hesiod come to town with a straw in his mouth. Will Rogers and Worzel Gummidge (the hayseed with whom the Labour leader, Michael Foot – in fact a metropolitan intellectual – was cruelly compared in the General Election campaign of 1982) were among the last of the breed.

* * *

When we first went to Ios, it would not have seemed unrecognizably alien to Hesiod. Standing in the middle of their stone threshing floors, the peasants lifted the slippery corn on wide wooden shovels and threw the grains into the breeze to be winnowed. As the sun set behind it, the wheat became a shower of dry golden rain. On the beach, we would see the goats dropping calmly down the hillside on the way home from some distant pasture. They seemed invisibly tethered, by the clank and chime of the bells around their necks, to the lame goatherd (who might once have worked for Odysseus). He wore a fraying straw hat and leaned – like the three-legged man in the riddle of the Sphinx – on a tough stick. Two black dogs were busy for him.

In front of the village cafés, mustachioed old men sat on upright, raffia-seated wooden chairs in baggy Turkish trousers, braided waistcoats and cloth caps. Smoking pipes, or hookahs, they played *ntomino* (dominos) or *tavli* (backgammon) with emphatic snap. In the spear-leaved shade of eucalyptus trees, haltered donkeys nodded and nodded, but never quite agreed. The eucalyptus has a Greek name (the well-shading tree) but, although it is now to be seen all over the Mediterranean, it was a post-Hesiodic import from Australia.

As in ancient Athens, where poets could also be generals and priests (and its wisest man doubled as a common soldier), one islander in his day played many parts. Michali, the postmaster who wore two pairs of spectacles simultaneously, one for close work, the other to look at his customers, sported an official cap in the mornings, went out in his caique to fish in the afternoons and short-order-cooked in his brother's *kapheneion* at night.

76 Ios.
Ah, the old days!

There was no television and little contact with the outside world. Ios was in some respects more isolated than it had been two and a half millennia earlier, when it had a large population (some said as many as 10,000) and a fleet to go with it. Our Ios did, however, have a telephone. The only available line to the mainland went through Naxos. If we needed to call London, Michali would crank a handset and yell "Naxos", quite as if hailing the next island from a cliff-top.

Greeks continued to bring gifts. In those days, you could not pass an islander without him giving you something. If he was empty-handed, he would take the flower from behind his ear (a common decoration) or reach inside his *hypoukamiso choriatiko* – the typical collarless, striped cotton shirt we too came to wear – and bring out a tomato or a biscuit whose age prompted more gratitude than appetite. The meeting would always involve a staccato inquisition – like a vestige of tragic stichomythia – of which the first words were almost always *"Poo pate?"* (Where are you going?). The destination was always evident since – in true Heracleitan fashion – the single path led either up (to the village) or down (to the sea).

The question was a civility, not an inquiry, and often carried its own annexed answer, so that it ran: "*Poo pate, sto chorio?*" (Where are you going, to the village?), if you were going uphill; or "*Poo pate, sto limani?*" (Where are you going, to the port?), if you were coming down. Should the islander be on his donkey, he was certain to offer more substantial gifts than if on foot: sometimes beans, sometimes fresh eggs, and – as Easter approached – *kokkina avga*, the specially reddened, hard-boiled eggs which Greek Christians cracked, one against the other, in celebration of Christ's *anastasis*. After the *coup d'état* in 1967, the Colonels would call their uprising "*ee anastasis*", thus seeking to vest their unholy mutiny in sacred lineaments.

Some gifts were more Greek than others. I was surprised one day by one of the village grocers (another of the several men called Giorgos) when he not only added some olives to my white canvas fisherman's bag of provisions, but asked us to lunch at his house the following Sunday. I should perhaps have guessed than it was unlikely to be for the pleasure of our uncertain conversation. As the *dolmathes* were served, in a glutinous white sauce, it became clear that I was better at delivering my mugged-up Greek phrases than in understanding the replies: the latter were not only quickly spoken, but accented in a way which encrypted them beyond easy access.

Giorgos and his wife had dressed themselves with sudden bourgeois formality. As we sat in their sitting room, we were touched to find ourselves under the aegis of two large colour prints, in gilt frames, of Edward VII and Queen Alexandra in full courtly regalia. When I observed how impressed we were by the iconic standing of the British crown, Giorgos found my Greek as Delphic as I did his. After I explained, in slow words, who the two dignitaries in the portraits were, he butted his chin forward in ritual surprise. He had had no idea of their identities; they looked impressive, so he had given them pride of place.

At the end of a long, awkward meal, the real purpose of our invitation was revealed. Not surprisingly, although absurdly, Giorgos had taken me – simply because we were foreigners – for a rich man who might care to be his partner in a chicken farm, of which the clucking first inhabitants were visible from the terrace at the back of the house. Was it vanity, embarrassment or a silly wish to be a part of village life that impelled me, to my own amazement, to act as though I was honoured to have been selected for fleecing?

I declined the partnership, which even I had enough wit to see was likely to be more profitable to one partner than to the other, but I was then asked whether I would at least, "as a friend", lend a few thousand drachs. Giorgos had interpreted my earlier words to convey that (for him) happy meaning. Even as I handed him 5,000 drachmai, no small sum in those days, I knew that I was being a fool. Edward VII and Queen Alexandra witnessed my folly with imperial dignity. *Noblesse oblige* was our common badge.

I repented at leisure, but there was no way of recouping my cash (we soon needed it) except from Giorgos's shelves, which were not remarkable for their variety. I pillaged regularly, and with righteous persistence. One day, I asked if he had any of the local honey. He brought down a big-bellied earthenware jar from a high shelf and, as I filled my canvas bag with the least rusty of his tins of bully beef and sardines, he poured from it, thickly, into a large tin. Since the island's hills are a pungent herbarium, Ios honey has always been particularly delicious. In the ancient world, mortal recipes for *ersatz* ambrosia (by definition the food – and balm – of immortals) mixed wine with honey. I returned to our cottage with the feeling that I had retrieved at least a few of our drachs in ambrosial kind. When I poured the honey from the tin into a jar, I noticed that it seemed to be filled with what looked like plump raisins. Was this a *choriatik* additive on which Hesiod might have smacked his usually joyless lips? No; forensic inspection proved that the glistening black beans were in fact embalmed bluebottles. The whole jar was a mausoleum of suspended flies. I retrieved the rest of my silly loan almost entirely in sardines and NouNou condensed milk.

We were accepted on the island as *metoikoi*, foreign residents, with the warmth which our two small children earned for us. Another Giorgos (Galatsios), the donkey-man who insisted on being our local *daimon*, suggested one day that he take Paul and Sarah (who was under two years old) off our hands for the day: his wife, Kyria Maroussa, would make lunch and – "*Dthen piradse!*" (never mind) – he would bring them home later. How innocent we were! What parents today would allow a stranger, however sweetly intentioned, to lift their small children onto his donkey and disappear down the valley with them?

Given a few easy hours to ourselves, we had no misgivings; until we did. As the shadows thickened and lengthened, I was suddenly a demented, Demeterian father, running along the rock-littered pathway up towards the village, calling "Paul, Sarah", with increasing volume and alarm. I ran from the village back down to the end of the long green valley, stumbling and lurching like a mad man in my clumsy sandals. Then I saw Giorgos riding serenely towards me, Sarah on his arm, Paul astride Phryne, the donkey, in front of him. Giorgos was bouncing his horny heel against Phryne's flank and grinning. He knew very well how alarmed I had been. At one with the donkey that seemed to be part of him, he looked like an asinine centaur.

The butcher kept his best chickens (he said) for the children, and the occasional cut of fresh meat, and liver. He also made cheese at a "factory" on our way to the empty beach. We would meet him, Anatolian-smiling, with a bleating lamb for a scarf, its feet buckled by his two hands: the posture of the gentle killer in the sixth-century *Moschophoros* (calf-bearer) in the Acropolis Museum.

* * *

*T*he commonplace was transfigured in Greek sculpture. The quotidian meshed with the sacred: the priesthood, if venerable, was an honorary, part-time dignity. Fresh meat supplied both a rare feast and a votive sacrament: "To what green altar, O mysterious priest, / Lead'st thou that heifer lowing at the skies / And all her silken flanks with garlands drest?"

Keats recognized how the sacerdotal slaughterman flattered the beast he was due to kill. Once at the altar (more likely red with blood than green with foliage), the heifer was offered a dish of its favourite grain. Bowing its head to eat, it was taken to have assented to its sacrifice. Modern slaughterhouses mimic this antique courtesy by setting bales of hay at the entrance. Doomed beasts are duped by pleasure on their way to death. Condemned animals too can get the last breakfast of their choice.

At one great festival, after the victim's blood was shed, the Athenians, in grave pantomime, "tried" the sacrificial axe, found it guilty and threw it into the sea. After the execution of the Nazi war criminals, Winston Churchill agreed to meet, but would not shake hands with, the hangman Pierrepoint. During the Thargelia, the city's accumulated sins were loaded onto human scapegoats. Like psychic garbage collectors, the outcasts removed the civic miasma incurred during the year: taking its guilt with them, two trashy characters (often convicts) were driven from the city into exile. Tradition promises that they were often lashed on the genitals as they fled. We still relish, and are purged by, the ritual humiliation of scapegoats: the politician, footballer or celebrity whose sexual conduct – although widely emulated, or envied – is outed by tabloid headlines. There, by the grace of editors, goes a victim other than ourselves. The horror with which our eroticized society reacts

77 Athenian delivery boy.

78 Holman Hunt's scapegoat.

to sexual deviance, especially (today) to paedophilia, is both rational and ritualized. How different is the violence of demands for their sequestration, and even for their castration, from whipping culprits on the genitals and driving them out of town?

René Girard maintained (against the structuralist current) that scapegoats were originally put to death: hence the vestigial cruelty in festive ceremonies of eviction. As Orestes exemplified (until redeemed by Apollo's advocacy), exile was a living death: there were wandering Gentiles before they were wandering Jews. Rites of eviction were antique recipes for banishing evil: a sublime form of human sacrifice. There were undisguised reversions to it in Greco-Roman history: Themistokles was accused (if slanderously) of the ritual slaughter of three Persian nobles before the battle of Salamis.

If true, this would clash with another accusation that seeks to darken Themistokles' reputation, that of having *genuinely* warned Xerxes, on the eve of the battle, that the Greek ships were about to disperse, and with them the Great King's only chance of catching them all in the same net. Even if Themistokles *was* hedging his bets (in order to come out a winner whichever way the battle went), would a man of his intelligence so ostentatiously have murdered three prominent Persians ahead of the time when he might want to make his peace with, and claim his reward from, Xerxes?

The Romans despised the Carthaginians for their cult of infant immolation, but, after the disaster of Cannae, they too had recourse to human sacrifice. For Girard, the scapegoat mechanism finds its critical instance, on which it founders, in the case of Jesus. Part of the Gospel's Good News was that God had no appetite for blood. After being brought to realize that, in Jesus, a blameless scapegoat had sacrificed Himself for them, how could men imagine that they could ever again excrete their sins or gratify (or dupe) the Godhead by sacrificial mechanisms?

Social and architectural structures sustain, and reflect, religious logics: after the Roman destruction of the second Temple in Jerusalem, and the onset of the Diaspora, Jews abandoned the habit, as they lacked the site, of formal sacrifice. They became the People of the Book, the portable "Temple" on which they based their long, wandering piety. The abiding orthodox horror of bloody meat remains a hint that it was once reserved as God's portion.

The modern abhorrence of animal sacrifice does not inhibit us from the "humane" killing of the same range of domesticated animals to satisfy our own appetites as were once despatched to placate the gods. Mythic figures – for instance, Minos when he spared Poseidon's white bull – were punished for denying the gods the meaty pleasure which we continue to relish, despite its uneasy affinity with cannibalism (from which, like Zeus, we rear back in humbug horror). If civilized people ever entirely outlaw their diet of blood, it will probably be less because they fear the spirits of their victims than for the sake of honouring our one surviving mythological totem: the cholesterol-conscious Narcissus, who puts a taboo on whatever endangers his health.

Only a few years ago, when a red cow was said to have been born in Israel, it was enough to revive among the pious, or the cracked, the memory of a biblical prediction that such a birth signalled the imminence of the Messiah and that, once grown, the magic cow would lead (literally) to the recovery of the Temple Mount for the Jews. The television crew with whom I happened to be working, on a programme about gods, drove out to the farm where the miraculous creature was being fattened for its redeeming role. It did not look markedly crimson to me, but then I was wearing sceptically-tinted Channel-4 spectacles.

Unsentimental, secular Israelis called for the creature's summary execution, but the superstitious insisted that scripture offered a divine guarantee that the Arabs would be evicted by its parade. The notion that God or gods interfere directly in human affairs was dismissed in logical terms by Spinoza, as it had been, more gently, by Epicurean agnosticism, but the idea that duly solicited divinities can take an irresistible hand in mundane life is implicit in the plaited fears, and anthropocentric self-importance, of human mythologies.

Homer's gods are projections of human beings, graced with beauty and immortality, but ill-tempered, capricious and with no marked concern for humans unless they happened to be their favourites or their own offspring (no god could make love to a mortal woman without impregnating her, which littered the earth with consequential children). Sacrifice was more a form of hopeful insurance than of grateful tribute. Zeus had the lineaments of Auden's tyrant who "knew human folly like the back of his hand /...When he laughed, respectable senators burst with laughter, /And when he cried the little children died in the streets".

If Homer depicts the Olympians as willing to laugh, it is seldom kindly, but occasionally at each other. When Hephaestus enmeshed Aphrodite, his wife, and her warmongering lover Ares under that artfully gilded net, so publishing their adultery to the other Olympians, the gods' amusement was ambiguous. The divine craftsman had been so keen to display his ingenuity that he forgot that a cuckold was a cuckold for all that. Like sexual shame, sexual embarrassment, and the laughter that goes with it, scarcely originates in Christian prudery: Pindar depicts Apollo laughing (unusually) at the huge erections on the donkeys which the Hyperboreans are sacrificing to him (donkey salami is still eaten in Hellas). Sex and comedy are an old double act. But can we imagine Apollo – the original smiler with a knife – being a good loser, as Priapus was, in a first-century B.C. epigram of Antipater: "Seeing Cimon's dick erect, Priapus said, / Good lord, I'm an immortal beaten by a bigger prick than me"?

Greek gods were docked of their sense of humour when Plato required his ideal state's divinities to be inexorably moral. In his *Politeia*, human beings were denied the democratic luxury of coarse laughter: the ideal state would sponsor no Aristophanes, who had made a laughing stock of Socrates. The latter had endured the pillory in good part; his hagiographer was not amused.

In line with Platonism, the Christian God has no sense of humour: Jesus wept, but the New Testament never indicates that Jesus, or His father, was amused. In the perfect Godhead, as in the cult of totalitarian leaders (its mundane counterfeit), there is no comedy. Nietzsche thought Socrates a better model for mankind than Jesus. Among his more generous range of human responses was the "smile that tempered his seriousness and the wisdom full of mischief which is the most handsome human attitude of mind. Furthermore, Socrates is more intelligent".

Aristophanic comedy was funny both because it broke the rules as often as its characters broke wind and because such outrageousness was licensed only on a few days of the year. The Attic comic theatre was an off-season entertainment aimed at mainly domestic audiences. Visitors to the city were more likely to frequent, and be impressed by, the great tragic festivals.

Aristophanes' most impertinent satire (the anti-war *Lysistrata*) was staged when Athens was fighting for its life and the tourist trade negligible. In earlier years, when Aeschylus's *Oresteia* was presented, solemn diction and themes dignified Athenian culture and her imperial role, though even then the satyr play – a burlesque postscript – licensed the relief of residual emotion in brief hilarity. The *Oresteia*'s appended satyr play, which has not survived, was a domestic sitcom showing Agamemnon's brother, Menelaus, and little wife Helen back home, in rueful bliss, in post-war Argos. Kenneth McLeish and I did a mock-up of this for BBC television. In her last public performance, the late Diana Dors, a sex symbol of the 1950s, played a middle-aged Helen opposite a Menelaus more eager to get to the golf club than to return to her bed.

The (probably Hellenistic) critic Demetrios, in his essay "On Style", defines the satyr play as "tragedy at play". The only extant example is Euripides' *Cyclops*. There is, however, no shortage of fragments and synopses to make it clear that subtlety was not at a premium: in Sophocles' *Syndeipnon*, the Achaean warlords engage in a blokeish binge, ending with one of them, perhaps Odysseus, having a pisspot poured over his head.

Aeschylus made light of Oedipus in his *Sphinx*, and in his *Prometheus Pyrkaeus* the eponymous hero becomes a fire-raising *Poneros* (rogue or trickster). If Euripides failed to appreciate the fun that Aristophanes poked at him, he was not afraid to make a joke of himself: the *Cyclops* seems to have been a parody of his own *Hecuba* (recently revived, triumphantly, in London, with Clare Higgins in the lead). The tragedians have come down to us with solemn faces, but they were capable of assuming the mask of comedy with versatile enthusiasm. Self-mockery seems to have been their speciality.

The notion of sincerity in art is implicitly questioned by the alternative use of myth as both solemn and comic topoi: the masks of comedy and tragedy indeed hang from the same hook. Duplicity is the mark of both Prometheus and Daedalus, the archetypal Makers. The amputation of the comic codas which the great playwrights pinned to the end of their trilogies was, no doubt, as much a matter of chance as the Venus de Milo's loss of her arms, but it has lent the tragic theatre a doctored solemnity which conformed nicely with the aesthetics and ethics of the scholars' Hellas. The interplay of tragedy and comedy in Athens (and of ribaldry with morality) was deemed unedifying by Victorian teachers and dons, who were often in Holy Orders.

In the solemn centuries of the British Empire, the classical education was a preparation for dominion over palm and pine. The ruler had to be taught to keep a straight face. Even one's own jokes were not to be laughed at. In Terence Rattigan's *The Browning Version*, the desiccated classics master, Crocker-Harris, remarks, almost chidingly, to one of his pupils: "You laughed at my little joke, Taplow." The boy later gives him Browning's translation of

79 Archaic Dionysus toting raw materials.

Aeschylus as a leaving present, thus moving the bitter old man to painful tears.

Once imperial pretensions (and the obligatory straight-facedness) were abandoned, reticence and modesty ceased to be virtues: deconstruction then ascribed them to hypocrisy, or to mis-reading. In the wake of Nietzsche and E.R. Dodds, modern taste has more appetite for the Dionysiac than for the Apolline. In satyr style, the Union Jack has been lowered from the flag of empire to a motif for underpants.

By licensing licence, Dionysus looks more sincere than strict-tempoed Apollo with his golden meanness. Dionysus encourages the uninhibited conduct which, in today's culture, belongs to rock music, sexual freedom and day-light yobbery. Dionysus's sexual ambiguity gives him postmodern glamour. The swinging god of wine passes for an advertisement for a Club Med world, whose immoderate trade mark is "Everything in Excess". Today, Apolline mean-mindedness is honoured only by squares. Their Apollo wears a tie; Dionysus rips it off.

Bacchantes typically ran out of the city and into the hills to binge on raw nature: as females, they represented the wantonness, the lack of civic propri-ety which Pentheus, the repressive king of Thebes in Euripides' *Bacchae*, was not alone in deploring. The Bacchantes' male equivalents were the satyrs, with their grotesquely elongated erections: large genitals were an embarrassment, unaesthetic and, in flaccid form, the mark of senility. Male Greeks were haunted by dread, and envy, of uncontrolled female desires and pleasures. Tiresias told them, as usual, what they both wanted and did not want to hear: that women had nine times more pleasure from sex than men. Even today the female capacity for unlimited orgasms is the stuff of uneasy comedy: the famous scene in *When Harry Met Sally* proves both how much women can enjoy sex and, worse, how easily they can fake it.

As for righteous grief over the death of sons and husbands in war, that risked being unsociably sincere. Perikles deplored prolonged lamentation and

put a tight limit on public mourning. Even now, it is given an official term, when it comes to royal deaths or national disasters. If matriarchy did indeed precede patriarchy, male policing of "emotional" outbursts suggests abiding fears that the other sex might stage a counter-revolution, especially when men have done something unforgivably crass or cruel, such as going to war.

In *Lysistrata*, Aristophanes envisages females taking control and, by a sexual strike, making peace a necessary preliminary to making love. Such a strike had, however, to be depicted as a comic prospect: in a state of rampant tumescence, how could Athenian males still be capable of dignified politics, or waging war? If the comedy derived from a (wo)manifest *reductio ad absurdum* of proper politics, in what other society, ancient or modern, might a playwright, during a destructive war, make fun of the warrior ethos and suggest that the whole enterprise was a farce? If the Greeks' arts and gods came – as Bernal and others claim – from elsewhere, the willingness to entertain, and be entertained by, counter-cultural possibilities was wholly theirs.

The condemnation and execution of Socrates prove that there were limits to the latitude of Athenian tolerance. Yet his fate hardly amounts to evidence that democracy was a capricious aberration. The freedom and wit with which Plato expressed his criticism of democratic Athens would have been inconceivable in any society of which Plato himself might approve.

Gilbert Ryle, in his *Plato's Progress*, depicts Plato as a frustrated playwright whose dialogues were secret scripts for a public stage he never occupied. Ryle guesses that Plato hung around drama festivals in the hope of picking up "sixteen-year-olds" (very British of him to posit so advanced an age group). Ryle – most probably a lifelong virgin – confessed, on a train journey with his quondam pupil A.J. Ayer, that had he abandoned celibacy, it would "probably" have been with a male partner.

Ryle too deployed drollery to illustrate his philosophical ideas, not least in *The Concept of Mind*. I remember a lecture in which, with the required straight face, he dwelt at length on the relationship of two propositions, which he called p and q. The similarity of the latter to the former he referred to as "the p-ness of q", a performer's joke.

Greeks might be amused by excess but, like the Romans, they put a premium on decorum. While *parrhesia* had no rule against slander, public speakers had to observe a code of dress and gesture not unlike that of modern legislatures. They might accuse their enemies of being the willing (or rented) target of buggery, or even of having parents with ignoble occupations such as sausage-making, but they had to do it with the expected style. If panache warped truth, public decorum owed as much to religious propriety – in which repetition of due forms was obligatory – as to democratic freedom. The Delphic oracle did, after all, speak in Apollo's name when it commended moderation. It continued to be revered by the average citizen, however much smart tongues might mock its venality.

Dionysus presided over the drama in Athens, but he was banned from the Olympic precinct, which was as symbolic of Hellenic culture as Delphi. As its contentious gods proved, Hellas was full of contradictory simultaneities: to claim that Reason was the guiding Greek principle, and prefigured St John's *Logos*, is to ignore how riddled with superstition daily life was. Reason emerged at least as much from diplomacy and military tactics as from philosophy. Might this go to explain why it was not associated with women? Reason and Unreason were, in Lawrence Durrell's favourite terms, "systole and diastole", the old in-and-out at the heart of Hellas. Reason is the last of the myths left us by the Greeks, just as hope was the last of the scourges to escape from Pandora's box.

Nothing was so foreign to Greeks as Bishop Butler's dictum, "A thing is what it is and not another thing". Mutability and double-talk were integral to their vision of themselves and of the gods. Their archetypal hero Odysseus was nothing if not duplicitous. He masterminded the "gift" of the Trojan horse. Having blinded Polyphemus, he told him that his name was Outis* (literally Nobody), which led the wounded Cyclops to tell his brothers that "Nobody" had hurt him, after which – assuming him unharmed – they left him to his fate. *Metis*, Odysseus's defining quality, is a variant of *outis*.

Finally, the hero returned to Ithaka disguised as an old beggar, the better to ambush his wife's suitors. As for his long nostalgia, that too can be read as devious humbug. Paul Rassinier, a French critic (and Holocaust revisionist)

---

* Isaiah Berlin was known to use the pseudonym O. Utis.

remarked that "Ulysses...each day added a new adventure to his Odyssey, as much to please the public taste of the times as to justify his long absence in the eyes of his family". Storytelling can be nursery-speak for lying, but not all stories – Rassinier should have learnt – are therefore lies.

Proteus – the Old Man of the Sea, who could take on manifold forms, as could Thetis (the daughter of Nereus, a sea god) – made magic and treachery of a similar, elusive piece. The Greeks never trusted the sea not to change its face. I remember sitting with Captain Adonis on the dock on Ios, on days when the Aegean was a smooth golden platter before us. When asked if he was going fishing, he shook his head (and raised his ouzo glass) and pointed to the calm water as if its treachery were palpable.

The strangest quality of Greece is that it is a little country, at least in modern cartography, but seems to stretch, like its myths, in all directions, mimicked, duplicated and travestied: there is an Athens in Tennessee, where I came across two Greek brothers running a 1950s retro hamburger joint and soda fountain. There is also a Sparta in the same state, which figured in Norman Jewison's film, *In the Heat of the Night*. Ithaca is in the state of New York, and so is a second Croton.

In Taos, New Mexico, we went to see D.H. Lawrence's paintings (still banned in today's Big Brother England) in the La Fonda hotel. We paid our dollar and went into the owner's office, where they were displayed. The room was stacked with books. Even the windows were shuttered with them. The walls were covered with D.H.L.'s innocuously ithyphallic daubs and with framed prints of heroes of the Greek War of Independence, including Byron in klephtic rig. It so happened that we owned three prints of the same series, one of Prince Mavrocordato, in buttoned cap and Phanariot spectacles.

While we were inspecting the display, a large, bald man came in. I took one look and said, "Of *course*: you're a Greek." "And you are a Jew," he said. "Now I take you to lunch and we talk." Saki Karavas was no Procrustes: he insisted we stay in his hotel, but – since we were immediate friends – refused to let us pay. *Philoxenia* was his passion. I have on my shelves volumes of Yiannis Ritsos and Cavafy and Seferis which he sent me with generous regularity. Saki made Taos part of Greece: Hellas is wherever there is a Greek.

It is said that the ancient Hellenes did not always acknowledge the sea as materially different from land: Greece did not stop where the sea started. At first, the sea was called simply *poros*, the same word as roadway. Etymologically, *pontos* (the open sea) is identified with *pons*, the Latin for a bridge. Even the sky was colonized by Greek gods, mythic heroes and awful warnings such as Ixion.

Greekness, like Jewishness, is a state of mind. I was once having a haircut in Barcelona and discovered that the barber was Greek. When I showed off a little by speaking the language, he asked if I was of Greek origin. Why else was I so dark-haired? When I said I was Jewish, he said, "*Miadzouni*": they're much the same thing. Yes and no: a Greek answer, and a Jewish one.

The doubleness of the gods – now protective, now vindictive – was matched by (because it sponsored) duplicities of language. Just as the "plain-speaking" of oracles had to be deconstructed by the intelligence, to tease out its "true" meaning, so the place of *apate* (fraud or deception) in art eliminated from Greek aesthetics the notion of "sincerity", which romantics take for evidence of merit. Heracleitus made the point that it is natural to love secrets, and secrecy: his Nature's way. First, Nietzsche and, later, E.R. Dodds insisted on the central importance of Dionysus (and of the Irrational, which his riot impersonated). Both scholars were intent on redressing academic overemphasis on the priority of Apolline restraint.

Today's anthropology – with its Herostratan streak – prefers to dig out the bitter roots of art rather than to relish its sweeter fruits. Jane Harrison, in her still delectable, if obsolete, *Prolegomena to the Study of Greek Religion*, was among the first classicists to take her cue from anthropology and strip off the Olympians' pious cladding to reveal the snakes and furies behind the arras; and the old bottles in the attic.

Yet the exception was not the rule: the Dionysiac was celebrated because it was aberrant (the god was, above all, a homeless wanderer). Part of what the Bacchantes demonstrated was the civilizing force of the rules which they flouted by their rustic excursion. They also proved, though it was scarcely their purpose, how strong society was. After all, once down from their high, the women did return to their senses, and to their cloistered duties. As in the Roman Saturnalia, those "best of days" (in mid-December) during which slaves were served by their masters, role reversal was evidence of how unchallengeable the social order was during the rest of the year. Prison governors still sometimes wait table at Christmas lunch. In today's Thessalian folk festivals, the locals stage travesty weddings in which two men play bride and groom.

In the fourth century, Aeschines looked back on the Golden Age of Athenian oratory, in which *kalokagathia* – a portmanteau word conveying, without irony, the qualities now ironically attributed to "the Great and the Good" – was the expected, and exacted, style. Men such as Perikles, Themistokles and Aristeides were said to be "so controlled...that it was considered a moral failing to move the arm freely". In the days of empire, talking with your hands was typically un-British. Superfluous gesture advertised a lack of what the Romans would call *gravitas*. Cicero, in one of his typically outspoken speeches, accused a senator of "dancing naked on the table" during a drunken party. "Naked" meant only that the reveller had thrown off his toga.

81 Dionysiac ravers going to it.

Ancient public behaviour was much more conventional than we choose to imagine: the "natural" was foreign to the city. Themis, the much revered goddess of limits, held the line between order and anarchy. The stiff upper lip was more admired than Euripides' *Bacchae* made it seem: Socrates was exemplary for having stood still, for all but twenty-four hours, while on military service at Potidaea. If he was, in fact, locked in some kind of catatonic fit, it was diagnosed as stoic, guardsmanlike endurance.

Keeping one's place was essential in fourth-century Athens. Demosthenes brought suit for *asebeia* rather than for *hubris* (common assault) against a rival, Meidias, who was said to have given him a sock on the jaw as he officiated, as *choregos*, in a quasi-magisterial role. A jury was more likely to be shocked by a breach of piety than by a theatrical punch-up. Taking it on the chin in his turn, Meidias seems to have settled out of court, for no small sum.

Athenian dramatic performers were probably limited in their range of gestures by rules similar to those which governed public speaking. Rhetoric too was a theatrical performance: deviation from the expected was, in either department, a false note. According to Plutarch, in his biography of the Roman general Pompey, using a single finger to scratch the head, without disturbing the coiffure, suggested (at least to Clodius and his rowdy claque) the effeminate narcissism of a homosexual. Pompey – in truth, an extremely uxorious man – did it, supposedly, to mimic Alexander the Great's hairstyle, as portrayed in the statue by his contemporary, Lysippus. Roman life imitated

Greek art, and so did Roman art. In his Nobel prize-winning *Les Mots*, Jean-Paul Sartre recalls how his grandfather became obsessed with his personal appearance (especially his profile) after the invention of photography had made him immodestly aware of it. Hardly less conscious of his own image, as an anti-bourgeois, Sartre refused the Nobel prize. He might have recalled the Duc de la Rochefoucauld's "He who refuses praise seeks to be praised twice over".

Tragedy survived the fall of the Athenian empire as a form, but how often did new authors articulate it to criticize the gods or society? Little of their plays has survived, perhaps not unjustly: had they had great merit, Aristotle might have cited some of them in his *Poetics*. In fact he stuck to examples from the great trio of Aeschylus, Sophocles and Euripides.

Comedy became pure entertainment: Aristophanes had reminded Athenians of the state they were in. He craved their applause as much as the next man, but he also goaded them to change, if only to change back, while there was still time. After the battle of Chaeronea, in 338, when Philip crushed Athens and her allies, there wasn't.

In the New Comedy, of which Menander (342–292) was the master, domestic themes, of love and marriage, indulged a public grown weary of practical issues and impotent to return to the old ways. Menander made light of the conservative tradition of the once obligatory marriage of an heiress to her husband's next of kin. Romance sugared tradition; personal preference (and happiness) made clan loyalties second to romantic love, in which passion trumps propriety. Like Marx's History, drama repeated itself, first as tragedy then as farce. Audiences became addicted to variations on anodyne themes: rather than surprise them, the comic playwright honoured their expectations. The tragic moment of recognition (*anagnorisis*) – such as when Elektra realizes that Orestes has survived and has returned to avenge his father – dwindled into the mutual recognition of star-crossed lovers in finales where ends were cosily and amusingly tied up.

As Aristophanes proved, insolence could win prizes in ancient Greece, but gods could rarely take a joke: to quiz them was to meet with a dusty answer. Prometheus was the only mythical figure to force a draw with the supreme deity. Paul Claudel epitomized the cleavage between the Roman Catholic and the rebellious God-botherer when he came out uncompromisingly in favour of Zeus against Prometheus. Diogenes (that cut-price Socrates) took the same view: his Prometheus deserved punishment because fire was the source of mankind's appetite for luxury.

*   *   *

*P*rometheus had rare nerve to play the rebel with Zeus, but he also had immortal blood: he was related to the pre-Olympian Titans, the gigantic dynasty befriended by Kronos. Their alliance – which the provident Prometheus deserted in order to side with the Olympians – was beaten in the cosmic generation-war by Zeus and his allies. Prometheus was also a pupil of the industrious Cyclopes, a breed which was given a bad name by Odysseus's captor, the man-eating Polyphemus.

The one-eyed monsters had a countervailing reputation as archetypal teachers: a Cyclops gave master classes in handicrafts to Hephaestus and Athene when they were neophytes. As their name implies, Cyclopes had an eye for rounded things. They were also reputed to have built the great walls of Tiryns (actually constructed around 1400 B.C.). Alone in the palace in the noonday heat, in the days before the site was fenced against tourists, I could share the ancient credulity that declared the builders of those fat walls to be superhuman. What human muscle could have put such massive, heat-glazed boulders so tightly in place? Only the Incas' black palaces in Cuzco have mortarless masonry to match it: in both places, you cannot insert a knife-blade between one trim block and the next.

The long gallery at Tiryns, with its ceiling of huge slabs of granitic rock leaning together in an inverted vee, was of a piece with the mysterious architecture (and triangular window apertures) of the Incas' sacred city, Macchu Picchu, at the end of the highest railway in the world, more than two miles up in the Andes. Menelaus is said to have been the king of Sparta, but it is tempting to imagine that his summer place was at breezy Tiryns, whose walls also recall the massive symmetry of the Inca capital.

Hesiod was the first to flesh out the story of Prometheus, the arrogant, ambivalent craftsman-deliverer, who both invented and then sided with human beings. Although the son of the Titan Iapetus, he had the wit to support the Olympians and earned their favour: he held Zeus's head while Hephaestus trepanned it to release Athene. Prometheus applied his craftiness to the creation of human beings, out of mud – clay is a common ingredient in recipes for creation – and from his own semen.

Athene was so amused by the clay models (Kenneth McLeish noted that the Greeks' slang name for dolls was "Prometheus's babies"), and so grateful for Prometheus's part in her delivery from Zeus's skull, that she blessed them with life. Zeus insisted that the little beasts be confined below stairs: they were relegated to earth, and then only for a short span. He also denied them heavenly knowledge.

Prometheus could not endow his babies with divine intelligence, but he enhanced their chances of physical survival by turning them into carnivores.

Having stolen one of the Sun's prize bulls, which he killed and jointed, he decked the bones and the fat in the hide and pouched the meal in the unappetizing stomach. Then he invited Zeus to make his choice: whichever receptacle he preferred would always be the gods' portion, the other mankind's.

In Hesiod's *Theogony*, Zeus agrees to be tricked by Prometheus (whom he calls "cleverer than anyone else") because he wants an excuse to take revenge on mankind. Since the king of the gods is said to be choked (literally, "angry about the lungs") when he realizes the deception, this looks like an *ex post facto* device for saving Zeus's face. If he had already guessed that Prometheus was setting him up, he did not take the result sportingly: he decreed that man should forever eat his meat uncooked.

Prometheus knew a trick worth two of that. While the Olympians were at table, he stole a spark of fire from Hephaestus's forge, hid it in a fennel stem and took it down to earth. Fire not only charred civilized men's steaks, and beefed up their powers of resistance, it also allowed them to cadge enough divine power to make them lords of the world. The Byzantines would later make a state secret of their formula for "Greek fire" – a compound of nitre, naphtha and sulphur – which enabled them to repel hostile fleets by flooding them with flame.

In postulating Hesiod's "untiring fire" as the principal element in creation, Heracleitus honours the myth whose author he scorned. Hesiod says that when Zeus spotted "far-beaconing fire among mankind", he lost his temper and despatched Prometheus to the Caucasus to be riveted to a rock and have his liver pecked by an insatiable eagle. Zeus, it appears, took the old soldier's line: "A joke's a joke, but fuck a pantomime".

Prometheus's rebelliousness is most probably explained by his Titanic blood. Foresight armed him to side with Zeus, but his heart did not follow his head. His half-brother Atlas had been loyal to the Titans. While many of the giants were punished by being buried alive under what turned into volcanoes whose eruptions were believed to vent their imprisoned rage, man-mountain Atlas had to support the heavens on his neck and shoulders (the cervical vertebra is still known as "the Atlas").

Prometheus was unique, in Greek myth, for his willingness to suffer for his playthings, mankind. Although insolence was no less characteristic of Hermes, the latter combined roguishness with being Zeus's dutiful messenger. If he too had stolen the Sun's livestock, it was only out of mischief. He could also play the policeman: he was *psychopompos*, the escorter of souls to Hades. Armed with his snaked wand, Hermes was Zeus's spin doctor.

Prometheus is the prototype of Lucifer, rebel angel, bringer of light to mankind (matches were once called Lucifers) and the most personable character in Milton's *Paradise Lost*. Thanks first to Aeschylus and later to Shelley, Prometheus was written up into a saviour more noble than his divine persecutor. Even Plato seems to have winked at him when he attributed the work of creating the world to a "demiurge" with Promethean energy and resource.

While he was chained to his rock, Prometheus's liver grew again each night, so that his torment might, as in the Christian hell, be unending. Tityus, who had sexually assaulted Leto, was similarly chained in Hades, where two eagles tore forever at his liver. In the anatomy of faculties, the Greeks associated the liver both with lust (Tityus's crime) and with divination. Could it be that Prometheus's punishment was as much for the misuse of prophetic powers as for the theft of fire?

He was sustained, during 30,000 excruciating years, by knowing that, as long as he withheld one secret vital to Zeus's own future, his torment would eventually have to be ended in a trade-off. The moment came after the voluntary death of the immortal centaur Chiron, who was modernized as a schoolteacher in John Updike's novel *The Centaur*. Though his name (like that of Palamedes) labels

82 Artisan Prometheus making prototypical brats.

him handyman, Chiron was also a teacher: among his old boys were both Achilles and Herakles. After that agonizing wound from a poisoned arrow while fighting on Zeus's side against the Titans, Zeus turned him into the constellation Centaur (more fanciful pundits say he became Sagittarius, a sour pun since the arrow he bore was the one that killed him).

Chastened by the horse/man's charitable suggestion that his place among the immortals be taken by another, Zeus sent Herakles to release Prometheus from the fetters with which Bia (the Enforcer, whose name came to be associated with rape) had clamped him to an outlandish Caucasian crag, and to propose a diplomatic trade-off in order to learn his secret.

Some sources say that Herakles himself (who was half-mortal) took Chiron's place among the fully-tenured Olympians, others that it was Prometheus, who was, until then, only a sort of privileged metic. If Herakles was the recipient of Chiron's chair at the highest table, he must, logically, have been in mortal agony when he unplugged Prometheus's rivets. This crux proves only that neither logic nor temporal sequence has any place in myth. Since Zeus was a supreme god never credited with omniscience, there was no contradiction in his knowing that the fettered Prometheus knew something that he himself did not. The omniscience and omnipotence of the monotheist's God pose more difficult problems for His apologists, since they must reconcile His ability to do everything with His unwillingness to do anything about human suffering: Christians posit His gift to mankind of free will as the reason for His inaction, quite as if some vestigial Themis kept Him within the bounds of His own rules. Nature was sometimes postulated as this regulatory agency. When Spinoza equated God and Nature, he "incidentally" rendered miraculous events illogical, since they are by definition supernatural.

Once reprieved, Prometheus was prepared to reveal the one thing Zeus needed to know: that the sea-nymph Thetis, whom the sea-god Poseidon was planning to marry, was fated to produce a "son even greater than his father". Someone greater than Zeus's brother the Earth-Shaker might unsettle, or even unseat, the King of the Gods. Forewarned (at last), Zeus aborted Poseidon's wedding plans and substituted a mere mortal as Thetis's fiancé. Peleus, the replacement, caught sight of her, mermaidenly naked from the waist up, from the deck of the *Argo*, of which he was a crew member. The result of their mixed marriage was Achilles: a hero indeed greater, but no less mortal, than his father. However, Thetis did seek to make her son immortal by immersing him in the waters of the magic river Styx. To avoid him drowning, she held him by one heel, which – because it remained dry – was in due time fatally vulnerable to Paris's lethal arrow. There is a fine statue of Achilles being dipped in the Styx by Thetis in the British Museum.

The game of sticking to the letter – but ducking the spirit – of divine promises and oracular pronouncements repeated itself in several plots involving the relations of gods and men. When in love with mortals, gods and goddesses were liable to make incautious offers of privilege. After Eos, the goddess of dawn, fell in love with Tithonus (brother of King Priam of Troy), she begged Zeus to make him immortal. In her passionate haste, she failed to stipulate – though she clearly intended – that his youth should endure with him.

Zeus yielded, but only to what Eos had specified. After many a summer, Tithonus shrivelled until he was nothing but a husk around his voice. His time having been denied a stop, he wizened into a cicada, which sounds like a watch being perpetually wound up. In the end, he longed for death, a wish repeated by the Sibylline prophetess, who – similarly desiccated – lived in a jar.

* * *

*T*he gods could be celestial shysters: the catch was in the fine print or in perversely literal interpretation. Despite Wittgenstein's dictum, logic does have its surprises. The trickiness of divine lawgivers was echoed by powerful mortals: masters of language, and of the law, gained mastery over men.

As tyrannical caprices bore down on men, a communal wish arose to have the laws written in stone and posted in a public place. People wanted to know exactly where they stood (the philosophical demand for definitions seeks to stabilize the world, or at least the language, as laws establish a state). One of the earliest instances can still be seen in the centre of Gortyn, in Crete, where – in the mid-fifth century – the tablets of the law were incised, for common scrutiny and reference. The centrality of truthful testimony, from the earliest days, is proved by provisions at Gortyn for the "ordeal by oath" in cases of suspected perjury.

When set in stone, Gortyn's laws became accessible to everyone, though justice was not dispensed in equal measure: rape could be punished only with a fine, computed on a sliding scale according to the status of the victim (of whichever sex) and of the rapist. As in Athens, the laws of inheritance were carefully tabulated, but Gortyn's slaves were not without rights: they could own property and marry free women, perhaps because they were at least as often prisoners (or the victims) of war as they were born servile. Gortyn had a long period of military and economic expansion in which to recruit them.

The wishes of the Gods were less easily tabulated, nor did they post standards to which they themselves had to be true. Plato's doctrine of *anamnesis* held that men's immortal souls had seen the Ideal in its immaculate perfection, but – on their way into human flesh – had to pass through Lethe, which blighted their memories. The Greek for truth, *aletheia*, originally refers to what is not blanked by Lethe's obliteration of eternal truth. A charming Jewish midrash says that Moses "forgot" some of Yahweh's laws on the way down Sinai. In consequence, no one can know everything that G-d demands of us: the fundamentalist claim to know in full what G-d or Allah requires of men is always false. Justice might be associated with Zeus, but he was not its paradigm: like the great princes of Europe, with their trains of lesser titles, and entitlements, the major Olympians had a portfolio of interests, attributes and spheres of influence, but – again like princes – they were bound more by their own idea of themselves than by any notion of obligatory virtue.

The monotheist's God is, by definition, all-powerful and all-good. The less He is taken to interfere in the world, the more He is assumed to be aloof from its lusts and cruelties: He becomes the absolute measure, and measurer, of moral qualities. When Plato wished his ideal society to honour (and poets to depict) morally responsible gods, he was proposing not only that divinities no longer be portrayed as skittish or adulterous, but also that the gods themselves cease to be those things.

In the sixth century, Xenophanes of Colophon had anticipated Plato's prim scepticism about the polymorphous, often perverse, Olympian gods who, it was prudent to say, had been ill-served by Homer and Hesiod. Like Akhnaton, the Pharaoh from whom Freud suggested that Moses got his monotheistic idea, Xenophanes posited a single deity, without anthropomorphic faces or mundane vices of the kind that men regarded as detestable in each other. His idea of god is not unlike that of Perikles' guru, Anaxagoras, who pronounced *Nous* (Mind) the ruling principle of the world. Perikles' domination of Athens, and Athens' of Hellas, was a pretty proof of *nous* in action. As a metic, Anaxagoras broadcast his heterodoxy too brazenly and, in 437, was expelled from Athens for *asebeia*. Unable to save his protégé, Perikles probably paid for his repatriation to Lampsacus, a Greek city in the Troad, on the south shore of the Hellespont, where (like Oedipus at Colonus) the *meteora phrontistes* (stargazer) was revered as a sage. Albert Einstein went from being an outcast in Nazi Germany to an elevated role at Princeton. No philosopher is on record as being charged with *asebeia* in any Ionian city, which may account for the plethora of free-thinking Ionian speculators.

The unworldly and solitary deity of sophisticated philosophers justified the view that material nature could be scrutinized without apprehensions of divine presence. The evacuation of god(s) from earth led to a grander, but blander, conception of the Deity. Its culmination was Aristotle's "Unmoved Mover", whose main activity, after setting the material universe going, as a man might push a pendulum, was self-contemplation. After the invention of the mechanical clock, nature itself could be said to function on the same principle: Pierre Hadot cites Nicolas Oresme who, in his 1377 *Treatise on Heaven and Earth*, conceives of the universe as a clock which, once wound up by God, continues to operate independently of Him. In our electronic age, Richard Dawkins proposes to dispense with the Great Winder Himself.

When Aristotle postulated a single-minded god, detached from the mundane, he sponsored the logical possibility that divinities were irrelevant to *ta physika*, the workings of the world. Scientists – the pursuers of knowledge – examined the field of forces abstracted from the gods who so long impersonated them, but they have often been careful to abstain from debunking cherished and enduring credulities (Descartes was particularly apprehensive of the Inquisition).

In his Character of the Superstitious Man, the fourth-century wit and philosopher Theophrastus was clearly drawing largely from life. Even today, who walks blithely under ladders or never touches wood or spills salt without tossing a pinch over one shoulder? Paul Veyne, in his *Les Grecs ont-ils cru à leurs mythes?*, confesses that he doesn't believe in ghosts, but still fears them.

The Zeus who, during the Trojan War, conceded victory to the side his wife supported, was said to "give ground willingly, but with an unwilling *thumos*

83 Superpowers Apollo and Poseidon confer on the Parthenon frieze.

(spirit)". Such an internal conflict is unthinkable in monotheistic gods, who continue, nevertheless, to be summoned to support one side or another in all the wars for which men would like to recruit them. Gentle Jesus is reported (inconveniently for some, if not for Crusaders) as saying that He brought "not peace" (of which He is elsewhere said to be the Prince), "but a sword". Using God as a warrant for bloodshed is a mutation of the savage belief that the gods needed blood to bring them to life. Islamic terrorists are the new Aztecs, with no Tenochtitlan.

At first, texts were spelt out in the fashion known as *boustrophedon*: in one of the inscriptions bearing a poem of Archilochos, alternate lines read from right to left and then turn back again from left to right, like a ploughman's furrow (*strophe* turn; *bous* ox). *Boustrophedon* offered literal turns of phrase. The Gortyn tablets of the law also employ it.

The wish for articulate legislation led philosophers to propose more prosaic rescriptions of the divine role. Empedocles and Parmenides delivered their ideas in quasi-oracular verse; but if prose was rare before the fifth century, it came to supply means for recording history and laws. Euripides – whose plays have theatrical genius but lack the lush poetic texture of Aeschylus – wrote his (lost) memoirs in prose.

Free of stylistic or metrical constriction, prose offered unmetred scope for the *parrhesia* on which social versatility, and increasing literacy, thrived. The Greeks who spoke of "the laws of the Medes and Persians, which never change", may have been in awe of their immutability, but the Athenians were busy legal innovators and – as in the case of the law *mee mnesikakein*, which restored the shattered cohesion of the state after Critias's *coup* – set an example of pragmatic magnanimity. It was in such *ad hoc* legislation, drafted to respond to specific social circumstances, rather than the result of some ideological scheme, that Karl Popper saw the lineaments of "the Open Society". Having experienced twentieth-century totalitarianism (of which religious fundamentalism is the latest mutation), Popper insisted on the merits of "piecemeal social engineering" as the way forward for civilized life. His own autocratic style was amusingly at odds with his tolerant doctrine, but does nothing to invalidate it. There is further irony in the view that, in a certain light, Popper's "ideal state" (with no higher ideal than the well-being of its citizens) is a recension of the vanished supremacy, and geniality, of the old Habsburg empire, without the emperor. Imperial Vienna's presumed tolerance of a variety of racial and social ingredients should not be unduly sentimentalized: when clemency was recommended to him, after the Hungarian rebellion of 1848, by the tsar of Russia of all people, Prince Schwarzenberg reminded his master, the young Franz Josef, "Mercy is all very well, but we must have some hanging first". And they certainly did. Pragmatism, too, can have its heartlessness.

Belief in the gods, or in the plausibility of divine intervention in the world, remained part of the machinery of poetry: most obviously in the tragic use of the *deus ex machina*. Prose writers broke the pious mould. Although Thucydides reports, with his usual straight face, that Nikias made a speech to the defeated Athenians, about to retreat from Syracuse, in which he seemed genuinely to hope that the gods would favour them, since he had always fulfilled his religious duties, the historian knew that no pity was, in fact, about to be shown to his compatriots. Indeed, it was Nikias's superstitious willingness to believe that an eclipse of the moon required him to delay his army's retreat from Syracuse, by several dawdling days, that sealed its fate. Long before Cavafy's god deserted Antony, Nikias had been abandoned by his.

Thucydides never ironized openly about the delusive faith of human beings in the benevolence of the gods: the prose medium itself removed from his history the divine upper register to be found in Homeric epic. The film *Troy* dispenses almost entirely with the gods, probably because of the practical difficulty of making them cinematically plausible. Michel Pic remarks on the coincidence of photography and positivism. Scott Fitzgerald once wrote a screenplay which required that a telephone call between two lovers be connected by an operator revealed to be "an angel" in headphones. The producer was at a loss to recruit one.

* * *

*A*ncient Greeks measured wealth, and social status, by income from land. Hence commentators were puzzled by the number of rich men in Megara, a city with little productive hinterland. In fact, there was small mystery: Megara had a rewardingly neat location, on the Saronic gulf. Most of its income derived from maritime trade: the equivalent of modern economists' "invisible earnings". The scorn which "trade" long excited among landed aristocrats (not least the English) echoes the Greek feeling that, in contrast with squires and landowners, merchants were rootless profiteers who conjured wealth without sweating for it.

Early in the sixth century, Solon classified Athenians according to their income. Their category would determine their voting privileges and eligibility for office. His rule of thumb was to assess how many bushels a man's acreage was likely to yield (the five-hundred-a-year men were the top people). Revenue from trade was irrelevant, if not despicable. Traders were always rated aliens, though Athens came to owe much of its prosperity to exports of silver, oil and ceramics and from the capacity of its travelling salesmen to make deals in the Black Sea, Egypt and Magna Graecia. The language of Athenian politics never embraced the notion of economic life as central to the city's well-being, still less to its cultural or spiritual vitality.

The uncertain status of *metoikoi* – sometimes welcomed for the commercial know-how, but later expelled (like the Ugandan Asians, under Idi Amin) – testifies to a marginality of which the Jews have been Christendom's correlative. The Germans regularly called the Jews (unwelcome) guests. Marx's typifying of them as "hucksters" reminds us of his early study of Greek philosophers.

Drafted in to resolve the social crisis caused by rural poverty, Solon set Athens on the way to democracy, if not very far, and only inadvertently. He had no preconceived blueprint, still less a radical agenda. His reputation for prudence meant that while the common people trusted him to be impartial, fellow-aristocrats could rely on him to be a safe pair of hands: when he produced his plan, the rich retained the greatest influence. All but the poorest citizens were, however, given rights, if only to indicate "yes" or "no" to motions they had no part in drafting. "All show" is a formula for gaining quick approval, much favoured by old-style English Trades Union barons: a forceful executive, or a glib tongue and visible peer pressure, can often dragoon the rest.

The secret ballot was first introduced so that no powerful lord or vested interest could oversee how people voted. Communists later argued that it fetishized private over public interests (that is, their own). They "compromised" by rigging the ballot and choosing the candidates. Recently, the countries with whaling industries were *refused* a secret ballot at an ecological conference so that their selfishness could be made manifest.

Rhetoric gave demagogues leverage which they became increasingly adept in exercising. The best early orators are likely to have been Eupatrids for whom free speech, among their aristocratic peers, was no novelty. Later, visiting professors of rhetoric, such as Gorgias (from Leontini in Sicily), promised golden tongues to those who attended, and paid for, their courses. In her novel, *A Severed Head*, Iris Murdoch alludes to the pagan ritual of placing a golden coin on the tongue of a chrysostomized head in order to prompt it to divulge oracular truths. Plato lamented that, as soon as government was subject to the recruited suffrages of voters, persuasion perverted truth, by which he meant the immutable standards set by his Ideas. They were postulated to establish a universal grammar of rectitude, against which democracy would, as it were, have no appeal.

A social crisis bad enough to need emergency measures, but which did not quite dispel the habit of deference, licensed Solon to propose a modest revolution. His *de haut en bas* concessions to the desperate peasantry made unavoidable concessions seem like generosity. As a modern analyst might put it (and no Greek ever would), the *seisachtheia* – cancellation of smallholders' debts – was the only means of both defusing violence and reflating the rural economy.

Athens ceased, in theory, to be the exclusive fief of the voracious aristocracy, but if the powers of the rich became less peremptory, Eupatrid security was enhanced: "old money" still established social status. At the same time, the peasants – retrieved from despair – abated their militancy. Yet if the *demos* remained limited in practical authority, it was made aware of the size, and potentially determinant force, of its constituency. A progressive despite himself, Solon began the process which led to the citizen body as a whole acquiring irreversible power.

The Athenians never possessed – nor did even the wildest demagogue imagine – anything like a welfare state, but the institution (by Perikles) of payment for jury service did supply a cross between the dole and a state pension. Such payment was resented by conservatives whose most carrying voice was that of Aristophanes. Modern jurors too are compensated, but they cannot turn up as a right and in unlimited numbers, as they could in Athens. In one famous case, 6,000 jurors were allegedly enrolled. One can imagine how closely they followed arguments or evidence. Too much democracy shades into ochlocracy: mob law. *Ochlon parechein* was "to give trouble" in ancient Greek, as *enochleo* is in modern.

Where the Romans had bread and circuses, the Athenians had theatre, open debate (of a kind) and litigation, which always had to be instituted by a private citizen. If popular juries were paid a pittance in Athens, selected upper-class juries were more regularly, and lavishly, bribed in Rome, especially in cases of peculation by provincial governors.

Like Mirabeau, who was midwife to the French Revolution while intending to abort it, Solon – while defusing an emergency – kindled hopes which he scarcely shared. Enlightened self-interest enabled him at the same time to save his own class from overthrow and to avert the dispossession of the rural poor. Those who had previously had nothing received little, but were primed to want more. Plausible and shameless, the Eupatrid populist Peisistratus would soon be offering it.

Solon's reputation for wisdom did not inhibit charges of duplicity against him. According to Plutarch, he was imprudent enough to tell three rich friends, ahead of publication, about his plans: he meant, he told them, to cancel debts, but not – as the poor hoped, and the rich feared – to redistribute land. The trio borrowed large sums, and bought up big estates at rock-bottom prices. When Solon's measures were proclaimed, the property market soared.

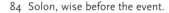

84 Solon, wise before the event.

The syndicate refused, quite legally, to repay its creditors and kept its purchases. The game had begun whereby – contrary to the spirit of the laws – speculators, lawyers and accountants find loopholes in legislation meant to help the disadvantaged, through which fat cats squirm, and then get fatter.

The accusations of insider dealing subsided only when it emerged that, so far from profiting from his own measures, Solon himself remained an unpaid creditor: submitting to the logic, and spirit, of his reforms, he had written off something like fifteen talents of debts owed to him.

One of his cleverest moves was to enact a law which, in the case of internal violence, made it an offence to remain neutral. Those who elected to wait and see how things would turn out were to be deprived of their political rights. Hence there could be no profit, and should have been certain loss, in staying passive. The modern pollsters' constituency of abstentionists and "Don't knows" was regarded as culpably fence-sitting.

Such indecision could indeed be fatal in Greek politics: in Corcyra, in 427, Thucydides says, "As for those who held moderate views, they were destroyed by extremists in both parties, either for not taking part or in envy at the possibility that they might survive." The killing of "moderates" who *almost* share their views is a priority with ultras who hate evidence of broadmindedness.

Solon's purpose was not, of course, to make sure that civil strife promptly engaged the whole population, but to encourage the citizens' arrest – there were no police to do it – of plotters who hoped to benefit from the *attentisme* of an indifferent public. It is, however, hard to see how lazy members of the *demos* would in practice be punished, or by whom, should a tyranny or oligarchy gain power as a result of their passivity. What arriviste enforces laws designed to block his arrival?

Perhaps Solon intended more to establish a civic principle than to inaugurate a viable measure. Some modern democracies imitate him, mildly, by fining voters who neglect to participate in elections. Others, like the USA and Great Britain, tolerate large minorities who, by failing to vote, think to dispense themselves of responsibility for the outcome. Solon's scorn for those who hedged their bets was echoed by St Paul when he condemned the people of Laodiceia, a nice little town in Asia Minor, for blowing "neither hot nor cold". Dante reserved a place in the inner ring of his Inferno for those who, through accidie, had failed to take moral decisions.

After setting his reforms in motion, Solon volunteered to go abroad for ten years. His absence would prove that the measures had nothing to do with self-advancement. The Athenians, in return, swore that they would adhere to Solon's constitution during his absence. During his tactful travels, Solon is said (unhistorically) to have visited King Croesus of Lydia at the height of his vanity. The king, so the story goes, had him shown round the palace and its treasury. It was typical of absolute monarchs to conceal their wealth behind high walls. Tyrants' residences were likely to be plain to the outside eye and gilded within. In democracies, revenues were devoted to the public good. Athenian grandees (unlike Roman) never lived in ostentatious seclusion: their houses were uniformly unpretentious.

When Solon had inspected the hoarded wealth of Croesus, the king asked if his guest knew anyone who was happier than he. Solon had the nerve and

wit to reply, "Yes, Tellos, one of my fellow-citizens." Tellos, he explained, had left behind him children and grandchildren whom everyone admired, had lived modestly well and had died gloriously for his city. Anyone else? Yes, there was Cleobis ("Famous for Life") and Biton, mythical Argive brothers distinguished for their love for each other and for their mother, Hera's priestess, to whose chariot they had yoked themselves in order to get her to the sanctuary on time. The grateful mother prayed to the goddess

85 On the verge of incineration, Croesus remembers Solon, Solon, Solon.

to give them the greatest possible blessing. Falling asleep in Hera's precinct, they died painlessly during the following night, without regret and – Solon insisted – covered with glory (St Teresa may not have been the first to remark on the dangers of answered prayers). There is an allegedly daedalic statue of Cleobis and Biton in the museum at Delphi.

Solon continued to tease his host with other mundane candidates for happiness until the king cried out, "What about me?" Solon was polite, but unaccommodating:

> God enjoined on us Greeks that we behave with moderation in all things, and this moderation gives us an idea of virtue which seems timid and common-place: nothing regal or flashy about it. When we look at the ups and downs which never fail to upset human lives, it stops us being proud of our posses-sions or admiring the happiness of anyone subject to the caprices of time. Everyone's future is mutable, and based on uncertainties. We regard as fortu-nate the man whose luck holds till the end. But to flatter the happiness of someone still alive, open to all the dangers of human life, that's like calling someone the winner, and giving him the championship, when the fight is still going on.

Herodotus tells of a Thracian tribe, the Trausi, who lament when a baby is born, since it makes them think of all the sufferings it is likely to face, but who bury their dead "with merriment and rejoicing" and point out how happy they now are and what miseries they have been spared. Sophocles put it with gnomic severity in *Oedipus Coloneus*: "*mee phynai ton hapanta nika logon*" (not to have been born beats all the chat about it).

Greeks had a habit of moralizing when addressing barbarian kings: the renegade king of Sparta, Demaratus, was a privileged adviser to Xerxes during his invasion of Greece in 480. Royal status emboldened him to tell the Great King that Greeks would fight ten times better than Persian conscripts because they were free men defending freedom. Darius's Greek fellow-traveller in 490, the vengeful Athenian Hippias, was like the archetypal exile against whose vain hopes and wishful thinking Machiavelli warned the Prince, but of whom no one reminded the CIA when it came to the Iraqi exile Chalabi's wishful information before the war of 2003.

Years after Solon's visit, Croesus was defeated by Cyrus, having miscon-strued that Delphic oracle which promised that if he "crossed the river Halys" he would destroy a great empire. If guileless, Croesus had not been precipi-tate: Herodotus says that he polled all the ranking oracles, from Dodona in the far north to Ammon in Libya, before his calamitous move against Persia.

Once captured, Croesus was condemned to be burned alive. Bound and handed over to the executioner, he raised his voice and cried out, "Solon, Solon, Solon." Cyrus wanted an explanation. Croesus's account of Solon's recommendation of modesty so touched Cyrus that he released Croesus and covered him with honours.

Herodotus repeats a melodramatic story that the pyre was already alight before Cyrus pronounced his reprieve and that a heavy shower fell from a clear blue sky, after Croesus had reminded Apollo, with tears in his eyes, of all the expensive donations he had made to his shrine at Delphi. According to Herodotus, Cyrus allowed Croesus to send the iron chains with which he had been bound as a reproach to Delphi. The messenger was told to inquire if Greek gods were usually so ungrateful.

The school motto of Charterhouse, where I served my time with Latin and Greek, was "*Deo Dante, Dedi*", nicely alliterative, if grammatically doubtful, Latin. "God Giving, I Gave" was the slogan of the school's founder, Thomas Sutton, a merchant who, it is said, hoped by his benefactions to secure prompt entry to heaven. Even in 1611, God was expected not to be unaffected by human largess.

The sententious Plutarch observes that Solon saved the life of one king and educated another. It is a pretty phrase, but Cyrus and subsequent Persian kings never realized the lesson that leeching taxes from their subjects and putting all the gold in the royal vaults was a way of impoverishing their own economic prospects. Jesus showed economic sense in recommending that talents, literal and figurative, be put to productive use.

Solon had not always been a man of measured responses. It is said that, some time around 600, before he became a senior politician, he was a loud advocate of Athenian expansion. In the interests of security, he urged the annexation of the fateful nearby island of Salamis. However, the first attempts to acquire it were so disastrous that the Assembly declared it illegal to continue even to advance such an idea.

Solon then pretended that he had lost his mind. In his focused delirium, he wrote a long poem lauding the banned policy. He declaimed his verses so incessantly, and intemperately, that the people were embarrassed into changing their minds. This showboating performance is wholly at odds with his later dignity. Aeschines would say of the statue of Solon, which, in his day, stood in the *agora* of Salamis, that it depicted the great man with his arm hidden under his robe, exactly as he was in the habit of appearing in front of the assembly. In order to abate his embarrassing delirium, the Athenians voted to give Solon's policy one more try. The result was the triumphant acquisition of Salamis. Victory and recovery were simultaneous. A few years later, Solon was elected archon and *diallektes* (the office which validated his *seisachtheia*).

As an old man, Solon was hardly less loud in opposing Peisistratus than he had been in his "mad" youth, but less effective. In the way of many bullies, Peisistratus contrived to appear a victim: one day he came into the Assembly, claiming to have been wounded by "the enemies of the poor". Against Solon's urgent advice, he was voted a bodyguard. Like Nazi brownshirts, his bully boys gave the rabble-rouser enough muscle to seize dictatorial power.

As his name suggests, Peisistratus was both persuasive and forceful: *Peisi-* derived from *Peitho*, patron of rhetoric; *stratos* meant an armed force. Solon could do nothing to stop the imminent *coup d'état*: the popular will had been made irresistible by the abuse of his own measures. Once in power, Peisistratus knew better than to make his opponent a martyr: he imitated Cyrus the Great and gave the retired sage fulsome, and empty, respect.

* * *

*P*eisistratus was that frequent figure in western politics, an aristocratic demagogue. His constituency were the *sans culottes*, mostly poor hill-farmers from around the estates of his own rich, landowning family. A star of political theatre, his speeches were for the masses; his ambition for himself.

At one stage, the other political "parties" (always a figure of speech in volatile Greek politics) combined to expel him, but in the 550s he returned from temporary exile in triumph and in a chariot which also contained a "tall, beautiful girl", sporting full armour. He claimed her to be Athene come in person to reinstate him. This *coup de théâtre* beguiled the simple and bemused the worldly: it is unwise to assume any class of Athenians to have been immune to credulity. In modern advertising, girls and wheels still go glamorously together to flatter male potency.

Peisistratus's *mise-en-scène* may have been inspired by a traditional festival: Herodotus reports one in "Libya" (North Africa) in which rival teams of girls paid honour to a "native deity which is the same as our Athene" by picking the best-looking girl and dressing her in "Greek armour and a Corinthian helmet". They then put her in a chariot and drove her "round the lagoon". Peisistratus's "Miss Athens" had African antecedents: anticipating Martin Bernal, Herodotus concedes that Greek styles in both armour and helmet could be of African origin.

Once restored, Peisistratus recruited the aid of another divinity, in 530, by bringing the image of Dionysus from Eleutherae, on the margin of Attica and Boeotia, and installing it in the same god's old temple. The March festival of the Great Dionysia, which began with a torchlight parade, was expanded to five days. Its dramatic competitions made Athens a magnet for cultural tourists. If part of Peisistratus's intention was to lull the people with civic entertainment, he (like Solon) began something of which he might not have applauded the consequences. The theatre created a public space in which the *demos* (all the free males) could see each other and become aware of their common power. Although dramatic prizes were not awarded on overtly political grounds, the development of the Attic theatre shows how a benevolent tyrant created a platform from which tyranny was regularly criticized. Kreon, in Sophocles' *Antigone*, is the very type of the man for whom the retention of power outranks humane and religious duty.

Pesistratus did not rely on hype alone: he had also secured the backing of Megacles, literally a Big Name, aristocratic boss of the prosperous coastal constituency of Attica. The tyrant was also folksy enough to trace his lineage back to the protractedly eloquent Homeric pundit, Nestor. The opinionated King Leopold I of Belgium gave himself similar, if metaphorical, airs.

Peisistratus had the wit to sing hymns both ancient and modern: he extended Athenian hegemony by playing the religious card and by practical diplomacy: he was simultaneously friendly with Sparta and married (for a while) to a woman from Argos, Sparta's main Peloponnesian adversary. His crowd-pleasing tyranny lasted until he died, in 527. Populism had been a cheap price to pay for lording it over the people.

If Peisistratus's tyranny was unique for its durable effrontery, his contemporary, Polycrates of Samos, was no less flashy; his island's wealth enabled him to become, temporarily, the power-broker of the Aegean. He could even afford to seduce the great physician, Democedes, to abandon public practice in Athens (where he was paid 100 minae) by offering a transfer fee of two talents, 20 per cent more than his Athenian stipend. Democedes was a star of the medical school at Croton, in Magna Graecia, which was regarded as better even than Cyrene in North Africa. Thanks to Hippocrates (under whose tree you can still find a cure for the midday sun), the island of Cos – the Harley Street of the ancient world – would later eclipse both.

Polycrates (his name implies "much power") was said to have irritated the gods, as he certainly did the Persians, by seeming to have everything he wanted. On the advice of Amasis of Egypt, he threw a prized seal ring into the sea, to allay divine jealousy. It was returned to him a few days later, by a fisherman, one of whose catch had swallowed it. Amasis read the omen to mean that the tyrant was doomed and renounced his friendship.

Public benefactor and patron of poets such as Anacreon, Polycrates flattered to deceive, and was eventually himself deceived by flattery: a Persian satrap – affecting to need him in a conspiracy against the Great King – lured him to the mainland and had him crucified. Polycrates' heir, Maiandrios,

86 405 B.C., Samos and Athens pledge eternal friendship for a while.

wisely declined personal power and handed it to the *demos*. Democratic Samos, unable to stand alone against Persia, would later be one of the Athenians' more reliable subject-allies, though it too rebelled from time to time.

* * *

*T*yranny has been given a bad name by posterity, not least by Plato, less because he was in principle hostile to it than because, in practice, it had paved the way for democracy. Tyrants often supplanted stagnant aristocracies, whose dominant interest was maintaining their own allegedly god-given status (even as he affected to be a man of the people, or at least the people's man, Julius Caesar would claim, straight-facedly, to be descended from Venus). Ancient tyranny has acquired an undeserved bad name: rude leverage was needed to evict hereditary grandees who could be more tyrannical, in the ugly sense, than many of those who supplanted them.

Like Thersites, tyrants claimed to speak for the under-represented, and with some justice; if they gained power by force, they could keep it only with popular support. Validated not by lineage but by results, survival depended on increasing the prosperity of their cities. This, in turn, could excite the jealous. Tyrants resembled *The Golden Bough*'s lonely monarchs of the glen, who retained authority only with the sword and to whom all comers were threats. The philosopher Thales was once asked what he considered the most surprising thing he could think of. "An old tyrant," he said, "because tyrants have as many enemies as they have men in their power."

Tyrants were occasionally succeeded by their sons, but dynasties rarely endured. Cypselus of Corinth (tyrant from about 657 to 625) was succeeded by his son, Periander, who reigned for forty years, despite (or because of) his ruthlessness. The Cypselid tyrants succeeded above all because their city's economy boomed: its pottery (in the "Ripe Corinthian" style) sold all over the Mediterranean. In the 550s, however, it was eclipsed by Athenian black- and, later, red-figure ware. Like Deucalion, Cypselus survived thanks to a chest (*kypsele*). He was not riding out a flood but being hidden, as an infant, from a family of earlier tyrants, the Bacchiadae, of which he was a bastard offshoot. Cypselus's chest was one of the oldest relics on show, in the Corinthian treasury, at Olympia, where it was seen by Pausanias, that tireless precursor of the *Antiques Roadshow*.

Periander is credited with having constructed the *diaulos* along which ships
could be dragged across the neck of land
linking the Peloponnese with northern
Greece (it was severed only when the
Corinth canal was cut). Herodotus
says that Periander acquired the
recipe for a long reign from
Thrasybulus of Miletus, who took the
tyrant's emissary into a field of corn
and lopped off any ears taller than the
rest. The Spartans were moved by the
same logic to cut down helots who
showed signs of being uppity.

Since tyrants had no legitimizing
way of passing on power without
bloodshed, what began with cheer-
ing crowds usually ended in palatial
paranoia. Incest was their typical vice:
as with the Pharaohs (who set a long
example), it was a way of keeping
everything in the family. The

87 Harmodius
and Aristogeiton,
tyrannicidal lovers.

incestuous tendency continued in ancient ruling families. In the fourth century, Mausolus of Halicarnassus in Karia married his sister. Incest persisted in Egypt until the Romans evicted the Ptolemies, who had aped the Pharaohs, although the first Ptolemy was one of Alexander the Great's Maecedonian generals. Having hurried to carve out a fief for himself in Egypt, Ptolemy I later hijacked Alexander's corpse (from Damascus), when it was on its way home to Vergina. The divine bones, enshrined in Alexandria, lent mana to a metic's kingdom.

∗ ∗ ∗

Solon's "mad" speech about Salamis was composed in iambics, perhaps to put him under the protection of the Muses, and of Dionysus. Although his verses were didactic rather than lyrical, the demonstration of how iambics could sing for a policy, and argue a point, may have encouraged their later use in tragedy. There is an abrupt contrast between the operatic elevation of the lyric choruses and the argued exchanges and measured narrative in the intervening, more pointed, iambic dialogue.

Scholars were once inclined to derive tragedy from solemn, ritual sources. In the Aristotelian tradition, historians like to give progress, in life or in art, a steady, measurable rise to maturity and then a fall into decadence. But how often do art forms (or societies) result from "natural" flowering and decay? Fresco replaced mosaic in Renaissance churches not least because it was quicker and cheaper, after which freer forms and a lighter touch seemed "inevitable". Its sweep allowed religious illustration to take persuasive, popular forms. But had fresco not been conspicuously, and economically, adaptable to the new architecture, the Sistine Chapel might as well have been embellished with mosaic, like Roger II's Capella Palatina, in the twelfth-century Palazzo Reale in Palermo. Invention follows the market; applause amplifies invention. In art as in war, what succeeds is reinforced.

Almost any prevailing ethos can procure beauty. When was there any direct rapport between the moral qualities of patrons or the "truth" of a religion, and the arts they encouraged? Aztec and Mayan sculpture of monumental genius decorated human abattoirs and celebrated gods as insatiable for blood as their servants were pitiless in supplying it. Myth says that the marble of the temple in Tauris, where Iphigeneia became the priestess, was always red with human blood. Nietzsche remarked that there would have been no architecture had man not built temples to often absurd gods.

Artists who served Fascist and Communist dictators were unlucky in having loutish masters who imposed their own aesthetics; otherwise we might be embarrassed by the quality of work created to advertise the grotesque creeds of monstrous masters. Attic tragedy was fostered in the first place by a tyrant who supplied funding and kudos for dramatists. Around 500, new festivals excited bigger audiences and attracted tourists. Did Peisistratus deliberately plan that theatrical illusion should distract the citizens' attention from his political despotism?

Dramatists soon learnt that popularity, and prizes, came of telling stories that pampered patriotic pride. "This happy breed" is an old notion. In the fifth century, Athens' ascendancy engendered confidence (in Athenians) that its culture enjoyed divine favour. If the population as a whole continued to cleave to antique pieties, the evidence that the gods were on Athens' side encouraged the ruling class to a vanity that issued simultaneously in political *hubris* and in scepticism (as often a function of prosperity as of disillusion). In much the same way, Elizabeth I's England became "this sceptr'd isle". Art followed, and waved, the flag. Freedom and freebooting went together.

Victory over the Spanish armada did not *cause* Shakespeare's genius to flower, but would it have been as prolific under a Catholic "occupation" policed by Philip II and a new and bloodier Mary? The Reformation may not have presented the theatre with its licence (which Puritanism would revoke), yet without the incitement to patriotic particularism primed by Henry VIII's insolent rebellion against the Pope, in what form, if any, would Shakespeare's genius have been licensed? Only after the clerical clamp had been removed, like Prometheus's rivets, could medieval mystery plays evolve into secular, antinomian drama.

Intellectual freedom and diversity came of the breach in Christendom which allowed art to flourish both as endorsement of the ruling ethos and as the means of prising even wider the space between piety and scepticism. The "windows" opened by the similes in Homer's *Iliad* were matched by those in Renaissance painting, which were eventually flung so wide open that the sacred subject was pushed out of the frame, and easel painting became a secular and often profane and revolutionary medium.

The golden link between power and art embarrasses purists; but artists are at least as often jesters and time-servers as they are seditious and transgressive, and sometimes both. The double helix of formal piety (based on an institutional grammar) and countervailing speculation generates the European genius. Some men, like Sir Walter Ralegh, are at once patriotic leaders and subversive poets: there is something akin to Euripidean dissidence in Ralegh's, "Say to the court, it glows / And shines like rotten wood; / Say to the church, it shows / What's good and doth no good: / If church and court reply, / Then give them both the lie".

* * *

*C*leisthenes' new electoral arrangements, introduced to cement his come-back in 507, are sometimes regarded as a far-sighted prelude to giving future (free, male) Athenians a full say in the running of the state. In fact, they had at least as much to do with revenge on the Peisistratids as with the realization of democratic ideals: the "hill-people", who had lent the tyranny their unanimous rustic block vote, had to be divided before the *demos* as a whole could be trusted to vote (against, in particular, the return of Peisistratus's exiled son, Hippias). Instead of their continuing to weigh together in a preponderant caucus, Cleisthenes allotted parcels of the "hill-people" to each of ten new "tribes", which became voting blocs. The "plainsmen" and the maritime constituencies of the Attic population made up the other two-thirds and diluted Peisistratus's supporters into insignificance: division preceded democratic rule.

It seems strange that the population of Attica agreed, apparently with small reluctance, to have tribal and social allegiances redefined to such an arbitrary scheme. However, Arthur Koestler once pointed out the sad ease with which human beings can be recruited to almost any cause that offers power over others or rewards to the members. Anyone who has played pick-up football in the park knows that – even without the smallest dividend – fierce, if transitory, loyalty can be recruited by the lifting of a selector's finger.

The new tribes presided, in rotation, in the new Council of Five Hundred. Hence no single pressure group could dominate Athens: compromise became less a procedural obligation than a social habit. The argumentativeness of Athenians made debate part of the new social machinery (and *peitho* its oil). Politics entertained, and tolerated, a multiplicity of opinions: Cleisthenes' constitution was like a dramatic production in which everyone had the hope of a good part.

Plato, whose dialogues were a fabricated derivative of free speech, regarded Athens' nationalized garrulity as an aberration. He preferred the Spartan oligarchy, which discouraged verbosity. Laconic wit was all brevity: anticipating Mies van der Rohe, "Less is more" was its spokesmen's policy. The Spartans' style outlasted their hegemony. The rite in which adolescents were whipped to see if they could, literally, take it ("it" being cheese from an altar), persisted in the exaggerated form of *diamastigosis*, the sadistic flogging described by Plutarch, as a tourist attraction, long after Sparta lost its military clout.

Cleisthenes' measures were a cleverly elaborated response to the abiding risk of political disintegration. The cleverness lay in the elaboration: it lent the grace of novelty to settling old scores. In the reshuffle of voting procedures, the new deal seemed to distribute trumps to everyone. The overall purpose, however, was to reconcile the Athenians in a union which gave a voice to all but the poorest, the *thetes*, who, if mute, were now given the right to vote on previously drafted legislation. As a radical conservative, Cleisthenes moulded the Athenians into a single society, but, like Solon, did less to upset the rich than he hoped the poor would think. He replaced Eupatrid aristocracy with plutocracy: the moneyed were made eligible for the archonship or the new tribal priesthoods (an honorary, never a vocational role).

By making their interests and those of the state coincide, Cleisthenes enticed the wealthy to justify themselves by public works: charity remains a showy form of insurance against resentment. Rich metics (assimilated or resident aliens) were urged – with whatever subtlety – to make similar liturgies, even though they had no voice in the assembly. The pressure on them was less legal than intimidatory. Islam had a similar habit of priced tolerance towards Christian and Jewish minorities.

Perikles boasted, in the Funeral Oration, of the Athenian acceptance of diversity and welcome to foreigners. He was, like Evelyn Waugh's Lord Copper, right up to a point. Even as a neighbour, the stranger had ambivalent status: under the protection of Zeus *xenios*, he might be privileged, but he was never integrated. The greater the stranger's success (and its consequent enrichment of the community as well as of the traders), the more the possessors of old money insisted on the social distinction between the landowner's autochthonous and inalienable merit and the arriviste's shifty provenance. Yet by becoming the reserve currency of the Aegean, the Athenian *stater* made Athens itself porous to outsiders. Their money was as good as (and indistinguishable from) that of the resident aristocracy. Metics brought prosperity to Athens, but the Athenians gave them no reliable standing. From the earliest times, immigrants were liable to be sent back to where they came from, or to some even more distant destination.

Citing Hecataeus, Herodotus tells a disobliging story of how, after helping the early Athenians to build the walls around the Acropolis, a number of Pelasgians – the mythical pre-Hellenic inhabitants of Greece – were allotted a patch of barren land beneath Mount Hymettus. Attica was notorious for the poverty of its soil, but the Pelasgians farmed it so diligently that the Athenians were seized with envy and drove them out, "without further ado, and without offering any other excuse".

Herodotus supplies a less flattering account: the Greeks in those days had no house-slaves, so they sent their own daughters to fetch water from the Nine Springs. The Pelasgians, "regardless of decency or respect", used to rape them. Finally, they were said to have plotted to usurp the state, and were expelled. The Athenians vaunted themselves on their magnanimity in not killing them all, but that sounds like one coat of whitewash too many.

Herodotus's story has a vile sequel, in which the Pelasgians who had emigrated to Lemnos, with the women whom they had got with child, found that they had two clans of young people – one full-blooded, the other half-Attic – who regularly came to blows. They avoided the growing risk of civil war by killing all the bastards and their mothers, a "Lemnian deed" to go with the myth about how the women of Lemnos killed their husbands ("and Thoas too", Herodotus tells us, thereby contradicting a version of the myth in which Thoas – Ariadne's son by Dionysus – escaped the Lemnian carnage through the love of his daughter, who pushed him out to sea on a raft). The Lemnian women paid the price of a stinking crime by giving off a vile smell. Lemnos is still an unattractive island.

The right to full Athenian suffrage was precisely defined as belonging to the offspring only of an Athenian father. After 451, however, in a reaction against metics, it needed two full citizens to produce a citizen. Need for and the concomitant dread of immigrants are nothing new.

As The Arrow, my fifth-form master at Charterhouse, put it, Cleisthenes' reforms had divided Athens into ten "houses", whose representatives rotated in running the place. A fortunate proviso was that though the nine annual *archontes* (chief magistrates) could not be re-elected, consecutive periods of office were permitted for *strategoi*, the generals. If this distinction was probably made for military motives (it allowed for – if it did not always procure – consistent, perennial strategy), it happened to furnish a way for Perikles – repeatedly elected general during the decade before his death – to wield *de facto* authority in political as well as in military matters, especially when war was in the air, as his aggressive policies made sure that it was.

If generals could have longer tenure than politicians in democratic Athens, their authority was limited: they too could be returned to private life if their tactics failed. When successful, a general such as Miltiades or Themistokles might be honoured by having his statue in the Tholos, which housed the presiding committee of the *Boule* (the Athenian "House of Commons", with fifty members from each tribe), but he was never guaranteed to keep his rank for life. Even Perikles went through periods of unpopularity to which he responded with emollient condescension. If Athens first set up the slippery pole on which democratic politicians continue to seek a firm purchase, what society before Cleisthenic Athens made provision for high officials simply to revert to private life as the price of failure?

* * *

*T*hen again, in what other ancient society might even success lead to impeachment? In 406, in the desperate last years of the Peloponnesian War, the sea battle of Arginusae, near Lesbos, ended in a crushing victory for the Athenian fleet. Yet the admirals' failure to pick up survivors from twelve sinking ships (in increasingly stormy conditions) led to their trial and execution, like that of the English admiral Byng, *pour encourager les autres*. The bloodiest self-inflicted wound in the history of Athenian democracy indicates the degree to which the power in the Assembly now lay with the once despised *thetes*, a class from which most of the drowned sailors may be presumed to have come.

The fact that Athenians had outmanoeuvred the Spartans and killed their old-fashioned admiral, Callicratidas, did little to abate the fury of those at home in Athens at the "unnecessary" losses endured by, in particular, the lowest class of citizens. What land battle ever led to the same measure of popular indignation, until cargoes of body bags were seen on TV being flown back to the US from Vietnam? The Vietnamese war is said to have been the first to be lost, or abandoned, because it could be seen close-up, from a distance. The Athenians had no sight of Arginusae, but public opinion, and imagination, at home contributed to their eventual defeat abroad.

The Spartan admiral, Callicratidas, the Laconic equivalent of a young fogey, deserves a wry salute. A *mothax* like the slightly older Lysander, whom he was deputed to replace, Callicratidas compensated for his uneasy social status, not by his senior's tactical flair and personal ambition, but by a parade of old Spartan qualities and, in particular, by contempt for the Mede and a sense of shame at Lysander's *realpolitik* in seeking barbarian cash to fund a contest between Hellenes. Being less than a gentleman turned Lysander into an adventurer of genius. Callicratidas preferred to impersonate honourable propriety. Depriving himself of the barbarian subventions which had compromised and funded Lysander, he went into battle in the honest old Spartan manner.

The tradition of warfare between Hellenes carried a hint of ritual formality: the best troops were always posted on the right of the line. The privilege of facing the best of the enemy suggests the undertaking of a sacrificial role. Epaminondas broke precedent, and the Spartans, by switching wings at Leuctra. Not until the fourth century did the Athenian Iphicrates think to give his men lighter equipment – and footgear – to give them new, winning mobility. Napoleon's military genius declared itself, in his Italian campaign of 1792, when he broke the rules by going through neutral ground.

In the Mayan ball game, it was sometimes the *winning* team, or captain, who was sacrificed to the corn god. When I asked a Mexican anthropologist whether this had ever made it difficult to raise a team or motivate its members to put the heavy ball through the high stone hoop on the side wall in the middle of the stadium (the same one for both sides), she said that I did not understand the Mayan social ethos: for an individual to die so that the corn might grow for the community was an honour. It is never wise to assume one fully understands, or can share, antique motives: the least likely can be the most irresistible.

Apart from class resentment, what else primed the Athenians' self-destructive fury after Arginusae? First, primal horror at unburied and unhonoured bodies. Sophocles' *Antigone* testifies to the solemn importance of proper burial. Antigone was willing to die rather than acquiesce in the dishonouring of her brother's body by the triumphant Kreon.

On land, there was a rarely breached consensus between warring Greeks that there should be a truce after a battle, during which the dead on both sides could be duly interred. The mound of Athenian dead at Marathon is still a shrine; so too is where Leonidas and his Spartans died at Thermopylae. Religion no less than class excited the shame and rage of the Athenians after Arginusae. To die at sea and be tossed by the waves in ignominious restlessness was an unnatural scandal.

A second possible source of the voters' rage were the words of the most revered of Athenian playwrights, who had been dead for fifty years. Aeschylus's skill as a war reporter had added unforgettable words to the group memory, of which the most painfully apt described the Persians' plight after Salamis: "...The sea was swamped with wreckage, corpses, / The beaches, dunes, all piggy-backed with dead." When they first heard these lines, in 472, Athenian audiences no doubt gloried in their terrible accuracy. In 406, they must have come back, almost literally, to haunt them. It has been claimed (perhaps fancifully) that ancient audiences were prompt to learn the texts of the great playwrights, almost as they heard them (modern audiences repeat the jokes). Aeschylus's remembered genius must have lent the unseen battle of Arginusae as much abhorrent vividness as television supplied from Vietnam. Can it be a coincidence that Dionysus chose to bring Aeschylus back from the dead in Aristophanes' *Frogs*, which was produced in 405?

In the face of what the Athenian civilians could imagine, their admirals' tactical skill – by forming a double line of advance, they had foiled the Spartan *diekplous* (a gambit learned from the Athenians' own earlier pet manoeuvre) – afforded no defence. The Spartan commander, honest Callicratidas, had been killed, and the whole course of the war in the Aegean had tipped in Athens' favour. Yet the *thetes* had their vindictive way: the best commanders in the Athenian navy – including the great Perikles' son by Aspasia – were voted to death (contrary to due process) by the public that might have been expected to applaud them. Socrates alone protested against the mass verdict. Perikles'

88 The sea battle as land battle on water. Seventh-century B.C. warship carrying outsize marines.

illegitimate son had been granted citizenship and eligibility for military command, in tribute to his father, when the great man's other sons died of the plague: his execution was a Euripidean irony.

Deprived of its best admirals, the morale of the Athenian fleet was destroyed. Within a year, the Peloponnesian War would end in utter defeat. A year after Arginusae, at the battle of Aegospotami, the foolish Athenian commander was tricked by Lysander, who had been returned to effective command, though supposedly in an advisory role. The master tactician went after the Persian gold for which Callicratidas had disdained to crawl, and used it to refurbish his fleet. He then gave the Athenians the impression that he funked a fight, and deceived them – as Themistokles had the Persians, in the run-up to Salamis – into expending energy in aggressive patrols, which he refused to confront. When he had convinced them that they could relax their guard, since the Spartans dared not launch their ships, he mounted a lightning attack on his enemies' beached ships and dispersed, tired crews. Of the Athenian fleet of one hundred and eighty ships, only twelve returned.

Their city faced immediate starvation: no grain could now reach her from the Black Sea. Her client states defected to Lysander; those who had feared Athens lost their fear, those who hated her found their voices. At Athens itself, democracy gave way to Spartan-sponsored oligarchy. Reactionaries, led by Critias, immediately disenfranchised the *thetes*, less because their folly, after Arginusae, had lynched their city's best leaders than out of hatred for the whole period of democratic rule which is now known as the Age of Perikles. Thucydides famously remarked that Periklean Athens had been *"logo men"* (in theory) a democracy, *"ergo de"* (but when it came down to business) "under the rule of one man". Although Thucydides' contrasting terms were a commonplace, the memory of Homer's use of *ergon*, to denote the business of war, flavours the cant phrase with a hint that Perikles' irreplaceable role was as a military commander, although his strategy at the outbreak of the Peloponnesian War has come to be regarded as autocratic, over-confident and unmindful of morale. Whatever the merit of his long leadership, there would never have been an Age of Perikles, had Cleisthenes' reform of the *polis* not allowed for the re-election of generals.

History can turn on the unintended and unexpected use of constitutional formalities: when the Fascist Grand Council voted Mussolini out of office in 1943, it used paper powers which no one had ever intended it to take seriously. The Council existed only to lend a formal dressing of cabinet rule to the Duce's autocracy. Its vote to dump him was the revenge of the rubber stamp.

Cleisthenes' constitution underwent radical emendation but, as long as Athenian democracy endured, it was never repudiated. Ostracism was his flashiest, crowd-pleasing measure to avoid deadlock in the running of the state. Although Cleisthenes may not have invented ostracism (so called because votes were registered on clay "slips" known as *ostraka*), he certainly refitted it as a political safety valve. The relegation of the *de facto* leader of the opposition to a safe distance, for a whole decade, left his surviving antagonist with a free hand. If the survivor's policies failed, however, he might soon find himself in the same boat which had exported his opponent.

Politics has rarely been a polite activity in Greece: the "left-wing" Athenian leader Ephialtes was murdered in 461, probably by followers of Cimon. Peisistratus's earlier fear, that the "enemies of the poor" might rough him up or kill him, may have been exaggerated but it was not implausible.

In 1922, six cabinet ministers were condemned to death, like the Athenian admirals after Arginusae, and shot after being held responsible for the fiasco which ended in the eviction of the Greek population of Asia Minor. Ernest Hemingway's *In Our Time* gives an "eyewitness" account both of the evacuation of Smyrna (where he describes the departing Greeks smashing their donkeys' legs with sledgehammers) and the executions themselves. Hemingway gives a callously unblinking, utterly convincing account of how one of the condemned men sat in a puddle. There is no evidence that he actually witnessed any of these things.

* * *

89 Ios *limani* (harbour) from the *chorio* (village).

*C*ritias and his junta would have admired the cowed orderliness of
1968–69. When it says, "An ox is sitting on my tongue", the apprehensive chorus in Aeschylus's *Agamemnon* catches the climate of terror
engendered by Klytemnestra and her usurping lover, Aegisthus. The Colonels'
ox was a formidable secret police force that sat on people's tongues with
clamping severity. Themistokles had been exiled, in his day, to Argos, and
Thrasybulus to Thebes; the Greek world was accustomed to sheltering political refugees, and, in general, whether ancient or modern, they benefited from
local *philoxenia* (and distrust of central authority of any kind). Papadopoulos
and his friends followed antique practice in despatching their more harmless
(and often innocent) opponents into internal exile. Others were treated more
savagely by the infamous Colonel Ioannides and his fellow-torturers.

Ios was one of the pleasanter places to which exiles were sent. One in
particular was a left-wing Athenian, who had, it was rumoured, been a Trades
Union organizer. I used to see him walking around the village, a somewhat
resigned figure, escorted, at least in the beginning, by a scarcely less resigned
minder. Loukas had nothing better to do than to observe the incipient tourism
of the 1970s with increasing interest. Some of the most alert and energetic
islanders were already beginning to make large profits from the rooms they let
or the meals (and drinks) they served.

Being a socialist, Loukas was not, in principle, an admirer of private enterprise and was, of course, opposed to the profiteering he and his ideology associated with the petty bourgeois trading class. But he could not help seeing that many of the islanders were making inept managerial decisions and failing to take commercial opportunities. Never having spent time in the sticks, he had taken the same view of the Cyclades as Solon, but now he put his intelligence at the service of people whom, without his eviction from Athens, he would never have known. He made himself so useful that he was welcomed as a partner in local businesses. Thanks to his contacts in the capital, he was able to raise a little money, which he invested on Ios. As the months passed, he became less bored, and less urgent to resume his political life. By the time the Colonels had themselves been evicted, Loukas had invested himself so thoroughly in Ios, both literally and metaphorically, that he was indifferent to recall. As the seventies ended and the eighties brought mass tourism to the island, Loukas was the most powerful and respected financier on Ios. He bought property; he arranged franchises; he opened cafés and a camping ground. Thanks to the Colonels, a man who might have remained an honest Trades Union functionary, on a limited salary, became a multimillionaire of no notable scruple.

One of our other Greek friends in the Colonels' ugly day was an ex-master mariner. Lefteris had the soft, lisping accent of an educated Athenian, but he was more outspoken than any other. One night he took us out to dinner in a taverna in Kiphissia. It was crowded with smart people who appeared to be

90 Oligarchs, 1967–1974.

doing well out of the corporate dictatorship. Good food and drink loosened, and loudened, Lefteris's tongue. His contempt for the Colonels began to exceed the bounds of our table and become more widely audible.

Lefteris's wife, Efdoxia, became anxious. Perhaps she sensed that part of her husband's rage was directed against her: she had made him leave the sea and help her run her dress business. She became increasingly apprehensive as Lefteris's scorn carried to the corner of the taverna, where a large man, in tinted glasses and silk suit, was dining with a group of similarly hard-faced men. His growing interest in what Lefteris was saying, and his murmured comments to those around him, suggested that our friend was drawing dangerous attention to himself. The more Efdoxia pleaded for reticence, the more explicitly Lefteris analysed the vulgar, tyrannical imposture to which Greece had succumbed.

Efdoxia's anxiety became almost tearful when the large man in the corner signalled to the head waiter and, with his eyes on Lefteris, began to write on a piece of paper. He folded it and indicated to the waiter to take it to our host. Lefteris took the message and read it. He looked over at the man in the corner and nodded, and was nodded to. Then (we were at the end of our meal) he stood up and said, "*Pame!*" Let's go.

Efdoxia said, "Aren't you going to pay the bill?"

Lefteris pursed his lips and lifted his chin, in silent, Greek negation. The owner of the taverna bid us goodnight and held Lefteris's elbow for a moment in his hand as he showed us out.

In the street, Lefteris showed us the note from the big man. It said that Lefteris was very unwise ("*para poly asynetos*") to have said the things he did, because they were all true. Since he had shown more courage than the big man ever had himself, would Lefteris allow his admirer the petty honour of paying for our dinner?

During the tyranny, Lefteris never lost his sprightliness. Greek exiles would arrive at our London house and ask for money, in his name. I gave it without question and was always repaid when we went back to Athens. After the fall of the Colonels, in 1974, I expected to find Lefteris in a state of euphoria. He was not. He appeared more morose than I had ever known him. When I began to explain how the English had greeted the return of Karamanlis, my Greek was inadequate and, since Lefteris's English was excellent, I switched languages. He was irritated, though he had never been so before, and chided me for having a house in Greece, a classical education and such lame modern Greek. Our friendship waned. He and Efdoxia abandoned their smart shop and began to sell souvenirs and more or less ready-made clothes. Later, I heard that he had bought two obsolete ships and had returned to the sea.

* * *

91 Melpomene, Muse of Tragedy. Note the column-like fluted drape of her skirt.

The founding figure of the tragic theatre was always said to have been Thespis, an actor/author/manager from the Attic village of Ikareia, where Dionysus, the player-god, had a sanctuary. Peter Green suggests that Daedalus originated from this deme, which was subsequently named in memory of his unfortunate son, Icarus. Thespis is credited with the radical innovation of having a single actor – almost certainly himself – stand out from the choral unison and impersonate the hero. Dialogue begins with the differentiation of the hero's speech, and reactions, from the dithyrambic lyric which, tradition promises, Arion of Corinth fashioned into dramatic choral recitations at the end of the seventh century. Thespis need not be accused of vanity in creating for himself a plum part in what had been an ensemble company. As Paganini would prove, virtuosity changes forms. Socrates said that tragedy was older even than Thespis: it was the means by which the Athenians took their revenge on Minos (by depicting him as a tyrant).

Rather as Democritus suggested that the collision of random atoms led to the creation of the world, so the clash between epic speech and ritual incantation engendered the dramatic *agon*, which may have begun over the tomb of a local "saint": heroic passion and narrative obituary addressed common ground. Synthesis, like synoecism, was an aspect of the Greek genius. No hermeneutic search for origins can trace it to a single source.

Anthropologists itemize many contributing influences, from initiation ceremonies, funeral *rites de passage*, the revelation of sacred objects (widened into the moment of *anagnorisis*, as when Elektra recognizes Orestes' hair), "catechism" (examination by the rat-tat of question and answer in stichomythia) to the "graduation" of the candidate in the *exodos* or passing-out parade. Why not? If present, the traces of these elements are digested into a transcendental form, their vestiges no more "explain" or account for plays than the flavour or look of a chef's meal can be included in a shopping list of its ingredients.

In tragedy, once the fracture of the choral ensemble revealed the possibilities implicit in dialogue, it was followed by more elaborate staging and choreography, the use of masks (never a feature of dithyrambic performance) and the introduction of a second and then a third actor.

Innovation was not always applauded. Athens was more conservative and superstitious than surviving texts, and scholarly glosses, suggest. Writers were ill-advised to take unpopular liberties or allow poetic licence to become blasphemy (they still are). The long career of Phrynichus offers an early paradigm of the vicissitudes of a writer's life. In at the creation of Peisistratus's expansion of the Great Dionysia, he won dramatic competitions in 511 and 508, and was, they say, the first to introduce female characters, as fruitful an innovation as could well be imagined. Somerset Maugham said that if you wanted your play to be put on (or your movie made, he might have added), be sure to write a cracking part for a woman. The Old Party knew a thing or two.

Phrynichus's career lasted long enough for him to enter the prize-winning *Phoenissae* in 476, when Themistokles was probably its sponsor. Aeschylus is said to have modelled his *Persae* (472) closely on his predecessor's work. Aeschylus's opening line (*tade men Person ton oichomenon*) is either a steal or a tribute to that of Phrynichus (*tad'esti Person ton palai bebekoton*). Aristophanes regarded Phrynichus as a stylish paragon of pre-Euripidean drama; he was admired for his ingenious stagecraft and (assuming Aristophanes was keeping a straight face) for the beauty of his lyrics. Yet nothing but a few fragments survive.

Posterity has served him badly; and his contemporaries not much better. Zeal for extending the range of the drama made him go too far for their taste. His *The Capture of Miletus* was a daring deviation from the standard mythical themes. The first "drama-doc", it was produced shortly after the events its unprecedented realism depicted: the crushing by the Persians of the rebel Greek city in Asia Minor in 494. Before seceding from the Persian Empire in 499, the Milesians had been egged on by promises of help from their Ionian brothers, the Athenians (not least the newly enfranchised *thetes*). The promises were not fully kept.

Phrynichus's play was more graphic than Athenian stomachs, and consciences, could endure. Miletus's calamity was too raw for tranquil consumption. The audience was devastated by shame and rage. As on the first night of Victor Hugo's *Hernani*, the drama moved from the stage to the auditorium. *The Capture of Miletus* provoked a riot: emotion recollected emotionally proved unacceptable. The Athenians were so chagrined that they took it out on Phrynichus for reopening their wounds: they fined the playwright a very large sum for "drawing unnecessary attention to the sufferings of fellow-Ionians".

Sympathy was hardly an invariable Greek habit. Herodotus says that the Milesians, in happier days, were so appalled by the destruction of Sybaris – a town virtually twinned with them, although a thousand miles away – that all the male Milesians shaved their heads in mourning. But when Miletus suffered its calamity, the surviving (transplanted) Sybarites failed to display reciprocal distress. Hedonism has no conscience.

By attacking Phrynichus, the Athenian public foisted their chagrin on the messenger. Interestingly enough, however, no one seems to have questioned whether his play properly belonged to the category of tragedy: all plays had, in fact, to go through a preliminary selection process. Phrynichus's history of inventive boldness suggests that tragedy soon burst the bounds of the origins which scholars have been assiduous to detect in its mature form. *Parrhesia* seeped into literary composition.

Aristotle's "rules" for tragedy (which, at times, became mandatory for both French and English playwrights) were deduced a posteriori from the Greek canon, not established preliminary to its composition. The origins of tragedy are endlessly interesting, but they never determined what came of them. *The Capture of Miletus*, for mould-breaking instance, is unlikely to have owed much to the dithyramb, or to rituals of initiation: there are big bangs in art as well as in cosmology. Phrynichus made one of them, though it can no longer be heard or seen. He was the first of an unended series of artistic insider/outsiders, at once applauded and suspected, sometimes popular, sometimes reviled, who belong to a European tradition of discomfiting entertainment.

What culture previous to sixth-century Athens, and what art form before the theatre, gave rise to such figures? Only the Hebrew prophets, with their regular, but never institutionalized reproaches to the people and kings of Israel, offer any kind of parallel. Revision, parody and plagiarism are the troika that advances tradition's chariot.

Not wholly deterred from *faits divers*, Phrynichus reverted to less vexed, but still painful, issues: his *Phoenissae* dealt with the contemporary anguish of Phoenician women after the disaster in which so many of their men died fighting for Xerxes. This time, however, by drawing attention to a national triumph, Phrynichus enjoyed one himself. Gloating and pity were sweetly married; the audience savoured the pathos without sharing the shame. Phrynichus's radicalism, in lending his voice to victims and the socially repressed, surely inspired Euripides at least as much as the sophists whose echoes scholars detect in his work.

Phrynichus's *Phoenissae* was very successful when it was produced in 476, probably sponsored by Themistokles in the hope that reflected glory would reverse incipient political eclipse. In writing *Persae* (first performed in 472), Aeschylus learned more than one lesson from Phrynichus. Taking his cue from *Phoenissae*, he too offered a (somewhat) daring take on a topical theme: *Persae* is the sole extant version of a "realistic" tragedy. If Aeschylus was bold in looking at the triumph of Salamis from the point of view of the humiliated Persian royal family (and especially of Xerxes' mother, Queen Atossa), he was also prudent enough – by making the play itself an implicit, but palpable, paean of triumph for the Athenians – to avoid incensing the public. Even Aeschylus, however, was not always exempt from censorious reaction: he later narrowly escaped a charge of impiety which, in theory, carried the death penalty.

In *Persae*, Aeschylus has been accused of writing imperialist propaganda. The play was "produced" – perhaps commissioned – by the young and aggressively expansionist Perikles. Scholars have argued that the climactic entry of the humiliated Great King was a cheap shot, designed to invite unsporting laughter. Xerxes' appearance in rags is indeed a parody of majesty, matched by Jesus' crown of thorns and shabby purple robe, but who knows how the Athenian audience greeted him? With tears and laughter? With jeering pity? Or with chastened apprehension that the Persians would – as they certainly did – rally from their disaster?

Aeschylus's originality lay not only in the authenticity of his play but also in the fact that none of its characters is either Greek or mythical. All are in a more or less dignified state of barbarian distress; yet the final effect is to celebrate what the text seems to bewail. What is not visible is also present. In the architecture of the Parthenon (not yet built when *Persae* had its premiere), the spaces bracketed by the columns have the form of amphorae: they contain a shaped emptiness, like statues made of air. In a similar way, *Persae* draws attention to what is never mentioned: the salvation of Hellas and the joy of the dreaded Athenians whom Xerxes had set out to punish.

How should a patriotic playwright abstain totally from adding a zest of triumphalism after his city had, only just, survived a war which would have extinguished its liberties for ever? If Shakespeare had written a drama, in the 1590s, in which the 1588 defeat of Philip II's armada was depicted entirely from the Spanish point of view as a national disaster and a personal humiliation for the king, what English critic would reproach him for a touch of pride in Spain's fall?

Some scholars have accused Aeschylus of dramaturgical incompetence: *Persae*, they say, lacks any proper clash of characters; the Messenger arrives at the wrong moment, and with stale news (as if good news, to Athenian ears, could not bear repetition). Such criticism fails to remark a signal instance of Aeschylean genius: his mastery of time, and timing. The Messenger delivers a vocal flashback, after which Xerxes' appearance, supposedly wearing the same clothes which he ripped mournfully when the battle of Salamis started to go badly for him, is a "jump-cut" into the future/present.

The "realism" of *Persae* is also a disjunctive montage, immune to literal-minded quibbles such as that Aeschylus was "in error" by putting Xerxes' capital and his father Darius's tomb "in the same place" when, in reality, they were hundreds of miles apart. The organization of space and time in Greek drama was more like that on a vase painting or in a mural, where spatial juxtaposition can imply temporal sequence, than it was like an atlas or a chronicle.

Aeschylus was a master of the arrangement of time, adept both in its acceleration and in slowing it down (by the specifics of his narrative), or even, as he does in *Persae*, in revising it from another perspective. Need the absence of surprise blight suspense? Knowledge of the Persian disaster does not lessen our morbid interest in how Queen Atossa will respond to it. (In *La Dolce Vita*, Fellini's paparazzi lie in wait for a smiling woman whose husband, they and we know, as she does not, has killed himself.)

Again and again, both in *Persae* and in the *Oresteia*, Aeschylus compresses and extends a scene, replays events and "flashes forward" (when Cassandra predicts the murder of Agamemnon and of herself). The technique of Fellini's narration is anticipated in Aeschylean dramaturgy. The Furies were revealed, at the beginning of *Eumenides*, in a combination of a "shock cut" and "special effects": just the kind of theatrical theatre which smacks of vulgarity to pedants, but thrills audiences.

Persae is sophisticated in its apparent simplicity and deceptive in its seemingly smooth and doleful progress. By declaring – never in so many (or too many) words – the ruinous vanities of absolute monarchy, it celebrates democracy without mentioning it. The want of "argument", and of the spirited dialogue which might carry it, suggests the stiffness of autocratic protocol. As Kenneth McLeish once said, *Persae* is "unsatisfactory" only to scholars who, "with their enviable ability to detect needles, sometimes fail to notice the haystacks".

Every Athenian knew that Aeschylus had fought at Marathon, and was possibly present at Salamis. His brother bled to death in the former battle, after his hand was cut off as he tried to prevent a beached Persian ship from scooting with survivors from their defeat. How different would western literature have been if the dramatist had died in his brother's place, instead of when he was (probably) in his seventies? His brother died nobly; the great tragedian's life is said to have ended farcically, when an eagle dropped a tortoise on his bald cranium, having mistaken the poet's head for a rock which might crack the tortoise's shell: if so, Aeschylus's world ended – like the satyr plays which followed tragic trilogies – not in pathos, but in fatal farce. In preparing an epitaph in which he refrained from citing theatrical credits or awards, was it in honour of his brother that he asked to be remembered only for serving at Marathon?

* * *

That the producers of ancient theatre continued to be called *choregoi* was a tribute to the unassuming and undifferentiated origins of tragedy in choral ensemble; but the competitive drive towards novelty emphasizes how different tragedy was from *any* contributing elements, including religious ritual, which derived its sanctity from the *repetition* of hallowed routines and formulae: Roman ceremonies always began again if there was the smallest stammer or slur. In modern rehearsals, the director will sometimes say, after a fluff or a dry, "Once again, from the top", in unconscious tribute to the *instauratio* required by Roman priests whenever anyone faltered or, as they say, lost the plot.

However often old stories were rehearsed (a term which has at its root the bucolic notion of "raked over again"), Attic dramatists could never win prizes without beating expectations. Whatever the reason for masking the actors, the effect was to privilege words and gestures. It also made feasible, if never intentionally, the introduction of female characters (played by men, as Shakespeare's were by boys). The unprogrammed consequence was that the repressed female voice often usurped the centrality of the male. Giving tongue to Klytemnestra and to Antigone (the tragic incarnation of the brave Greek *ochi* of 1940) prompted the writer to put on metaphysical drag and, almost against the prevailing ethos, inhabit the alien world of women.

Formalizing costumes liberated tongues. No other ancient society, and few subsequent ones, put an aesthetic premium on going against the grain. To butt against formal limits, while seeming to honour them, strikes creative sparks. Art can evolve, like a game, beyond the foreseeable scope of the original rules. Merely by not stipulating that rackets have wooden frames, those who drafted the original rules of Lawn Tennis licensed what they never even imagined (though many wish they had), in terms of metal frames making power and pace determinant in the "modern game".

Masks did not so much conceal the actors as announce the (almost always) well-known characters – or, in comedy, the types – that they were assuming.

92 No one went on
stage without one.

When the plot is a given, the beauty can be concentrated in the detail. Similarly, the labelling of figures on vases made sure that those who "read" them understood which myth was being depicted and could enjoy the nuances.

By assuming a mask, the actor blanked his own personal features, though professional actors travelled with and treasured their favourite – and, we may guess, recognizable – masks. Since their voices remained their own, the masked players both were and were not the stars whom the public had paid to see. Laurence Olivier made a fetish of false noses, but displayed no marked wish to be taken for anyone but Olivier.

It is tempting to see an "obvious" connection between tragic self-effacement and the royal impersonation of emblematic animals in rites which assimilate members of a tribe to its cultic denomination. We were once promised that the bull-religion of Minoan Crete involved the king assuming first the crown and the taurine panoply and then the sacrificial role in which a sacred bull later deputized for him.

The tragic stage did not hold the mirror up to nature but to the supernatural, and its penetration of the everyday. Hence the author was not shackled to the banal "realism" of today's film and television. What seems outlandish in tragic costume persists, vestigially, in the wigs and gowns of lawyers and judges: they become impersonations of justice by ceasing to look like ordinary men and women. The masked *Carnevale* of Venice dispenses the reveller from his or her normal caution, and morals. Such dispensation was never the purpose of dramatic masking, but by denying routine facial expressions their place in high drama, emphasis was concentrated on text, gesture and music. Tragic performance generalized the close-up: nothing came closer to the anguish of the human condition, yet formality avoided sentimental or histrionic self-indulgence.

The excellence of the acoustics at, for famous instance, Epidaurus, where you can indeed sit in the back row of the vast auditorium and hear a whisper at the centre of the orchestra, suggests that variations of tone – accompanied by the music which is now forever silenced – gave ancient theatrical performances an operatic richness which promoted what was heard no less than what

93 Epidaurus. You *can* hear a pin drop, they say.

was seen. Even warfare had its musical soundtrack. Life as performance was never confined to the theatre.

The differentiation of narrative into two dimensions (the actor and the chorus) was followed not only by additional actors, but also by conceits, annexes and digressions, which generated new perspectives, often from an unexpectedly low angle. In *Choephoroi*, the slave nurse recalls what it was like to care for the infant Orestes, whose death she is required, by the plot, to report to Klytemnestra. Her dawdling presence adds to the suspense and the irony (Orestes is, of course, not dead at all), but the accuracy of the nanny's affection for "Other People's Babies" (a well-known song in the 1930s) also opens a window on unheroic or servile characters, whose lives and feelings were very rarely worthy of attention in epic or in early tragedy. Eumaios, in the *Odyssey*, is a touching exception.

It might fracture the texture of the *Oresteia* to play the nurse's role for laughs, but it would be surprising – and untypical of an actor – if (s)he failed to prompt the amusement of recognition from the audience. Performance itself affects and extends dramatic, and comic, possibilities. This extension opened a window

94 Orestes and his nurse? Fifth-century B.C. Boeotian terracottas were mass-produced big business.

through which we can see the promotion of slaves (in other words, the defeated) to a place in public awareness. Low-life characters came centre stage in Menander's comedies, where slaves (like *Figaro*) can be cleverer, and funnier, than their masters. Tragedy did and did not honour the heroic past; it deconstructed, criticized, secularized and renovated it. For instance, only Sophocles ever had the idea of making Oedipus put his own eyes out, and (neat touch!) with a brooch taken from his wife/mother. Shock and horror, no less than verbal finesse or rhapsodic lyricism, won fame and fame's evidence, first prize. Despite Aristotle's aversion from such vulgarity, *opsis* (spectacle) was an applauded addition to tragedy. At the same time, questioning the obvious gave drama a common hinge with philosophy, which quizzed received ideas as drama did received stories about gods and heroes. How often did epic concentrate attention on the defeated?

Aristotle gave Alexander the Great an annotated copy of the *Iliad* before he set off to acquire Persia and kill Persians. Presumably the notes were of the essence, since it is also said that Alexander knew the whole poem by heart. It would have been tactless, but more humane, to give him the works of that quondam refugee at the Macedonian court, Euripides. Aristotle's convenient claim that barbarians were, of their nature, slaves is a sorry reflection on a man whose *Poetics* proves that he knew tragedy, and its implicitly humane lessons, very well.

* * *

*D*espite the piety to Zeus *xenios* which insisted on granting sanctuary to strangers (*The Suppliants* of Aeschylus deals with a vexed case), the Greeks did not have magnanimity enjoined upon them, as an article of faith, as the Jews did: God required the latter never to forget that they had once been slaves in Egypt. Aristotle's ethics were never better than grandly ethnocentric.

In the second half of the fifth century, Agathon (one of Plato's harder-headed symposiasts) tried to expand the range of tragedy by devising a fictional plot which owed nothing either to myth or to recent history. There may have been banal reasons why Agathon's play was a failure and set no precedent: bad writing or inept performance by actors (and audiences) uneasy in roles without a known history. The actor/author's daring may have been excited by vanity (Aristophanes – never one to give a rival an even break – accused him of being too pretty in face and style), but it sounds like a brave, doomed try that belonged to the category of showbiz of which a critic once observed, "They said it couldn't be done, and it couldn't".

The reason for the abortion of tragedy made from wholly new cloth may be no more abstruse than that the plays which "worked best" – the *Oresteia*, *Medea*, the *Oedipus* cycle, *Antigone*, and so on – all began with *something already known to have happened*: Ibsen's "dead man in the cargo". Ibsen's own tragedies could be domestic and parochial because the locus of bourgeois common knowledge was fathers and sons, wives and mothers: the primal scene was a universal human, not a cosmological, struggle. *Peer Gynt*, alone of his plays, seems bizarre to non-Nordic audiences, because it chimes only fitfully with alien mythology. Ancient Hellenes could be expected to anticipate, and relish, the principal elements furnished by their common culture: Troy has fallen, Medea is being dumped, Thebes is in the grip of a plague, and Agamemnon dead.

An original play, on the other hand, has to set its own terms: it cannot have the trimness of a text in which the author is confident that the back-story will already be familiar to the audience. Plays based on myths were all rescripts of common knowledge. Tragedy could deal with great moral and social issues without preamble: the Greek language was already articulate with metaphors and figures of speech, impersonated by gods and heroes, to which the dramatist added existential twists and more or less contemporary glosses.

George Thomson, a scholar who, back in the 1950s, seemed to carry the Marxist key to the society and literature of Periklean Athens, interpreted the *Oresteia* in the light of what, to a Communist, *had* to be the case: that a nascent, increasingly assertive "bourgeoisie" appropriated Athenian culture and ruptured the old forms. With the surefootedness of a man whose path is flashed with foregone conclusions, he – even more than the great G.E.M. de Ste. Croix in his magisterial (and tendentious) *The Class Struggle in Ancient Greece* – made a case, and selected evidence, that validated a preconceived ideology.

In the post-Peloponnesian War period, it is more plausible to accuse Athens, shorn of its imperial vanities, of wearying of the gods and their capricious tutelage. Philosophers such as Protagoras were by then as openly sceptical as the Athenian commander who recommended the Melians not to rely on divine justice. Where man was "the measure of all things" there was little room for pious credulity. If anything, stories of conquering heroes seemed to pass scornful judgment on a city with shrivelled prospects. Myths which, in the Golden Age, had given life a cruel coherence became antique furniture, like *Rule, Britannia!*

Today, ancient Greece itself is at once the laurel on the brow and the millstone around the neck of modern Hellas: as the Cretan-born Odysseus Elytis says in his *Axion Esti*, "*Neos polee kai gnorisa ton ekato chronou phones*" (Though very young, I came to know the voices of a hundred years). Greeks are condemned to the treadmill of an ever-present past.

Fear of displeasing a mass audience may not have been the only cause for Thucydides and Plato to elect to write in prose, but the risk of exciting outrage was reduced by using a medium read in private rather than heard in public. When Herodotus acquired enduring fame by reciting his prose account of the Persian wars to sports fans assembled at Olympia, he told them nothing that they were not thrilled to hear, and to applaud, which they did at length (echoing the welcome which had been given to Themistokles at the same venue over twenty years earlier). Herodotus's public success encouraged the use of prose, but what later historian ever excited the same enthusiasm?

Thucydides claimed to be fashioning a *kteema es aei*, a work for the ages; it was a wisely long-term ambition, since what he had to say was unlikely to appeal to a contemporary Athenian audience. When he came to analyse the conduct of the Athenians with regard to Melos, he adopted the dialogue form, but did not use the theatre to publish it. His astringent tone would not have got much applause at Olympia (though the Spartans might have given him a round), nor would he have fared better than Phrynichus if he went public, in drama-doc form, at the Great Dionysia.

Although Thucydides has been accused of depicting the Athenians' conduct towards Melos as unforgivable *hubris* (quite as if it typified decline from some higher, Periklean standard of public morality), their delegation's argument was of a piece with Solon's doctrine, which, in the case of internal *stasis*, stigmatized the wilfully neutral.

With more clarity than cynicism, Thucydides remarked that justice might be possible within states, but that between states there could be only *rapports de force*. Pacts between states work as long as they are not needed; when they are broken, only the stronger can enforce them. Moral scrupulousness may wish it otherwise, but in international practice dominant powers make the law. It is a point which Thrasymachus thrust, like a lance, into the opening book of Plato's *Republic*, and which the rest of the dialogue is an uneasy attempt to confront and confute.

The Melian dialogue took the poetry out of killing and replaced it with businesslike prose. In the theatre of war, the drama ends in unconcealed, and uncontrollable, blood. No reconciling deity empties the stage in an uplifting *exodos*. In Thucydides' war, nothing scans, little is heroic, no one is godlike (though Lysander, the most heartless of victorious generals, was indeed paid divine honours). History may be a kind of theatre, but not of the kind whose participants do not really bleed or in which gods can be wheeled out at the last moment to procure a salutary ending. Defeat in the Peloponnesian War triggered the feeling that the Olympians had turned their backs on Athens. In Plato's *Euthyphro*, the protagonist complains that anyone who talked as if the gods were seriously relevant to everyday life was laughed to scorn.

After the abject days of 404, it was Athens itself, not Miletus, that had come down in the world. The link between tragedy and social evolution, which has its majestic instance in the sombre optimism of Aeschylus's *Oresteia*, was ruptured. Domestic comedy became the popular form of drama. Menander was *the* successful playwright of his day. Like the derided Agathon, he was conspicuously effeminate. With his swivelling hips and flowing robes, as he pranced before Demetrios of Phaleron, the overlord of Athens in the 320s, he was "taken for a pederast", a charge repeated by Lord Queensberry (trust the inventor of the rules of boxing to hit below the belt) when he accused Oscar Wilde of "posing as a sodomite".

* * *

*S*how business begins with New Comedy. Infinitely pliable in pandering to prospects of praise, fame and revenue, it conceives of no higher purpose than success. Aristophanic comedy attacked the confident society on which it depended for laughs. Tolerance of his satire was a function of what the audience believed could never happen, and then did: the curtain descending on Athenian supremacy. New Comedy was calculatedly unabrasive. Distracting attention from sorry realities in favour of a world of timeless contrivance and larkiness, it supplied the quarry from which the Roman playwrights Terence and Plautus took their material. Shakespeare – blatantly, in *The Comedy of Errors* – would work the same vein, as did Boulevard comedy and Feydeauesque farce.

In the televisual mutation of the intricate joinery and stock characters of New Comedy, soap opera and sitcoms replace climax with protraction: the ratings-winning trick in television is to create appetites for more and more of the same thing. Like TV soaps, New Comedy furnishes a subdivision of Empsonian pastoral: a hermetic world of narcotic surprises which invites its audience to become inertly addicted. It is the very opposite of agitprop, which incites them, at the least, to politically correct prejudice and, in theory, to righteous militancy.

At the end of the Peloponnesian War, Athenian cohesion collapsed into a "Vichyite" reaction led by Critias (for whom defeat was, as France's was for Charles Maurras in 1940, a "divine surprise"). The tyranny was sponsored by Lysander, but was evicted, after a few months, by the Athenian democrat Thrasybulus (Mr Rash-in-Council), whom the Spartan King Pausanias encouraged to introduce the law *mee mnesikakein*.

Athens' Golden Age had lasted less than a century. Right-thinking historians have long accused the *demos* of endorsing the reckless policies which brought the city to its knees. In fact, the people almost always voted only for what, in most cases, their betters had proposed. Cleon was the butt of both Thucydidean spleen and Aristophanic snobbery, but how greatly did his intentions differ from those of the lordly (and over-confident) Perikles or the shamelessly recurrent Alcibiades?

Democracy remained a practical, not an ideological, device. It less destroyed the old ruling class than enabled it to continue, with popular support. Rather than any idealism, the nautical basis of Athens' power made politic the enfranchisement of the *thetes*, who toiled in its engine room. Loyal effort supplied a better pace than forced labour. However practical their motives, the Athenians were more humane than the Genoese, whose fleet, twenty centuries later, was fuelled by enslaved "Turks" who lacked the clout (or common ethnicity) to claim citizens' rights and were worked to death in the galleys of *La Superba*.

While enfranchising the *thetes*, Athens continued to be unashamed in its exploitation of slaves, both domestically and in the mines. There was, however, no New Comedy about string-pulling slaves in the slime and the dust, though there were (lost) plays about metal miners by Pherecrates and Nicomachus. We are unlikely ever to know their plots or purposes, but it is improbable that they advocated a shorter working week.

Athens' Open Society remains admirable, at a distance, but closer inspection hardly shows that it was the ultimate democracy which sentimentalists imagine or agitators wish to "revive". How certain is it that modern society would be better served by annual elections, press-button universal participation in all important political decisions or high office obtainable by lottery (to allow the gods to make their marks)? As for People's Courts, with verdicts indistinguishable from popularity contests and juries hectored by demagogues, were these things quite as sweet and reasonable as they sound?

"All vote now" may work in a quiz show, but what modern government, of states with millions of voters, could conceivably be rigged to function effectively on such a scheme? Those who dream of resuscitating history's "only genuine democracy" are counterbalanced by Marxists who, deconstructing the Athenian constitution into a façade for imperialist adventure and class exploitation, planned to replace it with the Dictatorship of the Proletariat.

Programmatic reactionaries prefer to fall in with Sparta's overt oligarchic discipline. In this way, extreme Right and extreme Left meet, round the back, in common distrust of the untidiness of *ad hoc* institutions and undragooned humanity. Sparta, with its "selfless" dirigiste elite, provided a maquette for both Fascism and Communism. The "closed" Spartan constitution was also generated by war, but instead of enfranchising its lowest class, as Athens did the *thetes*, landlocked Sparta enslaved both Lakonia and the adjacent Greek state of Messenia, whose citizens were set to work like farm animals. Their enslavement freed Sparta's best men, the *homoioi*, to rehearse their military machine without ever having to break off campaigning in order to bring in the crops. The brave Mayan revolt against Spain in the 1820s collapsed because the divine duty of harvesting the corn in Yucatan took priority over sustained military action. English history teaches the same lesson: peasant revolts may alarm urban rulers but they never overthrow them. In Socialist Realist paintings, Lenin consulted the peasants; in fact he coerced and dispossessed them.

Mercenary armies were an unsurprising development in later warfare: those who saved the sum of things, or kings, for pay did not have to get home for harvest. The early city-state was dependent on wealth created on the land, to which manufactures were rated a petty supplement. Its rural economy, and the socio-religious calendar that punctuated it, was never going to be suited to protracted warfare. Even the Spartan war-machine could be stalled until the Karneia festival had been honoured (inaugurated in the mid-seventh century, it celebrated the "end of civic discord", that is, the enslavement of all Sparta's neighbours).

The more successful Sparta and Athens were in war, the more difficult for a limited number of citizens to hold on to their winnings. The *polis* withered away because it lacked enough ground to go to seed: its exclusive organization, and territorial limits, aborted the expansion of its citizens' numbers. Macedonia knew no such inhibitions: its army did not vote; it marched when instructed by a king whose rule might depend on success but was untrammelled by constitutional brakes.

By the coerced incorporation of adjacent tribes, Philip of Macedon widened the base from which his army, especially the cavalry, could be recruited. No social or constitutional crisis followed: apart from "voting" for his coronation, his warriors were brought up to do what they were told. Yet even Alexander the Great's Macedonian freebooting army did finally weary of tracking his glory to the ends of the world and mutinied in favour of home leave. Hence those mass marriages at Susa, staged to create a baby-farm for future imperial policemen.

Athenian and Spartan purposes were not fundamentally dissimilar: both wanted, or at least needed, to maximize their capacity for war. More by chance than through preconceived high-mindedness, Athens provided a fruitful model for future, free-speaking societies. Sparta sponsored and – in blinkered eyes – its success validated militaristic uniformity. Its ruling caste, the *homoioi*

95 Good fifth-century B.C. Greek infantrymen: chins down, shields up.

– more *alike* than Equals – had similarities to Hitler's SS: the training which began at the age of seven made them a corporate elite virtually interchangeable with each other. Obedience was their first rule, imposing it the second.[*] To lend legal authority to practical brutality, Sparta declared war annually on already subjugated Messenia: cynicism and superstition validated terror, as it did with the Aztecs. Spartan cadets formed the *Krypteiai*, squads of secret policemen whose blood sport was murdering allegedly insolent helots.

In Mafia style, initiates were made men by learning to kill without emotion and on command. In a "gentle" version of human sacrifice, the killer boys had themselves often been flogged at the altar of Artemis, where they were expected (like later public schoolboys) to endure pain without complaint. Masocho-sadism was the deadly virtue of Sparta.

According to Pierre Vidal-Naquet, the Athenians had initiation rites not unlike those of the Spartans: before being admitted to full citizenship, young men – though not conscripted to murder – had to prove that they could live rough. Under the rubric of "Black Hunters", they fended for themselves on the margin of society, in order to qualify for full citizenship. Adolescents had to be as resourceful as young Theseus was when he lived dangerously on the way to claim his throne: he authenticated himself as a hunter by killing a wild sow called Phaia, even though it did not threaten him, nor did he need its meat. Plutarch, rationalizing as sententiously as usual, said that the sow was really some low-life wanton who died for her sins.

---

[*] The Jesuits, who cowed and enslaved the Mayas, and burnt their history (and their priests), were the *homoioi* of Catholicism.

However callous the Spartans seemed (and wished) to appear, their enslavement of the defeated Messenians was less scandalous to ancient than to modern, liberal eyes. In the ancient world, the defeated could expect enslavement and confiscation at best. Thucydides' Athenian delegation warned the Melians of what they already knew to be the case. Athenian *hubris* may have been highlighted by the clarity of the exposition, but what ancient society would have been shocked by its logic? The Athenians treated Melos as the Spartans had Messene (and once hoped to treat Tegea, in Arcadia) and as Cyrus the Great treated Lydia, not to mention many smaller, but juicy, objects of his greedy attention. There were, however, occasions when a great power agreed to be bought off, as the Persians were by the Egyptians, but only when the outcome was dubious and a high price offered for a draw.

The Spartans attacked the Tegeans in 550 or so, bringing with them the chains in which they proposed to fetter them. The brave Tegeans put them on the Spartans, but were later obliged to become the unenthusiastic allies of their big neighbour for two centuries: the break came at Leuctra in 371. Like Sparta, Tegea was at first a confederation of villages, with no central city for over a hundred years. The Tegeans were proud warriors and, in 479, challenged the Athenians for pride of place in the battle order at Plataea.

Hellenistic kingdoms regarded each other more with jealousy than with implacable enmity: diplomatic finesse could pay better than an expensive, protracted campaign. The post-Alexander, pre-Roman Fertile Crescent was ripe with profitable offers the parties would be unwise to refuse, and often went to war to secure. There was seldom any recognizable ethnic entity to generate fight-to-a-finish passion or fanatical obduracy (that came with monotheisms). War ceased to be a rite and became a business.

The Phoenicians, for prime example, were nautical traders no less than warriors. In accordance with their deal-making tradition, their colonists the Carthaginians imagined, after defeat in the Second Punic War (and the eclipse of Hannibal), that the Romans would keep their harsh bargain and at least not utterly destroy them. Cato thought differently, and persuasively. The destruction of Carthage in 146 was an act of ruthless policy by a self-centred, wilful and homogeneous people without parallel in devious, but usually compromising, Hellenistic *realpolitik*.

In the absence of written evidence to the contrary, the assumption has long been that helots responded to Sparta's legitimated violence only with mute and listless resignation. The same charge was often brought against the European Jews as a whole, not least by Raul Hilberg, the first sympathetic historian of their tragedy. We have since learnt of many displays of hopeless courage of which there was no written record. It seems at least possible that the helots were never as completely cowed as the supermanly myth of Sparta implies. Halfway between slaves and free men, the Lakonian helots were able to be converted, at short notice, into auxiliary soldiers of no little ability.

In 479, as Mardonius was advancing with a large Persian force towards the Peloponnese, the Spartans recruited thirty-five thousand such auxiliaries to accompany the five thousand Spartiates that marched to join the Athenians and other loyal Greeks at Plataea. This helot contingent at Plataea was, no doubt, militarily helpful, and may have been given a promise of emancipation, provided it held firm in battle. At the same time, the Spartan elite must have wanted to be sure to have the strongest of their Greek serfs where they could see them: a long way from the homeland which, with Sparta's best muscle absent, they might have tried to repossess.

A century later, after Leuctra, where the Theban phalanx dispelled the myth of Spartiate invincibility, the Messenian helots (whose forefathers had fought long and valiantly against their Lakonian neighbours) were hardly less swift to organize themselves into fighting units. The great Theban Epaminondas inspired them to establish a durable city, which the enfeebled Spartans scarcely tried, and certainly failed, to overset.

Thebes' tactics were not unlike those which Sparta had used at Dekeleia, and the Athenians at Pylos: by creating a refuge for runaways, they sapped the Spartan workforce, and confidence. In the same spirit, Epaminondas encouraged the creation of Megalopolis, a new town which became the largest in the Peloponnese, though never the most stable, while in the re-founded Messene, ex-helots established a sort of Liberia, where they recovered their dignity, though little effective cohesion.

The new, improved Messene (with Mount Ithome – the Messenians' Masada – as its acropolis) was calculated to intimidate not only the Spartans but also the citizens of Tegea and Mantinea, who disliked each other hardly less than their common enemy, Sparta. Today's Messene is a long belt of impressive walls without content. The extensive fortifications were hurriedly put up, but proved more durable than the city walls of Athens, which were constructed, in a prophylactic frenzy, at Themistokles' urging, after the expulsion of Xerxes and before the already sullen Spartans knew what was happening. In 404, when Athens had been defeated by Sparta (with the indispensable help of Persian gold), the Spartan general Lysander took vindictive pleasure in supervising a symbolic breaching of the Long Walls – connecting Athens with the Piraeus – to the sound of flutes.

Spartan distrust of their slaves was matched by Athenian distrust of Sparta (and vice versa). Even in their finest hour, the common front of the Greeks against the Persians was, like an old sweat's shield, full of dents. Before

Plataea (which secured Greek liberty far more decisively than Salamis), the assembled Hellenes obliged each other to swear an elaborate oath, with many clauses, promising not to desert or stab each other in the back, either during the battle or – should they survive – after it. The more fervently allies swear to their unbreakable resolve to stick together, the less reliably adhesive their relationship is likely to be. Until recently, blood brotherhood was often sworn annually in the Balkans. Just before the Serbs attacked Bosnia, Theodore Zeldin wrote a book which took this to be a symptom of the unusual warmth of human bonding in the region. Ethnic cleansing soon followed.

* * *

*A*mong the promises made by the Greek allies, before Plataea, was not to leave even one of the allied dead unburied: the same solemn duty which Antigone insisted on honouring, against the Theban tyrant Kreon's explicit veto, when she buried her "disgraced" dead brother, Polyneices. She was damned if she did not, and condemned (to be walled up alive, to avoid Kreon being tainted by the miasma of direct bloodshed) when she did. Sophocles posed no fabricated dilemma: as Arginusae proved, Antigone's self-righteous resolve would not seem exaggerated or hysterical to an ancient audience.

It is a curiosity of the Greek style that we know more about the characters, desires and even the physical appearance of a number of mythical figures, heroic and relatively insignificant, than we do of historical figures before the fifth century. Tradition and its glosses depict a more personalized Theseus (his deeds were tabulated "in chronological order" in the Treasury of the Athenians at Delphi) than Thucydides did when it came to men of the generation before Perikles. Biography, detached from a man's society or deeds, smacked of what the Funeral Oration called idiocy. In earlier days, a man's tomb and *kleos* (battle honours) were his claim on posterity's respect. Socrates' self-conscious insistence on giving priority to the "examined life" makes him an appropriate subject for early biographical studies, however tendentious, by Plato and by Xenophon, one of the pioneers of the form. The other was Isocrates, who wrote about Evagoras of Salamis, in Cyprus (to which Teucer, the illegitimate brother of Aias – with whom Evagoras claimed ancestral kinship – earlier repaired when ejected by Telamon). Evagoras, somewhat like Polycrates of Samos, was for a while a significant and subtle player on the interface between mainland Greece and Persia.

Socrates has no known shrine except what has been written about him. Over the posthumous years, his famously ugly face – that of a chaste Silenus – was graced by portraitists into that of the emblematic thinker.

96 Seventh-century B.C. hoplites kept in step, Spartan style, by a flautist.

Individual initiative, which Perikles claimed to be characteristic of his compatriots, might be vital at sea; but it was disruptive on land: once engaged, the hoplite was required only to hold steady in the ranks. They might stab, jab or even grab the enemy – as the legendary Spartans did, when out of ammunition in their last stand against Xerxes at Thermopylae – but infantrymen did not, as a rule, improvise. Above all, a hoplite's shield had to be in place to defend the man next to him.

Only a rare man such as Archilochos – egocentric mercenary warrior, poet of genius – had the nerve, as early as the seventh century, to shrug off having dumped his shield: "I can get another one", he wrote, "just as good". If Hesiod was the first to intrude personal history into literature, Archilochos was the first to grace even its least gracious moments with art (he made a poem out of premature ejaculation, just as Craig Raine did, over two and a half millennia later, of the anal sphincter).

A few years after Archilochos, Alcaeus of Mytilene – a poet of almost equal renown – followed his fugitive lead by throwing away his arms. The Athenians made a pious propaganda point by hanging them up in the temple of Athene. And after fighting, if only somewhat, at Philippi, in 42, on the losing side against Mark Antony and Octavian, the Roman poet Horace imitated Greek models, and prettied his brazen cowardice with poetic grace. Unlike his Greek models, however, he not only dumped his gear but also made a profitable peace: an indifferent subaltern became an inspired propagandist for

Augustus's new world order. He then had the curious felicity to write *Dulce et decorum est pro patria mori* (Sweet and proper it is to die for your country[*]), plagiaristic homage to Tyrtaeus, the seventh-century poet who composed Sparta's chauvinist marching songs and beat the drum for the Spartans to conduct their second, and conclusive, war against the Messenians.

The anti-Spartan tradition, both in Hellas and among liberal scholars, makes the enslavement of the defeated Messenians into a signal instance of internal colonialism. The war with Messenia was not, however, a case of coming down like the wolf on the fold: the Messenians resisted for nineteen years, during which the Spartans suffered losses and, no doubt, convinced themselves of the righteousness of their campaign. The truth was that Messenia, unlike Hesiod's Boeotia, had enviable territory: "good to plough, and good to sow". If heartless, the Spartans were scarcely the only predators in the ancient world: dog eat dog is a traditional Greek recipe. Though this is certainly true metaphorically, in practice dogs were sacrificed (to Artemis the Midwife and, by the Spartans, so Pausanias says, to Enyalios, a mutant of Ares), but they were never, I think, eaten, except perhaps when a besieged city had no other menu.

Tyrtaeus was the first Greek poet to make a virtue of dying for one's country: Homer glorified, but never sentimentalized, the brave deaths of warriors. His Greeks fought more for personal glory, and honour, than for Hellas. If, as legend says, Tyrtaeus was indeed literally lame, it would make him a prototype of Dr Goebbels, with his zeal for Total War: he incited others to march more quickly, and straighter, than he could himself. Byron too was lame, and urged the Greeks to war, or at least to righteous rebellion, but he put himself on the line with those whom he so fervently, and expensively, backed to eject the Turks. However, the myth that he "died fighting for Greece" is true only in spirit: he was indeed in Greece when he died, probably of malaria and septicaemia, in mosquito-ridden Missolonghi.

Some ancient sources refer to Tyrtaeus as a "general", but it may be that this was an honorary title for the cheerleading which was part of a war poet's office: he was there to be chanted, not read. Another legend (denied by staid authority) says that Tyrtaeus began his career as an Athenian schoolmaster and was seconded to Lakonia when the Spartans asked for a suitable poet to put snap in their step. It is tempting to imagine that his didactic militarism bored the Athenians, who were happy to give him good references and send him to electrify the Spartans.

---

[*] In the mid-nineteenth century, A.H. Clough ironized, in Amours de Voyage, "dulce it is, and decorum no doubt, for the country to fall /... Still individual culture is also something." Not in Sparta, it wasn't.

97 A dying warrior from once-powerful, early fifth-century B.C. Aegina puts a brave face on it.

Unlike Archilochos, Tyrtaeus owed a good deal to Homer; some of the debt was incurred deliberately: his verses were calculated to lend traditional lustre, and the promise of predestined victory, to the acquisitive march of the Spartan phalanx:

> You are the unbeatable race of Herakles.
> Heads up! Zeus won't look askance at you!
> Don't flinch at enemy numbers, fear them not:
> Shields up! Warriors go straight for the foe.
> Who wants to live forever? The black angels of death
> Beam down as bright as cheerful sun-rays.
> You know the savage deeds of Ares, the crock of tears,
> You've seen the moil of pitiless battle.

Yet in lines such as "Like donkeys borne down by heavy loads, / Bringing to their masters, under cruel duress, / Half of all the produce that their land supplies," there was a trace of the imaginative empathy with the losers which Homer initiated and which Aeschylus matched in *Persae*.

The communal nature of hoplite warfare, in which individual heroism could be a breach of discipline, was honoured in the tombs of the fallen: at Marathon, at Thermopylae, at Plataea, the glory of the dead was celebrated in a common mound. For those who chose to draw moral conclusions from the ancient world, the team spirit, in life and death, was a denial of the self-glorification which reached its superb, unedifying climax in the career of Alexander the Great. He was a travesty of heroism, not because he lacked courage, but because he made such a show of it.

* * *

*A*lexander's cult of self was unprecedented in the Golden Age. He pioneered the embellishment of war by taking with him embedded reporters, such as the historian Callisthenes, a nephew of Aristotle. In the hope of making poodles of the press and TV, the Americans packed journalists in their impedimenta on the way to Iraq, where Alexander had better fortune, and fewer scruples, than G.W. Bush.

Alexander wanted to be sure that he received favourable reviews for his lavish remake of the Trojan War, and much, much more. The vulgarity of his ambitions and the savagery of his methods were, for centuries, ignored by those for whom his adventures were their own justification. What, one wonders, would Thucydides have made of him? And how long would he have been suffered to live to tell the tale?

Callisthenes did all that was asked of him in endorsing Alexander's affectations of divinity and hyping the war as a righteous crusade conducted by a military genius. However, he flinched, too publicly, from literally crawling to Alexander and was put to death, almost certainly on faked charges, during the so-called Pages' Conspiracy. In his zest for purges, Alexander gave signs of the widening paranoid streak which would attain mass-murderous proportions in the tyrannies of Hitler and Stalin.

Alexander did not wait for death before building the monuments which would commemorate him. His passion for destroying cities was matched by his zeal for founding Alexandrias. The greatest was established in Egypt, but it had a rash of siblings on the way to the Hindu Kush and into India, where Arnold Toynbee noticed that the Buddha had acquired a Hellenic face.

Alexander wished, perhaps above all, to be memorable. In the midst of wrecking Europe and murdering millions of its inhabitants, Hitler found time for sessions with Albert Speer in which the two men planned fantastic palaces and utopian cities that would make the name of Adolf live through the centuries. In an access of maudlin projection, they even considered how best to glamorize the ruins of their still unbuilt paradises, not least Hitler's birthplace, Linz, where he once went to school with Ludwig Wittgenstein (but in a class below him).

Alexander's fame spread, after his death, to places he had never known or visited: Berlin itself would have its Alexanderplatz and the earliest surviving poem in French is a Franco-Provençal fragment by Alberich of Pisançon, about his boyhood education (an unconscious codicil to Xenophon's *Cyropaedia*). In the twelfth century, fatter versions of Alberich culminated in the extant confection *Roman d'Alexandre*, compiled by one Alexandre de Paris, where, it is promised, Alexander is portrayed as "a model ruler, generous and knightly, a man driven by intellectual curiosity". Callisthenes did not live to say as much.

The purpose of war has changed little over the centuries: men go and try to kill other men for a variety of greeds or vanities, and with a variety of implements, but the game, and the plans, and the excuses, have a sorry consistency. What has changed, as much as the weaponry, is the method of reporting what happens in the field. Until the advent of film, war was constantly touted as a glorious, manly contest (the American Civil War is "modern" because it was photographed). Homer did not conceal the cruelty and the pain and the unfairness of it, but his verses sang so sweetly that Hector and Achilles became the archetypes of those who do not grow old as we grow old. Photography made war more "real" to those who never witnessed it; but it has hardly affected its frequency or ferocity. Even the Greeks knew that violence was somehow a disgrace (and blamed the gods, in large part, for generating the Trojan War), but they sailed to wage it all the same. America may have abandoned the Vietnam War because of the body bags shown on television, but the defeat or "defeat" (the inverted commas are largely Republican) led, after not many years, to increased military budgets and a sense more of grievance than of shame.

The vivid, photographic reporting of war may appal, but it also entertains, however furtively, those who seem to share the danger without being in it. Perhaps if reports include the smells and the pain and draft them into comfortable homes, the long history of how the myth of war is conveyed to the civilian, in words and pictures, will end by killing becoming – key word in modern media – uncommercial. Terrorists thrive on publicity and pander to the zeal for horrors which even their declared enemies show to television audiences: they need what denounces them.

Alexander's life seems, in retrospect, to have been a race with death. He had to do everything, and at once, to shore up a myth against his ruin. Not unlike Theseus, he did more than enough to merit heroic status without ever becoming the hero one would choose to be. He was a Narcissus who loved his image best when he saw it reflected in a pool of blood.

A brilliant and brave leader, Alexander rewarded those who had shared his glory with suspicion and, often, with execution on flimsy or invented grounds. Black Cleitus, the old soldier who saved his life at the battle of the River Granicus, was run through and killed by his king during a Macedonian officers' binge. Alexander had a long, conscience-stricken hangover afterwards, but most of his victims, and friends, were subsequently consigned to execution with no sign of compunction or regret.

The civilizing mission with which the influential W.W. Tarn was pleased to bless him was hardly a corrective to unmitigated barbarism. The Persian Empire, which Alexander wilfully invaded and tore into pieces that were later fought over by his surviving generals (the so-called *diadochoi*), was a ramshackle, decadent affair, but it was probably much more pleasant to live in, as the Ottoman Empire was before its disassembly, than the bloodstained, factitious monarchies which succeeded it.

Egypt was probably the most delectable, and certainly the most easily defensible, of the vultures' portions grabbed by Alexander's top legates. The wars

that beset the other Hellenistic kingdoms touched, but seldom seriously threatened, the Ptolemies. Much of their revenues were spent on useful ostentation such as the Pharos, the lighthouse which advertised the great harbour of Alexandria just as the Colossus did that of Rhodos, until it was toppled. The Pharos too was eventually overthrown in an earthquake, but shone brightly for several centuries.

Both the Pharos and the Colossus figured among the Seven Wonders of the World listed by academic tabulators at the Mouseion (more university than museum, in any modern sense) founded and funded by the Ptolemies. Alexandria became

98 Alexandria's Pharos souvenir vase, found in Kabul, Afghanistan.

a luxurious fortress which the royal family made impervious not only to external enemies, but also to indigenous Egyptians whose Pharaohs they imitated (even in the practice of incest) without ever recruiting local loyalty. The Ptolemies introduced a non-negotiable currency (like the Spartan iron-bars, but flashier) to create a barrier to economic incursion.

Proconsular even in what they claimed as their own kingdom, they set a fashion for elitist foreign rule which was followed, if modified, by the Romans, the Mamelukes and the British under their "Consul-General", Lord Cromer. Lawrence Durrell's Mountolive (alias, in fact, Sir Miles Lampson), in *The Alexandria Quartet*, was the last of the line.

Alexandria (like Los Angeles) was literally built on sand. Its attractions were signalled by the febrile variety of its imported cultures. Its prosperity, however, was founded on the prodigious amounts of wheat grown in the hinterland farmed by the despised *felaheen*. At the founding ceremony, the limits of the city were strewn with grains of wheat which, so it was said, were promptly removed by a flock of birds who flew off in all directions, thus symbolizing Egypt's role as the granary of the Mediterranean. Alexander insisted that the creation of the city was meant as a service to the Athenians, who regarded it as detracting from their eminence: they need no longer depend on grain from the Black Sea, which came through the easily blockaded Hellespont. Sestos, on the north side, was known as "the breadboard of the Piraeus".

The great lantern of the *pharos* declared that the Alexandrian shop was always open. Love was not the least of its commodities: especially after the Roman sack of Corinth in 146, the city became that "wine-press" of love whose empurpled encomium Lawrence Durrell was only just in time to write, in four juicy volumes. The triune city which Cavafy celebrated, in which Christian, Jew and Muslim cohabited in fruitful and sometimes bloody friction, was always a precarious fabrication. Its readiest currency was written on paper: scholars, prophets, poets and dilettanti made Alexandria's famous library the world's greatest house of index-cards.

Poets such as Callimachus (though none was ever quite like him) combined servility to their patrons with intellectual arrogance and recherché ostentation. The allusive fanciness of Callimachan poetry was to the Ptolemies what Fabergé's bejewelled ingenuity was to the Romanovs: the quintessence of trinkets. In Alexandria, literature was a caucus race: even marginal genius might win tenured prizes. How right that its modern (perhaps last) *kteema es aei* should be the poems of Cavafy, whose early *Candles* warned of the brevity of the human lease, and whose later ones sought to reconcile him and the city to the moment when, as it did Antony, the god (of chance) deserted it!

* * *

*A*lthough Alexander's tomb was no doubt very fine, it never outranked that of a minor tyrant, Mausolus, whose fiefdom of Karia had its capital at Halicarnassus, the modern Bodrum in southern Anatolia, the birthplace of Herodotus. Mausolus was (somewhat intermittently) a Persian satrap who, by ruling from 377–353, had the good fortune to pre-date the predatory Alexander, to whom, we may be pretty sure, he would have offered small resistance and every facility. Mausolus's first loyalty was to himself and to his family. It was said of him that he would do anything for money. He was scarcely alone in that: Lydia – where Croesus had made his pile, and Gyges the first coins – was his neighbour. Since the area was inherently unstable – it had no defining racial, geographic or linguistic limits – coins advertised the identity, and certainly the scope, of its rulers and so helped to sustain their authority. There had been a Karian language, but it was losing currency in Mausolus's day and was extinct by the time of the Roman Empire.

Mausolus taxed Karia vigorously and built an impressive, hundred-ship fleet, but his military position was never secure, nor did he ever create a cohesive state. Not the least of Karia's endemic failings was that it lacked horses: military self-sufficiency on land went with the possession of cavalry, prestige with a parade of chariots. Mausolus was pitched between the devil of the Great King, to whom he pledged the loyalty which he suspended during "The Satraps' Revolt" (a *fronde*, primed by Orontes, who – unlike Mausolus – was a plausible pretender to the throne of the King of Kings), and the deep blue Aegean where Greek fleets prowled and pounced.

Mausolus was self-enlarged small fry: his family did not even have a representative in the royal harem, which Peter Brown called "that parliament of the regions of the Iranian hegemony". Hostages rather than bedfellows, how much room did the women have for debate? Under the Ottomans, a weak and pampered Sultan not infrequently fell under the manipulative spell of a comely wife (or a dominating mother). The harem was the headquarters of a regiment of women who, given the chance, laid down the law.

Playing both sides against the middle was an unavoidable part of the *règle du jeu* of the region. Mausolus was loyal only to his own interests, which included doing nautical business with the resurgent Athens, when it was once again a force, though his city owed it no favours. In the twilight of the Delian League, Alcibiades had extorted disproportionate tribute from cornered Halicarnassus, whose inhabitants had to pay their subscription to the Greek club, although without evident claim to, or profit from, membership.

Mausolus later turned against the Athenians, at the right (or dictated) moment, and – so Demosthenes declared – detached Rhodos, Chios and Byzantium from their second empire. It was convenient for the orator, and for his audience, the Athenian *demos*, to forget that, a couple of decades earlier, in 391, the Athenians under Thrasybulus had made a swift attack on Halicarnassus and made off with whatever they could load on their ships.

Mausolus was fat, sly, greedy and self-obsessed, but it is hard not to smile at his vices and slightly admire his vanity. His obsession with creating an enduring monument which would, once he was dead, proclaim a fame he never earned when alive (François Mitterrand's Louvre pyramid is a similar edifice) is a symptom of the precariousness of being a ruler with literally fugitive subjects: always a good place to get away from, Karia's inhabitants were notoriously available for mercenary service. Athenian slaves were often called "Karians": a fragment of comedy says, "Get out, you Karians! The Anthesteria is over." The Anthesteria (literally, Festival of Flowers) was a February holiday sacred to Dionysus in which classes and drinks were mixed. Today's Battle of the Flowers in Nice also takes place in February and is famous for its rowdiness.

When scholars observed the *difficilior potius* rule, some preferred to read *"keres"* (trouble-making spirits) where the majority saw Karians. The latter reading is now favoured: it accords with the sayings accumulated by Zenobius, the paroemiographer, who lived in the age of Hadrian, when epitomes and commonplace books were the fashion. Isaac d'Israeli, Byron's favourite author and Benjamin's father, was a latter-day paroemiographer. The Anthesteria's "festival of flowers" resembled the Roman Saturnalia and allowed brief licence for servile frolics.

Mausolus was more the parody of a monarch than the real thing. Unlike a successful tyrant, such as Polycrates of Samos, in the sixth century, his subjects had small reason to like him. Failing to guarantee their welfare, he ostentatiously indulged his own. The register of his accomplishments is quickly told: he moved the capital of Karia from Mylasa – where the majority of Turkish rugs are still made – and amalgamated eight coastal villages into an enlarged Halicarnassus; he expanded, and retained, his authority in a mutable region; he planned to build himself a great tomb; and he married his sister, Artemisia, who brought the project to conclusion after his death.

She was named after the earlier Queen Artemisia of Karia who had distinguished herself as a *taxiarchos* (admiral) at the battle of Salamis. After watching her in action, Xerxes supposedly said, "My men have become women, my women men." The Great King may have thought that he had seen her ship ram an enemy trireme, but Herodotus says that she collided with another Persian man-of-war. Did Xerxes mean only to say that Artemisia had, as they say, stuffed him? His elegant phraseology secured her a brave, perhaps undeserved, reputation.

99 Mausolus and Artemisia: incest was nicest.

Mausolus was never a man to hide his light under a bushel, nor did he plan his tomb to testify to his modesty. A tradition of dead heroes was that they should be buried inside their city, but in a secret place, unrevealed to their fellow-citizens and inaccessible to enemies who might abscond with the dead man's mana; hence the removal of Theseus's alleged remains from Skyros, and Themistokles' from Magnesia, to Athens. If no one ever wanted to abstract Mausolus's bones from their showy resting place, plenty proved eager to remove the artwork.

Although an Anatolian, Mausolus was the quintessential instance of Levantine mutability: almost certainly bilingual, with a conspicuously hybridized pedigree and a correspondingly eclectic view of life. When he married his full sister, he flouted Greek tradition to honour that of the Egyptian Pharaohs. If there is no reason to doubt the passion which united the couple, Louis Gernet argued that it was typical of tyrants, from as early as the seventh century, to contract incestuous marriages.

Artemisia's sister, Ada, also married her full brother, Hidreus, and so became Alexander the Great's honorary "mother". Vladimir Nabokov's novel *Ada* features an incestuous relationship, of the kind that Byron – whose legitimate daughter was called Ada – had with his half-sister, Augusta. Paronomastic as ever, Nabokov notes gleefully that incest is an anagram of nicest.

Claude Lévi-Strauss associates incest with stinginess (it kept the wealth in the family), but neither authority explains why it was abhorrent in some societies and venerable in others: Incas, Azande chieftains, the royal families of Siam and Burma, among others, practised it with pride. Oedipus would have been offside in all of them: none ever knowingly had children by his own mother.

Mausolus's marriage was happy, and Artemisia was so distressed by his death that her grief became proverbial. She is said to have drunk a potion made up of his bones and ashes, though this may have been evidence less of anguish than of a desire to assume his power, which she did. She reigned alone, apparently without challenge from her Asian subjects, after her husband/brother's death, something no woman ever managed in mainland Hellas.

The Rhodians, however, whom Mausolus had brought under his control, affected to be scandalized by a female ruler and attacked Karia. The assault failed, but Rhodos sent an appeal for help, as fellow-democrats, to the Athenians, whose rebellious allies Mausolus had supported in 357, during the "Social War". The Athenians responded only with advice, that speciality of the mature and the impotent.

Karians were a byword for duplicity, a consequence as much of geography as of individual character. The want of natural boundaries in the Middle East has always required endless agility, not least from minor potentates hoping to conserve power. As a satrap, Mausolus's father, Hekatomnos, was ordered by his master, the Great King Artaxerxes II, to make war on Evagoras, the dissident king of Cyprus. Hekatomnos then subsidized Evagoras, the better to make himself indispensable to Artaxerxes.

A dangerous game was, as it still is, the only one on the cards in the Fertile Crescent. Staying on top required clever balancing not only of external forces but also of local populations: Mausolus tolerated a degree of democracy at town council level, the better to keep supreme authority for himself. By beginning work on the Mausoleum, he made sure that his reputation would have a fine three-dimensional lodging.

Decked with a wealth of detachable sculpture, embellished with precious metals and stones, it turned out to be an invitation the dead man was unwise to flaunt. Proximity to Egypt exposed Karia to professional tomb-raiders who had had decades of experience among the pyramids. While he was alive, Mausolus had a secret harbour near his palace. It is now a marina that chinks with expensive rigging. A rapid reaction force was stationed there, ready for prompt police work. When Halicarnassus lost its defences, it soon lost its treasures too. The British Museum is only the most illustrious of the receivers of its stolen property.

The period between the end of the Peloponnesian War and the rise of Alexander precedes what is usually called the Hellenistic Age, but it was, in many respects, a happier one. The Persian kings demanded tribute, military service and deference, but – like the Ottomans – they allowed, or could not prevent, a large measure of local autonomy. Successful empires (notably the Roman and the British) seduce their subjects into sharing their world-view.

Favours no less than threats procure the "voluntary servitude" analysed by Etienne de la Boétie in the sixteenth century. The Persians tolerated many cultures, including that of the Hellenes, whose genius was as admired as their loyalty was suspect.

Mausolus commissioned a tragedy in honour of his supposed ancestor, the Sun, from the Lycian-born Theodektes, who doubled as playwright (he won seven victories at the Great Dionysia in Athens) and diplomat. George Seferis matched him by both winning the Nobel Prize for Literature and capping his diplomatic career by becoming Greek ambassador to London. Theodektes later composed a tragedy entitled *Mausolus* for the tyrant's funeral *agon*. I suspect that it ended in an *exodos*, from the adjacent theatre, to the uncompleted Mausoleum.

The Hellenistic taste for grandiose individual tombs was of a piece with the new habit of commissioning encomiastic biographies. Nothing so magnificent as the Mausoleum had ever been conceived for the heroes whose tombs lent their mana to the cities where they lay. Mausolus's palace is said by Vitruvius* to have been the first building made of brick and then faced with marble, a technique which would allow the emperor Augustus to claim that he had "found Rome brick and left it marble".

The Mausoleum had a core of limestone (a vestige of it is left *in situ* in today's unenchanting Bodrum), but it was faced with the best Pentelic and/or Parian marble. The sculptures on the friezes alone cost more than ten talents. Construction took over ten years on a building which carried eclecticism to new heights, and lengths. Plagiarizing homage was paid to Egyptian, Persian and Greek sources and monuments. Old enemies were reconciled in marble: a life-size battle between Greeks and Persians was tactfully costumed to resemble the Trojan War.

Since the Hekatomnids had changed sides with speculative adroitness as the fortunes of war tugged them in one direction or the other, the Mausoleum prefigured the homogenized culture of the Hellenistic Levant in which the great wars of the recent and distant past became motifs for art rather than the pretext – of which Alexander was about to make pseudo-Homeric use – for bloody remakes.

The Mausoleum was a very elaborate, multi-coursed dog's dinner (with a double-decker frieze to outdo the Parthenon) in honour of a local nabob with more money than taste: a tribute to all the clubs to which he wished he could truly belong. Mausolus himself was depicted as a centaur, a species noble in

---

* A military engineer – Julius Caesar's equivalent to Louis XIV's Marshal Vauban – who became the most important architectural historian of the ancient world.

some books but described by Euripides as "that four-footed embodiment of *hubris*". A four-sided projection of the same vanity, the monument gave employment to many, offence to none and – though not one of its multi-sourced treasures remains on site – procured precisely what its creator wished, the eternal fame of a Levantine Mr Toad.

Mausolus's facial likeness has been preserved for posterity, though different scholars take different views of it: Lorentz calls it "ruthless", but Bernoulli accuses it of "Christ-like mildness". Since Simon Hornblower, in his invaluable *Mausolus*, declares that a bust of Themistokles (found in Ostia) gives that "half-Karian" a look of "Neanderthal cunning", Mausolus could claim to have triumphed, at least in the image department, over a genuine hero of the Golden Age.

Like his father, Mausolus admitted, implicitly, the provincial limit of his ambitions by never attempting to make a name for himself in mainland Hellas. For all his philhellenic affectations, he refrained from claiming to be Greek enough to compete at the Olympic Games, where he might have been expected to out-Alcibiades Alcibiades in the number of teams he entered for the chariot race. It was not until 296 that a Karian (Sosiades of Tralles) got his name in the winner's frame.

* * *

*T*he kudos for winning the Olympic chariot race was slightly tarnished by accruing to the owner, not the jockey, of the victorious team. For this reason, the only female Olympic champion in the four-horse race – in both 396 and 392 – was Cynisca, daughter of the Spartan king Archidamus. Xenophon says that her brother, Agesilaus, put her up to it so that everyone could see that cash, not *andragathia* (manly virtue), was needed to win the event. Perhaps there was a lingering resentment in Sparta at Alcibiades' treacheries: how better to denigrate his Olympic triumph than to have a

100 An Olympic boxer between rounds in the second century B.C.

woman match it? Another Spartan female, Euryleonis, repeated the tarnished feat, in the two-horse race, some years later.

The only woman to make a rather more glorious name for herself at the Olympics was Callipatira of Rhodos, who – probably at the Games in 404 – dressed as his trainer to watch her son compete. At his victory, she leaped out of the trainers' box and, by doing so, exposed herself. The issue of a line of Olympic victors, she was forgiven (and nicknamed Pherenike, the bearer of victory); but a rule was made that trainers, like athletes, be naked in the stadium. In 720, Orsippos, who dropped his loin-cloth and won the sprint, had made nakedness a permanent fashion.

The longest-running clock of Greek civilization was supplied by the Olympic Games: if all Hellas ever had anything in common, apart from its gods, it was the measure of time by the four-yearly calibration of Olympiads: from 776 B.C. until A.D. 393, athletes, grandees, pimps, whores and tourists converged every four years on a remote Elean village that swelled, briefly, into a city of many thousands. "Zeus, protect me from your guides at Olympia" was one of the more fervent prayers of pilgrims requesting inoculation against tall stories, and taller prices.

The Olympian gods, whose home base, Olympus, was far away to the north-east, were presumptuous latecomers to Olympia. Pelops was worshipped there, as a fertility god, long before the Dorians burst into his "island". Throughout the millennium of the Games, a place was reserved (and roofed) in the *altis* (sacred enclosure) for a wooden relic said to be all that was left of the palace of king Oenomaus, with whom Pelops had that legendary chariot race (his and Hippodameia's marriage bed was, the guides would say, on show in Hera's temple). Archaeology has established that no kingly palace ever existed in the *altis*, but some scholarly tour leaders promise that the relic was the prehistoric winning post for a suitors' race whose winner impersonated some arcane god, perhaps Pelops, in sacred marriage with the winner of the girls' race. Pelops was appeased with a starring role on the façade of the temple in which Pheidias enthroned his Zeus.

Although Herakles was proclaimed as the founder of the Games, his sulky stepmother and persistent enemy Hera was the first Olympian to have cult there, in a wooden Heraeum. Girls from neighbouring Pisa raced in her honour long before Herakles established the men's foot-race in the stadium (feminists see evidence of primal matriarchy in the speed with which the females were off the mark). Herakles paced out the historic course – by setting one foot in front of the other six hundred times before he drew breath, and the mark, at 192.24 metres. Simple division shows that the commentators' original "big lad" would take size fifteen track shoes.

Like so much of Hellas, Olympia was an impacted palimpsest of claims for mastery, human and divine. The Dorian Eleans defeated the indigenous men of Pisa as guardians (and profiteers) of the site, in the mid-seventh century. Alerted to his genius by his chryselephantine Athene, a later generation of Eleans crowned their vanity by commissioning Pheidias to create a statue of Zeus. The sculptor had been forced to leave Athens in a hurry after being accused of *hierosulia* (temple-robbing, a capital offence). Zeus was the totem of the Dorians, but Hera's ancient influence could not be banished from Olympia: she had to be appeased with sprucer accommodation. Her renovated limestone Heraeum crested the hot sky with its acroterium, a huge fan of terracotta, flamboyant with black, white, red and yellow images. (At a remove of thousands of miles, and years, the same colour scheme was used in a sacred grove of the Mayas in Yucatan.)

Hera's temple was a tourist's "must" since it enshrined, among other sacred relics, the "quoit of Iphitus", a bronze disc on which the first Olympic charter was inscribed, in the same archaic *boustrophedon* script still to be seen in Gortyn. Although only briefly an impresario (when he accused Herakles of stealing his prize mares, the irascible big guy threw him off the highest fortifications of Tiryns), Iphitus is credited by one myth with being the "real" founder of the Games and regularizing the event, in association with Lycurgus, the quasi-historical lawgiver who is more famous for establishing *eunomia*, the Spartan rule of law before which only the best people were equal.

Part of the traditional sentimentalization of Hellas was to make the Olympic Games, and the truce that accompanied them, the symbol of the underlying sportsmanship and mutual respect of the Greeks.

101 Roman marble copy of Myron's fifth-century B.C. bronze discus-thrower. Jealous Zephyus, an ill wind, arranged for Hyacinth to be killed by one when working out with his lover, Apollo.

In fact, the Games were a continuation of rivalries, and often of violence, by other, ritual means. Like the funerals of modern grandees, they also afforded regular opportunities for diplomacy and more or less literal horse-trading.

Dark stories are told of prehistoric human sacrifice on the site, after which the officiating priests murdered each other in atonement. The survivor presumably became king of the nearby hill of Kronos. The classical boxing and wrestling competitions were sublimations of savage rites, but not as sublime as all that: contestants were known to be killed.

Only during the obligatory month of preliminary training, for which all entrants were required to report on site, was there a spirit of comradeship. Contestants worked out together and musclemen pelted each other with dust to toughen their hides.

In the first century B.C., a certain Nicophon of Miletus was said to have had a physique that would have made Zeus himself tremble. When he removed his travelling clothes, he literally outstripped his rivals. The mere appearance of Milon of Croton must also have disposed weaker spirits to think again. Scratching from the competition was not a total disgrace when confronted by godlike pecs and abs, though those who won by a walkover were happy to describe themselves as *akoniti*, dust-free. The term was metaphorically attached to any easy achievement.

To become a champion put a man, briefly, on a divine level. To come second, or worse, was no achievement at all. *Pace* the Baron de Coubertin, who founded the modern Olympics as an arena for amateurs who loved sport for its own sake (those were the days), no one competed at the ancient Games for any reason but glory for himself (and his city). The symbol of enduring championship was Zeus, who had fought more ferociously than fairly for mastery of Olympus.

* * *

*A*lthough Pheidias's huge chryselephantine statue of the king of gods and men was not made until the Games had been contested for at least three centuries, it was thenceforth the emblem of Hellas united in worship, if nothing else. The god and his sculptor were newcomers to Olympia. Zeus made himself locally useful in the guise of Zeus *Apomuios*, the Lord of the Flies, to whom the Eleans sacrificed a white ox as a reward for purging the site of flies. Since a hundred oxen were slaughtered on the third morning of the Games, *Apomuios* must have possessed a remarkable swat.

The first Olympic flames were not merely decorative: they consumed countless victims. By the time that Pausanias put his measure to it, the heap of their accumulated ashes was forty yards in circumference and over seven yards high. Steps had had to be cut in the hardened cinders to allow the officiating priest to add to its summit. As the appetizing smoke drifted towards Olympus, Prometheus's old trick guaranteed that the best steaks were left to feed the classier pilgrims.

Zeus had already taken many forms, and pleasures: one of the loveliest relics found on site is a terracotta of Zeus and Ganymede in which eroticism and dignity are sweetly harmonious. There was a close similarity between the vocabularies of athletics and of sex: love and war shared linguistic amenities. The athletes who competed naked in honour of Zeus became so symbolic of Greek virtue that the god himself began to be depicted as one of them. In 1926, fishermen off the island of Evia (ancient Euboea) netted a great bearded bronze, of a Zeus as naked as Orsippos, about to launch a thunderbolt.

The Evian version of the Father of the Gods as victor ludorum dates from about 460, not long before Pheidias promoted Zeus to a higher plane when he began work in his studio (later a Byzantine church) in the *altis* at Olympia. From the middle of the sixth century, Olympic victors were allowed to erect their statues in the *altis*, though at first they were forbidden to be likenesses (the old Jewish taboo had Greek cousins) or larger than life-size, lest Zeus take lightning offence. Over the years, statues of the god abounded, large and small, in the precinct. Many were paid for by fines exacted from cheating competitors or from the cities that put them up to it.

The Zeus from Evia was not the first athlete to be dredged from the sea. Theagenes of Thasos, a fifth-century Olympic victor, revealed his rare strength at the age of nine by picking up a bronze statue in the *agora*. When he himself had won 1,400 victorious crowns on the circuit, his own statue was erected there. After his death, one of his erstwhile opponents took to beating the unbeaten champion's image. One day it fell on him and killed him.

102 Look what I've got! Happy Zeus, smug Ganymede.

103 Second-century A.D. brazen Zeus,
imperial Roman style.

It was then accused of murder, condemned and flung into the sea.

Some time later, Thasos was afflicted with famine. The Delphic oracle recommended the recall of all Thasian exiles. When the island still remained hungry, the Thasians sent for a new prescription; the Pythia said, "You have forgotten the great Theagenes." Shortly afterwards, a fisherman netted the sunken statue. Theagenes returned to Thasos and fruitfulness with him.

As Olympiads went by, triple winners were licensed to put their likenesses in the *altis* (Pliny notes that these inhabitants of the outdoor Hall of Fame were called *iconica*). It was a matter of pride to get your image in place as quickly as possible: Eubatas of Cyrene relied on the veracity of a favourable Libyan oracle (close to his home town in North Africa) and brought his effigy with him when he competed (and won) in 408. In the same style, the great Ben Hogan was said to greet fellow-golfers on the opening day of a major tournament with, "So who's coming second?"

Pheidias's purpose was to create a Zeus to out-Zeus all others. The temple now adapted to house it had been built, for a more modest figure, in the 460s, by a local architect called Libon. It was of standard proportions, an armature for external and internal embellishment rather than a work of art in itself. Pheidias flattered his Zeus with qualities that belonged more to the artist's fancy than to his creation's mythical reputation. He worked on sections of his Zeus through several Olympiads. It grew to be one of the slowest surprises of all time.

Pheidias had the nerve, yet again, to plan something unlike anything seen before. His Athene, for the Parthenon, had scandalized as many Athenians as it had amazed. The brilliance of the new Zeus amounted to a revision more dramatic than that imposed on the Faithful by Vatican II. To start with, the figure was seated rather than standing, as cult figures always had been. A gigantic throne had to be prepared for it: the base filled the whole width of the nave of Libon's temple, and a third of its length, an area six and a half metres by ten. Its construction alone must have excited prolonged speculation about the appearance of the finished figure, which Pausanias describes as having

104 Pheidias's Zeus Pantocrator, resurrected by computer.

a crown on its head imitating the foliage of the olive tree. In his right hand he holds a victory in ivory and gold.... In his left, a sceptre adorned with all manner of precious metal, and the bird seated on the sceptre is an eagle. The robe and sandals are also of gold; and on Zeus's robe are imitations of animals and also of lilies. The throne is richly adorned with gold and precious metals and with ebony and ivory. Upon it there are painted figures and wrought images.

The massive head very nearly touched the roof, over thirteen metres from the floor. Strabo observed that if the god were able to stand up he would lift the translucent marble panels of the ceiling. Maynard Keynes said of Woodrow Wilson, "like Odysseus, the President looked wiser when he was seated". Zeus too perhaps.

Marble was not a common roofing material (it was heavy and expensive), but a single marble "tile" can be seen on a shelf outside the Knights of Rhodos's chapel in what remains of Mausolus's palace in modern Bodrum.

A spiral staircase took tourists up for a closer inspection of the gigantic bearded majesty of a head of which the only relic can now be held in the palm of one's hand: the sole visual record of it is stamped on a few modest Elean coins.

Pheidias simplified construction work by using a scale model (as the Rhodians would for their Colossus). The power of his Zeus was conveyed not only by its mass but also by its grace: the life-size statue of Victory which stood in the god's hand had not to appear too heavy a charge on him. Zeus's head and torso had to be equally impressive whether seen from below, as the tourist first entered the temple's *cella*, or from the gallery, where sunlight through those thin slabs of marble lent life to the divine features.

Pheidias was an old hand at meeting technical problems with aesthetic answers. He once entered a competition with his pupil Alcamenes, who worked with him on the Acropolis. A jury of the public were the judges. The entries were first paraded, convenient for inspection, ranged on the ground. Pheidias's work looked so grotesque that the jurors threatened to stone the artist, who seemed to be mocking both them and the gods. But when the statues were elevated to their plinths, the groundlings put down their missiles and applauded. Pheidias's entry now looked perfectly proportioned; that of Alcamenes ungainly.

However solitary in conceiving his work, Pheidias was eager for approval: it was said that he hid himself in the shadows to hear the first public comments on his Zeus (modern film-makers are advised to "Trust the cards", the forms filled in by preview audiences, and to re-cut their work accordingly). When each section of the statue was finally in place, assembled like a huge three-dimensional kit, its maker prayed for the divine nod. A benign bolt of lightning then rapped the floor of the *cella* just in front of the throne (it may be that the roof had not yet been closed). A bronze urn permanently marked the spot where the electric message came, just beyond the lip which caught excess oil from the god's regular facials: to keep the skin sleek and uncracked, it needed constant cosmetic attention. He was worth it.

Pheidias's Zeus took his place at Olympia in the high season of Greek confidence in their genius, and in his favour. The victory in his gift had been handed to them. When Pheidias stood in the shadows to eavesdrop the public's reactions, he is unlikely to have overheard cynical views about the work or the god. But as time went by, and Greek fortunes changed, so did the veneration with which Zeus was regarded. Five centuries after Pheidias, Dio Chrysostom said, in the first century A.D., that his Zeus resembled "Odysseus's old father, burdened with age and sunk in senile neglect".

Dio had been driven from Rome by Domitian, whom he had offended with his gilded garrulity. He made some amends to the Zeus in his *Olympian Oration* (composed as if it were spoken by Pheidias himself) where the statue was said to "rise above factions and races to represent the father of all mankind". Dio may have been implying flattery of Domitian (he still craved recall) when he described Zeus as a paternalistic emperor of whom his fictional Pheidias says:

> Our Zeus is peace-loving and gentle in all his ways.... I tried to depict him as an exalted being with an untroubled and serene countenance.... He joins all men together and wishes them to be friends, not enemies.... The similarity between his and the human form symbolizes the kinship between gods and men.... The overall impression is one of love, the noblest of all conditions and the source of all good.

Dio was engaged in a rhetorical exercise, not an aesthetic appraisal, but Pheidias's achievement had been to elevate a lecherous and tyrannical deity into a spiritual paragon. He probably took inspiration from the portrait of Zeus in book twelve of the *Iliad*, where Zeus promises Thetis that he will help Achilles: "Zeus, as he finished, inclined his sable brows, / The ambrosial locks rolled forward from the immortal head / And high Olympus shook..."

Pheidias's golden-haired image was glossed with a gravity that revised the passions of Homer's all-too-human god-king. He graced him with a gravity and an air of universal concern which transcended the partisan god whom the Dorians had toted with them when they broke into Greece some time before the eighth century. The notion of even-handed justice which Dio read into Pheidias's figure was both an innovation and a sly demand: it asked that Zeus become the magnanimous divinity that he should have been from the beginning. Men had always feared the gods, but had had small reason to love them or to expect their love.

Pheidias's mechanical devices (to which the detritus of his studio bears witness) had a spiritual theatricality. The play of filtered sunshine on gold and ivory gave Zeus an enlightening vividness, an aspect more divine (and more humane) than he had ever shown before. The olive wreath on Zeus's brow recruited him to the community of Olympic victors and suggested concord between heaven and earth. Pliny said that when men received their crowns, the coronation was a sacrament. Heroes returned, symbolically, to a common table with the god whom Tantalus made unsociable.

Pheidias's Zeus enjoyed centuries of eulogy. Epictetus, the first-century A.D. Stoic, was less of a gusher than Dio, but declared it to be the absolute embodiment of truth: "He looks you straight in the eye, as if to say, 'I can't take back what I have said, and besides it is true'." In the same century, Apollonius of Tyana greeted the image with, "Good Zeus, your goodness is so great that you even share yourself with mortals".* In the Greek Anthology, an anonymous poet put Creator and creator on the same level: "Either Zeus descended to you from heaven; / Or you, great artist, ascended and saw the god."

Yet over the years, the nobility of Pheidias's masterpiece ceased to speak with the same commanding authority. Caecilius of Caleacte, Sicily, a first-century B.C. *flâneur* who may have started life as a slave, and a Jew, called the Zeus "a defective colossus". In Greek eyes, its main defect was that it ceased to deliver to them the victories which it held in its hand. Foreign conquerors approached the site with respect (Aemilius Paulus in 167 ordered gargantuan sacrifices), but their alien presence diminished the credibility – and denied the quondam partiality – of the Thunderer who had sent Darius and Xerxes scuttling ignominiously homewards, but never deterred the Romans.

What had begun as a statue charged with supernatural force became first a work of art and then a curiosity. Caligula ordered it brought to Rome like any other piece of cumbersome booty (he had already lifted Alexander's breastplate from his tomb in Alexandria). Memmius Regulus, his legate, informed the emperor that it would break if moved. Caligula was assassinated before he could insist. The story ran that Regulus was given pause because, when he was about to erect scaffolding and disassemble the statue, the god let out a raucous laugh.

By Lucian's time (the second century A.D.), Zeus had become little more than a laugh. The satirist has him complaining to his brother, Poseidon, that things are completely out of control. Those who once came to Olympia

---

* Gibbon supplies the perfect footnote: "Apollonius of Tyana was born about the same times as Jesus Christ. His life (that of the former) is related in so fabulous a manner by his disciples that we are at a loss to discover whether he was a sage, an impostor or a fanatic."

for reasons of piety now came only for plunder. How else, Lucian has him ask, could sacrilegious scoundrels have escaped to Pisa after cutting off two of his "tresses" – perhaps a meiosis for his testicles – each weighing six minae? Lucian was later openly derisive of the god's senile impotence:

> Your much-vaunted, far-ranging and ever-ready weapon has...lost its fire and grown cold and can't strike a spark of anger against evil-doers. No one sacrifices to you now and nobody crowns you.... They'll soon depose you, oh noblest of gods, and cast you in the role of Kronos.

The Olympic Games never wholly lost their magic, though Zeus's waned. When Hadrian moved to transfer their prestige to Athens, where he planned to inaugurate pan-Hellenic Games in honour of the drowned Antinous, the professional athletes of the day ostentatiously sailed past on their way to Olympia. Perhaps it offered more prestige, and bigger prize money. Secularization had long robbed the Games of ritual significance. Sport was on the way to becoming the religion of the masses. Attendance at Olympia, once a privileged pilgrimage, became a distasteful chore: in the third century A.D., Aelian threatened to take a misbehaving slave with him to the Games if he didn't shape up.

* * *

*R*oger Fry, the Bloomsbury aesthete who formulated the theory of "Significant Form", once said that there were very few paintings that anyone would want to see more than two or three times. Pheidias's Zeus had been seen too often, by too many people, to retain its mystery. Not long ago, Anthony Caro attacked Michelangelo's *David* in terms hardly less scornful than Lucian's. Even the Parthenon marbles seem less miraculous each time one sees them. It is as if admiration leaches their magic from great works. The Parthenon has been rendered trite by the attention given to it. Flaubert, however, always remembered a single unadorned wall (of the *cella*?) which, he said, remained for him the perfect example of art that rendered the artist invisible in his own work.

I once heard a Frenchwoman demand to be taken to see the Zeus of Pheidias. Her tour leader displeased her with, "*Il n'y a plus de Zeus, madame!*" The last recorded sighting was by the sophist Themistius in A.D. 384. By 395, it had been evicted from Libon's temple and shipped, piecemeal, to Constantinople, where it was on show in the palace of a certain Lausus (one imagines a Byzantine Trimalchio). The great god was reduced to a curio. In 415, in Alexandria, the clever Hypatia, a woman who was a mathematical prodigy and a pagan, ecumenical philosopher who had many Christian friends, was murdered by a Christian mob. The dethroning of the Zeus and the killing of Hypatia presaged what Charles Freeman called, in his eponymous polemic against the effects of Christian ideologues, "the closing of the western mind": advocates of the True Faith always regard tolerance as a dirty word.

In 462, Lausus's house was destroyed in a great fire, and Pheidias's Zeus with it. Byzantium was a Christian theocracy, with its own Pantocrator. The old pagan god could never be at home there. The world no longer set its clocks, as it were, by the chronology of Olympiads. Zeus's lease had lapsed, and with it his spiritual dominion over Hellas.

If all the masterpieces of ancient Greece had survived, if we had all Pheidias's works, and all of Aeschylus, Sophocles, Euripides, not to mention the unfortunate Phrynichus, all Sappho, all Polygnotus (every one of whose paintings, like those of Zeuxis, is lost), if every despoiled temple and sacked city were immaculately resurrected, and every lacuna in our libraries filled with pristine volumes, our lives might well be spent on our knees in homage to the Greek genius. Why would anything else ever have to be written or art created? Yet the moment would surely come when some Herostratus would show up at Lausus's museum with a can of petrol and a match, and we might not strive officiously to stop him. As a recent fire in an art repository in London proved, vandals are not invariably enemies of culture. If we were loaded with the full repertoire of antique art and literature, who would not dream of being another Herostratus and freeing the world for something new to replace what, not altogether alas, we ourselves can never read or see? Oblivion too mothers Muses.

105 A third-century B.C. Zeus in cameo.

Introduction to a partial bibliography

The partiality consists in the fact that almost all the listed books are those in my own library. I have included a few which I know I have borrowed over the years, but I have no accurate record of them and must ask any author who imagines himself or herself to be the source of some idea to excuse me their inadvertent anonymity. I have preferred to list my sources here rather than bedeck the text with references, which would give it academic affectations. My reading has been that of an enthusiastic amateur. That enthusiasm was primed not only, or even mainly, by the "reliable" authors whose names I have cited, but also by another kind of partiality: a taste for those whose challenge, "irresponsibility" and energy (especially in the case of Marxists, anthopologists or feminists) brought improbable excitement to a once dusty subject. One of the first, and almost forgotten, of these was Naomi Mitchison, whose novels about ancient Greece I read in my lonely monastic boyhood. Far more than Mary Renault, she made the ancient world seem hotly present.

Of all the scholars who rekindled my eagerness for ancient Greece none have been more delicious to me than the French structuralists and neo-structuralists. Although he is by no means of the same *galère,* I should also mention a particular favourite, René Girard, of whose passionate view of myth as a cloak for violence, and a recipe for its civic use, in the repeated figure of the scapegoat, I became, for a while, a fully convinced devotee. I am inclined to take more water with his medicine these days, but recommend him, nonetheless, for the lucidity of his fervour and the shapeliness of his prose (at the least an excellent introduction to formal French).

Among English writers, none has been more prolific and more readable, over almost half a century, than my friend Peter Green, who – in a different, transient guise – was the first to accept a short story of mine for publication. My admiration for the breadth of his accuracies, and for the range of his artillery, is entirely independent of my affection for their author. No one has been more outspoken in dispelling antique pieties or discountenancing modern pundits. Peter has loud disdain for the system-builders who wish an ideological pattern or even some sublime purpose on ancient life and its great men. Of the former, G.E.M. de Ste. Croix, and his wilful Marxism, is a favourite target for Green's punctual scorn, but I am still enthralled by de Ste. Croix's fat texts and, in the case of the Melian dialogue in particular, convinced by his vindication of Athens (most nobly expressed first by George Grote). Of the latter, Green was a prompt sceptic when it came to W.W. Tarn's vision of Alexander the Great as a man with a civilizing mission to create One World in which Greek and Barbarian would share a common culture (Greek, of course).

I confess to, and the bibliography reflects, an addiction to the anthropologists and social critics of the ancient world. George Thomson's tendentious subtlety captivated me as an undergraduate, in the days when the first part of the classical tripos was a disappointing continuation of school work: Latin and Greek proses and verses were regular steps on our treadmill. I longed for wits that would break the codes of propriety which faced our studies and our society. Lord Raglan was another early liberator from conventional thinking about the ancient world of gods and heroes. I include Philip Slater here partly as an example of the plausible, yet aberrant reading which a clever man can attach to the Greeks and their gods, partly because – however misguided – his view of the Olympians and their hangers-on as suitable cases for psychoanalysis is very good fun. He seems cleverly unaware that it is the categories which the Greeks themselves supplied, and are instanced by their gods and heroes, that supply the vocabulary and, in a sense, the concepts by which he seeks to transcend them with his own diagnoses.

In addition to the listed texts, and many others which have, I daresay, left shreds of their intelligence in the disorderly compost of memory, I have read countless articles, offprints and reviews during sixty years of eclecticism. They too may have left their marks, for good or bad, on what I take to be my opinions, though none – cited or uncited – should bear the responsibility of them. None, of course, was as inspiring as the visit to Greece in 1962 which ended with our purchase of our first "house" (a donkey shed) and four terraces of olives, figs and cactus, on the then almost deserted Cycladic island of Ios.

As for personal friendships, none was so precious to me as that with Kenneth McLeish, who rekindled my eagerness for Greek drama and with whom I translated all of Aeschylus's extant plays and several of Euripides' and Sophocles'. *Miglior fabbro*, he was the perfect collaborator, quick, stringent and always *disponible*. We spent so many hours in conversation (often on the telephone) that there is scant written record of the ideas and readings which we exchanged or of the (on my part) often wild theories we floated. I cannot count how many suns we tired with talking until death robbed me of the most generous of critics and most loyal of friends. Of those happily alive, I am greatly indebted to Professor Paul Cartledge, who has saved me from many errors. Those that remain are my own.

"Athenian", tr. Clogg, Richard, *Inside the Colonels' Greece*, London, 1972

AYMARD, A. and Auboyer, J., *L'Orient et la Grèce antique*, Paris, 1953

BAKER, Howard, *Persephone's Cave*, Athens, GA, 1979

BARING, Anne and Cashford, Jules, *The Myth of the Goddess*, London, 1991

BARRETT, W.S., *Euripides' Hippolytus*, Oxford, 1964

BEARD, Mary, *The Parthenon*, London, 2002

BERNAL, Martin, *Black Athena*, vol. I, London, 1987

––, *Black Athena Writes Back*, Durham, NC and London, 2001

BERTHOLD, Richard M., *Rhodes in the Hellenistic Age*, Ithaca, NY, 1984

BILLOWS, Richard A., *Antigonos the One-Eyed*, California, 1990

BOARDMAN, John, *The Greeks Overseas*, London, 1964, fourth edition, 1999

––, *The Diffusion of Art in Classical Antiquity*, London, 1994

––, *The Archaeology of Nostalgia*, London, 2002

BOWERSOCK, G.W., *Hellenism in Late Antiquity*, Cambridge, 1990

BOWRA, C.M., *The Greek Experience*, London, 1957

––, *Periclean Athens*, London, 1971

BURKERT, Walter, *Structure and History in Greek Mythology and Ritual*, California, 1979

––, *Homo Necans*, California, 1983

––, *Greek Religion*, London, 1985

CAMPBELL, David A., *The Golden Lyre: The Themes of Greek Lyric Poets*, London, 1983

CANTARELLA, Eva, *Bisexuality in the Ancient World*, New Haven, 2002

CARPENTER, T.H., *Art and Myth in Ancient Greece*, London, 1991

CARROLL, James, *Constantine's Sword*, New York, 2001

CARSON, Anne, *Economy of the Unlost*, Princeton, 1999

CARTLEDGE, Paul, *The Greeks*, Oxford, 1993, revised 2002

––, *Spartan Reflections*, London, 2001

––, *Alexander the Great*, London, 2004

CASSON, Lionel, *Travel in the Ancient World*, London, 1974

CAWKWELL, George, *Philip of Macedon*, London, 1978

CHADWICK, John, *The Mycenaean World*, Cambridge, 1976

COOK, J.M., *The Persian Empire*, London, 1983

CORNFORD, F.M., *Thucydides Mythistoricus*, Cambridge, 1907

––, *The Origin of Attic Comedy*, Cambridge, 1934

DAVIDSON, James, *Courtesans and Fishcakes*, London, 1998

DAVIES, J.K., *Democracy and Classical Greece*, 1978, revised 1993

DE JULIIS, Ettore M., *Greci e Italici in Magna Grecia*, Rome, 2004

DETIENNE, Marcel, *Les Jardins d'Adonis*, Paris, 1972

––, *L'Invention de la mythologie*, Paris, 1981

––, *Apollon, le couteau à la main*, Paris, 1998

DETIENNE, Marcel and Sissa, Julia, *La Vie quotidienne des dieux grecs*, Paris, 1974

DETIENNE, Marcel and Vernant, Jean-Pierre, *Les Ruses de l'intelligence: la metis en Grèce Ancienne*, Paris, 1974

DODDS, E.R., *The Greeks and the Irrational*, California, 1951

DOUMAS, Christos, *Cycladic Art*, London, 1983

DOVER, K.J., *Greek Homosexuality*, New York, 1978, new edition, Cambridge, MA, 1989

DREES, Ludwig, *Olympia: Gods, Artists and Athletes*, London, 1968

EASTERLING, P.E. (ed.), *The Cambridge Companion to Greek Tragedy*, Cambridge, 1997

ELSE, Gerald F., *The Origin and Early Form of Greek Tragedy*, Michigan, 1965

––, *Aristotle, Poetics*, Michigan, 1970

FINLEY, M.I., *The World of Odysseus*, London, 1954, second edition, 1977

––, *The Ancient Greeks*, London, 1963

––, *Aspects of Antiquity*, London, 1971

–– (ed.), *Studies in Ancient Society*, London, 1974

FORREST, W.G., *The Emergence of Greek Democracy*, London, 1966

FREEMAN, Charles, *The Greek Achievement*, London, 1999

––, *The Closing of the Western Mind*, London, 2002

FRIEDRICH, Paul, *The Meaning of Aphrodite*, Chicago, 1978

FRONTISI-DUCROUX, Françoise, *Dédale*, Paris, 1975

FRONTISI-DUCROUX, Françoise and Vernant, Jean-Pierre, *Dans l'oeil du miroir*, Paris, 1997

GAGARIN, Michael, *Aeschylean Drama*, California, 1976

GEORGOUDI, Stella and Vernant, Jean-Pierre, *Mythes grecs au figure*, Paris, 1996
GERNET, Louis and Boulanger, André, *Le Génie grec dans la religion*, Paris, 1932
GIRARD, René, *La Violence et le sacré*, Paris, 1972
—, *Des choses cachées depuis la fondation du monde*, Paris, 1978
GODWIN, Joscelyn, *Mystery Religions in the Ancient World*, London, 1981
GRAHAM, A.J., *Colony and Mother City in Ancient Greece*, Chicago, 1983
GRAVES, Robert, *The Greek Myths*, London, 1955
GREEN, Peter, *Essays in Antiquity*, London, 1960
—, *Alexander of Macedon*, London, 1970, new edition, California, 1991
—, *Armada from Athens*, New York, 1970, new edition, California, 1996
—, *The Year of Salamis*, London, 1970
—, *The Shadow of the Parthenon*, London, 1972
—, *A Concise History of Ancient Greece*, London, 1973
—, *Classical Bearings*, London, 1989
—, *Alexander to Actium*, London, 1990
—, *The Greco-Persian Wars*, California, 1996
—, *From Ikaria to the Stars*, Austin, TX, 2004
GRIFFIN, Jasper, *Homer*, Oxford, 1980
—, *The Mirror of Myth*, London, 1986
GROTE, George, *A History of Greece*, abridged edition, by Mitchell and Caspari, London, 1907
GRUEN, Erich S., *The Hellenistic World and the Coming of Rome*, California, 1984
GUTHRIE, W.K.C., *The Greeks and their Gods*, Boston, 1950
—, *A History of Greek Philosophy*, Cambridge, 1965
HADOT, Pierre, *Exercises spirituels et philosophie antique*, Paris, 1993
—, *Le Voile d'Isis*, Paris, 2004
HALPERIN, David M., Winkler, John J. and Zeitlin, Froma I. (eds), *Before Sexuality*, Princeton, 1990
HAMMOND, N.G.L., *Alexander the Great*, London, 1981
HANSON, Victor Davis, *Carnage and Culture*, New York, 2001
HARRISON, Jane, *Prolegomena to the Study of Greek Religion*, Cambridge, 1903/1957
—, *Themis*, London, 1963
HARTOG, François, *Le Miroir d'Hérodote*, Paris, 1980
HAVELOCK, Eric A., *The Greek Concept of Justice*, Cambridge, MA, 1971
HORNBLOWER, Simon, *Mausolus*, Oxford, 1982
—, *The Greek World 479–323 B.C.*, London, 1983
HUMPHREYS, S.C., *Anthropology and the Greeks*, London, 1978
JEFFERY, L.H., *Archaic Greece*, London, 1978
JONES, A.H.M., *Athenian Democracy*, Oxford, 1977
JONES, John, *On Aristotle and Greek Tragedy*, London, 1978
KAGAN, Donald, *The Peloponnesian War*, London, 2003

KAHN, Charles H., *The Art and Thought of Heraclitus*, Cambridge, 1979
KERENYI, C., *The Gods of the Greeks*, London, 1951
—, *The Heroes of the Greeks*, London, 1959
KIRK, G.S., *Myth, its Meaning and Functions in Ancient and Other Cultures*, Cambridge, 1970
—, *The Nature of Greek Myths*, London, 1974
LANE FOX, Robin, *The Search for Alexander*, London, 1980
—, *Alexander the Great*, London, 1973
LEFKOWITZ, Mary R., *The Victory Ode*, New Jersey, 1976
—, *Heroines and Hysterics*, London, 1981
LEMPRIÈRE, J., *Classical Dictionary*, London, 1792
LEVI, Peter, *The Hill of Kronos*, London, 1980
— (tr.), *Pausanias*, 2 vols., London, 1971
LLOYD, G.E.R., *Magic, Reason and Experience*, Cambridge, 1979
LLOYD-JONES, Hugh, *The Justice of Zeus*, California, 1971, second edition, 1983
—, *Blood for the Ghosts*, London, 1982
—, *Greek in a Cold Climate*, London, 1991
LONG, A.A., *Hellenistic Philosophy*, London, 1974
LORAUX, Nicole, *Les Enfants d'Athéna*, Paris, 1981
—, *L'Invention d'Athènes*, Paris, 1981
—, *Façons tragiques de tuer une femme*, Paris, 1985
—, *Les Expériences de Tiresias*, Paris, 1989
—, *Né de la Terre*, Paris, 1996
—, *La Cité divisée*, Paris, 1997
LORAUX, Nicole and Miralles, Carlos (eds), *Figures de l'intellectuel en Grèce Ancienne*, Paris, 1998
LOWELL, Robert, *The Oresteia*, London, 1978
McLEISH, Kenneth, *The Theatre of Aristophanes*, London, 1980
—, *Myth*, London, 1996
MEIGGS, Russell, *The Athenian Empire*, Oxford, 1972
—, *Trees and Timber in the Ancient Mediterranean World*, Oxford, 1982
MOMIGLIANO, Arnaldo, *Sagesses barbares*, Paris, 1984
NILSSON, Martin P., *The Mycenaean Origin of Greek Mythology*, New York, 1932
—, *Greek Folk Religion*, New York, 1940
—, *A History of Greek Religion*, New York, 1964
NISETICH, Frank, *The Poems of Callimachus*, Oxford, 2001
O'BRIEN, John Maxwell, *Alexander the Great, the Invisible Enemy*, London, 1992
PADEL, Ruth, *In and Out of the Mind: Greek Images of the Tragic Self*, Princeton, 1992
PARKE, H.W., *Greek Oracles*, London, 1967
PARKER, Robert, *Miasma*, Oxford, 1983
PEYREFITTE, Roger, *La Jeunesse d'Alexandre*, Paris, 1977
PLUTARQUE, *Vies parallèles*, ed. Hartog, François, Paris, 2001
POMEROY, Sarah B., *Goddesses, Whores, Wives and Slaves*, New York, 1987

POPPER, K.R., *The Open Society and its Enemies*, London, 1945, fifth edition, 1966
POWELL, Anton, *Athens and Sparta*, London, 1988, second edition, 2001
RAGLAN, Lord, *The Hero*, London, 1933
—, *Jocasta's Crime*, London, n.d.
RAMNOUX, Clémence, *Héraclite, ou L'Homme entres les choses et les mots*, Paris, 1968
RAPHAEL, Frederic, *Byron*, London, 1982
—, *Of Gods and Men*, London, 1992
—, *Petronius, Satyrica*, London, 2003
RAPHAEL, Frederic and McLeish, Kenneth, *The Plays of Aeschylus*, London, 1991
—, *Sophocles' Ajax*, Philadelphia, 1996
RICHTER, G.M.A., *Greek Art*, London, 1959
ROBERTSON, Martin, *A History of Greek Art*, Cambridge, 1975
ROMILLY, Jacqueline de, *Pourquoi la Grèce?*, Paris, 1992
—, *La Grèce antique contre la violence*, Paris, 2000
RYLE, Gilbert, *Plato's Progress*, Cambridge, 1968
SAGE, Michael M., *Warfare in Ancient Greece*, London, 1996
STE. CROIX, G.E.M. de, *The Origins of the Peloponnesian War*, London, 1972
—, *The Class Struggle in the Ancient Greek World*, London, 1981
SANTOSUOSSO, Antonio, *Soldiers, Citizens and the Symbols of War*, Colorado, 1997
SCHIAVONE, Aldo, *Società romana e produzione schiavistica*, Cambridge, MA, 1981
SCHMIDT, Michael, *The First Poets*, London, 2004
SEGAL, Erich, *The Death of Comedy*, Cambridge, MA, 2001
SEFERIS, George, *A Poet's Journal*, Cambridge, MA, 1974
SHAW, Pamela-Jane, *Discrepancies in Olympiad Dating and Chronological Problems of Archaic Peloponnesian History*, Stuttgart, 2003
SIFAKIS, G.M., *Studies in the History of Hellenistic Drama*, London, 1967
SKINNER, Marilyn B., *Catullus in Verona*, Ohio, 2003
SLATER, Philip E., *The Glory of Hera*, Boston, 1968
STARR, Chester G., *The Economic and Social Growth of Early Greece 800–500 B.C.*, New York, 1977
STONEMAN, Richard, *Land of Lost Gods, the Search for Classical Greece*, London, 1987
SWADDLING, Judith, *The Ancient Olympic Games*, 2002
TAMINIAUX, Jacques, *La Fille de Thrace et le penseur professionel*, Paris, 1992

TAPLIN, Oliver, *Greek Tragedy in Action*, London, 1978
—, *The Stagecraft of Aeschylus*, Oxford, 1979
TAYLOR, Michael R., *Giorgio de Chirico and the Myth of Ariadne*, Philadelphia, 2003
THIMME, Jurgen (ed.), *Art and Culture of the Cyclades in the Third Millennium B.C.*, Chicago, 1977
THOMSON, George, *Aeschylus and Athens*, London, 1941
—, *The First Philosophers*, London, 1955
VANOYEKE, Violaine, *La Prostitution en Grèce et à Rome*, Paris, 1990
VERMEULE, Emily, *Aspects of Death in Early Greek Art and Poetry*, California, 1979
VERNANT, Jean-Pierre, *Les Origines de la pensée grecque*, Paris, 1962
—, *Mythe et pensée chez les Grecs*, Paris, 1965
—, *Religions, histoires, raisons*, Paris, 1979
—, *Entre mythe et politique*, Paris, 1996
—, *Figures, idoles, masques*, Paris, 1998
VERNANT, Jean-Pierre and Vidal-Naquet, Pierre, *Mythes et tragèdie en Grèce Ancienne*, Paris, 1972
VEYNE, Paul, *Les Grecs ont-ils cru à leurs mythes?*, Paris, 1993
VEYNE, Paul, Lissarrague, F. and Frontisi-Ducroux, F., *Les Mystères du gynécée*, Paris, 1998
VIDAL-NAQUET, Pierre, *Le Chasseur noir*, Paris, 1981
WALBANK, F.W., *The Hellenistic World*, London, 1981, second edition, 1992
WALCOT, Peter, *Greek Drama in its Theatrical and Social Context*, Cardiff, 1976
WEST, M.L., *Hesiod*, Oxford, 1998
WOODFORD, Susan, *Images of Myths in Classical Antiquity*, Cambridge, 2003
WORTHINGTON, Ian (ed.), *Persuasion: Greek Rhetoric in Action*, London and New York, 1994

No honest account of sources should omit the invaluable contribution of the Loeb editions, many of them now revised, which have supplied cribs and texts to generations of lazy boys, hurried scholars and perpetual amateurs. Of other translations, apart from my own and those of Kenneth McLeish, I have made negligible, or at least neglected, use. Many reference books provided much-needed back-up. The following were those to which I most regularly turned:

The Encyclopaedia Britannica
Liddell and Scott's Greek Lexicon
The Oxford Classical Dictionary
The Oxford Companion to Classical Literature
The Oxford History of the Classical World

Sources of illustrations

Frontispiece. Museo Archeologico, Florence; 1. Photo Paul Hetherington; 2. Kunsthaus, Zurich; 3. Private Collection, Vienna. Photo AKG; 4. Museum of Archaeology, Istanbul; 5. Natural History Museum, Frederiksborg, Denmark. Photo AKG; 6. Museo Archeologico, Florence; 7. Carlsberg Glyptothek, Copenhagen; 8. Museo Archeologico, Florence. Photo Alinari; 9. Lord Byron, *Works*, London 1832–34; 10. National Portrait Gallery, London; 11. Staatliche Antikensammlung, Munich. Photo Hirmer; 12. Photo Camera Press; 13. The Ronald Grant Archive; 14. The British Museum, London; 15. The Wallace Collection, London; 16. Museo Pio Clementino, Vatican City. Photo Alinari; 17. Giorgio de Chirico, *The Silent Statue (Ariadne)*, 1913. Kunstsammlung Nordrhein Westfalen, Dusseldorf, Germany. Photo Bridgeman Art Library. © DACS 2006; 18. The British Museum, London; 19. National Museum, Athens; 20. Kunsthistorisches Museum, Vienna; 21. The British Museum, London; 22. Woodcut, Basel, *c.* 1490. Photo AKG; 23. The British Museum, London; 24. Copyright Elizabeth Ayrton; 25. Museo Nazionale, Naples; 26. Kunsthistorisches Museum, Vienna. Photo AKG; 27. Bibliothèque Nationale, Paris; 28. Staatliche Antikensammlung, Munich; 29. National Museum, Athens; 30. National Museum, Athens; 31. Photo Paul Hetherington; 32. Museum of the Jewish Diaspora, Tel Aviv; 33. Staatliche Antikensammlung, Berlin; 34. Réné Magritte, *The Rape (Le Viol)*, *c.* 1935. The Menil Collection, Houston, Texas. © ADAGP, Paris and DACS, London 2006; 35. Villa Albani, Rome. Photo Alinari-Anderson; 36. From *Man, Myth and Magic*; 37. Staatliche Antikensammlung, Berlin; 38. Louvre, Paris. Photo Bridgeman Art Library; 39. The Ronald Grant Archive; 40. National Gallery, London; 41. Museo Archeologico, Florence; 42. Museo Nazionale, Naples; 43. Ostia Museum, Rome; 44. The British Museum, London; 45. Camera Press; 46. Photo Arts of Mankind; 47. The British Museum, London; 48. Metropolitan Museum of Art, New York; 49. Thyssen-Bornemisza Collection, Madrid; 50. Agora Museum, Athens; 51. Kupferstichkabinett, Berlin; 52. Ephesus Museum, Turkey; 53. Louvre, Paris. Photo Bridgeman Art Library; 54. Herzog Anton Ulrich Museum, Braunschweig; 55. The Ronald Grant Archive; 56. Paestum, in situ. Photo Paestum Museum; 57. The British Museum, London; 58. Staatliche Antikensammlung, Berlin; 59. Thessalonika Museum. Photo S. Tsardaroglu; 60. Musée Royaux des Beaux-Arts, Brussels; 61. Staatliche Museum, Berlin; 62. Museo Nazionale, Naples; 63. Photo Hutchinson Library; 64. Sparta Museum; 65. Photo Institute of Archaeology, Florence; 66. Sparta Museum; 67. Pinacoteca Nazionale, Siena. Photo Scala; 68. Museo Nazionale, Naples. Photo Scala; 69. Staatliche Museum, Berlin; 70. Priene. Photo Antonello Peressinolto, Padua; 71. Archaeological Museum, Istanbul; 72. Archaeological Museum, Istanbul; 73. Bibliothèque Nationale, Paris. Photo Bridgeman Art Library; 74. Kunsthalle, Hamburg. Photo AKG; 75. Andy Warhol, *Shot Light Blue Marylyn*, 1964. Private Collection. © The Andy Warhol Foundation for the Visual Arts, Inc. ARS, NY and DACS, London 2006; 76. John Flaxman, *Hesiod; Works and Days*, London, 1817; 77. postcard; 78. Acropolis Museum, Athens; 79. Lady Lever Art Gallery, Liverpool; 80. Museum of Reggio. Photo Leonard von Matt; 81. Badisches Landesmuseum, Karlsruhe; 82. The British Museum, London; 83. Louvre, Paris; 84. Acropolis Museum, Athens; 85. Museo Nazionale, Naples; 86. Louvre, Paris; 87. National Archaeological Museum, Athens; 88. Museo Nazionale, Naples; 89. Palazzo dei Conservatori, Rome; 90. Photo Camera Press; 91. Photo Nikos Koutos; 92. Carlsberg Glyptothek, Copenhagen; 93. The British Museum, London; 94. Photo Hirmer; 95. The British Museum, London; 96. Kunsthistorisches Museum, Vienna; 97. Museo Nazionale di Villa Giulia, Rome; 98. Glyptothek, Munich; 99. Kabul Museum. Photo Josephine Powell; 100. The British Museum, London; 101. Photo Michael Gidon; 102. Museo di Terme, Rome; 103. Olympia Museum; 104. The British Museum, London; 105. Reconstruction by Sian Francis; 106. Hermitage, St Petersburg.

Index

Page numbers in *italic* refer to illustrations.